THE BRITISH IN FRANCE

The British in France

*Visitors and Residents since
the Revolution*

Peter Thorold

continuum

Continuum UK, The Tower Building, 11 York Road, London SE1 7NX
Continuum US, 80 Maiden Lane, Suite 704, New York, NY 10038

www.continuumbooks.com

First published 2008

British Library Cataloguing-in-Publication Data
A catalogue record for this book is available from the British Library.

ISBN 9781847252340

Typeset by YHT Limited, London
Printed and bound by MPG Books, Cornwall

Contents

For my Grandchildren

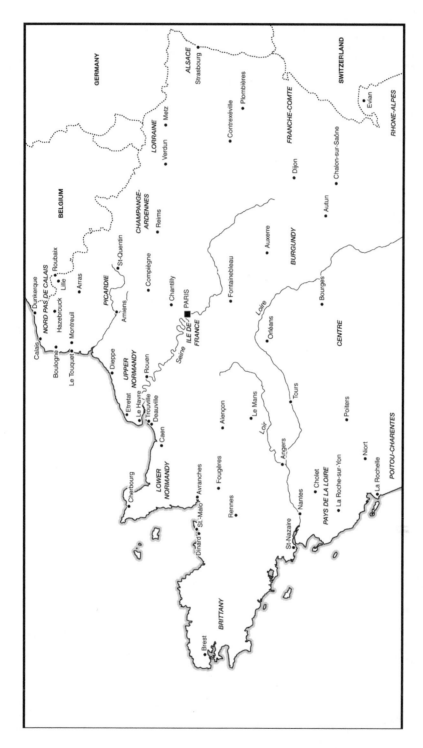

Northern France

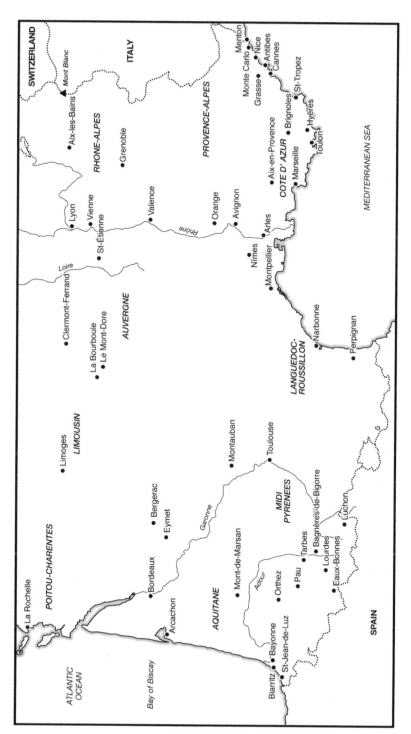

Southern France

Acknowledgements

I am much obliged to Madame Gervais-Aguer of the Université Montesquieu-Bordeaux for guidance on her survey of the British in Aquitaine. Mme Joëlle Devever of *Insee*, Aquitaine, and Mme Natalie Léon of the *Mairie* of Paulhiac, Lot-et-Garonne, kindly supplied detailed information on censuses, both historical and current. I owe thanks to Messrs Hérranz and Tomzack of *L'Aspig*, the preservation society of Decazeville, and to M. Joannes Payens, the president of the Dordogne Organization of Gentlemen, for the especial trouble they took in briefing me. I am grateful also to Ms Alice Cortes of Nestlé Waters UK for the background to the British connection with Perrier. I also want to thank Mme Grimaux of the *Bibliothèque municipale* at Hyères and to the staff of the libraries at Pau and Villeneuve-sur-Lot, as well as to Mme Karen Oberti Carpenter of John Taylor, Cannes. In London I was much assisted by the staff of the Imperial War Museum, including Ms Emma Gilbert who put me in touch with holders of copyright. Ms Andrea Gilbert, Librarian of the Wallace Collection, supplied some interesting information on the collection. Finally, as always, I owe thanks to the staff of the London Library and the British Library, and in addition to Ms Michelle Hockley who patiently steered me through the records at The National Archives at Kew. I would also like gratefully to acknowledge the help I have received from Solange Demangeat, Miles Gladwyn, François Gueriot, Linda Henry, Richard Klein, Ian Lowe, Olivier Paschoud, David Shapiro, and Robert and Sabine Wallace-Turner.

Note on French Names and Translations

Readers may notice anomalies in the rendering of French names, which generally speaking have not been anglicized. Thus, I write St-Tropez, not St Tropez, and Lyon not Lyons. However, in a few cases, as with 'Napoléon' and 'Monte-Carlo', the French form in an English book might appear pretentious.

It was only in the twentieth century that the French referred (sometimes) to *britanniques*. Before that *anglais* comprehended Scots and Welsh as well as English. Where a quotation is indirect I have usually substituted British for English. Direct quotations have been translated literally.

Introduction

Leaving war years aside, there are more British now in France than ever before. A great number live in rural departments, regions that in the nineteenth and much of the twentieth centuries were unknown to all but the most adventurous. Unlike their predecessors, they are usually more than willing to mix with their French neighbours. They are in fact a new breed, the product after all of the social change which took shape in Britain during the 1960s and 1970s, people who go to France because property is cheaper, because social services are better, because there you can easily find unspoilt countryside and warmer weather. It is very matter of fact. Anyway, in the twenty-first century, travellers and emigrants seeking something more adventurous have the whole world from which to choose.

For the British of the past, France was exotic, a contrast to the glumness at home, offering freedom from the insistent weight of moral and social propriety in Britain. 'Am I really here, in France?' exclaimed the young Katherine Wilmot, waking up on her first morning in a Calais hotel in November 1801 – 'I never remember, in all my life a moment of such unfeign'd extacy!' That is, in effect, the moment at which this book starts, when for rather over 18 months the bitter, long war between Britain and France that followed the great Revolution was in remission. The British came to witness the new republican and godless world, and perhaps to seek out old friends who had escaped the guillotine. Above all they went to Paris, familiar to many of them from the past, the cultural and the natural social capital of the world.

The wars over, in 1814 and 1815 they returned in much greater numbers – to gamble, for sex, for fun generally or just to enjoy the atmosphere. It was a time of carnival for the proverbial *milord*, so arrogant and eccentric – though happily free-spending – in French eyes. The grandees, however, would give place to a middle class, more conventional certainly, but who also relished the chance to travel abroad. The eminent Victorian historian J. R. Green wrote that it was only when he was abroad that the Englishman could be seen as 'nakedly and undisguisedly English'. At home the English are 'too busy, too afraid of Mrs Grundy, too oppressed with duties and responsibilities, and insular respectabilities'. Many of those who went to France to save money were also influenced by social pressures: the cost of living there was not necessarily lower – at times Paris was more expensive than London – but it was possible to adopt a simpler style of life without losing caste. Climate was another factor behind at least temporary emigration. In the days before central heating (and more advanced medical treatment), the cold and damp British winter drove countless people to the south, to the spas of the Pyrenees and to the Riviera. Robert Louis Stevenson described the 'shock of wonder and delight' felt by an invalid as he found himself crossing the line between north and south.

Stevenson's invalid was travelling by rail and would have crossed the Channel by steamboat. The transport revolution made travel much cheaper, much faster and much more comfortable. The railways greatly stimulated the growth of the resorts patronized by the British. Travel turned into a huge industry. Books on the subject found an enthusiastic readership, which writers of all sorts, among them Dickens and Thackeray and the Trollope family – and Stevenson – set out to satisfy. Periodicals such as *Blackwood's Magazine* published regular articles on France. This book is based on such accounts, which are supplemented by Foreign Office and other archival records. It is social history, concerned only peripherally with politics. In fact, the frequently turbulent relations between Britain and France during the nineteenth century seem to have little affected British tourists and residents. They kept coming over – or remaining in place – thrown off balance only in 1848 and 1870–1. However, their phlegmatic attitude was seldom a by-product of warm personal relations with the French. There was perhaps too much difference in background. An American traveller declared that 'to change from England to France is almost the transition from one planet to another'. The British tended to form self-contained and socially self-sufficient communities wherever they settled. Pau, Tours and Menton, their economy and their social life were virtually dominated by the British at one time or another. (Boulogne was also a favourite, though it was notorious as a refuge for debtors and social rejects.) The businessmen among the British community would have had regular contact with the French public, playing an important part in the wine trade of Bordeaux and, particularly in northern France, in textiles and engineering. But, leaving the Paris region aside, they were a minority. Relatively few of the British were employed for, unlike other immigrants, a high proportion were economically 'inactive', people who lived on investments or pensions.

The British and French regarded each other warily. Put at its simplest, the French viewed the British as morose and hypocritical, while the British

considered the French frivolous and unreliable. But such basic character-
ization was sometimes hotly disputed. Then there was Paris, bewitching the
world, it seemed, in the years leading up to 1914. The capital of sex, so it
was held. If the soldiers arriving with the British Expeditionary Force during
the First World War knew anything about the French it was that they were
sex-mad. That was the legend. Yet it was pointed out that, by and large,
unmarried French girls were prim when compared to their flirtatious British
and American opposite numbers.

The First World War disrupted travel and the day-to-day life of the
British in France. It was also the prelude to a period of unaccustomed
political and financial uncertainty which was to culminate in the catastrophe of 1940. In the 1920s the British surged into France, encouraged by
a strong pound; in the 1930s, the pound devalued, the trend was in reverse.
The social pressures at home had modified, there was less John Bullishness,
but virtually no demographic change: residents stayed clustered in their
traditional localities. There was little incentive to move: motoring opened
up new possibilities, but the French countryside between the wars, impoverished and depopulated, was uninviting. The transformation of tourism and place of residence would wait until well into the second half of the
twentieth century.

Chronology of Events

1789–94	The French Revolution
February 1793	War between Britain and France begins
October 1801–May 1803	The Peace of Amiens
1814–15	The war ends; Napoleon goes into exile; Louis XVIII becomes King of France; Napoleon returns; the Battle of Waterloo
1824	Death of Louis XVIII and succession of Charles X, formerly Comte d'Artois
July 1830	The 'July Revolution'; Charles X abdicates, to be replaced by Louis-Philippe, Duc d'Orléans as 'King of the French'
February 1848	Revolution; Louis-Philippe abdicates; the Second Republic established
1852	Louis-Napoleon Bonaparte, already President, is declared Emperor, taking the title of Napoleon III
1854–6	The Crimean War, with France and Britain allied against Russia
1870	The Franco-Prussian War begins; the fall of Napoleon III; the siege of Paris
1871	Capitulation of Paris; the insurrection of the Commune; inauguration of the Third Republic
September–November 1898	Anglo-French stand-off at Fashoda in the Sudan, the climax of their colonial dispute over Egypt
1899–1902	The Boer War

1904	The Entente Cordiale
1914–18	The First World War
October 1929	The Wall Street Crash, the start of the Great Depression
September 1931	Britain abandons the gold standard
May–September 1938	Crisis over German demands on Czechoslovakia; the Munich agreement
September 1939	Britain and France declare war on Germany
May–June 1940	Defeat of the French and British armies; the Pétain government makes peace with Germany
July 1940	The British navy sinks the French naval squadron at Mers-el-Kébir
1942	American and British forces invade French North Africa
1944	The Allies land in Normandy
1945	Defeat of Germany
October–November 1956	Anglo-French forces occupy the Suez Canal
August 1961	Britain applies for membership of the European Economic Community (EEC), its application being rejected in January 1963
May 1968	Riots and strikes throughout France
1973	Britain formally enters the EEC
May 1994	The Channel Tunnel opens

The False Start

The best way to understand the English of the upper and middle classes is to think of us, the French, as we were before the Revolution, as described by Saint-Simon and La Bruyère. That was the advice of the writer André Chevrillon, member of the French Academy, to his readers in the 1920s. It is there, he went on, that we find the coldness, the self-discipline, the respect for custom, which strike us so much about the English today.[1]

Chevrillon's theme, a startling one, may well deserve a treatise, perhaps a book. Here, though, it serves more simply, to cast a sharper light on the completeness of the separation between Britain and France in the years following the Great Revolution. For a period of 21 years, from 1793, with the Revolution well into its bloodiest stage, until 1814, with one short interruption, Britain and France were at war. That they should be fighting each other was nothing new: in the previous hundred years they had done so for more than a third of the time. What was new, distinctive, about the Revolutionary and Napoleonic wars was their intensity and the time they lasted. They demolished ties between the two countries, which in past wars had survived only mildly damaged. No longer was there question (or virtually none) of a leisurely Grand Tour designed to instruct British noblemen and gentry in the manners and graces of the wider world, with opportunities for some exciting sex thrown in. It was not France alone that was out of bounds, but as a result of the sweeping French conquests, much or all of Italy and Switzerland, and in later years of Germany too. By the time the wars ended, a great deal had changed. France would again be the centre of the arts and fashion, but, financially exhausted, her young men slaughtered on innumerable battlefields, she would never again rank as the dominant power.

But if the English kept many of their old characteristics, they too changed, turned in on themselves. Mary Berry, the intimate of Horace Walpole and his spiritual heir, had lived at the heart of that cosmopolitan and civilized society which gave such lustre to the later eighteenth century, She was admirably placed to judge what had happened: in Harriet Martineau's description,[2] she was a woman 'acutely conscious of changes in taste'. To her mind, the British of all people, reserved and uncommunicative by nature, were ill-equipped to resist the cultural dangers of isolation. Mary Berry wrote in her book *Social Life in England and France from the French Revolution in 1789 to that of July 1830*, published in 1831:

> Among the many evils arising to England from the disastrous state in which the French Revolution had placed Europe, must be reckoned its influence on the character of our youth, by debarring them from all powers of seeing various modes of social life, or living in any society but that of their own country. Foreign travel, however incapable of supplying the wants of a neglected education, must surely be considered as particularly necessary to the development of mind, in the inhabitants of an island.

There was though an interruption. The desire to travel abroad again, to refresh fading memories, to renew old ties, would lead Mary Berry and many others to cross the Channel, to head for Paris, when in October 1801 Britain and France signed a provisional treaty of peace, to be confirmed the following March at Amiens.[3] The peace turned out to be no more than a nineteen-month truce, but for a moment it seemed as if the world might be patched up. Many of those who crossed the Channel were people who had known France well before the Revolution. Some had been there while it was in progress; it was natural that they should return with some trepidation to a Paris that they had last seen when 'she was possessed, like a Demoniac, with a spirit of carnage, and reeked in ... blood'.[4] Mary Berry, last there in 1790 and very briefly in 1791, before the carnage properly started, went back out of curiosity and an anxiety to see old friends, and also a simple need that she felt to '*shake* out of English ways, English whims, and English prejudices, which nothing but leaving England gives one'. Arriving at Calais in March 1802, accompanied by her close friend the sculptor Anne Damer, she was to a point reassured by finding Dessein's hotel, an old favourite with the British, as clean and comfortable as ever, even if the cooking and wine were unimpressive. But, eager as she was to see France again, she was too dispassionate an observer to allow herself to yield to any gust of emotion. In this she was unlike the 28-year-old Katherine Wilmot, also at Dessein's, writing to her brother about waking up in the morning for the first time on French soil. 'You will laugh at me,' she wrote, 'when I confess to the flash of transport I experienced in saying to myself "I absolutely then am in France," and in drawing aside the Curtain of my Bed to prove it to myself, by contemplating the Painted ceiling, the white marble Tables, the looking-glass panels, the polish'd oak floor, and all the little circumstances of difference in the Apartment; without exception I never remember, in all my life, a moment of such unfeign'd extacy!' She puts up her hand to see if 'her Nightcap at least was not turning into a "Cap of Liberty" '.[5]

Excited, curious and often apprehensive to find themselves in the land of caps of liberty and, more sinister, the guillotine, the British arrivals were struck by how strange France seemed. One of them, Anne Plumptre,[6] could say that 'Nothing can be more dissimilar than every object that presents itself on the opposite sides of the water'. And another, 'I found myself in a new world; the language, the physiognomy, the manners, all different'. Mrs King, the wife of an English parson, gazing over the Channel from Calais at Dover Castle and the White Cliffs, exclaimed, 'We seemed among a new race of people, their cast of countenance, manners, and dress, were so different from our own'.[7]

The sense of disorientation persisted as they travelled the road to Paris. The simple need to adjust physically had something to do with it; unfamiliar wine, for instance, could cause an upset stomach. Yet, even if there were no guillotines by the roadside – and anyway they were used to gibbets in England – there were reminders everywhere of the Revolution. The travellers were taken aback by the poverty, by the multitude of beggars. Anne Plumptre, a tireless and adventurous traveller (who drew the line only, it seems, at Bedouin camps in Arabia or dining on steak cut from a 'live ox on the plains of Abyssinia'), talked of the intolerable number of beggars who swarmed around the carriages whenever they stopped, and whose importunity, she said, exceeded all description. She, like others, noticed that mainly it was women, assisted by old men and boys, who worked on the roads, evidence of how the wars had drained away the men. Old hands remarked how few carriages were to be seen – the journalist Francis Blagdon thought no more perhaps than a tenth of the number he recollected in 1789 and 1790.[8] Another visitor recorded that at Lille, while he and his party counted 12 or 15 'excellent' hackney carriages, they saw not one belonging to a gentleman, and that in a town which before the Revolution had contained no less than 300 of the *noblesse*.[9] At Amiens, Katherine Wilmot had a more direct experience of the republic. Just as she and her companions were sitting down to supper, they heard, outside their inn, loud applause and cries of *Vive la Nation! Vive Bonaparte!* Joseph Bonaparte, the First Consul's brother, was arriving for the final round of peace negotiations with the British. For many, the most pungent reminder of the terrible and recent past lay in the sight of ruined chateaux along the way. And of the churches, or what was left of them. For here was what none of the visitors would have encountered before, a godless society. The banker John Dean Paul and his party were taken with a lively and hard-working chambermaid in one hotel, but 'we did not ask her if she found time to say her prayers; that would be a needless question, as I believe no one in France does, who is under sixty years of age'.[10]

It was at Paris of course that the search for familiar landmarks was at its most poignant. Francis Jackson, the acting ambassador, last in Paris 14 years before, found it greatly altered; the squares and streets, still less the buildings, public or private, little resembled what he had known.[11] One visitor wrote that 'every street in Paris has become notorious for its events; for the concealment of the proscribed; for the catastrophe of some inhabitant; for some singular combat, or for the birth or death of some venerable patriot'. The site of the Bastille was a timber yard; Versailles was gloomy and poverty-stricken, its gardens desolate; the Tuileries was defaced by revolutionary slogans still visible on its walls.[12] The sumptuous Hôtel de Richelieu, once the palace of the Richelieu family, was now a very comfortable and luxurious hotel in the English sense of the word. Some private mansions retained their original function. That belonging to the Prince of Monaco, for instance, had been undisturbed. The Prince had been obliged to flee from Paris before he could finish breakfast. Returning years later – from England with a British wife – he found the remains of his breakfast were still on the table.[13] Miss Berry though was disconcerted when taken to call on Madame Bonaparte, the First Consul's mother; she had known the house well before the Revolution when it belonged to her friends, the Montfermeils. There was another surprise, one of a different sort, attached to a meeting with Josephine, the First Consul's wife – she was introduced by a Swiss tailor. As one might expect, protocol and social convention were not what they had been. Nevertheless, the new egalitarianism was something of a shock to the British. Since the Revolution, noted Mrs King, 'the lower orders are become extremely familiar'. The easy relationship between master and servant was remarked on by Fanny Burney for one.[14] She was married to an ex-émigré, the Chevalier d'Arblay, with whom she had just arrived in France. When an old friend embraced her husband, whom he had not seen for years, a servant 'exclaimed aloud with that familiarity in which the French indulge their favourite servants'. Another visitor noted that at the Théâtre françois in Paris one actor specialized in the role of servants on a footing of especial familiarity with their masters, and described it as a part that did not exist on the British stage. Years later, the writer Amelia Opie reflected on the civility of the French lower class in recent years and quoted La Fayette, who had declared that, 'If our revolution has done nothing else for us, it has, at least, done this; it has taught men to look their fellow-men in the face, and feel their own dignity'.[15]

While nobody was able to tell Mary Berry what had happened to the

Montfermeils, she did her best to track down other old friends. This was difficult. Madame de Staël was there, but many were dead, or deep in the country nursing depleted fortunes, or refugees either in England or somewhere else abroad. She called on the Princesse de Beauvau and her sister Mademoiselle de Mortemart, lately emigrants in England, who spoke English very well, although that hardly mattered to Mary Berry. There was a gathering of fashionable guests, French and English. One was the Duchesse de la Rochefoucauld, a widow, whose husband had been assassinated during the Revolution, another the Duc de Rohan-Chabot. The British included Francis Jackson and the young Lord Henry Petty (in a few years to become Chancellor of the Exchequer at the age of 25) who, as Marquess of Lansdowne, was to become one of Miss Berry's closest friends. The venue though was less imposing. The Princess and her sister were lodging in a small house, 'the apartment more like an English than a French one in size and furniture', while supper, observed Miss Berry, was served 'in one of the coldest dining-rooms I ever felt'. But whatever the temperature, it was a kind and generous gesture, the supper being specially laid on to welcome the English, for 'few or no suppers are now given here, either by the new or the old set'. Returned emigrants were usually badly off, wrote Francis Blagdon, although those who had stayed and survived the Terror had often managed to preserve more of their property. Not, though, that the nobility were demoralized, let alone converted to republican principles. Aristocratic French society, according to Blagdon, profoundly disliked democratic ideas and forms. In conversation it was essential – where appropriate – to address whomever you were talking to by his or her title. When referring to dates, one did not do so in terms of the new republican calendar. The same with weights and measures; they used the old measurements not the decimal version. In this society too, one should stick to the *ancien régime* names for the French provinces, not speak about 'departments'.[16]

Had the Princesse de Beauvau attempted to entertain more than a tiny proportion of the British upper class in Paris at this time, she would have spent everything she had left. As one French historian put it, 'All the idle captives of the land of fogs shook their damp wings and prepared to take their flight towards the regions of pleasure and brightness'. In the words of another writer,

> Paris is for foreigners merely a huge inn, where they come to examine the consequences of the Revolution and admire the masterpieces stolen from Italy and Flanders.

It has been estimated that two-thirds of the House of Lords visited France during the Peace of Amiens. They included a future Prime Minister, Lord

Aberdeen, a future Lord Chancellor, Lord Erskine, five dukes, three marquesses and 37 earls. Jeremy Bentham, much respected in France, went over and so did Thomas Malthus and John Kemble, the glittering star of the London stage. Another theatrical personality was Philip Astley, the circus proprietor, intent on recovering rent due for his old Paris circus, which had been converted into a barracks. There was a heavy weighting of Whigs and radicals: though few had approved of the Terror, many had welcomed the Revolution. Lord Holland and the Duke of Bedford had consistently opposed the war, and Lady Holland, a 'West Indian', was in the course of developing a fervent admiration for the future Emperor. Some were extreme radicals, like Horne Tooke, indicted for treason in Britain, though acquitted, and his old political ally Sir Francis Burdett, who was to be committed to the Tower of London. The now repentant Henry Redhead Yorke, another visitor, had been imprisoned in England as a revolutionary. The Irish Lady Mount Cashell, with whom Katherine Wilmot was travelling, was a radical. Her education had been supervised by Mary Wollstonecraft, and she had been a close friend of the Irish nationalist Lord Edward Fitzgerald, killed while resisting arrest for treason.

Henry Redhead Yorke's description of his return to France during the Amiens Peace is particularly interesting.[17] The original purpose of his visit was to discover the fate of a relation 'so dearly beloved and so long lost'. It seems that in this he was unsuccessful. He was anyway much depressed: 'a thousand painful recollections obtrude themselves upon my mind,' he said. Should he look up old comrades? But some would have been British sympathizers with the Revolution, with whom he had quarrelled at a meeting at a Paris hotel in November 1792. A resolution had been passed, congratulating the Convention on the success of the Revolutionary army, and inviting them to 'liberate enslaved England', a clause strongly opposed by Yorke. To him, Paris in 1802 was a city of ghosts. A fellow guest at a dinner party, an Irishman, was someone Yorke believed to have been hanged long ago by the English. He eyed him for a long time before venturing to speak. With difficulty he tracked down Tom Paine, the author of The Rights of Man, ex-member of the Convention, who had ended up, like other British revolutionaries, imprisoned by the Jacobins. Yorke remarked that Paine was deeply depressed, a man now far more odious in France than in England, and living in the filthiest apartment he had ever seen. Yorke was taken to the studio of the painter Jacques-Louis David, now at the height of his fame, who as a member of the Committee of Public Safety had signed the warrant for Paine's arrest. He did not remember, said David, there were so many arrests.

The painting and sculpture on view at the Louvre, enriched by booty seized from all over Europe, were a great attraction to British visitors. The museum was an obvious magnet for professional painters such as Joseph Farington, Henry Fuseli, John Opie and John Hoppner, and also for the young Bertie Greatheed, who had just exhibited at the Royal Academy. He had come to Paris with his rich and cultivated parents, Mary Berry's friends Bertie senior and Nancy Greatheed of Guys Cliffe, near Warwick. Bertie senior declared that 'such an assemblage of the treasures of art never existed before either in ancient or modern times'. And there was the prospect of at least a glimpse of that phenomenon of the age, the First Consul, Napoleon Bonaparte, the man who had transformed France and, through his prodigious victories in the field, the balance of power in Europe. He was to be seen reviewing his troops, and sometimes at closer quarters. A friend of John Dean Paul, for instance, an officer in the Wiltshire Militia, dressed in uniform, was viewing pictures in a gallery of the Tuileries. He was tapped on the shoulder and, turning round, discovered the tapper to be General Bonaparte himself, who enquired to which regiment he belonged. (It was anyway not a bad idea, commented Paul, to wear a uniform in Paris; it got you extra attention.) Mary Berry, after a moment or two's conversation with Bonaparte at a reception at the Tuileries, thought him very simple and unaffected, and Josephine, his wife, someone who united dignity with much civility. What struck her though was that Josephine 'like all the rest who have not emigrated, seem [sic] to have totally forgotten all the very little they ever knew about England or English people'.

While Mary Berry felt the attraction of the First Consul, she found the Second Consul, Cambacérès, 'an uncommonly ill-looking, shortish, thick man, with his eyes sunk in his head'. Too much in fact like the men she saw in the streets, all equally ill-dressed, their coats too long and too big, 'like coats made by a village tailor'. She described her impressions after a visit to the opera:

> Indeed, it is at the *sortie* of the theatre that one of the wonderful changes that have taken place in Paris is very decidedly visible. That of the Opera, where one used to see brilliant groups of all the young people of fashion, and all the fashionable *filles* who rivalled and surpassed them in appearance, is the strangest collection of odd, blackguard-looking people that can be conceived.

Katherine Wilmot and Lady Mount Cashell met many of the new elite and enjoyed themselves. They were anyway young, and adventurous – they had, for instance, smuggled a proscribed *émigré* into France with them. By temperament they were more adaptable than Mary Berry, or for that matter Fanny Burney who wrote at the time that 'in select French Society there is a

Life, a Spur, a spirit of pleasure, that give it a zest rarely indeed to be met with in England'.[18] By 'select' she did not mean the republican ruling class. Maria Edgeworth, another visitor, declared that she liked French society enormously, but then explained that she had seen only the best, 'the men of literature and *ancienne noblesse*'.[19] Still, even Mary Berry would have allowed some advantages. Paris was safer than London, and she could hardly have objected to the lack of highwaymen on the roads outside. She relished the vitality so evident in the Bois de Boulogne on Sundays. The difficulty for her and for Bertie Greatheed was that they felt it a duty to make contact with the new elite. Early in her visit, Jackson, the acting ambassador, had taken Miss Berry on a round to meet the wives of government ministers. Greatheed complained in his journal, 'this is stupid work, but all these *sans culottes* must be seen'.

Francis Blagdon, who described the aristocrats so acidly, had little good to say either of the new rulers of France. They were self-made, speculators, people with 'a conscience not too nice', who lived expensively indeed on the scale of the old Court. Their etiquette too was rigorous, but the atmosphere was uneasy; this was a society whose members were too much on their guard. George Jackson, an unpaid attaché at his brother's embassy, considered it necessary to distinguish between the men and the women. He too thought the men vulgar and awful. On the other hand, writing to his mother, he reported that though the French women at an embassy dinner wore little in the way of clothes, what they had they carried gracefully. And their manners were lively and attractive. The English ladies, he added, seemed 'half-frightened' by them. (Their daughters, granddaughters and great-granddaughters would feel much the same way.)

The Jackson brothers were inevitably involved with the new society. Even more so, and even more significantly, was Charles, Marquess Cornwallis, the British negotiator at Amiens, where the provisional agreement reached in London was to be made final. Cornwallis's American biographers call him a 'typical eighteenth-century diplomat' – an unsatisfactory description.[20] His career, despite the surrender to the Americans and French at Yorktown – a disaster considered by no one to be his fault – was of exceptional distinction. He was twice Governor-General of India, and an outstanding Lord-Lieutenant of Ireland. In France at this moment, at the very start of the new century, he gave out an aura of those great British eighteenth-century *seigneurs*, legendary in their wealth and extravagance. In the case of Cornwallis, in France between November 1801 and March of the following year, lavish spending was a deliberate act of policy, intended to make manifest British opulence and state. He travelled from England with a town coach, a town chariot and a travelling coach, all notable for their magnificence, and was accompanied by sixteen servants to look after his own needs and those of his son Lord Brome and a small staff. There were also three king's messengers attached to keep in touch with the Foreign Secretary in London. Cornwallis's freehandedness on the road exasperated travellers in his wake. He had spoilt all the innkeepers and hoteliers, they complained: 'Lord Cornwallis had done all in his power to turn the heads of these fellows and set them agog for English guineas. For every thing that was supplied to him or done for him ... he paid double, and the higher their extortionate charges, the better he expressed himself pleased.' Bonaparte himself, much impressed by Cornwallis when they met in Paris, added to the impression of prodigality by despatching – soldier to soldier – a cavalry regiment to Amiens, to carry out manoeuvres in his presence, *pour lui servir de récréation.*

Amiens had been chosen for the negotiations because it lay more or less equidistant from London and Paris, and thus was well placed for the constant communications necessary between the negotiating teams and their respective governments. The discussions dragged on over four months, not least because the two governments intervened ceaselessly. A certain lassitude crept in. When Mary Berry called in on her way to Paris, she was told by Lord Cornwallis's deputy that Joseph Bonaparte, the chief French negotiator, did not get out of bed before one or two o'clock in the afternoon. The British got very bored. While Cornwallis found Joseph Bonaparte to be a very sensible and 'gentlemanlike man', fair and open in his dealings, the same, his delegation thought, could not be said of his team. Madame Bonaparte, reported one of them, was very short, very thin, very ugly and very vulgar. The Dutch Ambassador – Holland was a French satellite – was considered 'rather above par' and so was his wife, but the Prefect of the department was 'a very ill-looking scoundrel', a man remembered too as having voted for the King's death. As for the wife of the Mayor of Amiens, she 'has more the appearance of a lady of easy virtue than any of them'.

If the British did not feel at home with the French ruling class, they in their turn cannot have been very congenial. Cornwallis was an attractive man, with a pronounced sense of humour. For instance, years before Amiens, he had written to his son at school to say he will have heard that 'I was elected knight of the Garter, and very likely laughed at me for wishing to wear a blue riband over my fat belly'. But in a letter from Amiens to a friend he conceded that 'I am too much a *John* [Bull] to delight in foreign society, and the French of the present day have all the disagreeable qualities of the old French, without the accomplishments'. The negotiations then were not exactly a model, but even had they been so, the differences between the two nations were all but insoluble.

In August 1802 Charles James Fox arrived in Paris, a man who in most respects could hardly have resembled Lord Cornwallis less. They looked very different for a start. It is all but impossible to visualize Cornwallis without a wig, or without all the trappings of an eighteenth-century nobleman. Fox, on the other hand, is barely to be imagined with a wig at all, or even with his hair powdered. Slovenly dress and a five o'clock shadow were more like it. (In his youth, five o'clock in the morning shadow.) He arrived in Paris not as a grandee – although by birth he was certainly that – but as a representative of the Enlightenment, a francophile to the core, and a friend of Talleyrand and La Fayette. Fifty-three years old in 1802, he had first visited France with his father at the age of 15,

> when he ought to have been at Eton School. He talked French admirably & employd it in declaiming against Religion with a fashionable grace that wd. have charmed Voltaire himself. He gamed deep; had an arranged intrigue with a certain Mad.e de Quallens, of high fashion.

To quote a recent biographer, 'In a broad sense, France was Fox's university, not Oxford.'[21]

Fox possessed an international reputation as a statesman and as a resolute and long-standing opponent of the war with France. While he had never approved of the execution of Louis XVI, or of the Terror, he had found consolation in the Directory which followed. In his view, Bonaparte did not intend wars of unremitting conquest. To Fox, the fall of Pitt and the peace signed at Amiens were the vindication of the policy he had for so long propounded. In Paris, he was greeted with great enthusiasm by the public; at the theatre to see *Phèdre*, the audience rose from their seats amidst near universal applause. If the peace was to be more than a truce he was well placed to push it that way. And Bonaparte recognized the fact: later he was to declare Fox to have been 'a model for statesmen' and to express the opinion that, had he not died prematurely when Foreign Secretary in the 'Talents Ministry' of 1806, a peace could have been achieved.[22]

However, Fox was cautious. He was in France, so it appeared, to study the French archives in search of material for the history of the reign of James II on which he was working. (James was a relation, for Fox's mother was a great-granddaughter of Charles II.) When John and Amelia Opie encountered him in the Louvre, he seemed to be paying more attention to the pictures than to a military parade immediately outside attended by the now First Consul-for-Life. He was unsettled by all the pomp, less republican than monarchical. His wife, who was with him, remarked on it too. Indeed, Fox was so reserved that Katherine Wilmot, meeting him at a party given by the

British expatriate Helen Maria Williams, was disappointed: he really was rather maladroit and embarrassed in his manners. John Opie, who was at the same party, explained to Joseph Farington that Fox had felt too hemmed in by the people crowding around him, and that he had left early. He was in a difficult position. Any success he might achieve depended on his not being perceived in England as 'Citizen Fox', a francophile who neglected his own country's interests. Only reluctantly did he attend Miss Williams's party at all, for she was an ideologue – perhaps, says her biographer, the only person who remained an enthusiast to the end for the Revolution. He was already in trouble for an unplanned meeting with the exiled Irish nationalist Arthur O'Connor. What were clearly of utmost importance were his meetings with Bonaparte. They were, however, a failure, and for Fox a great disappointment; it was impossible to find enough common ground. They disagreed particularly over the necessity for large standing armies and freedom of the press. Bonaparte was clearly no closet Whig. Although on his return to England Fox was to argue in the House of Commons that 'I am sure we have nothing to fear from France', he had no illusions now as to the nature of his country's antagonist.

Then, in May 1803, 14 months after the signing of the full treaty, it all broke down. Amiens had proved a false start towards reconciliation between Britain and France in the modern, post-Revolution world. The experience of Dr Peter Roget (esteemed by grateful writers and others for his thesaurus, the encyclopaedia of synonyms) shows how one set of travellers was affected.[23] Roget was supervising a modest version of the old Grand Tour, in charge of Burton and Nathaniel Philips, the sons of the owner of the largest cotton mill in Manchester. In May 1802, having spent three months in Paris, they left for Geneva in a carriage. Also of the party, in his own carriage, was Maria Edgeworth's brother, Lovell. The journey across France took two weeks, and appears, so far as they were concerned, to have been dull, an expedition through 'deserted and forlorn' plains on long, silent roads bordered by avenues of trees. Geneva when they got there was quite fun, enlivened by the presence of numerous other British. They stayed on and on, passing a generally uneventful winter. By the spring of 1803, however, rumours started to circulate of a deterioration in Anglo-French relations. The boys' father, Mr Philips, sent reassuring messages from London and so they stayed put. After all, thought Roget, while Geneva was under direct French rule, they were within six miles of what was then the Swiss border and, if they had to, could get moving at an hour's notice.

There was a rude awakening. At a party given by General Dupuch, the commandant at Geneva, Roget noticed that he and his party were the only English present, and that Dupuch, previously so friendly, was now markedly cold. The Philips boys picked up news that the British at Lyon had been taken into detention, and the next morning they were told that those at nearby Sécheron had fled across the border. But now it appeared that they would be no safer in Switzerland, since the French intended to apply the same rules there as in France. Anyway it was too late. Madame de Staël, met by chance at the hotel, said to Roget in English, 'I have very bad news for you. You are all going to be sent to Verdun. I have it from an unquestionable source'.[24]

The rules proclaimed by the French government on the outbreak of war stated that British males aged between 18 and 60 – those considered capable of serving in the forces or militia in Britain – were to be detained as prisoners of war at Verdun and other towns. Such drastic treatment of enemy civilians was not unprecedented, for it had occurred during the Revolution. But it seems to have been assumed by those affected that they would simply be expelled from French and French-held territory, that any detention might be unpleasant but would nevertheless be temporary. That explains their general lack of urgency. For instance, Mrs King and her clergyman husband had reckoned in April that they should leave Paris, but that they would have time to see the Normandy countryside on the way home. But as they made their leisurely way, they came upon fellow-countrymen increasingly anxious to escape. The rumours now were very alarming; at Calais, where the hotels were filled with people waiting for a passage, the talk was of French invasion plans.

In fact, Peter Roget was all right; he had been born in Geneva and could claim Genevese citizenship, and the Philips boys were both under 18. Their companion from Paris, Lovell Edgeworth, however, was not; he was to spend 11 years in detention in France. What is more, the rules were tightened, and people whom no one would consider to be militia material were caught in the net. One of them – briefly – was the dowager Marchioness of Donegall, even though she could swear like a trooper. Another was Augustine Sayer, aged 13, sent to France by his parents for his education. Mary Berry, Bertie and Nancy Greatheed and Katherine Wilmot were all in difficulties. Five months after leaving France in April 1802, Mary Berry had returned, this time accompanied by her father and her sister Agnes, bound for a winter and spring (and perhaps the summer too) at Nice. But by May 1803, indeed on the same evening that Roget and his pupils attended the alarming party at the commandant's, they too were in Geneva, on their way to Germany and Husum, near the present German–Danish border, where they were to catch a boat back to England. While still at Nice, Mary Berry wrote to Nancy Greatheed in Paris proposing that they all spend the summer together in Switzerland. But the Greatheeds did not move, anxious that their painter son should be able to finish a copy he was making of a Correggio in the Louvre. By the time another Berry letter arrived, written from Cassel, it was too late. No passports from the French were forthcoming in spite of an appeal made direct to the First Consul's mother. The Greatheeds were detained in Paris under parole, and eventually, still under parole, allowed to go to Germany, whence they slipped away to Italy.

Katherine Wilmot and Lord and Lady Mount Cashell were trapped in Italy, in territory under French control. However, they had had time to enjoy themselves. Encounters with high ecclesiastics figure in Katherine's letters home. There was an audience of the Pope on Good Friday. And a reception by Henry Stuart, Cardinal of York, otherwise – according to himself and a dwindling residue of Jacobites – Henry IX of England. While protocol at the Cardinal's court was strict, it was not inhibiting; Katherine could write that 'the blithesome gaiety of this pious conclave of holy men was very pleasant and amusing. I never saw a more joyous crew, nor a set of human beings who forfeited less of cheerfulness than themselves, for having renounced the pleasures of the world!' A third encounter involved the Church of Ireland Bishop of Derry, who was also the fourth Earl of Bristol, a different kettle of ecclesiastical fish altogether.[25] He was, in Katherine Wilmot's words 'one of the greatest curiosities alive, yet such is his notorious character for profane conversation and so great a reprobate is he in the most unlicensed sense of the word, that the English do not esteem it a very creditable thing to be much in his society'. In fact, it was hardly an encounter for she did not actually meet him. He was a neighbour in Rome whom she watched drive out in his carriage, dressed 'in white bed-gown and night cap like a witch, and giving himself the airs of an Adonis'. Lord Cornwallis put on a magnificent show, but Lord Bristol was the doyen of English lordly travellers, forever on the move, extravagant, a devoted collector of art, the man whose fame launched countless hotels in France and Italy. (Even now there are in Paris two top class 'Bristol' hotels, the restaurant of one rating two stars in the *Michelin Guide*.) By the time Katherine Wilmot saw him, Lord Bristol was close to death. He had been detained by the French in 1798, and probably only escaped the same fate this time by dying first.

News of the war and the regulations hit Katherine and the Mount Cashells on 1 June. They were stuck, for Lady Mount Cashell was seriously ill. The Mount Cashells stayed on in Italy, she permanently with a lover, he until 1805 when he escaped through Germany. Katherine managed to get out first, also through Germany, finding herself on the same boat from Husum as the Berrys. A delightful person, with a gift for writing, her experiences illustrate admirably the difficulties faced by British travellers during the wars. A few years after France and Italy she was in Russia. The Tsar signed an alliance with Napoleon, and once again she was on the run.[26]

Greatheed and – in this respect – the Mount Cashells were fortunate; they were detained but not shut up in a detention centre. Yet high social standing was by no means necessarily an advantage.[27] The Earl of Elgin, at the height of his diplomatic career, found none. While his famous Marbles went straight through to England, Elgin and his wife had stopped off at Paris on their way back from Greece. With the resumption of the war, they were sent first to Tours and, in his case, on to captivity at Lourdes. Elgin's detention was unjust, not to say ironic, for while Ambassador at Constantinople he had persuaded the Turks to release French subjects imprisoned in the Ottoman Empire. It was contrary to the usage of civilized nations to imprison civilians, he argued. The Marquis and Marchioness of Tweeddale were particularly unfortunate. She was ill and they had come to France for her health. They were too prominent, and were held as hostages, both dying at Verdun in 1804. Even those who might have expected sympathetic treatment by virtue of their political ties might fare hardly better: the sons of Lord Thanet, a leading Whig who was to be a pall-bearer at Charles Fox's funeral, were sent to Verdun. Also unlucky were two Americans arrested by mistake and compelled to spend several months in confinement.

On the other hand, as in the case of the Greatheeds, good connections might help. Sir Elijah Impey, previously Chief Justice of Bengal, had known Madame de Talleyrand in India and was on good terms with her husband. He was soon allowed home. While Talleyrand as Foreign Minister was powerful, he was also notoriously venal and very expensive. Lord Cornwallis had been determined to avoid negotiating with him partly because he was so unscrupulous, and partly too, perhaps, through wariness of his outstanding intellect. (No doubt the British had heard of the plight of the hapless American envoys several years before who could not persuade Talleyrand to sign a treaty without a large bribe.) Sir James De Bathe found a more high-minded intercessor – the Pope – who, the story goes, was persuaded to intervene by the argument that if De Bathe were not released, his children at home might be turned into Protestants.[28]

Others who appear in the French list of captives were two bankers. One was Walter Boyd of the Paris firm of Boyd and Ker, the other his one-time partner, the old East India hand Paul Benfield, who would have been extremely embarrassed had he been repatriated to Britain, where, so bad was his reputation, he would have been most unwelcome. One Englishman to be sent home was the eccentric Lord Camelford, remembered in history as the man who insisted on his right to appoint his black servant if he so wished as MP for his pocket borough of Old Sarum. In 1803 he was arrested on disembarkation at Calais on the basis of a report that in London he had boasted he intended to kill Bonaparte. Camelford was briefly imprisoned but then quickly despatched home. Another would-be assassin, or alleged as such, was the ex-Whig MP James Greene. There was no plot. The pretence of one, according to a witness, was an excuse to justify Bonaparte's order of 13 May 1803 for the seizure of British shipping. Actually it was not the First Consul but the French police with whom Greene wanted to get in touch; he arrived at Calais asking to be taken as a prisoner of war. It seems to have been the only way he could think of to escape his creditors![29]

One British subject who had no trouble was Maria Cosway, described in the *Dictionary of National Biography* as a history painter and educationist, an extraordinary woman who seems to float free, only mildly discommoded by the traumas of her time. It is easy to get the impression that she knew everyone who counted – she was a friend of Miss Berry, Bertie Greatheed, Henry Redhead Yorke, Jacques-Louis David and 'Madame Mère', Napoleon's mother. The godparents at her daughter's christening in 1790 were General Paoli, the Corsican patriot and Boswell's original hero, and the widow of Prince Charles Edward, the Young Pretender. A Catholic, she left Paris in May 1803 for Lyon where she was to open a school sponsored by Cardinal Fesch, Madame Mère's stepbrother, a man with whom she was to carry on a correspondence for the next 32 years. Her most famous lifelong correspondent, however, was Thomas Jefferson, with whom she had conducted the intense affair during his time as American Minister in Paris just before the Revolution which is celebrated in the Merchant and Ivory film *Jefferson in Paris* of 1995.[30]

There were others who survived the purge. British businessmen and industrialists who were well established in France were unlikely to be disturbed; they were too important to the national economy. The American Colonel Pinkney, touring France in 1807 and 1808, noted the British residents at Amiens, an important textile centre. While they lived on excellent terms with their French neighbours, they knew very well that they were watched by the police. Some, Pinkney added, pretended to be American.[31] Again ordinary artisans who had been employed in France for more than six months were customarily left in their jobs. Peter Bussell, a seaman, lately master of the *Dove* of Plymouth, and captured with his ship by a French privateer in 1806, came across two English weavers in prison at Arras. One, named Rice, who had worked in Brittany, died of a fever soon after his arrival at the prison; the other, a Lancastrian, had lived in France for 20 years, had married, but lost his job when the factory which employed him went bankrupt during the Revolution. When Bussell met him he was warden in a hospital. Bussell also encountered another veteran prisoner:

There is one female prisoner here, they call her Nelly. It seems she has been in France a long time, some says [sic] she was a soldier's wife during the time the Duke of York was on the Continent.* She has one child, and has a room to herself, where she washes for some of the prisoners, and keeps a gin shop. She is of Irish extraction, not very tidy in her dress. She is as happy as can be, and speaks French very well.

Women were usually in an easier position. Even if they could not get home they were able – unless they accompanied husbands or lovers – to avoid the detention centres. One who struck lucky in 1803 was Catherine Davies, a nanny, whose British employers in Paris passed her on to the First Consul's sister Madame Murat, later Queen of Naples, who, war or no war, preferred English nannies for her children. In fact she already had one when Catherine joined her. Her brother, worried about spying, was not happy, but she was firm. Catherine Davies must be one of the very few British subjects during the war to have had a private, albeit undemanding, conversation with the Emperor.[32]

There are several accounts of the hardship suffered by the men, by artisans. Many of them – often from the industrial north and the midlands – lived in small villages spread over the various departments of France, working perhaps as shoemakers or curriers or hatters or coachmakers. Charles Sturt, ex-MP for Bridport, emphasized that they did not regard themselves as permanent settlers; they had come because it was easier to earn a living in France than in England. Even to get to the detention centre to which they were allocated they found themselves having to pawn 'their tools and cloaths [sic] for a mere nothing'. If that was impossible or failed to raise enough to pay for transport, they had no alternative but to walk. And it was not just artisans and labourers who were in difficulty. Then, as later, British rentiers lived in provincial France because it was cheaper. William Wright, who had been English interpreter to the commandant at Calais, described their situation. People 'who at Calais had always appeared as gentlemen' were sent marching off with knapsacks on their backs, bound for Valenciennes, 100 miles away, their families left to the charity of such of their countrymen who remained. One husband, reported Wright, took his wife and young children with him on the march. But they could not keep up.

That left the rich and the reasonably well-off. While there were occasional hiccups, they were in principle able freely to draw on their money at home. In fact, whatever their foibles and self-indulgence (which were considerable),

* He commanded the British army in Flanders, 1793–4.

they were to take their responsibility for their destitute compatriots seriously, subscribing to a fund for their upkeep and for schools. Money was sent from England, particularly by the Patriotic Fund, established by Lloyd's, which provided regular and generous support for hospitals and schools, and towards the maintenance of the more elderly captives. Through a committee at Verdun the money was distributed between the various depots where the British were held. The whole operation seems to have been admirably managed. In one report to its subscribers the Patriotic Fund's committee commented:

> It is but justice to add, that the officers who form these committees, the medical gentlemen who attend the hospitals, and the clergymen who officiate in the schools, appear to have devoted their time and attention to the several duties they have undertaken, with the most laudable disinterestedness, judgment, and zeal.[33]

While initially there were a number of depots (the word used), Valenciennes, Nîmes Arras, Fontainebleau and others, Verdun became the most important, and the one where a large number of patrician detainees were concentrated. Reallocation meant more forced marches. J. H. Lawrence, author of *A Picture of Verdun*, remembered that 'many a party from Valenciennes had the appearance of strolling players'. East of Paris, not far from the French frontier, its name later to ring with such tragic resonance, Verdun entered British consciousness in the nineteenth century as a prison.

James Forbes, archaeologist, botanist, and a fellow of the Royal Society, left one of the best accounts of life in the town. He was picked up late in the year in Paris, another victim of complacency, and also of his concern that his daughter Eliza's education should be improved by study with the 'superior masters of the French capital'. At least, Forbes, and his wife and Eliza, who insisted on following him into confinement, had no need to walk. They travelled to Verdun by coach. And when they got there it hardly seemed like a prison camp. They were comfortably lodged in a physician's house to which they had been recommended in Paris, and what with teachers available for French, music, dancing and drawing, there was no problem about Eliza's education. Detainees in Verdun were on parole, being obliged to report at 10 each morning at the town hall and submit to a curfew after 9 p.m. Forbes spent his mornings reading, writing and drawing. In the afternoons the family, which now included his brother, who owned a villa in the Touraine, went out together on the public promenade. Sometimes they walked on the town ramparts and Forbes even obtained permission for

modest expeditions outside the town gates. A tolerable life, but monotonous. Anyway, the Forbeses' stay was shorter than most. Scientists were
sympathetically considered by the French government and they were
released in 1804 with the help of Sir Joseph Banks, President of the Royal
Society, and Edward Jenner, the pioneer of vaccination.[34]

James Forbes's account of his confinement in his book *Letters from
France, written in the years 1803 and 1804*, published in 1806, proved
unpopular with those still imprisoned. So mild did it represent conditions
to be, that it was feared the British government would relax its protests over
the illegal detention of civilians. And, as it was, conditions at Verdun were
more severe than they had been, and the corrupt commandant General
Wirion proven much less amiable than he appeared in Forbes's book. It was
dangerous to take him or the rule-book lightly. Anyone misbehaving, for
instance caught trying to escape, was despatched to the fortress of Bitche,
near the French border, where conditions were harsh. A less comfortable
prison also awaited those who ran badly into debt. Cells could quite easily
replace lodgings.

The number of detainees at Verdun between 1803 and 1814 varied
between 600 and 1,100 – as against an indigenous population of around
10,000 – but in later years more and more were authentic prisoners of war
rather than civilians. The mix was reasonably varied. The records, not
entirely complete, list many as 'gentleman', a number as 'clergyman', others
as 'merchant'. There were Henry Greathead, the inventor of lifeboats, and, it
appears, John Pinkerton, a geographer and historian – both, like James
Forbes, released early. Others were Jamaican planters; a fellow of Queen's
College, Oxford; a cook from Brighton; a cobbler from Bristol; a hairdresser;
a student, a 'spy and traitor'. And the doctors praised by the Patriotic
Committee, several of whom anyway gave free treatment to the poor outside hospital. Some of the detainees, like the Tweeddales, died in captivity,
one went mad, many were released, some escaped. Among the last was
Philip Astley, the circus proprietor. James Hare, not at Verdun, a leading
Whig Member of Parliament, died at Bath in 1804 partly, it appears, as a
result of his treatment in France. Peter Bussell recalled an Anglican clergyman at Arras who later turned recluse as a result of his experiences.

While James Forbes discovered one view pleasantly reminiscent of India,
Verdun was not a place, it is safe to say, where most of the prisoners would
have actually chosen to spend a night. While before the Revolution it
contained 20 churches and 18 convents, by 1803 these were mostly abandoned. By then too there existed no more than three or four decent shops;
the remainder, according to one witness, sold nothing more ambitious than
gingerbread and firelighters. As to fashion, the middle-class women dressed

like servants, 'with not a white stocking to be seen among them'. The change seems to have been dramatic. By James Forbes's time, the College Hall had been converted into an Anglican church and the theatre was thriving. The whole town became alive, the shops 'were ornamented with crystal glass windows as at Paris' and were selling jewellery and fashionable clothes. New shops opened, notably 'Stuckey, Tailor and Ladies Habit-Maker', and 'Anderson, Grocer and Tea Dealer', each, their signs announced, from London. (Mr Stuckey and Mr Anderson were detainees.) Monsieur Houzelle, a haberdasher, nicknamed 'Hustle', established himself as the principal banker for the newcomers. His street in the lower part of town became the 'morning lounge' and was called Bond Street by the British. The local library was transformed, with new books arriving. As to the townswomen, now they were dressed in silks and muslins.

An Englishman, captured at sea on his way to the West Indies and interned at Verdun in its later days, left a vivid description:

> To a stranger the Grande Rue, of Verdun, at the hour of three o'clock in the afternoon, presented a curious scene. Here were carriages of various descriptions belonging to Englishmen, others on horseback attended by their grooms; it did not seem as if we were in captivity. There were shops kept by the English, eating houses, club houses, livery stables, news rooms, and an English church; the sight of the congregation issuing thence was singular. Our countrywomen (of whom there were many who had preferred remaining with their husbands and parents detained at the commencement of the war, as well as others coming to France) ... almost inspired the English spectator with the idea that he was once more at home.[35]

Indeed the detainees lost no time in doing what they could to create a familiar way of life. Early on, some fields three miles out of the town were rented for horse racing. A Jockey Club was formed. James Forbes wrote that 'all the inhabitants of Verdun, high and low, rich and poor, captive and free, assembled about a league without the walls to see an English horse race, which you may be sure was a novelty in this country'. A Mr Drake, by profession a 'livery-stable keeper', was one clerk of the course; another was Mr Green, also knowledgeable on horses through his old job as 'highwayman'. Certainly the inhabitants were getting some fun out of the new arrivals, and, like Monsieur Houzelle, were making money. The news got about. Professional French gamblers turned up from out of town. The casino opened at one in the afternoon, closed at five to allow time for dinner, and then reopened at eight with play continuing all through the night. Obviously racing and gambling required the approval of the commandant, General Wirion; he gave it in return for a large rake-off. (In the end he overdid things and an attempted extortion on his part led to an official enquiry in Paris and his suicide.)

It will be clear that the intellectual James Forbes and the conscientious doctors and clergymen were not typical. The patricians shut up in Verdun were much more likely to be Regency rakes,[*] notoriously extravagant and unrestrained. The young men, it was said, behaved as if they were at home, 'playing, dancing, singing, and drinking all day long'. As for their elders, as a French historian has put it, many of the *milords* had been in the habit in Paris of daily debauchery, and the pimps and courtesans, British and French, who followed in their wake provided a continual problem for the commandant and the police.[36] There were beagling and duck shooting, while a momentary bar to duelling was soon put right. Theatricals were organized by another detainee, the well-known London impresario Richard Concannon. Along with the Jockey Club and Bond Street came, so to speak, St James's – in the form of clubs. While the Carron (sometimes Caron) and the Upper Club were sedate and popular with families, the Créangis and the short-lived Taylor's were distinctly dashing and chic. William Richmond, a prisoner of war and future admiral, described a party for some 120 people at the equally select Cod Club, where facilities included billiard rooms, a large library and a cock-fighting ring. The party opened with a play performed by professional actors; then came a lavish supper; and from 2 a.m. on, a ball which lasted until 6 a.m., when a splendid breakfast was served. 'The ladies' dresses outrivalled anything of the kind ever seen at Verdun', noted Richmond, observing that one lady had paid 150 guineas in Paris (say £7,000 in our money) for her costume. Food and wine, it should be added, were of the highest quality at Verdun parties. Guests were sometimes French; a party held to celebrate the Prince of Wales's birthday in 1805 was attended by many French officers and local notables. In 1807 townspeople were invited by four of the detainees to a masquerade ball.

In January 1814, Verdun, threatened by advancing allied armies, was evacuated, with its prisoners sent off westwards. The original prisoners – again unless they could afford transport – ten years older and presumably less fit than before, were back tramping the roads. Their younger prisoner-of-war companions, many of them captured on merchant ships, did not find the evacuation too disturbing. They seem to have been quite jaunty, and most, wrote one witness, were accompanied by their French mistresses 'who had acquired a surprising mastery of English sailors' oaths'. Some of the captives left reluctantly; a few would stay on in France after the peace.

---

[*] Officially the Regency did not come into being until 1811.

The townspeople too had mixed feelings. The town registers show more than 600 births, deaths and marriages relating to captives and their wives, many of whom were locals. (Indeed, a Monsieur and Madame Michaud ended up with three English sons-in-law.) While there were many foundlings in Verdun during the period, the British fathers appear almost invariably to have accepted responsibility for births outside marriage. Anyway, it was a pity to see so much good money quit the town. There was though also some bad money, for the British left a lot of debts, partly it is true because they were given virtually no notice of their departure. Anyway, many years later Verdun creditors were still unsuccessfully pressing the British government for reparation.

So, to quote Michael Lewis, the poor and mean provincial town of Verdun blossomed for a few years, to become a reflection, a pale one admittedly, of Bath and Tunbridge Wells. The French historian Boutet de Monvel made another comparison: in its extravagant and raffish way, Verdun was a precursor of those British colonies which were to spring up in many other French towns over the next hundred years.

2

Travelling Before the Railways

Those who have seen an English family-carriage on the continent must have remarked the sensation it produces. It is an epitome of England; a little morsel of the old island rolling about the world … the ruddy faces gaping from the windows … and then the dickey loaded with well-dressed servants beef-fed and bluff; looking down from their heights with contempt on all the world around; profoundly ignorant of the country and the people, and devoutly certain that everything not English must be wrong.

Thus said Washington Irving in the 1820s. Rich, aloof and smug, a generalization, but one that represents a common French impression of the British, not just in Irving's time but for years to come. And the 'rolling about the world' – what one visitor, Henry Best, in a book published in 1826, called their 'locomotive propensity'. The English, he said, 'are assuredly a most enterprising and restless people: they form establishments at the Antipodes, and plant colonies on the banks of the Loire, in an enemy's country, after a war of twenty years'.[1]

In May 1814 Napoleon had been forced into abdication by the allied powers of Britain, Russia, Austria and Prussia, who then installed the Bourbon Louis XVIII, brother of the late king. Peace had come, even though it was to be briefly interrupted the following year by the Hundred Days and the Waterloo campaign. Again, curious and suspicious, British visitors rushed over. It was Amiens over again but on a larger scale. In 1815, 8,500 passed through Calais and Boulogne, the main ports of entry; in 1820 there were 12,000; in 1825, 23,000.[2] Occasionally they would come across fellow countrymen who had stayed out the wars in France. The painter Benjamin Haydon met an English estate steward who had all but forgotten his native language. In one case, the visitors suspected their English guide to have been a deserter. Many years later in the Pyrenees, the writer Mrs Ellis fell in with a 'canny' old English cotton-spinner from Blackburn, an internee who had just stayed on after the peace.[3] Some by now were French as much as British, or more so even, as with members of the business community at

Bordeaux, the centre of the wine trade. Here were old Jacobites, political exiles. A number were Irish, both Catholic and Protestant. They were very well established. The Bartons (an important name still) had arrived in 1715, to be followed a year later by William Johnston. The Skinners, the Lawtons, the Fosters, the Kirwans were other wine families of this type, as were the Hennessys in nearby Cognac. While they had intermarried with local *bordelaises*, they still kept their old connections alive, not least for reasons of business, and continued to do so during the war, whatever the inconvenience. For instance, in 1805, Guillaume Lawton sent his eldest son Jean-Edouard by a Danish ship through the British blockade to school in Bath, where he was later joined by his younger brother. Jean-Edouard returned to Bordeaux in 1809 with other members of *bordelais* families, this time travelling via Heligoland, Emden, Amsterdam and Paris.[4]

Though initially some of these families were threatened – and indeed were forced into exile – by and large they escaped internment in 1803. Other businessmen were less fortunate: the entrepreneur Christopher Potter, ex-MP for Colchester, with a factory at Chantilly, was packed off to Verdun. Still, he was suspected of being a spy, and anyway his work, the manufacture of earthenware in Staffordshire style, was not the sort to qualify for the special treatment afforded to the most technologically advanced industries, textiles and metallurgy. The Revolution had set the economy back and the British blockade had limited its recovery; inevitably, in the chaos of the time, foreign workers were likely to suffer. For instance, some workmen from Manchester who in 1791 had been induced to transplant themselves to Toulouse, though not interned, found themselves unemployed when the war broke out two years later. Still, they managed to set up their own workshops in smaller towns in the region.[5] The French badly needed assistance that could be provided only from Britain, and governments, Napoleonic and Bourbon, went out of their way to attract British expertise. Dieppe in 1814 put Henry Wansey in mind of Bristol 50 years before. But it was Manchester he thought of when he reached Malaunay (now a suburb of Rouen), and gazed on a flourishing industrial estate, with three up-to-date cotton mills, each belonging to an Englishman, equipped with steam engines, dye-houses and bleaching yards.[6]

Rouen was an important industrial centre. The Englishmen at Malaunay, Messrs Deane, Halme and Adlam, were experts but not pioneers. John Holker had manufactured spinning machinery there in the 1770s, and his example had encouraged James Milne and his son from Manchester to start up in France a decade later. Cheaper labour, cheaper land and often financial support from the French government acted as powerful incentives. People like the Milnes were not for the internment centres. Indeed they came over happily during the war, one of them an engineer, Mr Dobson, arriving with 20 workmen in Normandy in 1811. The incentives had to be substantial, for the British government had no desire for French competition: it stood firmly against the export of machinery or skilled workers during the war and for some years afterwards. In 1814, when the Jackson family, cotton millers and engineers, moved to France subsidized by the new (royal) government, their property in Britain was confiscated.[7]

Another traveller, passing through Malaunay not long after Wansey, was Thomas Raffles. He too was reminded of the North of England, but, he wrote home, here the factories were not a 'deformity to the landscape', they did not cover it in smoke, nor were they surrounded by black roads and dirty cottages with rude and filthy inhabitants. Raffles was an example of the British tourist who had very little idea of what to expect. How odd it was, he reported, to hear a language which we had been accustomed to associate with every idea of polish and of elegance, chattered with amazing volubility on the quay at Dieppe.[8] The following year Charles and Eliza Stothard arrived at Dieppe on what amounted to a working honeymoon, during which Charles, a painter, was to make drawings of the Bayeux Tapestry for the Society of Antiquaries of London. Mrs Stothard described Dieppe in her letters home as very picturesque, and the countryside around as interesting but strange, with inhabitants who looked prematurely old. But where – echoing that old question – where were the gentry? There was no trace of them or their houses. At her inn in Dieppe, dining at the communal table, she was disconcerted by the noise, and by the company, particularly by her neighbour, 'a French gentleman, of a most monstrous size, whose naturally fierce look was considerably augmented by a large pair of well-curled mustachios; he seemed a mixture of all kinds, and yet was neither decidedly, bear, monkey, or man'. Opposite him sat an old beau of 60, dressed in a sky-blue coat, his hands scented and his fingers covered with French-paste rings, his immediate neighbour a 'pretty, lively woman, who conversed so familiarly with all the gentlemen that I was greatly surprised when I found she was an entire stranger at the board.' Decidedly this was not like Jane Austen's England.[9]

Mrs Stothard may have found difficulty in adapting to the exotics of the *table d'hôte*, but she was alert enough to what was going on. At Granville, she was struck by a peasant girl – beautiful, polite, natural, with neat clothes – who sold her some wooden shoes. With some trouble, Eliza persuaded the girl to allow her husband Charles to draw her portrait. While the sitting was in progress the girl asked her, why, if England were so fine a place, and its people so happy, 'what could induce so many of them to wander about France?' 'A desire to satisfy their curiosity', replied Eliza. The girl responded that 'curiosity was a thing never satisfied; and that God intended all people to rest content in the land where they were born'. Most French would have agreed, although they might have expressed the thought differently; if it was not exactly unnatural to travel so much, it was certainly eccentric.

Curiosity was indeed what drove Mrs Stothard. She was perceptive and she examined her impressions. 'A Frenchman's whole life', she noted, 'is apparently a great *jeu de théâtre*'. And 'Monsieur is *au désespoir* if you are dying, he is equally *au désespoir* if he treads upon your toes'. In the sardonic classification of travellers compiled by Edmund Eyre (borrowing wholesale from Laurence Sterne) she, like Katherine Wilmot before her, would rank among the Inquisitive Travellers. The other types are less meritorious. Such as the Proud and Vain Travellers, ostentatious and extravagant, the dupes of everyone, who on returning home extol the superior advantages of other lands. Or the Idle Travellers, wealthy persons of either sex, who quit their paternal estates and leave the tenants to the mercy of avaricious stewards, people travelling in pursuit of pleasure, simply to kill time. Then come the Splenetic Travellers, blinded by national prejudice and predetermined never to be pleased; and Lying Travellers who make everything up.[10]

Whatever the motive for a journey, it needed to be a strong one, for travelling abroad before the railways was expensive, laborious and uncomfortable. Just getting started could be arduous. Mary Berry on her trip to Paris in March 1802 had found the road from London to Dover so deep in mud that four horses could hardly drag the coach – not a particularly heavy one – at more than walking pace for miles together. 'No great road that I know in England is so tedious to travel as this from London to Dover'; even at the best time of year, she reckoned, it would mean a very long day's journey. Then passports. Two were needed, one from the Foreign Office who charged for it and one from the French Embassy which came free. There were complications. The Foreign Office required references. Edmund Eyre had to write to his MP at Bath, who applied on his behalf to someone at the General Post Office, who in his turn wrote to Lord Pelham, the Surveyor General of Customs of London. The French passport allowed free circulation within France, but as it was sent on to Paris, you needed a supplementary version for the first stage of your trip. And as Bertie Greatheed found to his cost, you required another passport to leave the country.

The logistics for those travelling by public transport were simpler. Even in 1802 you could book a seat on the Paris *diligence*, a long-distance bus, which left Charing Cross each morning and evening. The fare, which included the passage across the Channel, was £4.13.0 (say £325 in current money), with a possible excess baggage charge. Taking your own carriage was more complicated as well as being more expensive. For instance, should you cross the Channel by the ordinary ferry or by an independent boat? At the time of the Peace of Amiens in particular, Dover seems to have been in chaos, with the captains of the independent vessels pursuing arrivals to their hotels. They had been so long deprived of business, observed one passenger, that 'they were now like a flock of hungry cormorants contending for their prey'.[11] Certainly they were eloquent, the banker John Dean Paul found. The 'packet master', as he was called,

> set forth in *all his force of colouring*, the many advantages attending the one, and the dangers and difficulties accompanying the other; nay, he would almost have had us believe, that there were two kind of winds, one that blows for vessels hired at great price, the other for the *canaile* [sic].[12]

The most popular route across the Channel was from Dover to Calais; being the shortest it was the most kind to those who suffered from seasickness. On a good day a sailing boat could make the passage in three hours – occasionally even less – hardly more than twice as long as it takes now, but in bad weather the story was very different. For instance, Lord Cornwallis (travelling in November) was at sea for 15 hours. Peter Roget's brother-in-law made a crossing from Boulogne to Folkestone in three hours – but only after contrary winds had shut him up in Boulogne for a week. Some people preferred the longer sea journey from Brighton to Dieppe, since, once arrived, the road to Paris was shorter. Disadvantages were the tricky winds and the lack of a quay at Brighton. That could oblige passengers to scramble through breakers to reach a rowing boat, which hopefully an hour later would deposit them on board the ferry. And if embarkation could be difficult so could disembarkation. Here is Dr Roots's description:

> After a five hours' sail we got into Calais Roads, but not in time to save our tide; the consequence was we got into a French row-boat, and had to row about three miles to the shore, and then we could not get near enough to land without being carried on men's backs a quarter of a mile. This is really a frightful and unpleasant consequence of losing the tide, for they come in shoals round the vessel up to their middles in the water, and without asking permission seize hold of you, and by main force drag you off on their backs or shoulders, or anyhow, half in the water and half out, and gallop off with you to the shore, where down they set you over your ankles in the mud.

What is more, the 'rescuers' might be women. Deplorable, thought the British, most unseemly.[13]

As we have seen, the British who had arrived during the Peace of Amiens were apprehensive; they knew so little of what they would find. John Dean Paul and his party, by no means a timid lot, were surrounded on disembarkation at Calais by what Paul described as hundreds of the strangest figures imaginable: women with odd caps and no shoes or stockings, men half-naked and in rags, wearing weird – to nineteenth-century eyes – gold earrings. And the confusion was atrocious, the horses terrible and the people not just unsightly but dirty and disorderly too. Then Paul recollects himself: these after all are the people we thought would never get themselves together and now find 'form conquering armies'.[14]

There were French too on these cross-Channel boats. On Paul's for one: out of what he labelled a 'motley group' of fellow passengers, the most amusing, he thought, were two old French women with three young girls under their care. In 1802, Anne Plumptre (herself in company of a French lady and gentleman) was on a boat entering Calais that arrived just behind one filled with released French prisoners of war. They were singing, dancing, laughing, shouting and scrambling to see who would get on shore first. 'I never saw greater appearance of delight among a number of human beings', she said. Sir John Carr, however, witnessed a very different return to France, one that was sombre and poignant. At Southampton, he had noticed on the quay a pile of old portmanteaus and battered trunks, and became aware that they belonged to *émigrés*, refugees from the Terror, who after years of exile were taking the opportunity of the peace and a generous policy of amnesty, to return home. At Le Havre the usual fearsome-looking crowd was assembled, but it turned out to be there simply to have a look at the British and to carry their baggage. The *émigrés*, understandably much alarmed, were received in a sullen silence. What was more, the 'Revenue Officers', not celebrated for their kindness, treated them gently. Anyway, thought Carr, who respected them, they could have had nothing much to declare; 'they who brought nothing into a country but the recollection of their miseries, were not very likely to carry much out of it'.[15]

Sir John Carr took the *diligence* to Paris, John Dean Paul his own carriages, or rather one of them only. The coach that transported two servants and the luggage presented no particular problem, but the other, a barouche – a four-wheeler with seats facing each other – carrying him and his party, two gentlemen and three ladies in all, looked to be unsuitable. That it was potentially fast seemed rather academic after a day spent following in the wake of a lumbering coach. Worse, it was doubtful whether it could cope with French roads. Better, thought Paul, to have hired a good chaise at Dessein's hotel and left the barouche to be picked up on the return journey. Hiring though was not always straightforward: the British were bulkier; a cabriolet intended for three French might accommodate only two British.

An old English post-chaise – another light carriage with removable hood – might well have been Paul's best choice, but it was too late for that now.

Travellers could bring their own carriages with them, paying a deposit at French customs that was refundable on the return journey, but they had to leave their horses behind. The result, the mismatch of horse and carriage, could be ludicrous. Mrs King thought nothing more odd than the sight at Calais of some miserable horses, more dirty and forlorn than the shabbiest English carthorses, attached to Lord Guildford's elegant English carriage.[16] The Earl of Cholmondeley and his family, who needed 25 horses to pull their carriages, must have looked even more peculiar. You needed horses, and normally you needed postillions to manage them. The postillion mounted one of the wheel horses – the near horse of the leaders – and controlled the others with his whip. Those unfamiliar with a French postillion could find him amusing, advised *Galignani's New Guide to Paris* of 1822. He 'was on and off his horse's back twenty times in the course of one stage, without ever stopping the vehicle', was one description. But with all their leaping about – looking like 'as many Robinson Crusoes' – they were judged much more humane to the horses than their opposite numbers in Britain.[17]

How difficult travel in France could be at the beginning of the nineteenth century is illustrated by the journey made by Miss Berry, her sister Agnes and their father, at the end of October 1802. Their objective, as related in Chapter 1, was Nice, the purpose – as with so many British then and later – good health. (In fact, Mary Berry, whose health was most in question, was to survive another 50 years, by which time she was touching 90.) The trip started smoothly enough: the party had their own coach, spent a week in Paris on the way, and rolled gently south admiring as they went the forest of Fontainebleau in its glorious autumn colours. There were some difficulties on the approach to Lyon, however. At one place they found postillions but no horses, at the next, neither one nor the other. The horses that they eventually located were so feeble that on hills the passengers were obliged leave the carriage and walk. Still, it was after Lyon that things got out of hand. Torrential rain made the roads impassable, so the Berrys hired a boat to carry them, and their carriage, down the Rhône. It was hardly a cruise; the wind mounted, forcing them to take refuge ashore. The courier, with Mr Berry, went ahead to fetch horses and a lighter carriage, but by the time he returned, it was dark, windier yet and threatening more rain. So they stayed where they were, the sisters sleeping in the coach, the party taking turns to keep watch. Finally they made Vienne, the sisters reunited with their father, and set off once more down the river. Again they were forced ashore to spend what turned out to be two nights at Tain l'Hermitage, a village with two inns to choose between. The one they picked was in the event so unremittingly noisy that they moved on to the second. It sounds like a Gothic nightmare. And even if few people – after life with Horace Walpole – could have been better acclimatized to the Gothic mode than Mary Berry, the overwhelming gloom and the sinister inhabitants were enough to cause them to station their English servant in Mr Berry's room, his pistols at the ready.

One has the impression that by the time the party reached Avignon they were to an extent inured to the difficulties of the journey. Not that it became easier. They returned to the road and struggled on through renewed floods, their horses wading through the water. Twice the carriage got stuck. The first time they were rescued by a muleteer and his team, the second by soldiers quartered nearby. The inns hardly improved, for many years later Mary Berry remembered the one at Tourves (to the east of Aix-en-Provence) as the worst she had ever stayed in. But she remembered too their relief when three days later they walked along the rocky edge of the Mediterranean between Cannes and Antibes.[18]

Sixteen years later, Frances Carey and her husband also travelled down the Rhône to the South of France and encountered some of the same difficulties. Nevertheless, in general, conditions were less daunting. Roads were improved, carriages were lighter and better sprung and, whatever *Galignani* might say, the postillions looked less freakish, more like their English counterparts. The Careys experimented with their transport, hiring from *voituriers*, livery stables in English. They also went by the ubiquitous public *diligence*, which Frances Carey described as looking like 'a barn set upon wheels, with a cow-shed in the front and a haystack in the rear'. The traditional *diligence*, which might weigh up to five tons, was slow, with four miles an hour a likely speed. Another traveller related how on one trip he and a fellow passenger would get out and walk alongside in order to enjoy the fresh air and to be at liberty to talk more freely. Mrs Carey's 'cow-shed', the *Coupé*, its seats the most expensive, held three passengers and provided the best view of the countryside. *Murray's Guide* recommended it for ladies; provided they could secure all three places for themselves, it was possible to travel almost as comfortably as in a private carriage, so it advised. At the centre of the *diligence* was the *Intérieur*, with room for six people. In summer it could be oppressively hot, and if passengers were accompanied by dogs, disagreeably smelly. Children also were a nuisance, complained the writer Selina Bunbury, the French made too much of them. Behind the *Intérieur* was the *Rotonde*, dismissed by *Murray* as 'the receptacle of dust, dirt and bad company', and on top, above the main compartment, the *Impériale*, next to the conductor, popular with some British for the fresh air it allowed. However, it meant a climb to get up to it. The *Impériale*, described by Victor Hugo as the place for dreamers and artists and those who had gone down in the world, could be very uncomfortable if you were travelling in remote parts of the country, said Mrs Ellis. You had people clambering all over it, and there was a mass of luggage. A stranger might conclude, she thought, that a French *diligence* transported the whole population of a village.[19]

By the 1820s, a network of public coaches existed in France, and on main roads, just short of six English miles apart, post-houses were established where horses and postillions were changed, both for public and private transport. What is more, there was a greater choice of the former. Vélocifères on the Calais and Rouen roads to Paris were closer to an English stagecoach than was the *diligence*, and the new mail-coaches (*malles-poste*), carrying two or three passengers along with the mails, took priority at post-houses, and, for double the *diligence* fare, almost halved the journey time to Paris.[20] But most important of all for travellers was the introduction of steam-driven transport at sea and on the more important rivers. The first steamship had crossed the Channel in 1816 and by the early 1820s these boats were readily available. 'Our wheels dashed through the water in magnificent style', noted a traveller in her journal, although she found less agreeable the smell of oil and the noise of the engine. 'The continued shake, shake, shake of these boats' was another criticism. William Hazlitt put the technological leap forward more imaginatively: 'People wonder at the steam-boat, the invention of man, managed by man, that makes its liquid path like an iron railway through the sea.'[21]

The run from Dover to Calais in good weather now took two hours, although fog could still delay a boat for a long time. To the conservatively minded, though, it must have been some relief to find that the steamships' captains were of the same old breed, in there fighting off the competition. Did you cross by an English or a French boat? was the question. A correspondent for *Blackwood's Magazine*, travelling with his wife, chose the first, partly because the captain 'seemed such a hearty thorough-going Englishman'. But which boat goes the faster? he asked the captain; sometimes one, sometimes the other, was the reply. And it had to be admitted that the French boat was particularly good to look at. 'Ay, ay – no doubt' answered the captain to this, 'all outside though – like all the French'. Anyway, the boats got going, and it clearly was a race, with the French boat taking the lead. But then a mist came down and the Frenchman ran aground.[22]

Yet even by 1840 the application of steam power to water transport made little difference for those engaged in an extensive tour. True, London to Dover by road was now a matter of three hours, no more the 'very long day' of Mary Berry's time. John Ruskin, in Normandy a few years later, made forty to fifty miles a day; good carriage horses went at six or seven miles an hour.[23] The railway system developed late in France; in 1840 there were still only 410 kilometres of line in operation. The long, straight, empty roads of central France, which 80 years later would so delight British motorists and make the journey from one place to another a joy in itself, were a very different matter for those who, day after day, found themselves hitched behind horses plodding along at something a little over twice walking speed. It was very boring. Another contributor to *Blackwood's Magazine*, writing in 1834, did his best to find some excitement in it all. Imbued with romantic fervour, he set off for the Pyrenees. Not for him the dull old *diligence*, rather a pair of Norman horses on which to ride the whole way. Putting his valet (now his *garçon*) on one of them, they were, he announced, Don Quixote and Sancho Panza. Certainly he shared some of the Don's unconcern for facts, believing that the Pyrenees were 'the land of the Provençals'. How far the two of them looked the part, we cannot tell, but certainly the scenery was in tune, for it appeared to them as dull and flat as La Mancha itself.

> The truth is, that nothing can be more proverbially tiresome than a Continental high-road. The infinite length to which it stretches in a straight line, and its utter absence of all stirring objects, living or dead, tire the eye; the *stops* in the journey consisting only of the *façades* of villages that would dishonour a group of wig-wams by the comparison; no groves, no gardens, no farm houses, no showy equipages flitting along from one fine mansion to another – no fine mansions, no village steeples peeping up from their 'embosoming oaks' . . .

Escape from the 'eternal gabble' of the city was what the Don Quixote character desired, a contrast to Paris, and, like many of his countrymen, he got more than he bargained for. Few British understood the profound differences in atmosphere and people. The journalist William Playfair remarked that it was almost impossible for Englishmen to conceive how unlike each other were the Parisians and the peasantry, even those who lived within two or three miles of the city. Stendhal warned that you could never learn in Paris about the southern half of France, and another French writer of the time put it that 'even idleness itself differs: that of one [the country people] is a torpor, a monotony, a material existence; of the other, an unexplained bustle, purposeless motion. What is commonly called perpetual lounging'.[24]

In Paris or the provinces, British travellers clearly needed French money or access to it. Some of them were surprisingly vague. For instance, the visitor to Calais mentioned above, he who had to choose between an English and a French ship, having established himself and his family in a suite at the best hotel, discovered – or so he said – that he was without francs or a draft on a banker. With some enterprise he managed to borrow some money from the captain of his boat. John Dean Paul, after all in the business himself, had paid over pounds to a banker in Dover in return for a draft on his opposite number in Calais. Even he ran into some minor trouble: he had omitted to check the weight of the *louis d'or* with which he was supplied, only to discover later on the road that some of them were underweight and therefore discounted. Paul experienced another setback in Paris, though it probably came to him as no surprise. Back in 1792 he had deposited money with the highly respectable banker Perregaux. Unfortunately it was denominated in old revolutionary *assignats* which by now were virtually worthless. Perregaux, or Perregaux and Lafitte, were particularly useful to travellers. After the Restoration, Dr Roots, with a letter of credit, called on them to find that one office in their bank was reserved for British customers, and that by entering his name in a book any English letters which arrived would be forwarded to him. By then there was no problem about buying French currency in London, although the exchange rate was poor. It was apparently better simply to carry guineas and exchange them in France. For larger sums, bills of exchange were one possibility, though they were less favoured than the more flexible letters of credit from a London banker which, through Paris, could be used even in remote parts of the country.

Galignani could supply you with advice on money, with travelling maps and diligence routes and timetables. The booking, at least from London to Paris, could be made from home, private carriages could be hired in advance. A (French) courier to deal with hotels and inns and to act as a guide could be reserved. However, particularly if you intended a visit to the more distant provinces, a guidebook was helpful. As there was no *Murray* until 1843, and no English edition of *Baedeker* until 1861, it was necessary to rely on what was sometimes rather idiosyncratic advice. One thing was for certain – to anyone believing that travel in France was a carefree business, these guides would have been disillusioning. First of all, advised Dr Kitchiner MD in his *The Traveller's Oracle; or Maxims for Locomotion*, make your will before setting out. (And why not, he suggested, consult his book on the subject.) Actually the proposal was less melodramatic than it sounds; it was not that long ago since anyone travelling over any distance from the country to London, had done so more or less as a matter of course. Do not travel on a Sunday, Kitchiner warned, not merely to satisfy your own scruples, but because grooms and coachmen need rest. Be very careful about buying second-hand carriages: like second-hand cars later on, worn-out carriages could be marvellously freshened up with paint and putty.[25]

Guidebooks make plain how much preparation was necessary. The 1824 edition of the respected Richard's *Guide du Voyageur en France* suggests the traveller take along with him vinegar, strawberries, fresh lemons, some bottles of good wine, since local wine was often adulterated by innkeepers, and, for medicinal purposes, *eau-de-vie*. In any event, the British traveller, according to French lore, always carried soda water. Kitchiner counselled a stock of pins, needles, thread, a sketchbook and a notebook, which apart from more general use could be handy for autographs should you come across 'any extraordinary person'. He also mentions medicine chests. (Stendhal would have been doubtful on this; in his view you needed an excuse to call in the local doctor, who could tell you a lot about provincial life.) The recommendations get more and more onerous. Take your own sheets, with dressed leather covers to put over the mattress, urge both Richard and Kitchiner. The dangers of the bedrooms in country inns are hair-raising. Flowers in a room can impart tuberculosis, and contaminated cotton sheets, claims Richard, have been responsible for the plague that has devastated parts of the countryside. The first thing you should do on entering your room at an inn, he insists, is to sprinkle scent around and open the windows which, however, must at all costs be kept firmly shut at night.

> All doctors agree that the night air is impregnated with harmful vapours given off by plants, trees and marshland. In summer after rain, even the earth itself fills the atmosphere with miasmas of varying strength.

The toxic night air is a reason for never travelling at night; you must always reach your inn by nightfall. But it is not just Nature which is threatening. Dr Kitchiner makes Mary Berry's Gothic innkeepers sound really quite typical. As soon as you have opened or closed windows, he says, look under the beds and in the closets. It is not a bad idea to have pocket-sized door bolts with you. And weapons. An umbrella with a sword in its shaft and double-barrelled pocket pistols with spring bayonets have much to recommend them. If it is possible to do so – accidentally as it were – make sure the landlord of the inn sees you are armed.

Whatever the uncertainties appertaining to inland inns and hotels, many British required no advice in respect of Boulogne or Calais. At Boulogne, the Hôtel de l'Angleterre was for years run by an Englishman, Mr Parker. Two of the Amiens travellers, Henry Redhead Yorke[26] and John Dean Paul, were saddened to find him much reduced by imprisonment during the Revolution and, no doubt, by the shortage of customers since. 'He greeted me with unfeigned pleasure', said Yorke, though he was shocked by his appearance. He seemed to have little authority over his staff, wrote Paul, complaining of the indifferent food and an impudent waiter. The Calais hotel was Quillacq's, usually called Dessein's after its former owner. Many customers remembered it from the old days, but an especial fame was due to its place in Laurence Sterne's *A Sentimental Journey*. Sterne was still virtually an oracle for British travellers; his name appears again and again in their books, and was familiar to the French as well. When Dr Roots complained of damp beds and noisy rats to the landlord of his inn at Montreuil, all he got in response was a shrug and the answer that it was curious he should find fault with the same bed and room in which Sterne had lately slept. Roots's comment was apt considering that Sterne's visit had taken place near enough 50 years before: 'from my heart I verily believe he must have been the last occupier of it, from its filth and musty appearance'. Even in 1802, when it had been deprived of British guests for years, Quillacq's boasted 140 bedrooms, with 42 servants living in. Thackeray described it as the great hotel of Europe. The wit Sydney Smith, writing in 1835, gave it the heartfelt eulogy that so well expressed the feelings of excited British arrivals.

> To compare it with any hotel in England is a violation of common sense in breakfasting and dining. Such butter was never spread in England, no English hen could lay such eggs, no English servant could brew such coffee.[27]

The American Colonel Pinkney, touring England and France in 1807 and 1808, declared Quillacq's to be the only inn in France that could enter into a reasonable comparison with any of the respectable taverns either in England or America. Nowhere else have they any idea of the importance of 'that first of comforts to the wearied traveller', a clean and housewife-like bed. At the same time, discussing the inns south of the Loire, Pinkney remarks how much cheaper they are than their equivalents in England, how too their food is better, how French cooks are infinitely obliging and how the wine is far superior. The drawback is simply that they are primitive. Too often the bedroom serves also as the dining room, its walls are merely whitewashed or covered with 'execrable' pictures, there are no curtains, and no soap, water or towels are provided. The furniture is wretched.[28]

'He who travels must learn to bargain, or be both cheated and laughed at', pronounced the veteran traveller Thomas Holcroft. 'In France all cheating is fair, and if the subject be an English milord, meritorious', insisted John Mayne. Mix such warnings with a natural ignorance of local customs and there is a recipe for mistrust, confusion and bitterness. Katherine Wilmot recorded that at her hotel in Paris, three men attended me up to my bedchamber, to my utter consternation there were none other but themselves to act the part of chamber maids. One had been a soldier, and had invaded Ireland, but in the true malleability of the French spirit had dwindled from a hero to a *fille de chambre* ... At l'Hôtel de l'Europe we stay'd but a couple of days, as a system of cheatery commenc'd and Lord Mount Cashell was obliged to have recourse to the commissary, on account of extortion.

However, Lord Mount Cashell managed to obtain immediate justice.[29]

Keep your wits about you on the road, warned Dr Kitchiner, never allow a stranger to join you if you can possibly avoid it, whether his appearance be shabby or genteel. And you never know where a postillion may take you if he can – as the Revd Mr Shepherd found. His postillion, a boy aged about 13, drove his cabriolet to the wrong hotel at Rouen, to the Hôtel de la Marine rather than to the Hôtel de France. It was dark and Shepherd discovered the mistake by enquiring of a passer-by. After a lot more driving around in the narrow streets the postillion landed them at another hotel. Except that it was not; it was still the Hotel de la Marine, the back entrance. Anyway this gentle adventure ended satisfactorily, and Shepherd and his companion, exhausted by the day, went early to bed at the right hotel. They did not sleep long. For at about 11 o'clock a cacophony (at least to them) of musical instruments shattered the silence of the town. This was not some bizarre French usage, but the work of a fellow countryman. 'An English baronet, travelling, I suppose, for improvement, – he had great need of it – had supped in state, and had drank [sic] Burgundy all night to the sound of horns, violins, and bassoons, which he had collected from all quarters of the town.'[30]

However, it is time to get the French view of some of these visitors. Here is an example.

Amid the clutter of the old rattle-trap [a *diligence*] one noticed first a leg, that judging by the expressive 'Goddam' with which its owner accompanied a further kick at a wretched dog, appeared to me to belong to an Englishman. Then it was possible to make out the rest of the traveller: an Englishman wrapped up in a frock coat as thick as a blanket, his head covered by a felt bonnet with chain, who from time to time put his hand to the leg bitten by the dog; whistling, he looked out on the countryside around Chartres, and swallowed some mouthfuls of rum, a supply of which he carried in a leather-covered flask ... he took another swig, closed his flask and replaced it in his pocket.

Another 'Goddam' and a fight with one of the passengers followed.[31]

There are other examples of rude, if not aggressive, behaviour on *diligences.* One problem was that the British often considered them a low class of transport, and therefore a demeaning one in which to travel. Thomas Campbell wrote home of one trip, 'Our company from Rouen was composed of two English compatriots – a man and a woman – a French-man, and myself. The English were people of fortune, reduced by some accident to travel in a Diligence. They were therefore sullen, timorous, and afraid of losing their dignity, by speaking to poor creatures, as unfortunate as themselves in having recourse to such a vehicle. They never exchanged a word, English or French, with us for seventy-two miles! The Frenchman and I talked the whole time.' Selina Bunbury encountered a fellow English traveller on the *diligence* to Boulogne who could not speak a word of French, and who, in a filthy temper, scolded the conductor for not understanding English.[32]

William Hazlitt was particularly trenchant about British failings:

> The rule for travelling abroad is to take our common sense with us, and leave our prejudices behind us. The object of travelling is to see and learn; but such is our impatience of ignorance, or the jealousy of our self-love, that we generally set up a certain preconception beforehand (in self-defence, or as a barrier against the lessons of experience,) and are surprised at or quarrel with all that does not conform to it. Let us think what we please of what we really find, but prejudge nothing. The English, in particular, carry out their own defects as a standard for general imitation; and think the virtues of others (that are not *their* vices) good for nothing. Thus they find fault with the gaiety of the French as impertinence, with their politeness as grimace. This repulsive system of carping and contra-diction can extract neither use nor meaning from anything, and only tends to make those who give way to it uncomfortable and ridiculous.[33]

How badly even the most cultivated of travellers might behave is illustrated by Lytton Strachey when he recalled a trip to Paris made by his grandfather and Thomas Carlyle. On reaching their destination, the postillion asked for a tip. He was curtly refused, Strachey's grandfather adding 'Vous avez drivé devilish slow!' Fifty years before, as Lytton Strachey points out, a cultivated Englishman would have piqued himself in answering the postillion in the idiom and accent of Paris.[34]

There were of course, mainly in Paris, gallicized British, who copied what they thought were French attitudes and modes of behaviour. They were considered rather ridiculous. Some, with the best will in the world, tried to enter into what they thought was the right spirit by acting with boisterous enthusiasm when they were in the company of French people. But it is Washington Irving's impression of what he calls 'the English family-carriage on the continent', quoted at the start of this chapter, the insularity, the self-satisfaction, which remain in the mind. A French satirist catches a similar coach load arriving at the Hôtel Meurice in Paris. They appear, he says, in a pretty *berline du voyage* with four horses and two servants up on top. In front comes a courier with gold lace braiding to his uniform. Four people get out: three of them young men with the same brown hats, blue silk handkerchiefs at the neck, identical jackets and trousers and grey boots. The fourth person is in black from head to toe, the mentor but in effect a servant. Some young French girls at the hotel windows start laughing. One of the young men pulls his hat over his nose, raises a spyglass and starts talking in unintelligible French to a maid, whom he calls *la pucelle*. 'A nice bit of work', he drawls to one of his friends.[35]

But, explains the author, these were not genuine milords, who might possibly have behaved with more discretion, but 'commercials', over for a fortnight's holiday. Guillaume de Bertier de Sauvigny in his *Nouvelle Histoire de Paris – la Restauration* quotes a disillusioned hotel employee who lamented that in the old days only the well born travelled. But 'nowadays you see thousands of grotesque people, perched like parrots on top of a diligence arriving inexpensively to visit Paris ... A bunch of penniless Goddems or miserly rentiers, officers on half-pay, eccentrics of ludicrous appearance, workingmen, artisans on foot, dining in low-class eating houses, drinking cheap wine ... and never settling the bill without making the most fatuous comments'. And the writer John Scott relates that one of his companions on the *diligence* to Paris in 1814 was a young English shopkeeper, come over for a week, determined to see the Louvre, who spoke no French, knew no one in Paris, and had not bothered with a passport or money. He brimmed over with self-confidence and 'would like to see a Frenchman refuse a Bank of England note'.[36]

Before the wars, the place to find the 'penniless Goddems', the debtors and the disgraced was on the Channel coast, above all at Calais, Dunkirk and Boulogne. It was near to hand and it was cheap. Henry Redhead Yorke, an early arrival at Boulogne during the Peace of Amiens, noted that while he was ahead of returning debtors, they were expected soon. Anyway, he thought, Boulogne would suit them better than the woods of America, among the rattlesnakes and savages. Life might be less dangerous in the Channel ports but it could be depressingly drab. Still, that is not the word to use about one household, crammed into a second-floor apartment in the Rue St-Michel, Calais, a year or two after Waterloo.[37]

It comprised four members, all Verdun alumni, all in a bad way. The brothers, the Honourable Charles and Harry Tufton, later tenth and eleventh Earls of Thanet, belonged to a family that once ranked among the very richest in Britain, but now, through gambling, found itself in deep trouble. (Their father, the ninth Earl, Fox's friend, was no help: he was preoccupied at the time, losing at the tables in Paris.) The other two members of the group add spice and illustrate another important function of Calais and Boulogne, their place as havens for lovers. Captain the Honourable Evelyn Dormer was a cavalry officer captured by the French in Spain, his lover Edith Jacquemont, was the daughter of a French colonel. They had met at a moment when the beautiful 15-year-old Edith, on her confessor's orders, was parading down the highway with her hands tied behind her back. They fell in love and she accompanied Dormer to Verdun, and later shared with him the discomforts of the forced marches westwards that followed the allied advance into France. Then there was a break; Edith went off to Paris with a French count who soon dumped her. She then rejoined her old lover in London, in time for another flight, not this time from advancing armies but from the sheriff's officers.

The story has a more or less happy ending. The Tuftons succeed to the family fortune, or what is left of it, and so does Captain Dormer. Back in London, in 1819, the bailiffs are actually in his house removing the furniture – or so we are told – when the news arrives of his brother's death and his own succession to the family peerage and money. As to Edith Jaquemont, she transfers to Harry Tufton who installs her in a comfortable villa in St John's Wood.[38]

Calais 'seems to have become a sort of purgatory for half-condemned souls', observed Lady Granville when she found her old friend Lady Oxford living there in lodgings. It was there too, in January 1815, that Nelson's Emma Hamilton had died. On the strength on his experience of Boulogne in the 1840s, the poet Thomas Campbell would probably have agreed with Lady Granville. While he was not in flight from creditors, he needed to save money, partly in order to pay for his niece's education. Though Boulogne was more expensive than many other parts of France, he said, it was cheaper than London: £200 there went as far as £300 in London. (In fact, thought one British traveller, the real saving in living abroad came from dispensing with comforts that would have been considered essential at home.) As to the French, Campbell thought them rather unfriendly, but at least there were some agreeable English. And some very disagreeable ones too, gangs of swindlers who preyed on the shopkeepers. But, oh, after a few months, how dull life was.[39]

Campbell died after a year of exile, a straightforward and accommodating man when compared to George Brummell, for whom it was a 24-year sentence. Beau Brummell, 'the very glass of fashion' in Thomas Raikes's description, the exquisite of exquisites, the dandy of dandies, his conversation, in the words of Virginia Woolf, 'flickering, sneering, hovering on the verge of insolence, skimming the edge of nonsense'.

> The French Revolution had passed over his head without disordering a single hair, Empires had risen while he experimented with the crease of a neck-cloth and criticised the cut of a coat.

Intimate of the Prince of Wales, admired, beloved even, by men and women, he too had run out of money. And of royal favour, for his tongue had taken him beyond the verge of insolence. So in May 1816, aged 38, he stepped ashore at Calais, never to return to England. To start with, it could have been worse. What was left of his capital, meagre though it was by London standards, went a long way in Calais. His lodgings provided a dining room, a drawing room and a bedroom, his meals were brought in from Quillacq's. He tried hard, he was funny, popular with his landlord and, having improved his French, became popular too with local French society. It was ridiculous, he told one of his visitors, Harriette Wilson, to go to the Continent, whether you were there from necessity or choice, merely to associate with other English. His friend Lady Granville heard in 1824 that he was the happiest of men, living chiefly with the local people and entering into all the 'little gossip of the place'. Just as he used to do in London. (But, nevertheless, he was always on the quay when the English boats came in.) In 1830, the King having died, the Duke of Wellington, the Prime Minister, appointed him consul at Caen. He travelled there via Paris, where he was entertained by Talleyrand and by the British Ambassador. But from then on it was downhill without a stop. For, like so many of his ineffable generation, Brummell was congenitally incapable of living down to his income. The consulship was abolished, through his own fault, and in 1833 he spent ten weeks in the Caen prison for failing to pay his debts. He was rescued (again) by his friends, who contributed to an annuity, one of the subscribers being the new King, William IV. Even in prison he spent hours a day in dressing and bathing. Now all that came to an end. He suffered two strokes, his mind failed, he gave imaginary receptions for long-dead friends, new debts accumulated. By 1838 he was filthy, looked like a ghost and acted like an automaton. He was taken by an English friend who lived in Caen to the asylum of Bon Sauveur, where, in 1840, he died, by that time an improbable Victorian.[40]

3

A Tumultuous Entente

Where shall I begin with the endless delights
Of this Eden of milliners, monkeys and sights –
This dear busy place, where there's nothing transacting
But dressing and dinnering, dancing and acting?

Thomas Moore, 'The Fudge Family in Paris'

To many British visitors France offered a delightful freedom from cant and inhibition. There was William Hazlitt in a public coach on the road to Brighton, bound for a cross-Channel ferry, when a fellow passenger, a Frenchman, started to play his guitar. 'It was a relief to the conversation in the coach, which had chiefly been supported in a nasal tone by a disciple of Mrs Fry and amanuensis of philanthropy in general. As we heard the lively musician warble, we forgot the land of Sunday-schools and spinning-jennies. The Genius of the South had come out to meet us'.[1] It was Paris that epitomized the special allure, the romance of France. For Dr Roots, his wife and their two young children arriving from Dover in 1814 shortly after the peace, their holiday started badly. The Customs officials were surly, there were rats in their rooms at Montreuil, and at Chantilly an incompetent blacksmith charged too much to fix the wheels of their carriage – 'a piece of Jack Frog's imposition', grumbled Roots. But his delight as they entered Paris wiped all that out; it recalls Katherine Wilmot waking up in Calais thirteen years before. 'We now exclaimed', he wrote, ' "Are we asleep? Is it all a dream, or are we really and truly at this very moment in the gay, the magnificent city of Paris?" '[2]

Visitors did not expect or want Paris to be like London. The tempo of life was different. In London, the people in the streets hurried, oblivious to the world around them, their demeanour grave and collected, all with business in mind. Time in England, it was said, passed more quickly than it did elsewhere. Here in Paris, noted the writer Anna Jameson, 'as a little girl observed the other day, all the people walk about "like ladies and gentlemen going a visiting." '[3] Generally the British who knew the city back in the old days thought it improved physically. A friend, John Ward, wrote home to Mary Berry that 'Bonaparte's improvements to Paris are quite magnificent and in the best possible taste'.[4] Sir Walter Scott, in Paris partly to gather material for a book on Napoleon, wrote in his journal of the magnificence of the buildings. We could not achieve the like in Britain, he thought, for 'royal magnificence can only be displayed by despotic power'. (Happily, he was wrong – witness the Prince Regent's rebuilding of the West End of London.)[5] The improvements, wrote another visitor, one who had come over in 1802, 'will go near ... to make Paris the queen of cities, and sovereign of the world, in grandeur and magnificence'. Samuel Rogers, upset by the smells for one thing, was less admiring, yet he wrote of the neighbourhood of the Tuileries that 'it strikes you as the city of a great king', as opposed to London, 'the city of a great people'.[6] But Anna Jameson raised a pertinent question: charming as it all was, was this in the end real life? She thought not, visualizing Paris as a 'place to live in for the merry poor man, or the melancholy rich one ... but to the thinking, the feeling, the domestic man, who only exists, enjoys, suffers through his affections, to such a one, Paris must be nothing better than a vast frippery shop, an ever varying galanty show, an eternal vanity fair, a vortex of folly, a pandemonium of vice'.[7]

Many people would have agreed with Anna Jameson's doubts about real life. It was the reason they liked the city so much and would carry on liking it for another hundred years or more. It was Gay Paree, the place where anything goes. William Jerdan's book of 1817, *A late Visitant. Six weeks in Paris; or, A cure for the Gallomania*, is a warning, the author says, to the British now emigrating in shoals from their own happy native country. In practice, despite the minatory title, he merely bundles up old legends to produce some good fun. As in the days of the Grand Tour, there is a young lord, Lord Beacon, 'piping hot from the University of Oxford', a bit vain and impetuous, accompanied on this his first visit abroad by his tutor Dr Ferret. There is some modern dressing: the polished manners of the *ancien régime* and the 'amenity of disposition' in which Paris excelled the world have gone. 'The women (who were never famed for chastity) are now repulsive from their meretricious dress (or rather want of it) and offensive by their *double entendres*' – actually anglicized French – 'which they scarcely deign to veil so as not to be utterly offensive to the ears of modesty'. Anyway, Lord Beacon is delighted and, as they leave a restaurant where they have gained some personal experience of what are termed the women's free and easy manners, the plot changes. They are greeted by an English 'view holloa' from Beacon's old friend Sir Humphrey Homespun who, it turns out, has been dragged to Paris by his wife. He is hating it all, longs for some wholesome English food and can no longer understand what his wife is saying, for she will speak nothing but French. In any event, he sees little of her, since she has told him (in English presumably) that in Paris husband and wife, unless they want to make themselves a laughing stock, must never be seen together by day and must have separate apartments at night. This last requirement does not matter much since she never returns to their hotel until 'three or five in the morning'.

Jerdan's was just one of many books. Over the past few years, one author wrote in 1819, it would be a very modest assertion to say that as many books on travels in France have been written as would fill a country gentleman's library.[8] None of them was more successful than John Scott's *A Visit to Paris in 1814*, which had run to four editions by 1816 and was followed by a sequel, *Paris Revisited in 1815*. Scott is intent on giving a rounded view of the city, its inhabitants and the differences to England in customs and attitudes. Architecturally, he declares, Paris is splendid, with houses that rise to twice the height of those in London, without a sign of monotonous speculative building – 'building rows by contract' – and with the streets leading off the main boulevard seeming 'to dart into a peopled and swarming confusion and uncertainty ... instead of being, like all the principal streets in London, self-imitators'. Paris is a 'glass bee-hive' where you see everything that is going on, for the 'essence of the existence of Parisians is a consciousness of being observed ... [They] live only for the bustle and notice of present society'. It is a place given over wholly to enjoyment.

> In the principal streets, almost every second house has a part of it devoted to amusement, or luxurious gratification of some sort. The shops appear to be almost exclusively occupied with embellishments and eatables, and certainly wherever superior ingenuity is shewn, on which Paris may fairly plume herself, it is in the manufacture of some decoration, some piece of virtù, some elegant trifle.

So far so good. Scott then turns to the contrast in social behaviour, British and French; on the one hand, what the French termed *formalisme*, in this context a conformity to rules, on the other, a marked lack of such constraint. Order versus disorder. Scott takes ordinary domestic arrangements as an example. In London, a mere glance from the street at the windows of a house will tell you how the rooms are used. One type of curtain indicates the dining room, another the drawing room, another a bedroom and so on. In Paris there is nothing so systematic. But principally he is concerned with ideas on social responsibility. A French family with a daughter of marriageable age, 'who must be put out in a marketable manner', will take a large and elegant *hôtel*, where they will entertain suitably. The daughter disposed of, they will sell or let the house and revert to a life of thrift and comparative obscurity. In England, such a public comedown would be regarded as shameful. Again, in London, should you keep a cabriolet – a smart one-horse carriage – you are required to live up to it; in Paris, you are perfectly at liberty to help defray the expense 'of this equipage of a gentleman by wearing a coat that an English journeyman would be ashamed to put on'.

More fundamental is the lack of what Scott terms 'moral symmetry'. The French, he claims, possess no 'fixed monuments of sound principle'. He finds it ridiculous, unseemly, that in France a dustman may take off his hat to a washerwoman. A Frenchman of the lower class, lacking 'a just sense of that to which he may pretend with propriety', will 'ape the etiquette of the higher orders, even while he submits to their insults'. Then there is the place of women in society. In well-to-do circles in Britain, he points out, the women leave the table as soon as dinner is finished. In France they remain with the men, sharing in the conversation, and by doing so they place themselves in an equivocal position, even though much less is drunk and the conversation is less licentious than in Britain. When he extends his analysis down the social scale, Scott runs into difficulty. He has no hesitation in conceding that 'the common classes ... are polished and conversable to a degree unknown in England'. Ordinary women, poor girls selling toys in the market, are reading Voltaire or Madame de Sévigné when not busy with a customer. Such erudition would be inconceivable in Britain. Moreover, Frenchwomen run their husbands' shops, control who he brings home with him, sit freely among crowds of men, wives mingling with prostitutes. And yet there is no drunkenness, no very gross breach of decorum. To Scott and to his readers such freedom is inappropriate, for moral order requires that woman should be, so far as possible, in her separate place, adorable and unsullied, already mounting what will be her Victorian pedestal.

For many visitors the romance, as in 1801 and 1802, was shadowed still by the past, by the memories of the massacres, of the guillotine, of the matchless armies which had ravaged Europe. Mary Berry was cautious about returning to Paris. After Waterloo she had written to Mrs Damer that 'the state of France appears almost as wretched as ever ... [T]hey have got rid of Bonaparte, it is true; but when will they get rid of the moral degradation which his reign fixed on them? ... for if peace and the *habits of peace* are not soon restored both to France and to England, we shall witness a new order of social society in *both* countries, when war will be the habitual state, and peace only occasionally recurred to'. However, she did come over in 1816 to stay with her friends Lord and Lady Hardwicke, and to find herself one of a crowd of upper-class British who, over two or three years, flushed with money, dominated French social life. Edward Stanley, a future bishop of Norwich, wrote home asking rhetorically,

> Where are the French? Nowhere. All is English; English carriages fill the streets, no other genteel Equipages are to be seen. At the Play Boxes are all English. At the Hotels, the Restaurations [restaurants] – in short, everywhere – John Bull stalks incorporate.[9]

Miss Berry soon found herself at home, though there was a bad start with her luggage going astray. (But that did not much matter since she was at once taken shopping.) Her approach to Paris life was unusual: she had always liked it, she wrote home, for it allowed one some quiet. Anyway she was soon fully in the swim; she resumed old contacts – she was, it has been said, almost as well known in Parisian society as in London's – she attended the theatre, and some sumptuous dinner parties. At one of these given by Pozzo di Borgo (the Russian Ambassador, and a bitter enemy of his fellow Corsican Napoleon) she sat next to a very old friend, the Duc de Richelieu, the Prime Minister. Two evenings later, at a dinner given by Comte Alexis de Noailles, her immediate neighbour was the Duke of Wellington, the commander of the Allied Army of Occupation. She enjoyed her stay but regretted that nearly everywhere too many of the guests were British. The French aristocracy were too short of money to participate fully, and Miss Berry noted that even on a wet Sunday in Hyde Park you saw 20 times more handsome carriages than there were present on Good Friday at Longchamp. (Good Friday was a gala day in France.)

Clearly not all the British arrivals were party-going patricians. The journalist Albert Vandam remembered in his youth staying with two of his uncles, British army surgeons, who had served during the Waterloo campaign and come on to Paris afterwards, never to leave again for any length of time. Vandam added that they had become effectively French, but with one reservation – they wanted to be buried near Amsterdam, for in Paris 'a man is forgotten in a fortnight by his best friends'.[10]

Had they known where to go, the multitude of British in Paris would have encountered some exotic fellow countrymen. The poet and ex-Girondin Helen Maria Williams, imprisoned by Robespierre, whose party Charles Fox had reluctantly attended on his visit to Paris, was one. Another was an amazing eighteenth-century survivor, Quintin Craufurd, as it happened a cousin of Mary Berry, a romantic hero indeed. Craufurd and his lover Anna Sullivan had been partners of Axel von Fersen in organizing the ill-fated escape of Louis XVI and Marie Antoinette from the Tuileries. They provided the fake passports and the lumbering coach which carried the couple to the border town of Varennes. And before that, Craufurd had been a notably successful soldier of fortune – the 'nabob of Manila' who acquired a large share in the ransom paid by Spanish-owned Manila when it was captured by the British during the Seven Years War. Craufurd's maxim was a straightforward one: 'Make your fortune where you like, but enjoy it in Paris.' He had arrived in 1783, accompanied by Madame Sullivan, whose husband was left behind in India. As well as being extremely rich, he was erudite and cultivated, publishing a two-volume study of India among other books, and building up a remarkable art collection. The Varennes affair had meant a lengthy exile, but the couple returned to Paris in 1802, married and, with the aid of Talleyrand (to whom Craufurd had loaned money and with whom he shared a passion for cards) and later, it seems, that of the Empress Josephine, survived Napoleon's purge of British subjects. On the restoration of the Bourbons in 1814, Craufurd arranged the purchase by the British government of what is still the British Embassy, while his own splendid house was to be the centre of the ebullient British community in Paris until his death in 1819.[11]

British *milords* were notoriously eccentric, but none more so than another Paris resident during the Empire, Francis Egerton, son of the Duke of Bridgwater and, later in life, himself Earl of Bridgwater. Born in 1756, he arrived during the Amiens peace, and stayed on until he died in 1829. He did better than just hang on: he lived in great magnificence, occupying palaces abandoned by their owners during the Revolution, the Hôtel Richelieu, then the Hôtel de Noailles. Egerton, absorbed in genealogical study, was unmarried – with an illegitimate daughter – and, like Craufurd, enjoyed entertaining. There was, though, a problem: he was difficult to get on with, and seems to have run short of orthodox guests. He found substitutes in dogs and cats who, dressed up in the style of fashionable men and women, were seated at his table as dinner companions. Apparently these friends of his, again appropriately dressed, were also taken out on carriage rides around Paris.[12]

For all the fun, it would have been strange if the French had not harboured resentment. This found particular expression in the theatre, in plays mocking the customs, the looks, the clothes of the British occupiers, and with such titles as *Les Anglaises pour Rire* (featuring *milords* Pif, Paff and Pouff) and *Le Spleen*, ill-temper being, it was supposed, an especially British characteristic. The hostility was particularly marked in the case of old soldiers, now unemployed or on half-pay. Captain Gronow,[13] late of the

British cavalry and living in Paris, recalled in his memoirs an episode that concerned a friend of his, a British officer, who was struck in the face by a French officer at the Palais Royal. In the duel that followed, the Englishman shot his opponent dead, only to find himself challenged the next day by one of the dead man's seconds. Again he fought a duel, this time wounding his adversary in the arm. But then more challengers were queuing up and the nightmare was only checked by the intervention of the French authorities. The humiliation of defeat was made the more bitter when the Duke of Wellington ('Lord Vilain-ton'), representing the allied governments, emptied the Louvre of the spoils accumulated during the years of Napoleon's conquests. Nor was reassurance for the French to be found in British politicians. To quote an historian of the period,

> In French eyes, when a British minister or publicist talks of humanity, he is thinking of himself; when he talks of philanthropy, he is planning domination by his country; when he talks of the general interest, he is calculating his own; big words indicate appetites.[14]

In 1821 the Duchesse de Broglie, Madame de Staël's daughter, liberal and with many British friends, wrote to William Wilberforce about the *horrible* slave trade, regretting that she and her husband could do so little to help him. There is, she said, 'so strong a national prejudice against everything that comes to us from England'.[15] A few years later, at a reception at the British Embassy, Lady Granville, wife of the Ambassador, found to her dismay that her French guests vociferously refused to mix with the British.[16] In 1825, in outraged terms, the *World of Fashion* reported the reception, or rather lack of reception, accorded on his arrival at Calais to the Duke of Northumberland who was on his way to represent George IV at the coronation of Charles X. The Duke, a man 'very fond of ancient state and ancient chivalry', was greeted by three half-ragged soldiers and escorted to his hotel only by his own domestics. No flag was waved, no gun fired in salute, except by the vessels belonging to the British convoy.

And behind the extravagant and ostentatious *milords* loomed, shadowy and more discreet, the industrialists of the Midlands and the North of England, possessed of an undoubted superiority in technology, and poised, unrestrained now by Napoleon's prohibition, to sweep into the French market. Hard men, from a hard country which lived for money. Even the British soldiers in Paris, members of the occupying army, disciplined and correct as they were, could be likened to automatons, suggestive of machines from Birmingham. What future had the ordinary artisan in a world where machines were all-powerful – a British-model poorhouse, perhaps? Britain was in the place that a century later would be occupied by the United States. 'England is too rich for the happiness of France', said a woman in a public coach to Benjamin Haydon.[17]

It was at Paris, or near Paris, that fear and hostility came to a head in a confrontation between British workmen and local people. Paul Gerbod,[18] an expert, has estimated that there were at least 16,000 British workers in France during the 1820s. Many were employed in Paris or nearby. Farry et Breitman was one British firm, well-known and highly regarded carriage-makers, but the largest were the engineers Manby and Wilson, who employed a British workforce of 250 at Charenton, just to the west of the city.[19] In the 1820s this firm proved spectacularly successful. Initially at Birmingham and then at Charenton and later at Le Creusot in Burgundy, they built the first iron steamships to be used on the Seine. With remarkable versatility they established a gas company, one of four brought into being to supply Paris with gas lighting. Manby also installed heating by hot water pipes in the Paris Bourse. British workers were attracted by high wages – the Jacksons, mentioned in the previous chapter, for instance, paid Sheffield rates – and a lower cost of living. They were, though, repelled by French customs and food. Turnover was high and their reputation was poor. A witness to a select committee of the House of Commons in 1825 declared that these emigrant workers, 'though able workmen ... in general [are] persons of extremely bad character, continually drunk, constantly quarrel-ling'. One reason for Manby and Wilson's success was Aaron Manby's knack of laying his hands on skilled workers, in defiance of the supposedly strict rules imposed by Britain intended to keep them at home. Ironically, only a few weeks after Manby was accused in the House of Commons of having 'carried off twelve men, in the inside and on the top of a coach out of Gracechurch Street', his firm's arrangements on employment were in crisis. According to a report in *The Times*, 50 of Manby and Wilson's English workers, armed with sticks, raged through the commune of Charenton, beating up everyone they came across, women and children included. A few days later, the paper produced an amended version of what had happened, reallocating the blame; this time the local population were held to be mainly at fault.

The late affair at Charenton was commenced by charbonniers [coalmen] and boatmen, who, it appears, have an inveterate hatred to the Englishmen at the factory, not only as Englishmen, but from the immense wages they earn, which enables them to detach their wives and women from them, giving rise to everlasting disputes and quarrels.[20]

For months past, it appeared, any lone Englishman was likely to be set upon by a gang of locals. The workmen had hit out in response. When three of the British were arrested and imprisoned by the Charenton police, the workers at the factory came out on strike, demanding their release. (Whether it was the British workmen only who struck is not clear.) On an appeal by Mr Wilson, the Paris police and a magistrate intervened and the British were released, with some of the locals going to prison in their place. For a moment it looked as if the matter might not end there. Some individual British, one a pregnant woman, were assaulted. Feelings mounted outside the commune. The students at the veterinary college had, it seems, to be locked in by their teachers to prevent their joining the fray against the foreigner. A 'plot' to march 500 or more men from the Faubourg St-Antoine – that incubator of violence – to Charenton was revealed in the nick of time. Or so the report went.

It turned out to be something of a storm in a teacup; for, after all, nobody was actually killed, nor was there a sequel, at least for some years. It helped that in the 1820s most of these British were in France only temporarily; part of their job was to train French replacements. Few of the more typical British men who came over to Paris had any job at all and, sexually adventurous as they might be, were unlikely to be in a position to 'detach' the wives and women of the French working class. In fact, the *milords* or *milord* types had little in common with Mr Manby or Mr Wilson themselves, let alone with their employees. However, from the point of view of the French authorities, they were not all harmless, just out for a good time and to spend money that would help revive the weakened French economy. Some were fervent supporters of the exiled Emperor. In November 1814 – that is only a few months after the peace – the Earl of Oxford was, with Wellington's permission, arrested for seditious involvement with Bonapartist supporters. Lord Oxford was generally regarded as a fool, but there were others to be taken more seriously. In December 1815 three British officers helped the Comte de Lavalette, a close associate of the Emperor, to escape from prison. The Prefect of Police complained of the impudence of 'by far the greater part' of the British residents in France, who take, he said, every opportunity to ridicule the Royal Family and to compare the present government unfavourably with the 'Usurper's'.[21]

Under the Empire, the police had kept a close eye on foreigners. The surveillance was continued after the Bourbon restoration. After all, Louis XVIII was imposed on France and though he was supported by old royalists – some objecting, however, that he was too cautious in turning back the clock – his hold on power was far from secure. In August 1818, Joseph Fouché, the veteran Minister of Police, was warned by one of his agents that a plot against him was in preparation at the Craufurds. Most dangerous was the radical Lord Kinnaird, an Englishman 'with very wide connections', reported to be close to the Austrians and to La Fayette (always opposed to the Bourbons), a man who 'mixes in everything, and is certainly engaged in a large-scale intrigue'. It could not be doubted, stated the report, that Kinnaird was the chief agent of the Duc d'Orléans. He was ordered to leave France a few months later. He did not, however, give up, and was compromised in one of the two attempts to assassinate the Duke of Wellington.[22]

What would happen when the army of occupation was withdrawn? Again in August 1818 – the withdrawal now imminent – *The Times* thought it likely that many of the 62,000 British currently in France would come home, adding darkly that the French police knew the addresses of the lot of them and could carry out arrests within 24 hours.[23] As it happened, the soldiers left, there was no revolution and the British remained. The Bourbons, for the time being anyway, were safe on the throne. Yet there was a question: how far was this the traditional France? Stendhal, writing articles for the British press in the 1820s, reflected that Europe always saw French society as it had been depicted 40 years before. He insisted on the change in manners and behaviour, giving as an example the difference between Mary Berry's friend, the Duc de Richelieu, the most temperate of men, and his father, the Duc de Fronsac, a man so licentious that he had even managed to scandalize his eighteenth-century contemporaries. Strange as it seems, wrote Stendhal, the French character changed less between 1500 and the time of Louis XVI, than it did between 1780 and 1824. 'The Frenchman of 1824 is at once rational and cold, strict in his reasoning, thirsting for deep emotions, in a word he is half English.'[24]

That the French were innately theatrical, frivolous and libertine was taken more or less for granted by all but the more informed British visitors; it was a cherished legend. It was true that on the streets you still saw a type familiar from the London stage, an old beau with silvered hair and white silk stockings, 'the very pink of fribble and gallantry'. And Mrs Stothard's neighbour at the Dieppe dining table certainly looked the part. But it was also true that there was in evidence a new, post-Revolutionary type, quite different to look at, 'mostly in a sort of military undress costume, with complete mops of black hair *à la Brutus*', and terrific whiskers. And even the old beaux were no longer what they had been. Lady Homespun's dictum that husband and wife should never be seen together was quite out of date. A lady of unquestionable authority told the Irish writer Lady Morgan that conjugal love was now much more usual than it had been before the Revolution, adding that the old jokes about men who attended to their own wives were considered to be in extremely bad taste.[25] Lord Granville returned from a political dinner in Paris to tell his wife (daughter of the famous Duchess of Devonshire) that it had been much like a dinner of the same sort in London. His fellow guests, he said, had been very unlike Frenchmen. Admittedly they were liberals, people who had little in common with the spirit of the old Versailles Court. But then, not long afterwards, a Frenchman from quite a different set, one who 'passes his life in the foyer of the *Théâtre français*', called on Lady Granville, to lament the decadence of the times. How bored the poor women are, he told her; 'gallantry has disappeared, husbands are safe, you have to go to England to find a seducer'.[26] Apparently the Englishwomen in Paris were equally frustrated. Captain Gronow reported one Frenchman – in whom 'gallantry' was still very much alive – as saying that 'these Englishwomen are really *très compremettantes*. They are not happy if they do not run away from their stupid, good-natured husbands, who only ask to be permitted to shut their eyes and see nothing'.*

In half a century we have changed places, declared Lord Normanby (a future Ambassador to Paris) in his book *The English in Paris*, published in 1828. Instead of being looked up to as moralists and philosophers, we are considered wanting in these points. 'It is now on all hands agreed, that we find the French a very grave people.' In turn, Normanby added, we are models of good breeding, our manners are refined, our air is distinguished. Even in the more difficult times, during the Occupation, it was admitted that by and large the British behaved well. Whether or not they resembled robots from Birmingham, the British troops were favourably compared to the Prussians. The Scots, with their open faces, their great height, their bonnets and bare legs, were particularly popular. To quote a French historian, 'There is a lot of whispering as they go by, they are watched surreptitiously, and pretty women, eyeing their little skirts with anxiety, murmur their fears into each other's ears, "Goodness, what happens if a wind gets up!" '[27]

The proper behaviour, the good manners on the part of the British and no doubt the shift in sensibility on the part of the French played their part by the later 1820s in promoting genuine good relations between the two peoples. The term 'entente' is justified. It helped that Louis XVIII and his brother and successor Charles X, both of them *émigrés* in Britain, went out of their way to pay attention to British visitors. The hoteliers liked the money the visitors brought with them, and so, for that matter, did the French aristocracy of the Faubourg St-Germain. There was a rush for what

---

* Chateaubriand, while Ambassador, found society in London more frivolous than in Paris.

was known as the *chasse à la dot*, the hunt for a dowry. The newspapers carried advertisements offering a reward to anyone who could procure the advertiser a rich English wife. In high society, the Prince de Polignac, close to the royal family and later a disastrous Prime Minister, married (consecutively) two Scottish heiresses, Miss Campbell and the Marquise de Choiseul, daughter of Lord Rancliffe. The Comte de Flahaut, a Bonapartist friend of Lord and Lady Holland, married Miss Elphinstone, daughter of the admiral, Lord Keith, who later became one of the most fashionable women in Paris. A less commercially conceived marriage was that made by Eliza Forbes, educated at Verdun while her father was a prisoner there; she married the emigrant Marc-René de Montalembert and became the mother of one of France's most famous historians.

The British were not put off by the new French propriety. Lord John Russell, speaking of course as a sophisticated visitor, put forward a common opinion:

> France, perhaps, affords the best models of an agreeable man. In [the French] we see the most refined politeness towards others, mixed with a most perfect confidence in themselves ... a skill in placing every topic in the situation which alone can make it amusing in conversation – a grace in treating the most frivolous matter, a lightness in touching the most serious, and a quickness in passing from one to the other, which to all other Europeans must seem quite unattainable.[28]

Others said the same thing. Lady Blessington for one, who in the 1830s was to run a salon in London which rivalled Holland House itself; the Cambridge don John Bowes Wright for another, who declared that he 'would not leave Paris ... for all the Carnivals of Italy combined'.[29] Lady Morgan was loud in her praise. Perhaps the conversation was too good: it has been suggested that one reason many of the British failed to shine in Parisian salons is that, at least in the 1820s, there was no talk there of hunting, shooting or racing.

As Mary Berry found, much of the entertaining was rather set-piece, and certainly in no way rowdy. For the French, some British customs proved tiresome, in particular the 'routs'. General de Castellane grumbled about the standing around, and then the walking and pushing, all in a stifling atmosphere. What the British missed – and so did some of the ex-*émigrés* – was the club atmosphere of St James's Street. In 1824, two cousins, the French Jean Greffuhle and the British Urbain Sartoris, jointly founded a club on London lines to fill the gap, and also to bring French and British together. There followed the establishment of the club of clubs, the Cercle de l'Union, its moving spirit the anglophile Duc de Guiche. It was very smart, and money alone was not enough to qualify for membership. So exclusive was it indeed that the historian of the earlier Parisian clubs suggested that even the late Lord Byron might have been blackballed had he applied for membership – the writing of poetry and association with literary hacks (*folliculaires*) could be thought to have compromised his standing. The diarist Thomas Raikes found the conversation better than in the London clubs, though he added that the noise and clamour at general meetings made rational discussion difficult. General de Castellane complained that the popularity of clubs with young men was undermining normal social life.[30]

The French, as many British observed, were a mercurial people. If they could blackball Lord Byron, they could do anything. For the French were swept off their feet by the Romantic Movement, by Byron, Walter Scott, Shakespeare and Sheridan. Particularly Scott. In March 1829, at the most magnificent ball of the time, the guests – in numbers almost equally French and British – wore fancy dress inspired by his novels.[31] The following year the Bourbon monarchy fell. The Duchesse de Berry raised an insurrection against the new government in the Vendée, her followers calling each other by names lifted from Scott.[32] And as to Shakespeare's contribution, an article in the *Figaro* declared that his genius had at last prevailed in France and had perhaps started the reconciliation between the two countries which politics had so long made impossible. Lady Morgan gives a vivid illustration of the effect of the new anglophilia. She goes into a shop in Paris to buy sweets for a child. In broken English she is told that they no longer stock sweets; instead they offer her plum cakes, mince pies, crumpets and apple-dumplings. She notices that the shop has changed its name, now proclaiming itself to be 'Tom or Jack somebody: pastry cook from London'. A cosmopolitan French friend explains to her that 'everything English, bar their politics, is now popular in Paris', is deemed romantic, and 'we have romantic tailors, milliners, pastry-cooks and even doctors and apothecaries'. Things indeed had come to an unexpected pass when 'L'Auberge de la rue Neuve-St-Augustin' renamed itself the 'Great Nelson Hotel'. And French grooms, whatever their real names, were called 'John'.[33]

Cultural fellowship was reinforced by political sympathy. In the 1830s, liberals came to power in both Britain and France, and the new king, Louis-Philippe, who spoke and wrote perfect English, was exceptionally anglophile. The high point of anglophilia generally seems to have been reached about 1835, but there was still enough around in 1845 for a correspondent of *Blackwood's Magazine* to report on the popularity in France of Warren's blacking for boots, and English razors. He told of a lunch where the English delicacy of raw crumpets was served, and where a Countess referred appreciatively to soap prepared by Mr Brown of *Vindsor*, and a poet of the romantic school (very pale with a satin waistcoat) spoke favourably of Shakespeare. What seems on the face of it more surprising was the sustained attraction of British ways to the old French aristocracy. The French historian Pierre Reboul has put it that:

> The French aristocracy, with nothing to do and troubled in its efforts to justify its wealth and honours, found in the imperturbability, the formality, the etiquette and the originality of the English nobility an overly seductive model.

It was hardly a conscious modelling, for few of them really knew much about Britain; it was rather, in Reboul's words, the result of osmosis.

Should they have needed them, the French nobility could have found plenty of models close at hand. Many appear in the memoirs of Captain Gronow, the journals of Thomas Raikes and Thomas Moore and in the sparkling correspondence of Lady Granville. Some are charming like Major Caradoc, later Lord Howden, or plain difficult like the Countess of Aldbrough, living out a long Paris life in the style of the past. Then there was Thomas Bryon, a huge man who encouraged an enthusiasm among fashionable Parisians for organized sport, a pastime closely associated with Britain and the British. Bryon introduced pigeon shooting in the great park of Tivoli Gardens – now disappeared – among a cluster of funfairs, theatres and restaurants. He was passionate about horse racing, in 1826 forming a club for its promotion and laying on a kind of mobile grandstand to ferry people to the races. In 1828 he published a studbook.[34] Above all there were the Seymour-Conways, marquesses of Hertford,[35] the most sensational and flawed of the Anglo-French, a family of great distinction in English history, and immensely wealthy. They are unique in leaving two remarkable and tangible memorials of their times, two great houses, both national monuments, one in London, the other in Paris. The first, Hertford House, home of the Wallace Collection, is a palace that lords it over Manchester Square in Marylebone. Its counterpart is the – much smaller – Bagatelle, in the Bois de Boulogne, a property with a double British connection, for its famous gardens were planned and established by a Scottish gardener named Thomas Blaikie for the original owner, the Comte d'Artois, the future king, Charles X. (Blaikie was another to be stranded in France by the Revolution. He fled Paris in the wake of the September Massacres of 1792, emerging after ten years of hardship to plan gardens for some of the surviving old nobility and the new Napoleonic aristocracy and industrialists.)

The Bagatelle itself suffered grievously from the Revolution, falling from grace to become a teahouse and a dance hall before, in the 1830s, being bought and restored by the fourth Marquess of Hertford who installed there much of the remarkable collection of fine art now to be seen at Hertford House. This was a very strange family. The third Marquess (1777–1842), then Earl of Yarmouth, a prisoner at Verdun, was released by Talleyrand in May 1806 to carry a message on possible peace negotiations to Charles Fox, then Foreign Secretary. He was then appointed chief British negotiator, although in fact the discussions got nowhere. After the war, Yarmouth was very much a part of the Anglo-French social scene, with his daughter marrying a French nobleman. At one time sociable and lively company – though exceptionally avaricious – his character deteriorated to the extent that he became the model for Lord Steyne in *Vanity Fair* and a byword for debauchery. His old age was far from elevating: Charles Greville wrote that 'broken with various infirmities, and almost unintelligible from a paralysis of the tongue, he had been in the habit of travelling about with a company of prostitutes, who formed his principal society'. Another account of Lord Hertford's last days has him driven round London to be carried every afternoon by two footmen up the steps of a brothel.

His son, the fourth Marquess, who purchased Bagatelle and put together most of the art collection, was in his youth regarded as a man of great promise, but a puzzle. Lady Granville, noting in the 1820s that he had taken to good company and was appearing at balls, wrote that 'He is the greatest pity that ever was. Such powers of being delightful and captivating, *grandes manières*, talents of all kinds, *finesse d'esprit*, all spent in small base coin. He walks amongst us like a fallen angel, higher and lower than all of us put together'. Her words 'the greatest pity that ever was' seemed justified many years later in Paris in 1870 when he died. Edmond de Goncourt was told by the doctor who treated Lord Hertford that he had carried himself nobly through great suffering, but, by now an extreme miser, he was governed, like others of his family, by a hatred of humanity. 'It is from Lord Hertford', added Goncourt, 'that we have that terrible saying, which he liked to repeat: "Men are bad, and when I die, I shall have at least the consolation of having never rendered a service to anyone." '[36]

There are two further members of this extraordinary family to discuss. One is Richard Wallace, whose (quite different) career falls into a later part of this book; the other, Lord Henry Seymour, conceived and born while Lord Yarmouth – happily with a mistress – was locked up at Verdun. Since Lady Yarmouth was Italian and the father probably the Comte de Montrond, Lord Henry was without any English blood at all. If one is to 'locate' him as well, it is on the course at Chantilly where the Jockey Club ran its races. He was its first chairman when the club was founded in 1836, its original meeting taking place at Bryon's premises in the Tivoli Gardens. He was a suitable choice, not only because was he passionate about racing, but because this eminently smart club was very much an Anglo-French affair. The statutes permitted membership to any member of the Jockey Club of England.

Legend surrounded Henry Seymour, who was much better known to the world at large than any other member of his family. He was an exceptional athlete, not just on horseback, but at boxing and fencing, with three rooms in his house turned into a kind of gym. His need to win whatever he went in for was demonic, and once drew him into serious trouble: driving his tilbury* hard, he cut in on the King's carriage, and only the efforts of his friends prevented his being expelled the country. Cruel, brutal even, misanthropic, avaricious, but also highly cultivated, he appeared a true member of his family, illegitimate though he was. While his friends were mainly French, the British found him less peculiar than they did. His style was Anglo-Saxon. It was the dandy in him.[37]

'Dandy' seems an odd word to use, suggesting to us now not an athlete like Seymour with 'monstrously developed' biceps, but a rather dapper person, a fop almost. But not then; a virile and forceful manner did not rule you out. Essential were a preoccupation with external effect and a desire to astonish, though not necessarily to please. Seymour was one type of dandy, but the perfect Anglo-French model is Alfred d'Orsay in whom the more virile dandy characteristics are tempered. One of his grandmothers was the Italian-born Anna Craufurd, ex-Madame Sullivan, his father was a dashing Napoleonic general, while his partner in life was Lady Blessington, whose stepdaughter he married. Equally at home in Paris and London, d'Orsay's conversation, according to Captain Gronow, was a successful mixture of French and English. A fine horseman, a good swordsman and a fair shot, wonderfully strong and active, his friends included Lord Byron and the future Emperor Napoleon III. Gronow described him:

> When I used to see him driving in his tilbury ... I fancied that he looked like some gorgeous dragon-fly skimming through the air; and though all was dazzling and showy, yet there was a kind of harmony which precluded any idea or accusation of bad taste.

D'Orsay was very handsome and had no intention of allowing his looks to be spoiled. Gronow recalled his words to his second who was making arrangements for a duel that he was about to fight.

---

* A gig, a light two-wheeler, devised by Mr Tilbury of North Audley Street.

You know, my dear friend, I am not on a par with my antagonist: he is a very ugly fellow, and if I wound him in the face, he won't look much the worse for it; but on my side it ought to be agreed that he should not aim higher than my chest, for if my face should be spoiled, 'ce serait vraiment dommage'.

Apparently he put all this with such charm that his second agreed with him; whether his opponent did we are not told.[38]

But d'Orsay loved show. He lived with the rich but he was always close to trouble. In fact, his last years in Paris came about as a result of pressing creditors in London, where he and Lady Blessington had entertained in the most extravagant style. Show was expected and respected. The Duke of Northumberland's inadequate reception at Calais in 1825, described above, was seen to be in offensive contrast to the sheer magnificence of his entourage and accoutrements. Like Lord Cornwallis before him, he was travelling, intent on spending money as ostentatiously as he could. His retinue, it was reported, included several relations of the Duchess, 12 'Gentlemen', four Secretaries, 12 Maîtres d'Hôtel and numerous domestic servants. Four young noblemen 'of illustrious families' also accompanied the Duke. Since he was representing the King, more was required of him than would otherwise have been the case. Even so, in private life the very rich could live and entertain on a huge scale. William Hope, an Anglo-Dutch banker living in Paris, was described as 'Croesus', with the Duchesse de Dino insisting that his palace of a house and his style of living were on a par with those of Louis XIV at Versailles.[39]

The Duchesse was writing in 1842, by which time British visitors lacked much of the Restoration glamour. The American Hezekiah Hartley Wright, touring England in the mid-1830s, observed that travel was now so generally popular as to have become unfashionable in high society.[40] By then, too, the patricians who had rushed to Paris at the time of Amiens and in 1814 and 1815, their minds enriched by the cosmopolitan values of the Enlightenment, had been largely replaced by the insular generation so deplored in her book by Mary Berry. A French paper's description of the British to be found at Paris balls in 1840 is not complimentary. They have, it declared, a scarlet tinge about them. There is not a gentleman tourist or a businessman retired from the City of London who at galas, royal or private ones, does not wear a superb lobster-coloured costume surmounted by two large epaulettes made of gilded leather. However, the British were not of themselves lowering the social tone. The patrician French often looked on Louis-Philippe and his government with downright hostility and were not apt to attend royal galas. Early in the reign, Thomas Raikes was told of a lady at one of them who complained that her shoe was pinching.

Immediately, her partner in the dance whipped out a business card which described him as 'shoemaker to the King', and offered to call on her next morning.[41]

According to Raikes's descriptions, many of these British were in no position to sneer, for they were by no means fashionables themselves and sometimes quite at sea in Paris, where they made easy prey for unscrupulous Parisian conmen who were apt to appoint themselves counts or barons to help along whatever game they were playing. (It was a theme that Thackeray would take up.) Raikes himself was a sophisticated West End clubman whose father had been Governor of the Bank of England. He was very sociable, too much so, for he neglected the family's banking business and was forced into exile in Paris to avoid some of the consequences. Raikes was a close friend of the fourth Marquess of Hertford and kept a record of British society in the city. He does not, however, mention two other exiles who, given their past experience of life in France, might have been expected to prefer some other country. One was Lord Elgin, who had experienced a particularly uncomfortable internment after 1803. Still, divorced and remarried, he died in Paris, where he had been living for years, leaving the enormous debt of £120,000.[42] The other was a genuine hero, who had indeed, in the words of a recent biographer, something gallic about him, a Gascon swagger and gallantry. This was Admiral Sir Sidney Smith, who, by fire, destroyed what amounted to an entire French battle-fleet. Captured, and imprisoned at Paris, in solitary confinement at the Temple, he escaped with the aid of French royalists in February 1798. It gave him time, through his successful defence of Acre, to play a decisive part in the ruin of Napoleon's expedition to Egypt and the Middle East. But, in retirement, he also spent too much money and, taking refuge in Paris, irritated Wellington with a series of what the Duke labelled 'vaporous' projects. Increasingly eccentric, Smith stayed on, dying in the city in 1840.[43]

As debtors flocked across the Channel their creditors attempted counter-action. In his skit *Six Weeks in Paris*, William Jerdan brings together Sir Humphrey Homespun and a Monsieur Jacquie, a Bond Street hotelier, who meet by chance in a park. Monsieur Jacquie, representing himself and others of his profession in London, is in Paris to chase up 'numerous birds of passage' who have either forgotten or just neglected to settle outstanding bills before they took wing. Jerdan's book could hardly have been better timed, for in its year of publication, 1817, General Crewe was arrested in France for a debt of £600 on the suit of Monsieur Brunet, who ran a hotel in Leicester Square. The French lawyers doubted whether the case was tenable, and, reported *The Times*,[44] 'it may be readily presumed that all the persons who have run away to the Continent to avoid the payment of their just debts are of the same opinion'. The lawyers were right and the charge did not stick; still, it must have been a nasty moment for a lot of people.

The memoirs of Raikes and Gronow are filled with anecdotes about ruined British, usually gamblers, on the run. If the British did not lose their money in London they lost it gambling in Paris. Some played in private houses, like Sir Charles Potter, married to a Frenchwoman and mentioned by General de Castellane in his journal. He was one of a group that met for cards every Wednesday at the house of the Duchesse de Luynes. Sir Charles would take the bank: should he lose, he did so with excellent grace. But he too ended up half-ruined. The Marquis de Livry, who reassuringly looked very like the Prince Regent, proved helpful to early arrivals after the peace, organizing play at the Salon des Etrangers in the Palais Royal. On Sundays he stepped in to entertain at his country house where there were ladies as well as gambling. Of the guests, said Captain Gronow, 'the male portion ... were bent on losing their money, whilst the ladies were determined to get rid of whatever virtue they might still have left'.

Along with the salons de Frascati, the Palais Royal near the Louvre was the centre for gaming. Founded by Cardinal Richelieu, it had been developed commercially by the Duc d'Orléans in the 1780s, his inspiration the London pleasure gardens such as Vauxhall. Benjamin Haydon described it as follows:

> It is a beautiful palace in the midst of the city and is a fine enclosed square, the alleys full of shops, and the houses full of gaming and brothels. After nine never was such a scene witnessed! The whole is illuminated, the walks & gardens which form the Square full of villainy & depravity, stuffed full, that as you enter you feel a heated, whorish, pestilential air flush your cheek & clutch your frame. The blaze of the lamps, the unrestrained obscenity of the language, the indecency, the baudy, bloody indecency of the People, bewilder & distract you. Such is the power & effect of this diabolical place that the neighborhood, like the country around the poison tree of Java, is mad by its vice and infected by its principles.[45]

It is hard to make out who gambled the more furiously: the French or the British. The traveller Dr Charles Maclean asserted that the French took to games of chance with an ardour he had seen matched only by the Malays in the East Indies: 'when a Malay has lost all his property, he will sell his wife and children; a Frenchman will sell his clothes; if, after that, their affairs become irretrievable, the one will *run a muck*, the other will drown himself.' Certainly the British in Paris, ruined though they might be, did not run amuck (a word incidentally borrowed from the Malay language). It would have been out of character. Their reputation, whether they were throwing money around or blowing their brains out, was for the most perfect sangfroid.

One after another they went down: Mr Stibbert, living on in Paris in great want; Henry Baring, whose gambling meant exclusion from the family bank; Colonel Sowerby of the Guards, 'a considerable loser'; Lord Thanet; Ball Hughes, 'perhaps the greatest gambler of his day', who lost three-quarters of his fortune; Mr Lumsden, dying in poverty; Mr Gough who killed himself. Particularly poignant is the story of Scrope Davies, a very close friend of Byron, scholar (a Fellow of King's, Cambridge), womanizer, ace tennis player, a manic drinker and a reckless gambler, regarded by his friends, who included Gronow, as a typical dandy. He fled London for Paris in the 1830s to escape his creditors, and lost there all the money he had left. John Cam Hobhouse, best man to Byron at his wedding and later a Liberal cabinet minister, found himself one day in 1851, in London, accosted by 'an old man, shrivelled and bent, who, in a feeble voice, asked me if I knew him. I told him I did not. He said, Scrope Davies'.[46]

Thomas Raikes died in 1848. Captain Rees Howell Gronow carried on until 1865, a monument to the past. He was Welsh, immersed in the fashionable world, one of the very few army officers to belong to that most exclusive of London clubs, Almack's. He lived in Paris for years and married twice, each time to a Frenchwoman. He knew Lord Henry Seymour, so he said, better than any other Englishman. There is a sadness to his memoirs: his friends are mostly dead; times are not what they were; the young nowadays take their pleasures so soberly and stupidly. He does not appear to have been a fervent gambler himself, though back in 1815 he had made enough money at cards to fit himself out for the Waterloo campaign. Even so, he died (in Paris) almost destitute. A French journalist described Gronow when he was 'about fifty' (so, in the 1840s), the picture of an ageing dandy. His hair is thinning and his moustache neatly trimmed and dyed brown.

> All day he was to be seen, dressed in an eternal blue frock coat, tight-fitting, closely buttoned, allowing just a narrow line of white waistcoat to show ... He passed his life sitting at the window of the Petit-Cercle [his club], his famous cane to his lips, watching his Paris go by.

He was, added the journalist, 'evidently intimate with everybody of note in Europe'.[47] It really is in France that we see a sputtering-out of Regency England.

4

Pau and the Spas

Those who know the English colonies abroad know that we carry with us our pride, pills, prejudices, Harvey-sauces, cayenne-peppers, and other Lares, making a little Britain wherever we settle down.

W. M. Thackeray, *Vanity Fair*

It is not difficult to place Colonel Thomas Thornton of Thornton Royal, Yorkshire – he is the Proud and Vain Traveller. Proud and vain at home as well: in 1795, commanding the West Yorkshire militia, he was court-martialled for permitting (no doubt encouraging) his soldiers to draw him into camp in a triumphal carriage. Not for him, in 1802, other than inci-dentally, visits to the Louvre and excursions to landmarks of the Revolution; he went to France for the sport, bringing with him a dozen foxhounds from his own pack in Yorkshire, transported together with an array of guns and fishing tackle in a carriage he had himself designed. The Colonel was not uncritical of what he found. He was displeased with the champagne, and to some extent by French women; like the Prince of Wales, 'an excellent judge of the fair sex', as he remarked, he favoured more *embonpoint* and a better complexion. However, according to letters home sent to his friend the Earl of Darlington, his visit was a great success, indeed near enough a triumph. He was very well received. At Dieppe he was welcomed by the Prefect of the department in person; at Rouen – a very sporting place, he said – former *émigrés* were anxious to repay hospitality. At Rouen too was a Mr Hartley, married to a 'French lady of fashion', who in the old days had hunted with the Colonel's pack in Yorkshire. His hounds were much admired and, when he moved on to Paris, he won a shooting contest at a Versailles gun factory. Anglo-French relations were well served: the Colonel felt able to say that in the French gentlemen he met he 'found precisely the same *ideas*, the same *keenness* and the same *frank character* which marks [sic] our Yorkshire sportsmen'.

Colonel Thornton hoped to buy an estate in France. His aspirations were lordly, indeed princely, and, returning after Waterloo, he rented Chambord

(444 rooms), one of the most magnificent of the Loire *châteaux*, and named himself the Prince de Chambord. For good measure he also assumed the title of Marquis du Pont, on the strength of an estate he bought at Pont-sur-Seine. It all fizzled out and Thornton died in lodgings in Paris in 1823.[1] Other British too, if with more modest aspirations, ventured into the French property market as soon as the war was over. Benjamin Haydon was touched by a couple he came across in 1814 who were 'going to France to settle, ignorant of the language, ignorant of the manners, young, thoughtless, & just married'.[2] Secondary homes flourished, particularly after the arrival on the Seine of Manby and Wilson's steamboats. Homeowners could land at Le Havre and reach their property much more quickly than by sail or *diligence*.

French land as an investment was a subject that intrigued the American Colonel Pinkney during his tour in 1807 and 1808. It was so cheap. He gathered that a 500+-acre estate in the Nivernais (Burgundy) or Bourbonnais (in the middle of France), half arable, a quarter forest, a quarter waste, could be bought for about 5,500 guineas (£5,775), a third of what such a property would cost anywhere in England. (In England the forest and the waste would be brought into cultivation.) A 600-acre estate close to the Loire would cost £5,000, its equivalent in England at least £20,000. An American friend, a diplomat, told him that the problem was the obstinacy and ignorance of French labourers: 'if we could import English or American workmen, or bring French labourers to English or American habits, no good farmer would hesitate a moment as to settlement in France.' Should American, English or Swedish gentlemen wish to settle here, the friend goes on, the best choice would be Touraine or the Limousin where there is good soil, vineyards and gardens admired by painters and poets, and where rainy weather usually occurs only in the spring.[3]

In fact, the British needed no prompting to migrate to Touraine, or more precisely to its capital Tours, although they did not go to farm. For one thing it was cheap in comparison to other French towns. Among the British families there in the 1820s were the Burtons including the young Richard, later to become the legendary Victorian traveller Richard Burton. The historically minded might recollect a trailblazer in the person of Alcuin, an eighth-century monk from York, who turned Tours into a centre of learning. Indeed, education was still an important draw for Alcuin's countrymen, since it was here that the French language was held to be at its most pure. While the country around was scenically uninteresting, the town itself was handsome, with a splendid main street, the Rue Royale. Colonel Pinkney made comparisons with Bath. The effect of British money was marked: inns were improved, lodging houses became suddenly neat, carpeted and comfortable, shops brightened up, pastry-cooks extended their skills. The milliner now called herself 'Parisian'; her wares, she declared, came straight from Paris. Prices rose, and local inhabitants let their houses and moved to cheaper quarters. Mrs Boddington, who gave this description in a book published in 1837, added, however, that decline had set in. 'Now Tours is French again, or nearly so, to the despair of the innkeepers, who wail after their prey like disappointed sea-gulls,' she noted. She seems, though, to have been rather premature, for *Murray's Handbook for France* of 1843 observed that a very considerable number of English lived in and around the town.[4] The colony thinned out after 1848, when political disturbances in the region appear to have persuaded some at least of those who remained to move out and to head for the more tranquil south. It was more or less brought to an end by the floods which in the autumn of 1866 completely inundated the surrounding country.

The main reason for the British to go south was, at least in the earlier part of the century, to remedy ill health, often some form of tuberculosis, referred to generally at the time as 'consumption', because its victims were almost literally consumed. Tuberculosis was the scourge of the age, 'the white plague', a killer which in 1838 for instance was responsible for a sixth of all deaths in England and Wales. While the urban poor were worst affected, plenty of wealthy or reasonably wealthy victims came to France, and especially to the Pyrenees, in hope, if not of total cure, of at least some alleviation of their suffering. Death itself could perhaps be held at bay. The faith in 'watering-places' or spas (named after Spa, near Liège), in the therapeutic power of their waters, to be sipped, swallowed and bathed in, had been held by the Romans, and for many years past by the French and the British. In Britain there were many spas, Bath, Tunbridge Wells, Buxton, Harrogate and Cheltenham being some of the better known, and, earlier on, to the north side of London, Sadler's Wells and Bagnigge Wells. London in fact unsurprisingly produced a sizeable proportion of health-seekers. General de Castellane, spending three weeks there one November, never managed to see across to the other bank of the Thames because of the smog. The French and other continental spas offered sunshine and clean mountain air, in themselves important to a cure.[5] An advantage of the Pyrenees was the splendid scenery, the more desirable since invalids were likely to be accompanied by members of their families or by friends, who could enjoy walking or riding or sketching in the mountains.

It was in the Pyrenees, or rather on their edge, that there was established the most complete of the British 'colonies' in France. In the words of the historian Pierre Tucoo-Chala, Pau became *'la ville anglaise'*, a morsel of Victorian England transplanted to the foot of the Pyrenees.[6] Now a bustling commercial city with its own airport, and enriched by the discovery of natural gas deposits nearby, Pau in the nineteenth century was primarily a resort and above all a British resort. Little is evident now of the British presence – a Rue des Anglais, a Rue Alexander-Taylor (named after a well-known doctor who proved very good for business), a few pictures in the Fine Arts Museum, that is about all. Pau had always been important: it was capital of the old French province of Béarn, the birthplace of the great French hero, Henri IV. Then, in March 1814, the British arrived – dramatically. Following their decisive victory over Joseph Bonaparte at Vitoria, Wellington's army pushed on over the Pyrenees. To their astonishment they were greeted at Pau not by a hostile population but by cries of *Vive l'immortel Wellington! Vive Henri Quatre et ses rejetons* [descendants]*!* This was true Bourbon country. The relationship between the people of Pau and the British could hardly have got off to a better start.[7]

Five and a half years after Wellington, the fifth Lord Selkirk appeared. He was a philanthropist, and a man of note in Canadian history as a tireless proponent of colonial settlement in the West. But in 1819 he was in the last stages of tuberculosis, and indeed died at Pau in March 1820. Accompanying him as his doctor was Dr George Lefevre from Edinburgh, of an old Huguenot family, who for his own health needed to spend the winter out of Britain. They arrived in mid-October in lovely weather. Lefevre was staggered by the beauty of the scenery: 'the four seasons seemed to be blended into each other, and present at the same time. The meadows still wore the aspect of spring. The hills were covered with the rich luxuriant grape . . . the blood-red beech and other forest trees began to show, in their party-coloured leaves, the garments of autumn.' And all against the backdrop of the mountains. He marvelled at the wildlife – a country, he thought, which to a sportsman would be an earthly paradise. With winter, however, came the cold. A local doctor, pointing to the snow-capped mountains, told Lefevre that Pau in winter was too cold for tuberculosis sufferers.[8] But confusing the climate of the Pyrenees with that of the South of France was to be a common failing of British visitors. The townspeople in their mufflers and thick woollen coats would gaze with surprise at invalids who walked about dressed for summer.

The Pyrenees and its resorts were a long way from anywhere, 'a sort of end of the world' in one description, the culmination of a difficult journey. In the dawning romantic age, that was in itself an attraction. Joseph Hardy set out from Bordeaux several years after Selkirk and Lefevre. The first 30 miles of his journey up the Garonne were covered by steamboat, less romantic than downright modern. And entertaining, too, for the machinery on these boats was English, as was the engineer, 'between whom and the pilot, in their necessary communications, the strange *mélange* of French and

English often occasions great laughter'. The next stage of the journey was spent in a very slow *diligence*, pushing south through the bizarre territory of the Landes, marshy scrub land of forest and sand, described 20 years later by Hippolyte Taine as a desert, a place not for men but animals and plants. What men there were could in the dry season be seen mounted on stilts four feet high. The road was formed by trunks of pine laid transversely, giving, Hardy commented, a most unpleasant motion to vehicles. Eventually, at the village of Villeneneuve-de-Marsan, by now in a hired cabriolet, he caught sight for the first time of the Pyrenees, a distant chain of mountains, covered in snow, glistening in the sun. 'My delight was of a kind to be felt once in a life', was his reaction. They appeared, remembered another visitor, 'like a barrier between earth and heaven'.[9]

Hardy's *A Picturesque and Descriptive Tour in the Mountains of the High Pyrenees*, published in 1825 and later translated into French, was a great success. However, it was followed by so many other accounts that a clergyman traveller in the 1840s could write that 'Pau and its environs have been so copiously and frequently described that perhaps few places on the Continent are more accurately known to readers of travels'.[10] The 'end of the world' theme played an important part. Even the Pyrenean cows, it was reported, behaved outlandishly: as active as monkeys, they leaped about the rocks and climbed the crags in a way that bewildered the stranger. In one story, the peasants of the Landes on their stilts become 'two figures of gigantic height which I at first thought to be two isolated fir-trees bending to the blast of the wind'. In another, a 'young dandy', after a long day's ride, seeks shelter with some peasants in the mountains. Skulking about are Spanish smugglers with whom his hosts do business in wool and tobacco. Indeed, in real life you had to be careful about the border. An English-woman who ventured over complained that in Spain women are subjected to 'insult and outrage' even when accompanied by a guide. An article in *Fraser's Magazine* in 1851 warned about Spanish Customs Officers, the writer declaring of the two who stopped him that 'a more cut-throat looking pair of ruffians could not easily be encountered anywhere'.

The fictional 'young dandy' referred to above is asked by his peasant host a local version of the question posed by the girl in Normandy to Mrs Stothard: what brings you here? 'God knows what charm our rugged mountains, dark forests, and brawling rivers can have for you. The inhabitants are unfortunate enough in being forced to live in such wilds; but to come into them by choice, and find pleasure in climbing rocks and glaciers, and the like, is something we don't understand.' For by no means all the British were invalids or companions to invalids.[11] Some came to hunt: Captain Gronow said that it reminded him of Wales. Others came simply to ride or to walk. At Pau you could hire horses, and carriages too if you required them, for trips into the mountains. In the 1850s, solitary ladies were advised of an 'elderly and respectable', if chatty, Polish major, who was available to accompany them. Quite a number of visitors were in search of unfamiliar plants or came to study the geology and collect stones. (According to a French historian, this last enthusiasm was termed *elginisme*, after Lord Elgin who had been detained near Pau after the resumption of war in 1803.) Yet others, as the dandy's host said in the story, were climbers. Charles Packe, acclaimed as the greatest of Pyrenean mountaineers, declared that these mountains might be less high than those of the Alps, but they were much more picturesque.[12] The first recorded ascent of Vignemale, at 3,298 metres one of the highest peaks, was made by the intrepid traveller Anne Lister in 1838.

The dandy's host may have found British tastes bizarre, and locals generally may sometimes have been confused about the difference between Wellington's troops and the English soldiery of the Middle Ages. Nevertheless, the opportunity was there and they hastened to bring in specimens from the mountains for collectors, and to act as guides. They expected to be treated with respect, and an English nobleman, arriving to shoot chamois, who was too offhand with his guide, found no sport over a whole two weeks.[13] One visitor considered that the locals resembled the Portuguese, Italians and Irish in their estimate of truth, but he added that 'this is probably the only country in the world where you may be sure that even a drunken man will be civil'. Indeed, the local people, so courteous and friendly, were one of the attractions to visitors. Mrs Ellis, at Pau, enjoyed watching them as they walked to and from the market. No one, she said, walked alone, all went in groups, 'for in France there seem to be but two evils greater than nature is able to sustain – loneliness, and bitterness. Many are the offers I have had, not impertinently, but kindly meant, of companions by the way, accompanied by a few words of condolence that I was *all alone*'.[14]

Mrs Ellis was not untypical of her time. She admits that walking about the roads in the way she does might be questioned on grounds of taste. Like others who let loose their Pyrenean reminiscences on the public, she was a professional author, best known for her *Women of England* published in 1832 under her maiden name of Sarah Stickney. She was at Pau for about 18 months from December 1839 while her husband, a prominent missionary, recovered from a pulmonary illness contracted in Madagascar.

Her first morning at Pau she looked out from her hotel room in the Place Royale on to a wide and handsome square to see, as the day advanced, a tide of respectable and fashionable-looking English people setting in towards a certain point ... The bright sunshine blazed upon the scene, and there were ladies in light dresses, with their parasols, without which it is scarcely possible to look steadily at any object when the sun is shining here; while others rode forth in happy looking parties, with their hats and habits, just as in Hyde Park, only somewhat differently mounted. Nor was there wanting the usual proportion of dandies, still evidently English, notwithstanding all the pains they have taken to look French.

She leaves the hotel for the Parc National, running along beside the river, to observe

a motley concourse ... [I]nvalids of every stage, from mere delicacy down to hopeless disease, are seen basking in the sunshine, or leaning on the arms that would be stretched forth, if it were possible, to snatch them from the grave.

The 20 years that had passed since Lord Selkirk's time made a great difference. Then Pau was barely known to most British; in fact, until he and Dr Lefevre reached Paris and obtained advice, they had little idea of where to go. Now, in 1839, Pau was a popular resort. One effect was a change in the relations between the French and British. Lord Selkirk had rented a house from one of the last appointed of Napoleon's generals – demoted to colonel after Waterloo – who was most attentive and who, after Selkirk's death, provided Lefevre with a letter of introduction for an excursion he made into the mountains. This ease of relations between the two peoples was to be a feature of the early period in Pau. The first British residents were often ex-officers in the army who, with their families, stayed on or returned. Lady Fowles, the widow of one of these officers, was remembered for the huge receptions she gave annually in her splendid apartment for French and British. The Hay family opened the first British salon in the town which, when the parents died, was carried on by the two daughters. While it was no mere copy of a Paris salon and retained always a *physiognomie britannique*, it was very much open to the French. In their turn, the Misses Hay, evidently highly cultivated, were received by the best French society. Clubs and theatre groups were closely linked: members of the *Cercle béarnais* and the English Club, for instance, were said to be virtually interchangeable.[15] There was intermarriage, most famously in the union between Alfred de Vigny and Lydia Bunbury in 1825. Vigny, an army officer discharging his national service at Pau, had a taste for English blondes – an address given at a 1978 conference on Vigny at Pau was entitled '*Alfred de Vigny et les blondes anglaises*'. The wealthy Hugh Bunbury, Lydia's father, at Pau to cure his rheumatism, had bought the Château de Billère, just outside the town. Vigny did not appeal to him; for one thing he was not rich enough. However, Vigny's friend, the Baron Duplàa – there is a Rue Duplàa at Pau – gave a party and won over Bunbury with liberal doses of alcohol.[16]

This easy mix did not survive the 1830s. Misunderstandings of each other's customs and conventions were partly responsible. In the 1850s the departmental Prefect organized entertainments intended to bring together locals and foreigners. The British considered the balls he laid on 'horribly unexclusive'; a lady was expected to dance with anyone who asked her or not to dance at all. And the steady increase in the numbers of visitors was important. The British were forming something of an enclosed world, and by Mrs Ellis's time the *ville anglaise* was starting to take on its definitive shape. In Pierre Tucoo-Chala's words,

> The English, even when surpassed numerically by the French and financially by the Americans, installed themselves with us according to the principles equivalent to those put into practice by the subjects of Her Majesty, in all latitudes, during the 19th century, transposing there their own model of society.

In this society, protocol was treated seriously. In 1860 Elizabeth Carne published *Three Months' Rest at Pau*, under the name of J. A.Wittitterly, a character from *Nicholas Nickleby*. (The spelling is very slightly altered.) She noted that Pau was much cleaner and more hygienic than before, and that the British on the spot were helpful to newcomers about accommodation and doctors. She warned, though, of the social conventions. A newcomer was not expected to call on an old inhabitant without some form of excuse, a claim to some mutual acquaintance perhaps, or a prior meeting in the newsroom or at a party. Your conversation when you did call must be cautious and dull. She is free with other advice too, some of it very sensible. Bargain with hotel-keepers, she urges, and be careful to select in advance the spa or resort which best suits your particular ailment. Doctors, she reminds her readers, are not always objective: for instance, there are famously 'Malaga doctors', 'Nice doctors', 'Pau doctors'. She does not care for the climate of Pau: it was so relaxing that it sapped her energy; it was like, she said, a 'sort of warm Penzance'.[17]

Yet Miss Carne does preach rather a lot, which makes it something of a relief to turn to an (unpublished) journal which, while not particularly admiring of the town and its inhabitants, is light-hearted. Harriet Jephson, in her twenties, is hearty, rather ingenuous, though with plenty of commonsense, and 'merry', not an adjective the French of the time would usually apply to the British. She stays, first with a girl friend and then with her husband, at a comfortable hotel in the Place Royale, in a room facing south over the famous view of the mountains. None of them speaks more than a smattering of French, and language muddles play a notable part in her journal. The landlady suggests that she and her friend lodge *en pension*, assuring them – though they are a bit taken aback by the price – that it will be 'very sheep'. At one moment, Mrs Jephson asks for an *assiette*, meaning a chair, and of course is given a plate. Her husband, rather older than she, a bluff, no-nonsense Commander in the Royal Navy, arrives from England at one in the morning, demanding of the night porter and of the hastily summoned landlady that he be shown to his wife's room. It takes a good hour before he is accepted as genuine, the delay caused not just by language difficulties but because – as in the old joke – he has difficulty in remembering the colour of his wife's eyes and hair.

Mrs Jephson is in Pau on doctor's orders, to recover from a bad bout of bronchitis. Nevertheless, she finds the energy to explore the great *château* where Henri IV was born, and goes with her friend to call on the descendants of his wet-nurse, a family held in much esteem by the town. She sketches, in the approved Victorian manner; her friend joins an expedition organized by the hotel to Lourdes, by now celebrated for its miracle. Happily she is observant, and perhaps the most interesting section of her journal is its description of her fellow-guests at the hotel's *tâble d'hôte*. All seem to be British, with the possible exception of a smooth young man with – according to a drawing by the friend – a suspiciously Continental moustache, and of two American ladies who amused the table by their quaint language, their 'reckoning' and 'guessing' that they will have 'an elegant time of it' in Pau. At the centre of the table sits a prim governess, bolt upright and ready to emit instant disapproval, in particular should one of her charges, apparently an heiress, get on too well with the continentally moustached young man who is placed next to her. There were also, in this distinctly Dickensian ambiance, a strong-minded travel bore who rambled on about her trips to St Petersburg and Japan, and a 'poor gentleman', evidently not much of a traveller, who mistook the paper frill that came with his cutlet as a French delicacy, and ate it.

Harriet Jephson ended her visit with serious misgivings about Pau. True, it was wonderfully situated, with a glorious panorama of the Pyrenees. True also that Henri Quatre provided a title to fame. Yet it lacked the art galleries that were to be found in almost every Italian town. It offered no antiquities, no studios to visit, no beautiful churches, while 'the little English Colony pass their time in hunting, & going three times a week to the bank, varied by an occasional dance at the Casino, & a mild Afternoon tea party'.[18]

She and Elizabeth Carne shared much the same views on the British colony. Those of the mountaineer Charles Packe appear to have been even more harsh. Writing home to his brother, he mentioned that he received invitations from 'the prodigious number of English at Pau', adding that the life these people lead is more artificial, more effeminate and much more frivolous than in London.[19] Miss Carne, however, who was by profession a writer on social and ethical subjects, put her assessment within a wider context, and considered the effect more generally of residence abroad:

> I have known several families intimately, who have spent some years abroad, and in every instance have witnessed the same injurious effects. They come back improved in French, Italian, or German, with their English awkwardness and bashfulness rubbed off, with increased fluency of tongue and ease of manner, and with a large store of new topics and impressions, if not always new ideas; but – they come back restless and dissatisfied with the damp, dark English climate, or the stiff, dull English society, or the insupportable bondage of house and home ties and duties. And how should it be otherwise? Think of what this Continental life is: in its whole aim and essence, it is pleasure-seeking, and nothing else.

It seems in so many cases to have been a fairly harmless sort of pleasure-seeking. Elizabeth Carne does not accuse the British at Pau of gambling or drinking or even of going to parties on Sundays. There is no hint that they were promiscuous. Yet the utter dullness does not seem to tally with the description given by the French writer and illustrator Bertall who included Pau in his book *La Vie Hors de Chez Soi* of 1875, a few years, that is, before Harriet Jephson's visit. He provides an extraordinary picture of a British-dominated society. Where are the French? he asks – 'in this world there is little or no place for the poor Frenchman'.

> The English ... have transplanted their manners, their customs, their pleasures; for they are the uncontested masters by the force of banknotes, pounds and shillings, this artillery more invincible than that of Krupps and Armstrongs.

All over the place are signs for 'Family Hotels', 'Boarding Houses', 'Boarding Schools'. And everywhere the horse: English horses, with English coachmen and English grooms. There was racing and polo, 'a type of game that resembles cricket'. At a polo match, Bertall noticed particularly the babies, pink and white, the old ladies with long teeth that protruded so preposterously, and the 'ravishing blonde girls destined later to become, if one went by precedent, bony, dried-up matrons'. And the men? Laden with bushy beards. (Why do the men here grow such great crops of hair? demanded Elizabeth Carne – because, answering her own question, they have nothing else to do.)

How Bertall could see a similarity between polo and cricket is a mystery, but while at Pau he must have seen a cricket match. He might well have seen people playing golf as well, for it was there, in 1866, that the first golf course on the Continent was laid out.[20]

But above all, expensive and very fashionable, was the foxhunting. Back in the 1830s, James Erskine Murray, in the Pyrenees partly to climb mountains, went out hunting. It was an amateurish affair. The hounds were virtually useless, he said: 'they potter about like a parcel of pigs in an Indian corn field.' (It was not a sport for the ailing: if you were hunting you needed to quit your bed by 4.30 in the morning.)[21] By the 1870s, however, the hunting was much more organized. During the season, the Pau Hunt was out three times a week, hunting country north and south-east of the town. To quote Monsieur Tucoo-Chala, 'to feel more at ease, the British did not hesitate to baptize the individual parts of the hunting country, with English names'. One became the 'Home Circuit', another the 'Hill District', another – where traditionally the Duke of Wellington had hunted – 'Old England'. There was also an area that received the accolade of 'High Leicestershire'. As in the real Leicestershire, it was necessary to compensate local farmers for damage caused to their property. In fact, the farming families, and the peasants more generally, were happy enough with the horse culture introduced by the British. There was money to be made in breeding and selling, and by working in the stables.

The master of the Pau Hunt needed to be wealthy, for he was responsible for the considerable expenses which were not covered by members' subscriptions. There was Lord Howth, master in 1878/9, a very successful season, who recorded his time in a book *Leicestershire in France or the Field at Pau*, translated into French in 1907. Another master was an outstanding all-round sportsman, Sir Victor Brooke, the father of perhaps the most distinguished British subject born in France, Field Marshal Lord Alanbrooke, chief of the Imperial General Staff during the Second World War. The best known internationally, however, was an American, J. Gordon Bennett, the newspaper owner who had sent Stanley to find Livingstone. For in the years around 1880, Pau, whatever the impression given by Bertall, had become very cosmopolitan. Americans bought large properties in the town or on its outskirts; the Parc Lawrence and the Rue Beverly are named after them. Lavish parties enlivened the winter season; the dressmakers were reported to be overwhelmed by work. In 1870 a fully fledged casino had been opened, to be followed by the sumptuous Hôtel Gassion, for a few days, in each case, the place of residence of ex-President Grant and the Earl of Chester, otherwise the Prince of Wales.

This is Pau at its fashionable climax. In 1880 it possessed an indigenous population of around 30,000 (about 80,000 now) and winter residents who, not counting their servants, totalled 6,000, numbers of whom returned year after year. While the high season was October to December, many people who were not full-time residents stayed on, although, because of the heat, doctors advised leaving in May or early June. Some would spend their summers at the spas. Louise Costello, another professional writer roaming France, arrived at Pau at the beginning of one October to witness the autumn changeover, the return of invalids and others from the various spas.[22] They were, she said, in a bad temper since it had been raining all summer. Indeed, it rains a lot here in the mountains, observed Hippolyte Taine, and there is fog; the English would think themselves in London.[23] Indeed, at high altitudes it was not only the visitors who left for the winter months; the villages too were likely to be abandoned by their inhabitants, left to shepherds who had no alternative but to remain.

The Pyrenean range, Atlantic to Mediterranean, is 250 miles long, with mean altitudes comparable to the French Alps. However, the spas patronized by the British were largely concentrated in an area 60 miles long and 30 miles wide, with Pau at its western end. The waters, in the Pyrenees mainly sulphurous, might feature as part of the diet treatment for tuberculosis, but were more directly intended for other diseases or conditions. For respiratory problems you might go to Luchon, for arthritis and minor nervous complaints to Bagnères-de-Bigorre. The waters at Barèges were famous for their therapeutic effect on wounds. Your doctor's advice on where to go was backed up by books, notably by other doctors. There were Dr Taylor in 1842 with his *On the Curative Influence of the climate of Pau and the Mineral Waters of the Pyrenees*, Dr Althaus in 1862 on *The Spas of Europe*, Dr Lee in 1865 with *The Health Resorts of the South of France* and others.

For some, usually hypochondriacs, spa-visiting was a craze. They moved on from place to place, drinking at every source, and consumed 50 or 60 glasses of spa water a day. For drinking purposes, the waters could then as now be taken in bottled form but, therapeutically speaking, they were held to be more effective consumed on site. And safer it would seem: *Galignani's Messenger*, an English-language newspaper, reported the case of a young man from Caen, married only a year, who was told by his doctor to drink *Eau de Barèges*, supplied by the local chemist. He drank a glass and a few minutes later dropped dead. Apparently the chemist had by mistake sent *Eau de Barèges* bath essence.[24] The actual 'cure' was only one attraction. A description of the visitors at Bagnères-de-Bigorre, one of the principal spas, gives an idea of the mix of interests and of nationalities.

> The young man flirtatiously eyes the pretty women, strangers and locals; the moralist marks up his notes at the sight of this crowd of oddities from all nations; the naturalist gives ear to the murmur of far-off mountain streams, to the fall of disdainful rocks; the artisan, the parasite, are come to speculate on the vices of the rich; the gambler presents himself, with no other instinct than the taste for gold.

No mention here of invalids. For many spa visitors, British or otherwise, were increasingly holidaymakers or travellers, people often brimming with good health, up to trekking on foot over the mountains for miles. One British traveller in the Pyrenees remarked,

> Nothing seems to me more singular among all the singular tastes and practices of our world, than the fashion which brings miserable sufferers, anxious invalids, and gay fashionables, or restless pleasure-seekers, congregated together at what is termed a watering place.[25]

The sick have little part to play in George Sand's tale of the Pyrenees, *Lavinia*, of 1842, where the principal characters are Sir Lionel and Sir Henry, dandies as Sand describes them, and Lady Blake, the Lavinia of the title. The world-weary Sir Lionel, unenthusiastically engaged to the heiress Miss Ellis, decides he should return to Lavina some love letters dating from a romance between them ten years before. Miss Ellis is jealous, and, as the smugglers who infest the mountains might seize them for purposes of blackmail, he intends to return them in person. Accompanied by the younger, irrepressible and chronically amorous Sir Henry, he sets off on a hard ride through the mountains to the tiny and remote spa of St-Sauveur where Lavinia is staying. There is no illness about her either: she is held to be the best woman dancer in Europe, and in fact when the pair arrive, she has to be retrieved from a ball. Lavinia is more attractive than ever, not least because, as George Sand assures us, she has now acquired all the beguiling grace of a Frenchwoman. Sir Lionel is on the verge of falling in love with her all over again, but now it is no use, she is a free spirit and sick of men. The story is one of contrasts: between the patrician Englishmen, between Sir Lionel and Lavinia, who is the widow of an English peer, but who is herself Portuguese and Jewish and between the high life of a fashionable spa and the simplicity of St-Sauveur.

What it also illustrates is the prominence of the British, rich and sophisticated British, in the Pyrenees generally. While, according to the records, they were not particularly numerous in the spas, they were popular customers expected to spend lavishly. The *Blackwood's* contributor who travelled as Don Quixote (see Chapter 2) found himself at Bagnères-de-Bigorre when a party of British appeared.

> The noise of their *calèches** brought out the idlers, who, excepting the waiters at the inns, form the whole population. We received them in front of the 'Grand Hotel' with due honours, that is to say, in our dressing gowns, white slippers and straw hats ... The party made a prodigious 'effect', for they came in four large *calèches*, and the whole four completely full.

The local population, he said, watched the arrival of travellers as 'crows watch a carcass'.

The spa of consequence nearest to Pau was Eaux-Bonnes, which specialized in cures for rheumatics and bronchial disorders. The Englishman Clifton Paris has left a homely memory. He walked the 28 miles from Pau – very properly wearing the tall top hat of the period – to what he called 'this little mountain city'. He wrote that 'you can have no idea what a lively scene the place presented at ten and five, the *hours for feeding*: all the inhabitants were then lounging about; and as the clock struck, innumerable garcons sallied from their respective hotels, and sent into the air a hundred iron-tongued calls, which were duly bandied about by the surrounding mountains'. As a lone traveller, Paris especially relished the sociability of the French. After the meal was finished, he commented, you adjourned to another room, the *salle de la musique*, where there was a piano and cards. A lady settled down at the piano, the others played whist or talked and danced. This sort of arrangement, and the existence at hotels and inns of a communal dining table, the *table d'hôte*, was helpful in bringing French and British together.[26] However, not everyone was happy: Hippolyte Taine complained that there was too much music at Eaux-Bonnes. As one ate, an orchestra played waltzes and popular airs and bits and pieces from opera, ravaging the repertoire.

But Eaux-Bonnes was not just homely, indeed it was grand, patronized by the Empress Eugénie who came there for a cure. That made it. In particular it made Dr Darralde, her physician, who came to be in such demand that people queued all night to make sure of seeing him. (Happily, you could hire a substitute for the queue.) There was a queue for hotel rooms too. A

---

* In English, calash: a light carriage with a folding hood.

new arrival one July was promised a room for sure by nine in the evening, the doctor responsible stating that the person currently in occupation would not last out that long. Eaux-Bonnes was also – and still is – very beautiful, a slate village set tightly in the mountains among waterfalls and a forest of beech and pine, with splendid walks. The political economist Nassau Senior, who knew France well, wrote in his journal that it was here on the mountain immediately above Eaux-Bonnes that were he a millionaire he would build a house to pass July and August in 'the finest air and some of the finest scenery in Europe'. It possesses still its grandiose baths and the casino deemed necessary by the later part of the century for any aspiring resort. But its attraction now is nostalgic, the atmosphere perhaps more Victorian than Imperial, an historical gem. You enter the village beside the Jardin Anglais (originally the Jardin Darralde), a small park running up the hill, with, to your right, a positively huge building, once the Hôtel des Princes, derelict, interminably awaiting conversion into flats, a stark reminder of past glories.[27]

People like Clifton Paris walked in the mountains sometimes for enjoyment, sometimes because alternatives were limited. Mary Eyre made the journey from Pau to Eaux-Bonnes by *diligence*. In a book she wrote about her travels in 1865 she was admirably forthright. There were many books written on the 'South of France' (as the Pyrenees were termed in her day), she stated, but none of them by anyone as poor as she was, and as a result they omitted much about ordinary French life. She hoped the originality of her book would strengthen its chances of making a profit and gaining recognition for its author. (It did.) Moreover, she wanted to 'show other poor gentlewomen, brought up like myself to no occupation, that they may do better than stay lamenting over their past prosperity in gloom and isolation and discomfort at home'. She travelled, she said, in what was for a lady a rather peculiar fashion, carrying a small waterproof bag containing a spare dress, a thin shawl, two changes 'of every kind of underclothes', two pairs of shoes, pens, pencils, paper, the 'inevitable' *Murray's* guide, and a prayer book. As companion and protector she took along a Scotch terrier. She did her own washing, since she was never in one place long enough to make use of local washerwomen. Anyway, she was by nature casual about clothes, disapproving of foreign women travelling in crinolines: 'dress is the thought and passion of their lives', she remarked. She had little money, but insisted that one could eat well for weeks on fruit and bread, reckoning that she spent little more than she would have done living in cheap lodgings at home. What was hard, though, was to be looked down upon for economizing when one could only pay one's way by the sternest self-denial of the common daily comforts of life. It was also hard that an English person, everywhere and in everything, must expect to be charged twice as much as a Frenchwoman.[28]

While Mary Eyre's tour of the watering-places was deliberate, that made by Selina Bunbury in the 1840s was largely involuntary. Miss Bunbury was a very successful novelist: her *The Young Widow* was hailed by *Hunts London Journal* as 'one of the very best novels in the English language'. It turned out to be a very rushed tour, with things going wrong from the beginning. She arrived in Pau by *diligence* with high hopes, expecting a lively and fashionable sort of town. She was disappointed; it was a plain, grave-looking place, she thought. It was not much of a start, but worse was quickly to come. The friends she planned to stay with had not yet arrived; they had sent a message that they were at 'The Waters'. Others were at the waters too, and Miss Bunbury came to the conclusion that 'all the inhabitants of Pau were immersed'. Anyway she was resolved to track down her friends and looked up a Monsieur M, an invalid and a companion on the journey down. Happily, Monsieur M was finding Pau too hot and was keen to try the waters. Happily, too, he was a restless man and prepared to keep moving, which, until she located her friends, obviously suited Selina Bunbury. So they set off together, arriving first at Cauterets, 42 miles away, right up in the Pyrenees close to the Spanish border, with an abundance of Spaniards and priests. She was unimpressed as she watched the 'sour-looking', chronic invalids being carried in what resembled sedan chairs. And not just invalids; sometimes the chairs were occupied by people whose chief malady, she considered, was idleness.

Still, she was not to be there (or anywhere) long. A friend of Monsieur M turned up and persuaded them that the waters of Lavinia's St-Sauveur were superior. So off they went, this time across the mountains on horseback. Maybe the friends would be there – indeed they had been, but had now gone on. While Miss Bunbury took to St-Sauveur, Monsieur M was impatient; he had heard of a promising doctor at Barèges, the spa renowned for treatment of wounds and for those suffering from rheumatism and gout. Barèges was less than three miles off but entailed a climb from 737 metres to over 1,200. No friends there either, and it turned out to be a place of which a later visitor wrote that 'everybody – inhabitants and visitors alike – seems to be ill; and those who come here, if not ill already, appear soon to become so, from the effects of the damp and dreary climate'. Leaving Monsieur M behind, Selina Bunbury carried on, riding with a guide to Bagnères-de-Bigorre, where she almost fainted after a glass of the local water, and then to Bagnères-de-Luchon. But she never did find her friends, and came to the conclusion that she did not really like watering-places.[29]

Bigorre, 'the Cheltenham of the Pyrenees', and Luchon were the most fashionable of the Pyrenean spas. Even now, when spas have lost so much of their appeal, the first remains a charming, elegant town, as well as being distinguished as a centre for Pyrenean history and folklore. The 'Don Quixote' traveller left a short description of the Bigorre baths 'in which my countrymen stew themselves down from London dimensions into pale, flabby, consumptive skeletons'. Luchon (which is where George Sand planted the heiress Miss Ellis) was the most beautiful spa in Europe, declared Dr Burney Yeo in 1890, and is the one Pyrenean spa that Dominque Jarrassé in his *Les Thermes Romantiques* allows as among the top five in France during the second half of the nineteenth century. Luchon continued to attract a substantial British clientele – in 1881, for instance, 70 per cent of all visitors were British – but the vogue for the Pyrenees in Britain was fading. At Eaux-Bonnes for instance, there were 228 British visitors in 1861; 157 in 1865; and 129 in 1870; this at a time when numbers otherwise were increasing. The Romantic period with its relish of wild country and its curious inhabitants was over, and the short summers, undependable weather and difficulty of access were putting the Pyrenees at a disadvantage to the Alps. Dr Burney Yeo, despite his praise for Luchon, could remark that generally there seemed to be few British in the Pyrenean spas.[30]

This lack of interest affected Pau less. In 1878, a group of British residents formed a real estate company to develop the area around what is now the Rue des Anglais. Nevertheless, whatever the spending power of the British in the seventies, the period described with such effervescence by Bertall, their numbers were down. The peak had been reached in 1858 when they composed two-thirds of all *hivernants*, of all winter visitors. While Pau continued to attract British residents and visitors up to the Second World War, the great days were nearly over. For one thing, the atmosphere had changed. In *Where to go Abroad* (1893), edited by A. R. Hope Moncrieff, the entry on Pau contains the following comment:

> The tone of English society here has long been, if not fashionable, at least eminently respectable, but complaints are now made by old *habitués* that rich Americans have introduced a more fevered strain into the enjoyments of the place.

In the top five French spas, along with Luchon, Jarrassé places Le Mont-Dore in the Auvergne, Vichy, Plombières in Lorraine, and the alpine Aix-les-Bains in Savoy. Le Mont-Dore was popular with the British, but is considered in a later chapter. Vichy is perhaps the best known spa of all, very popular with the French and other nationalities, but less so with the British, at least until the end of the century. A contributor to *Blackwood's* in

1846 rather ill-naturedly put it that 'we should not, in speaking of Vichy to a friend, ever designate it as a *comfortable* resort for a family; which, according to our English notion of the thing, implies both privacy and detachment. Here you can have neither. You must consider yourself as public property, must do what others do – *i.e.* live in public, and make the best of it'. What is more, 'the physicians don't permit their patients to read any books but novels ... Every unlucky headache contracted here, is placed to the account of *thinking* in the bath'.[31] (Still, all was not boredom at Vichy; it had a reputation for sexual freedom.)

Of Plombières at the start of the nineteenth century we have a charming record in the form of a journal compiled by the 18-year-old Sarah Newton, a great-granddaughter of Isaac Newton. Born in Britain but brought to France at the age of seven months, she came to Plombières in 1808 – that is in the middle of the Napoleonic War – in the company of the Marquise de Coigny. Sarah is resolutely British: 'Je ne sais rien de mon pays paternal; je suis Anglaise, God Bless the King! voilà tout.' She prefers English writers to French, adores Shakespeare and is taken with *Pilgrim's Progress* which she has read in both English and French. While Madame de Coigny approves of Sarah's reading, she criticizes her dislike of the Romans which, she says, springs from that English pride which makes her so difficult with other people. For her part, Sarah wishes that Madame de Coigny, with whom she gets on pretty well, would not go on so about Poland and Polish heroes, about Mockranowski and Radzivill, and her passion for Braniki, and, as Sarah puts it, all the *ki*, 'always vanquished, always so unfortunate, desolate, lost and ruined'. In her opinion, Clarendon on Lord Falkland in his *History of the Rebellion* is much more interesting. While the people taking the cure look happy, she says, nobody talks about anything other than their health, and really it is terribly boring. However, she loves the mountains and the walks, though not having to eat frog. In fact, she does not get much fun, and the nearest she gets to romance is a major, limping because of a bullet in his knee who, while jolly and taking Sarah's teasing in good part, is a bore. And when he leaves Plombières, he embraces Madame de Coigny and Sarah in such a way that 'one trembles from it still'. A more sophisticated arrival is a friend of Madame de Coigny, the great banker Monsieur Greffulhe.[32]

Plombières in 1808 was already one of the most important of French spas, offering a wide range of cures. It was, though, still quite simple. Sarah Newton was taken by a doctor to the public bath where the sick – men and women, young and old – were piled in together. It was a horrid sight, she wrote, the bathers lost all dignity. As the century progressed, facilities improved. So of course did medical knowledge, but it was directed more towards acute diseases, rather than to what were termed chronic maladies of the sort for which the spas catered. Plombières, as described in a guide of 1880, was opulent. There are four pump rooms, with the water from the source near the old Roman baths especially recommended. There are seven bath-houses, the largest, the Grand Bain des Nouveaux-Thermes, containing four swimming pools, 52 cubicles with 60 baths, 56 'douches Tivoli', six 'douches écossaises'* and seven other types of shower-bath. At the Bain National, the most popular of these bath houses, facilities included a Turkish bath so hot that it went by the name of the 'Inferno' (*l'Enfer*). The pool in the Bain de Capucins (named after a monastery once on the site) was particularly in demand from women hoping to cure sterility.

One reason for the success and enlargement of Plombières and of spas generally was the encouragement given by Napoleon III and his wife, the Empress Eugénie. (At Plombières, the Parc Impérial and the Thermes Napoléon are still there, reminders of the Second Empire.) Also significant at this time was demand from the French middle class, wealthier than before and converted to the idea of holidays. We need these holidays, wrote the journalist Charles Brainne in the 1860s, not just as a distraction, something to do, but because we work harder than our forefathers, we are under greater pressure.[33] Spas were a place to make friends, even if these friendships were usually cruise-ship type rather than permanent, and generally to have fun. Bath-houses and Douches then were not enough; above all, you needed casinos which came to provide a major source of revenue for spa investors. The casino at Plombières was huge; along with rooms for gambling, it provided a theatre for 300 spectators, a reading room, a billiard room where you could also obtain refreshments, and a ladies' room.

Plombières and its peers such as Aix-les-Bains, Vichy and Evian were in direct competition with Baden-Baden and other spas in Germany and Austria. For them the type of clientele was more important to their reputation than the nature of the waters they provided. The spas had long been attractive to the French nobility: they allowed a life patterned on old, more prosperous, or at least more prestigious, days, one in which social rank retained a consequence that it was losing in the real world. It was a way of living that appealed to the British, and indeed to patricians everywhere in Europe. In such places, centres of cosmopolitan high society, it has been said, that 'one felt as a cousin much more than one thought of oneself as English, German or French'.[34] Most fashionable of all French spas was Aix-les-Bains in the Savoy, a province which in the early 1830s, when Lady

---

* A fierce hosing-down in ice-cold water.

Granville and her husband spent an August at Aix, was not part of France at all. It had been returned to the kingdom of Sardinia from which it had been seized in the recent war. The Granvilles loved it, revelling in the view of Mont Blanc and the luxuriant alpine countryside, walking and driving, and cruising on the Lac du Bourget in flat-bottomed boats 'like Robinson Crusoe's rafts'. Lady Granville marvelled at 'the highest and most picturesque Alps – all I love – vineyards in festoons over *treillages* and round down about every cottage. Plums, apple, and walnut trees of uncommon size and beauty for hedges. Light yellow cows with bells round their necks, women with straw hats and milk pails, goats that look as if they had been blown in glass, Indian corn like a fairy forest'. This was country familiar to discerning British, an inspiration to the Romantics, visited by Wordsworth, Southey, Byron and the Shelleys. By the end of the 1830s the town of Chamonix, placed immediately under Mont Blanc, was established as a popular resort, with *Murray's Guide* recommending the Hôtel de Londres et de l'Angleterre as extremely comfortable. Ruskin in the 1860s even dreamed of settling there. This was of course mountaineering country, highly favoured by British climbers, and a centre for the Alpine Club which was founded in 1857.[35]

In 1860, the Savoy was once again French, ceded by Sardinia in return for Napoleon III's decisive assistance against the Austrians. The Emperor might well have felt special pleasure since at the age of five he had been brought to stay at Aix-le-Bains by his mother Queen Hortense of Holland. Certainly, Amadée Achard, an accomplished publicist for the resort, would have been pleased; in his book *Une Saison à Aix-les-Bains* he had demanded, 'is not Savoy still and always France?'

Another enthusiast for the town was Dr Thomas Linn, an American doctor practising at Aix, who addressed himself to the British public in a book written towards the end of the century. Linn recommended the Aix waters as especially beneficial for what he called the 'very English maladies' of rheumatism and gout. He mentioned the presence in the town of an Anglican church and a Presbyterian chapel, and the advantage that, unlike other spas, almost all of its French doctors spoke English. He distinguished Aix from competitors in two other ways. What often makes a cure, he claimed, was not the intrinsic qualities of the waters but the way they were applied: the speciality at Aix of massage or shampooing under hot water was carried out with a perfection unequalled elsewhere in the world. There were other refinements: after the douche and rubbing down, the patient was carefully wrapped in a warm blanket and taken to his hotel room in a bath chair. Then Dr Linn turned to the problem of boredom. He made no bones about it: most places with mineral springs were 'insufferably dull', but then at Aix there were two casinos, reading rooms, the best music, operas and plays performed daily. On top of that, there was a racecourse open in July and August, and pigeon shooting and lawn tennis. Emile Daullia for Evian, also in Savoy, writing at the same time as Linn, extolled his town's fine new hotels, sumptuous villas, the *crockett*, the *foot-ball*, the *lawn-tennis*, the shooting, the riding, but he had to admit that because of the terrain Evian could provide no racetrack nor rival the huge swimming pools at Aix. If you really wanted something more exciting, he said, you had best go down the lake to Geneva.[36]

Then there was sex. From all accounts, for that, the Pyrenean resorts provided little competition. Vichy did, as we have seen, and so at the end of the century did Contrexéville in the Vosges. Contrexéville, popular with the British, was virtually taken over by the Persians, with the Shah leading the field. (The town's tourist office is currently at 116 Rue du Shah de Perse.) At Aix, sex hangs heavy in the air, according to Amadée Achard. At the Casino you can imagine yourself among the best company of the Faubourg St-Germain, where 'the Queens of the Ball' come from everywhere, from France, Germany, Russia, England, America. 'And what about the husbands?' demands Achard rhetorically; 'one has to be frank, there are none at Aix-les-Bains, or if there are you never see them.' He is poetic: after midnight, under 'the wandering moon' shining on the lake, 'the tinkle of glasses, the champagne, the songs, the indiscreet lights in private rooms'. It is at this hour, he declares in something of an anticlimax,

> that the young English girls, yielding up the long tresses of their hair to the embrace of night, sip tea laced with a drop of milk; it is the auspicious hour of gentle dreams and slices of buttered bread! They bite into their toast and reflect on the mysterious Child Harold [sic] whom every daughter of Albion carries in her heart.

Well, perhaps, but then perhaps not.

There is a story Achard tells of an English girl, a pretty Miss Harriet, who arrives at Aix with a dreadful mother, large, thin and yellow, wrapped in a boa, whose passion is whist. The spirit of Aix wins. One night, the mother is at her whist, and Miss Harriet is on her balcony, listening like Juliet to words of love declaimed by the handsome Lionnel. At the corner stands a post-chaise; they elope; eight days of bliss. Brought back by the police, Harriet is greeted by her mother, still at whist, by 'Ah, there you are. You should know that your escapade has cost me fifty pounds. Go and change and come back to serve tea'.

Wanton, but above all, Aix was smart, by 1890 'perhaps the most elegant spa on earth', a magnet for British society, and 'inconceivably expensive'. The management would have been wary of too many illicit winking lights. The Shah of Persia chose Contrexéville, Queen Victoria chose Aix, approving of it so much that she commissioned a house for herself there.

5

The Transport Revolution

Railroads have unlocked the doors of districts hitherto barred against the masses of people.

Thomas Cook

At the end of December 1881 Harriet Jephson and her husband left Pau on the first stage of a journey to San Remo. It was of course no longer a matter of lumbering for days along monotonous roads; there were railways from start to finish. Leaving Pau station at 10.30 in the morning, they were at Toulouse by 4.25 in the afternoon. But the next lap, Toulouse to Nice, was less relaxed. The Jephsons wanted a private sleeping compartment, a *coupé-lit*. First, an application in writing was necessary; after that came half an hour of what amounted to negotiations with two officials, accompanied by what Mrs Jephson described as 'a great deal of bowing and smiling'. There was less reason for smiles when they came back that evening to catch the 11 o'clock train: it was irritating – having checked in their luggage – to be cooped up for half an hour in a waiting room, and maddening, when released, to find after all that no *coupé-lit* was available. Anyway, their supplementary fare refunded, they settled down in a first-class compart-ment, empty except for a young man who got out at Carcassonne. Happily, Harriet Jephson – as she put it – 'pulled off my boots, enveloped my feet in bedroom shoes, deposited my hat on the network above, shook loose my hair & lay down snugly amidst rugs and cushions'. Then there was 'a violent shake, followed by a thud on my head, & a perfect hailstorm of boots, hats, brushes, bandboxes, bags, & bundles startled us not a little'. The train came to a sudden stop. People started shouting. Understandably the Jephsons were rather more than startled, and less than pleased by the appearance in their carriage of two noisy Catalans who 'talked Spanish in a most excited and angry way'. At Montpellier they were replaced by a fat old man who sat on Harriet's hat. The unfamiliar smell of garlic prevented their getting much sleep that night.[1]

By 1881 France was well advanced into the railway age. But for a long time travellers endured a patchy service, part rail, part road. Over the New Year of 1854, John Stuart Mill made his way back to England from the South of France, initially retracing, but in a reverse direction, the journey made by Mary Berry, her father and her sister 50 years before. Again the weather was appalling. The first part of his trip was laborious, but at least it was more comfortable than the Berrys' experience. Mill too intended to go by water, but the river was impassable, iced over, so he made do with a long, freezing ride by coach. More precisely it was a series of rides, beginning with a first lap of 23 miles from Arles to Avignon. At Avignon, Mill spent most of a day waiting for a *diligence* to take him over the much longer stretch to Lyon. In fact he had to change *diligences* four times on the way. At Lyon, in much distress from the cold, he transferred to a small (eight-seater) omnibus to cover the journey on to the railhead at Chalon-sur-Saône. From there to Paris he was spoilt: the train's carriages were heated. Then it was back to normal. His train on to Boulogne broke down in the snow. The passengers waited seven hours for a relief engine which never arrived. Happily, the old engine recovered sufficiently to get up steam; unhappily, after plodding on a bit, it gave up once more. For Mill, it was back to an omnibus and a very long stay in the waiting room at Abbeville station.[2]

The British tended to find that, in those days, French trains were slower than at home, although often they were more comfortable. One British businessman,[3] looking back 50 years from the start of the twentieth century, fondly remembered the footwarmers provided in first class which were changed regularly during the journey, hour by hour. But everyone detested the waiting room, a 'sheep pen' as one traveller called it, where, like the Jephsons, you were held for half an hour before departure usually in the care of a notoriously strict and inflexible official, probably an old soldier, known to passengers as a *gendarme*.[4] Still, in the end, this was obviously no more than an irritant. There were more serious matters to bother about – above all obviously the risk of an accident, but also dangers to health. As late as 1861 a French doctor warned that a concantenation of sensations, nervousness, the jolting and speed, the inability to hold outside objects visually steady, 'ordinarily' led, to a greater or lesser extent, to the sensation of an enormous weight on the head. Whereas in the old days travellers risked 'diligence leg', now they might be faced not only with varicose veins, but with the pernicious 'railway spine', defined as a microscopic deterioration of the spinal cord due to mechanical shock caused by an accident. Even at the end of the century, a travel writer could warn of the dangers of hurrying to catch a train, particularly soon after a meal.[5]

For all this, it was indisputable that the railways shortened enormously the time taken on a journey. Whereas the star performers of public transport in the coaching era, the mail coaches (*malles-poste*), could manage 20 km an hour, an express train of the early 1860s sped by at 80 km an hour. The doctor quoted above may have wildly exaggerated the physiological dangers of the railways, but he was perhaps right in drawing attention to the 'inability to hold outside objects visually steady': the speed of the train meant that travellers came to see, to apprehend, the landscape through which they passed in a new way. Mr Justice Talfourd,[6] on his way to Southampton and a holiday in France, wrote with pleasure of 'gliding along' in his first-class carriage, watching a 'thousand lovely little pictures' flash by. In 1833, Louis-Napoleon, the future Emperor, noted of a train journey in England, 'all the objects pass before your eyes with an unparalleled rapidity, houses, trees, fences, all vanish before one can take them in'.[7] To Victor Hugo, everything – towns, steeples, trees – got mixed up madly on the horizon. The train was a 'projectile', to Charles Dickens, a 'great rocket', that 'rattled among the house-tops, and among the ragged sides of houses torn down to make way for it, and over the swarming streets, and under the fruitful earth, until it shot across the river: bursting over the quiet surface like a bomb-shell, and gone again as if it had exploded in the rush of smoke and steam and glare'.[8]

In his *The World the Railways Made* (1990) Nicholas Faith describes the railways, in their inconsistencies, charms, drama and comedy, as a truly Dickensian form of transport. Certainly Dickens wrote extensively on train journeys and was indeed himself caught up in one of the most alarming of nineteenth-century railway accidents in Britain. In his story 'The Calais Night Mail' the train hurtles on to Paris through a terrific storm. The guard, to check tickets, comes clambering along the outside of the train, from compartment to compartment; Dickens grips his collar to hold him against the whirlwind. There are his fellow passengers: one is an Englishman who insists that they should keep London time in France, the other a young priest with a tiny bird in a tiny cage. The priest puts the bird on the rack where 'he advances twittering ... and seems to address me in an electioneering manner'.[9]

Dickens and Thackeray each give a picture of the passage over to Boulogne by steamboat. On Thackeray's boat it is the wives with elderly stout husbands, nursemaids and children who predominate. But there is a also a *danseuse* from the opera on her way to Paris, accompanied by a maid and small dog, who steps out on the deck in real dancer fashion, ogling all around. And a group of young ladies off to Paris to learn how to be governesses, making a striking contrast to a pair of splendidly dressed ladies, milliners from the rue de Richelieu, returning to France having delivered the summer fashions to London. There are young men too, several of whom are trying to get their moustaches to grow, 'for they are going on the continent'. And some younger ones yet, pupils of the Rev. Mr Snodgrass who is conducting them to his establishment near Boulogne, 'where in addition to a classical and mathematical education ... the young gentlemen have the advantage of learning French among the French *themselves*. Accordingly, the young gentlemen are locked up in a great rickety house, two miles from Boulogne, and never see a soul except the French usher and the cook'.[10]

Dickens's fellow passengers are less flamboyant. He sees a few shadowy Frenchmen with hat boxes, a few shadowy Germans in immense fur coats, and a few shadowy Englishmen 'prepared for the worst and pretending not to expect it'. However, there is nothing shadowy about the arrival. As in Brummell's day, 20 years before, the Boulogne English assemble to watch the ferry and the disembarkation of its seasick passengers. The locals are in their best clothes, the better, Dickens says, to enjoy the degradation of their 'dilapidated fellow-creatures' as they struggle along the quay.

> Even we ourself (not deficient in natural dignity) have a lively remembrance of staggering up this detested lane one September day in a gale of wind, when we were received like an irresistible comic actor, with a burst of laughter and applause, occasioned by the extreme imbecility of our legs.

Dickens loved France; he was a constant visitor from 1844 until his death in 1870, in some years spending more time there than he did at home. He came to speak and write excellent French, he knew Victor Hugo and Lamartine (whose wife was British), he was close to d'Orsay. He had met the Emperor at Lady Blessington's Gore House in London. What is more, for the French, next to Walter Scott, he was the most popular British novelist of the nineteenth century. Genial, gregarious and animated, he was far removed from the stereotype of the Englishman implanted in French minds. Boulogne was his favourite resort in the 1850s. It was, he considered, a pleasant, cheerful town full of children and governesses reading novels. He admired the hard-working fishermen and fisherwomen and was particularly fond of his landlord, from whom, over two summers, he rented a house. In 'Our French Watering-Place' he turns him, Monsieur Beaucourt (in the article, Monsieur Loyal Devasseur), into something like a character from one of his books. Monsieur Beaucourt was a convivial and hugely popular figure locally, and eccentric too.

> It is never going to rain, according to M. Loyal. When it is impossible to deny that it is now raining in torrents, he says it will be fine – charming – magnificent – tomorrow. It is never hot on the Property, he contends. Likewise it is never

cold. The flowers, he says, come out, delighting to grow there; it is like Paradise this morning; it is like the Garden of Eden.[11]

To Dickens, Boulogne was a 'watering-place', a seaside resort, as it was to many. Like other Channel ports, it benefited not only from the increase in passengers and boats using its harbour, but also from visitors arriving by rail from other parts of France. The Pyrenean and Alpine spas too were greatly affected. The railway reached Tarbes, 25 miles from Pau, in 1859 and Pau itself four years later. The railway, arriving in 1873, does much to explain the spectacular success of Luchon: 9,000 visitors in 1865; 25,000 in 1887; 36,000 by the beginning of the 1890s. Aix-les-Bains, on the line from Paris to Italy, was particularly well placed: 3,000 visitors in 1830; 10,000 in 1869; and 30,000 by the end of the century. More generally speaking, the railways were of enormous demographic consequence. The geography of the country is changed, so a French writer of the time expressed it. On the one hand, you find an unknown village, become populous and rich, that wakes up one fine morning to discover itself a town. On the other, a town, in sudden decline, deserted by its inhabitants where, in 20 years time, an inscription on the wall of its last remaining house will proclaim 'Here lieth a one-time sous-préfecture'.*[12]

If Luchon and Aix gained a great deal from the railways, Archachon, on the sea 40 miles west of Bordeaux, could almost claim to have been created by the railway. 'Almost', but though not entirely, for it had been a summer station for British merchant families from Bordeaux who went there for sea-bathing. By mid-century it existed as an out-of-the-way summer resort buried in the deep pine forests of the Landes, unapproachable by road because of the surrounding bogs and marshes. In 1854, John Mill, arriving by rail at the nearby, 'rather shabby' village of La Teste, walked for six hours in the forest and on the beach, visiting Arcachon which he described as a long line of houses stretched along the seashore. By the time of Mill's visit, Arcachon seems to have existed as a resort – a strictly summer resort – for about ten years. Ten more years and it was about to enter the railway age. What was critical was the heavy investment in the region by the financier Emile Pereire and the active support of the Emperor. There was a policy to reclaim the barren country around, and a systematic planting of trees, partly to stabilize the shifting sands. The railway was extended from La Teste as Pereire and his brother saw the possibilities for tourism on the Bassin d'Arcachon. It became a favourite seaside resort for the British and was to be entitled the Bournemouth of France and the Southport of Bordeaux.

---

* An important town in its Department.

(Indeed. it might have been called the Whitstable of France given that it was famous for its oysters.)[13]

Not everyone was delighted by the advent of the railways. The Duchesse de Dino, for instance, while admitting that they were a marvellous invention, considered them a cheerless form of travel. There was no time to see anything; you charged straight across fields, missing all the towns and villages, the only relief being cold and humid tunnels in which you were stifled by smoke from the engine. Moreover, if you had your own carriage with you, a lot of time was wasted while it was loaded on to the train and then unloaded. And the saving you made, she thought, was nil, given the charges for transporting the carriage.[14] In the case of Dickens, though, there were few regrets. He welcomed liberation from the long straight roads of France that ran through monotonous countryside, and from the 'horrible little villages we used to pass through in the *Diligence*'. He was glad to see the end of those 'beggars who turned out at night with bits of lighted candle to look in at the coach windows, the long-tailed horses who were always biting each other, the big postillions in their jack-boots, the mouldy cafés that we used to stop at'. More neutrally, Edouard Siebecker could write that 'gone are the diligences, the wagoners, the inn-keepers, in their place are navvies, hoteliers and porters'. Robert Louis Stevenson was enthusiastic. As he travelled south to regain his health, he delighted in watching familiar sights. There were the children who occasionally cheered and waved at the passing express, the sheep browsing, a girl who sat balanced on the projecting tiller of a canal boat. 'Here, I think, lies the chief attraction of railway travel', he wrote: 'the speed is so easy, and the train disturbs so little the scenes through which it takes us, that our heart becomes full of the placidity and stillness of the country.'[15]

The eminent Victorian to argue most vehemently against this new world was John Ruskin, another constant visitor to France. He deplored the disruption to the countryside, the ruin of dear and familiar haunts, holding too that the railways, by making travel so easy, had taken away the pleasure.

> If the attention is awake, and the feelings in proper train, a turn of a country road, with a cottage beside it, which we have not seen before, is as much as we need for refreshment; if we hurry past it, and take two cottages at a time, it is already too much; hence to any person who has all his senses about him, a quiet walk along not more than ten or twelve miles of road a day, is the most amusing of all travelling; and all travelling becomes dull in exact proportion to its rapidity.

Moreover, Ruskin objected to the collective life inseparable from the railway. By 1848, making an (especially well-documented) tour of Normandy with his wife Effie, he used a variety of transport: train, *diligence* and hired carriage. His heart, though, remained with recollections of youthful tours accompanying his parents, his nurse, another domestic or relation, and a courier. He recalled the visit beforehand to Long Acre, the centre of the London carriage trade, to order a coach, and to devise its ingenious fittings, the storage space under the seats, the concealed drawers and pockets, the comforts of the small apartment in which they would spend so much of their time over a six-month trip. The notion of an 'apartment' is an important one, for this was private travelling in one's chosen company, to be enjoyed at one's own pace. It was to be one of the attractions of the motorcar that it gave back privacy and choice.[16]

It seems that it was not just the countryside that was being spoilt; it was the people as well, the travellers. Too many of them were turning into the Proud and Vain type. To go by *Blackwood's*,[17] the deterioration had early set in, even before the railways had a chance to play a part. 'It is astounding to behold', ran the article, 'the confidence with which, on the strength of a week or two at Pau, a few pints of water imbibed at Barèges, or a distant view of the Maladetta, [travellers] discourse of three hundred miles of mountain'. In a later issue, another article in *Blackwood's* criticized the distinguished mountaineer Count Henry Russell (French, but with an Irish father) for describing himself in inn registers as an 'ascensionist', doing so 'with as much frankness as was shown by those four American girls at Lucerne last year who stated their occupation to be "looking for husbands"'. The spirit of the times was changing: mountains now are taken for granted, wrote Anthony Trollope in 1866. A few years back, to have gone up Mont Blanc 'was a feat which almost opened the gates of society to the man who did it; but Mont Blanc is now hardly more than the equal to the golden ball on the top of St. Paul's Cathedral'. As to the American girls with their candour and self-confidence, they were nothing special. One need not worry about women travellers, said Trollope; what he called 'the unprotected female tourist' is generally much stronger-minded than her male opposite number. Certainly than those he terms 'United Englishmen', aged under 25, who are a great nuisance to other travellers, longing to shock and still 'enjoying the irresponsible delights of boyhood at a time when others less fortunate are already immersed in the grievous cares of earning their bread'. The solitary woman is not like that at all. (Nor for that matter are the 'United Frenchmen', on their travels so discreet, anticipating already the life of middle age.) The Englishwoman knows how to handle her money and knows exactly what she is about, speaks French fluently and possibly something of German and Italian. The self-confidence, however, seems to have gone to the head: sometimes, another article revealed, 'the unprotected females' inspire terror by the sternness of their looks, their thirst for information and their determination to engage in impracticable or dangerous enterprises. They all sketch, it announced, and they are mostly short-sighted and wear thick boots and spectacles. The younger ones are reserved, the older gushing. And they may well be intending to get their experiences into print. The writer adds that he has frequently witnessed the panic in a foreign community when the news spreads of the imminent arrival of a literary spinster.[18]

It was all getting out of control, proclaimed *Blackwood's*. Railroads and steam-boats are very useful in their way, but they have covered all Europe with tourists, 'all pen in hand, all determined not to let a henroost remain undescribed, all portfolioed, all handbooked, all "getting up a journal", and all pouring their busy nothings on the "reading public", without compassion or conscience'. They go on about America, Vienna, the North Pole or Antartica or wherever. Another takes a sweep at the French coast 'and showers us with well worn-out romance and modern vapidity'.[19]

Yet these formidable women could not be called typical. Indeed, Trollope concedes that they were a small group. In 1863 the Reverend George Musgrave, under the pen-name of Viator Verax in his *Cautions for the First Tour*, thought it necessary to address a warning to 'Husbands, Fathers, Brothers, and all Gentlemen' accompanying female relatives on Continental excursions'. The time has come for the plain speaking shirked by guide-books and journalists. Viator Verax has pleasant memories of France back in 1815 and of its people, lively, polite and friendly. But things have changed,'in my humble opinion, very little for the better'. (He means very much for the worse.) He gets going with so much vehemence that for a moment or two one suspects a spoof. But in fact he is serious, and, as it happens, some of his comments on contemporary travel are supported by a book of a very different sort, *Physiologie des Chemins de Fer*, also published in the sixties. Its author Edouard Siebecker recalls the old *diligences*, how everyone chattered away, so that by the time an hour had passed the coach had become a '*salon* on wheels'. But it was not like that with the railways – 'the manners of the cafés have turned us all into bears and egotists'. And there is the attitude to women, which is the core of Viator Verax's attack. Our fathers, says Siebecker, 'those old *rococos*', as soon as they saw a woman approaching the *diligence*, with a quick pat to their hair, stretched out a hand to help her aboard. If no seat were free they gave up their own. Now, with the train – as many British complained – there was a frenzied rush for seats, and no priority for women. Siebecker explained that once you, a man, had got a seat, your great fear was of a woman advancing on your compartment. She would object to your cigar and, were she susceptible to colds, would demand that you closed the window. The best thing to do was to stand in the doorway, your cigar in hand, look as ugly as possible, and swear.[20]

While in the USA trains were fitted with through-carriages, in France and Britain the carriages were divided into compartments. The French compartments were linked by a small pane of glass, in effect a tiny window which, due to the national predispositon in favour of privacy, did not happen in Britain. It meant that French trains were safer for women, observed one Englishman.[21] However, such spy-holes could be far from desirable. Viator Verax had plenty of grumbles about travelling conditions, but his ire was concentrated on hotels – first-class hotels, he emphasized – in the provinces. By now there was no need for pistols, or bolts for hotel doors, although some disagreed about bolts. Instead, Viator Verax equipped himself with a foot-rule with which – when he was not looking under carpets for dirt – he measured the width of the beds. That done, he said, check the panels of any door in your room that communicates with another room. Almost certainly you will find holes bored through them by Peeping Toms. Another essential was to inspect the *cabinet*, the lavatory, for indecent graffiti. In any event, these places were usually so filthy that it was best for ladies to carry in their baggage a specially designed chamber pot, which looked like a hatbox, that could be purchased in Leicester Square. By that means they could escape both the squalor of the lavatory and the risk of an encounter in the corridor with 'the moustached foreigner ... , his waistcoat unbuttoned, cigar in mouth, and his hands fumbling at his braces'. In Fleet Street, advised another writer, you could buy a special fllter to insert in your tumbler as a protection against tainted water.

Viator Verax advised hiring a courier, but generally, by the 1860s, that was considered unnecessary, and anyway was beyond the pockets of most travellers and tourists. Before mid-century, though, they made it easier to select the right hotel, particularly outside Paris. Francis Coghlan in his *Guide to France* of 1828 tackled the problem as far as Calais was concerned, recommending two of them, the 'Flying Horse' and the 'Brittania' for those who needed to economise. (Coghlan went on to produce no less than 30 guides between 1830 and 1860, initially in relation to steamboats and then to railways.) In the 1860s, *Bradshaw's Railway Guide*, important in any event because of the problems of coping with the large number of competing railway companies, recommended 54 hotels, out of which, it is worth noting, 20 had names with British associations – examples are the 'Saint-James', le 'Bedford', le 'Prince Albert', the 'London and New York', the 'Paris and Albion'.[22] Then there was the famous *Murray*, of which it was said that every British traveller carried a copy. Certainly John Ruskin did on his visit to Normandy in 1848, authority though he was on many of the places listed. But *Murray* was voluminous and solid reading; moreover, what suited Ruskin was unlikely to be ideal for the increasing numbers of British who were less erudite and less interested in churches and monuments. Later on anyway, many preferred *Baedeker*. In pre-railway days, it was observed, you could read guidebooks for fun, but now they had become too condensed for that. *The Complete Vade-Mecum for Tourists in France* (1856) declared itself to be especially intended for 'that large and increasing class of tourists who cross the Channel for a few weeks' and who required a cheap, easy-to-carry handbook containing the information they needed and nothing more. The reader is told, for instance, that at Rouen omnibuses are waiting at the station to take arrivals to their hotels, and the guide recommends the 'Hôtel d'Albion' run by Mrs Smith. And, as most of the likely readers would possess little or no knowledge of French, the guide provides some useful phrases. Very practical and un-milord like they are too.

'Tell me your lowest price'
'It is too dear – too much'
'This is dearer: can you not let me have it lower?'
'You ask too much'
'What deductions do you make for ready money?'

Some guidebook tips on language became celebrated as jokes for later generations; such was 'The postillion has been struck by lightning'. Still, at one time or another, the postillion phrase may have come in handy, more so, for instance, than this offering from Ahn's *Manual of French Conversation*:

'The gay and charming landscape sets off the long line of carriages full of the most brilliant and elegant company one can see collected in a single spot.'

Few travellers (or, for that matter, the schoolchildren for whom the book was also intended) can have found that very useful.[23]

In the eyes of purists, the sort of people that favoured the *Vade Mecum* were of a different and inferior type. W. H. Mallock in the 1890s asserted that the species, traveller, fell into three categories. The only true travellers, he says, are those who love change for its own sake; they take it into their system 'as a smoker inhales smoke'. All others are travellers merely by accident: they go to distant places for some definite object, one which is to be had at a distance only – a picture gallery, a gaming-table, or a good climate in January – which they would like as well, if not better, if they could find it nearer home. His third category, the 'Excursionist', is someone 'who in the course of a single holiday is "personally conducted" through India, Japan, and America'. It can hardly be said that he has ever left home at all. 'He has virtually sat still and looked at a moving peep-show.'[24]

The Excursionist was above all the creation of Thomas Cook[25] – carpenter, printer, nonconformist preacher and teetotaller – born in Derbyshire in 1808. And of the railways, without which such a person could not have existed. The first commercial excursion organized by Cook took some 300 customers from Leicester on a round trip by rail to Liverpool in 1845. Later ones could go almost anywhere. Mallock mentioned India, Japan and America; add, by the end of the century, Egypt and the Nile, Palestine and South Africa, along with virtually all Europe. In 1872 Cook led a small group, comprising British, Americans, a Greek and a Russian, on a 29,000-mile, 222-day journey around the world. The price for that was 270 guineas a head, in our money say £20,000. That was hardly cheap. But essentially his business was founded on cheap tickets, on concessionary fares obtained from railway companies, who, having once covered their costs, could find it profitable to fill the last 20 per cent or 30 per cent of their seats at a low price.

Cook did more than offer a good price; he provided very good value for the money, particularly important for foreign tours where a more comprehensive service was necessary. He was courier (with an interpreter's backing), guidebook and companion in one. He sorted out the hotels, squeezing them too for special terms. (He would have spotted those holes in the door panels.) He dealt with complicated rail schedules. He encouraged liveliness and fun on his excursions; people who were not genial and sociable, he said, should not come. He might not drink himself, but in his professional life he made no difficulties for those who did.

Cook's first excursion to France was planned to coincide with the Universal Exhibition in Paris of 1855. Four years before, he had achieved astonishing success with those he organized for the Great Exhibition in Hyde Park; around 165,000 people attended under his auspices, a very encouraging precedent. More immediately, his negotiations with Scottish railways on fares had broken down, and he needed to think out alternative plans. At best, however, the French project was no more than a partial success. Cook failed to persuade the Belgian and French railway companies to allow him special terms, and could get his excursionists no further than Calais, although he did substitute a round trip via Antwerp into Belgium and Germany, which passed through Paris on the way home. From his point of view, the experience had proved disappointing: he gained some goodwill and experience, but he lost money and heart, and was not to venture outside Britain again for another six years. Indeed, his firm's magazine, its eyes on a competitor Henry Gaze, pushed Scotland (where Cook was once more especially active) as against France. There were too many spies and *gendarmes* there, was his argument.

In 1861, when Cook organized his next trip to France, passports were no longer necessary for British visitors. Here was an opportunity to sell excursion tickets to people who up to then had never aspired to foreign travel. In fact, the 1861 tour to Paris was actually called the 'Working Man's Excursion', and its participants were mainly working class, mostly from the north of England. They included 200 employees of Titus Salt's cotton mills in Bradford. That the excursion took place at all was due to the encouragement and support of Sir Joseph Paxton, MP and architect of the Crystal Palace, and also President of the London Committee of Working Men, known to Cook through his involvement with the Great Exhibition.

The excursion, covering six days at Whitsun, was accompanied by a reporter from the *Illustrated London News* and a photographer. Some of the participants were veteran Cook's travellers, but very few, it appears, had ever been before outside the British Isles. Hence, said their *Illustrated London News* companion, even allowing for the guides and interpreters, they felt 'something like misgiving' about how the tour would go. In fact, fears were largely put to rest by the warm welcome they received at Boulogne. At Amiens, they paused for refreshment, which for the more adventurous included *eau de vie*. There were difficulties at Paris. For instance when the party assembled the first morning in the Champs-Elysées, they were dispersed (politely) by the police for infringement of the rules against public gathering. But the hotel keepers, initially wary of working-class customers, were helpful, the weather was good, expeditions were undertaken to Versailles and St Cloud. Everyone seems to have been happy: the excursionists, the French, and the reporter who, while gently criticizing some defects in the organization, forecast that this would be the first of many such trips.[26]

It had been very cheap, and Cook, a year or two later, could point out that it was now possible to travel from London to Paris as quickly as from London to Edinburgh and at half the price. But again he had lost money, and was faced with the recurring problem of how to make these French expeditions pay. It was the more serious since he was having his customary difficulties with the Scottish railways. Once more, Paxton, a director of several railway companies, came to the rescue, intervening with the London, Brighton and South Coast Railway. As a result, Cook's French ventures were put on a more solid foundation. Using the ports of Newhaven and Dieppe,

Cook, in the five years from 1863, conveyed 70,000 tourists to and from France.

Looking back over 40 years, the journalist Albert Vandam, resident in Paris for most of his life, could say that the Paris Exhibition of 1855 was a milestone in British tourism; it marked the beginning, he stated, of 'middle-class excursions'. Not, it should be noted, of 'working-class excursions'. And it is to the point that James Bertram, passing through Paris in the early 1860s – a Paris swarming with British tourists – singles out as an exception a 'very intelligent' cabinet maker whom he comes across.[27] At the same time, extending the advantages of overseas travel to the working class appealed to both Cook, the ex-lay preacher, and to Paxton, the son of an agricultural labourer. Cook called the 1861 Whitsun trip 'a work of love minus profit', and Paxton's committee intended that the British workmen would 'shake hands with the Parisian ouvriers, and assure them that, whatever may have been the case many years ago, this nation has now no other feeling towards France but that of good will'. The idea of moral purpose lay behind the two great exhibitions, London in 1851 and Paris in 1855. After the first, one author could state, rather naively, that, now writers representing the French people as frivolous and fantastical would be laughed at and disbelieved.[28]

The practical effect of good intentions is often hard to assess, but it is interesting that Bertram's cabinet maker was so impressed by the cooperative workshops he had discovered in Paris that he was returning home determined to start one in his own trade. Moreover, there was the belief that 'travel broadens the mind'. In Britain at a time when electoral reform was clearly imminent, it was arguable that broad minds lower down the social scale might sooner or later be very important. In 1867, the Society of Arts sponsored a scheme to send over workmen to the second Paris Exhibition. Paxton by now was dead, and his place was taken by Austen Layard, chairman of the Society's sub-committee. Layard, a Liberal politician and archaeologist, himself born in a Paris hotel, secured a parliamentary grant for the scheme and personally conducted 2,000 of his Southwark constituents on a trip to the exhibition. *The Times* reported some of what was happening, mentioning for example the selection of 25 'artisans' as their representatives by the Birmingham Chamber of Commerce. *The Times* also published letters from participants expressing thanks, and in one case a description of the exhibits so comprehensive that the writer's local clergyman thought it necessary to follow up with a letter of his own vouching for its authenticity.[29]

The Paris Exhibition of 1867 put its predecessor in the shade. It was also the culmination of Cook's Paris excursions. His son John Mason Cook, as entrepreneurial as his father and more ruthless, took charge of the cheapest tickets which were priced at £1 16s. 0d. (say £126) for four days' board, lodging and travel. Much of the firm's publicity centred on the prospect of the new Paris, the city so magnificently rebuilt by Baron Haussmann. The organization was meticulous and included a discussion with the Emperor's private secretary. A large house in the Rue de la Faisanderie at Passy, previously a school, was rented and renamed 'Cook's Anglo-American Exhibition Hotel'. It was comfortable and cheap, providing, as Cook promised, 'good English fare'. Demand was buoyant, so more apartments in the street were taken and temporary housing erected on some empty land. Customers who fancied luxury were lodged in a mansion on the boulevard Haussmann, once occupied by Benjamin Franklin and a 20-minute walk from the Exhibition grounds on the Champs de Mars.

Between 1830 and 1870, the number of passengers disembarking at Calais, Dieppe and Boulogne increased from 29,300 to 112,313, with the proportion of British fluctuating between 60 per cent and 68 per cent. Many were people who in an earlier generation would never even have dreamed of a foreign holiday. Such an increase in numbers and such a change in the type of person were inevitably distasteful to traditional British travellers and expatriates.[30] They were unhappy that the places they cherished and enjoyed in peace would be overrun, that their ears would be jarred by uncouth French (and English) and their sensibilities offended by rough manners. 'Popular tourism was regarded first as a social menace and then as bad joke', so Piers Brendon put it in his history of the firm of Thomas Cook. The most violent denigrator of Cook and excursionists was the humorist Charles Lever – a 'bear-leader', he wrote of Cook, 'who conducts tribes of unlettered British over the cities of Europe'. It was astonishing, he declared, that the characteristic independence of Englishmen would accept a plan 'that reduces the traveller to the level of his trunk, and obliterates every trace and trait of the individual'. Cook protested at Lever's extravagance, but as a rule he just shrugged his shoulders: 'Those who wish to live for themselves only, and to have the exclusive enjoyment of earth's provisions, had better make a tour to Timbuctoo, or to any other uninviting regions.'[31]

Lever asserted that the excursionists were damaging Britain's reputation on the Continent, an argument hardly advanced by his own description of the old days when, he said, 'John Bull was permitted to bully at railway stations and thrash waiters, on the simple condition of paying fourfold for everything'. Whether, in an increasingly democratic time, the new excursionists really hurt British standing is doubtful. It is certainly noteworthy that the sixteenth edition of *Murray's Handbook for Travellers in France*, published in 1882, uses almost exactly the same words as its 1843 predecessor to explain why the British were unpopular on the Continent.

Loutish excursionists might, one would have thought, have affected the way it was put.

As time went on, Thomas Cook and his son shifted their attention to a more upmarket clientele, providing tours to almost anywhere, and catering increasingly for those who did not want to travel in a group, to whom they supplied Hotel Coupons which gave the independent traveller the right to demand lodging and meals at any hotel on a list supplied, at a fixed price. Their attention now was less directed towards France and more to countries that lay further afield.

Anyway tourism in its traditional form had changed. An article in the *Quarterly Review* in 1890 explains what had happened. To the British of our day, it declares, countries that lie nearest to the British Isles are less well known than they were two generations ago even though the numbers of travellers have increased enormously. The article turns particularly to France; Paris, it argues, is a special case: look at the provinces. No question now of letters of introduction to local people or friendships in local society. Modern travellers never even see the local people except in glimpses from the express train that rushes them through the countryside, perhaps to a strip on the Mediterranean, perhaps to the hunting country in the Pyrenees. Not one in 20,000 of the 'hordes of gamblers, triflers and valetudinarians' knows as much about the land they pass through as does 'a Western pork-packer of the ethnology of the Indians who once inhabited the regions on the track between his marts at Chicago and Omaha'.

We have reached what might be regarded as the climax of the Railway Age.

6

Rosbif and Frog

To believe in any war in which England and France will not be rivals, is to entertain Arcadian hopes, fit only for shepherd and shepherdesses of the drama.
                                                            Fanny Burney in 1816

With a son half-French and half-English, and a history of incessant warfare between the two countries, it was no wonder that Fanny Burney was worried. Happily, it was a disaster that never came about. Indeed, after 1815, Britain and France were actually allies in the only major war, the Crimean, in which Britain was involved during the nineteenth century. There were, though, nasty moments galore: during the first half of the century, in 1830, when the Polignac government threatened to annex Belgium and sent troops to Algeria, then ten years later over the Middle East and in 1850 in the aftermath of another revolution in France; and later, with repeated scares over the sheltering of terrorists, about Nigeria, Indochina and Egypt, all culminating in the confrontation at Fashoda in the Sudan in 1898. An authority on Anglo-French relations declared in 1895 that 'our experience of the last few years is that France is about the only Power, great or small, with which England cannot come to an understanding'.[1]

Sometimes British residents in France lost their nerve, abandoned their houses and fled and, after all, political tension of this sort could not but complicate relations between them and their French hosts. For instance, at Bordeaux in the 1830s, the legitimists, supporters of the deposed Bourbons, blamed Britain and the British for the liberal values that had played so large a part in the installation of the Orléans monarchy. Yet most people just carried on, and the tourists, their numbers always on the increase, kept arriving. Moreover, as François Crouzet has written, however deplorable the state of relations between the two countries, they nevertheless continued to borrow ideas, institutions, techniques and works of art from each other. When it came to it, the French could usually shrug and see Britain as eternally ambivalent, a neighbour – as it was put later – that remained the natural home of Dr Jekyll and Mr Hyde.[2]

One way to gain an idea of how the British in France lived during the
nineteenth century is by running through the pages of the English-language
daily newspaper, *Galignani's Messenger*. It was owned and run by the
Galignani family who had moved to Paris in 1800. They set up reading
rooms in many of the towns to which the British went to live or to visit,
local centres that took the place of the fashionable booksellers' libraries that
were to be found in English spas. The firm published and sold books in
English (neglecting to pay royalties) and *Galignani's New Guide to Paris*
which was revised annually. But to return to the newspaper. The issues of
1840 and 1841 are especially interesting in view of the political crisis of the
time over the Middle East. Understandably, the editorials take a pacific line:
'certain warlike' Paris papers are rebuked, but so is the British government,
which is accused of 'faithless conduct' that may result in hardship to British
citizens in France. Looking on the bright side, the *Messenger* reports that the
King, Louis-Philippe, was very courteous to English gentlemen and ladies
introduced to him on his visit to Dieppe. As a matter of course there are full
reports of debates in the French Chamber and, necessarily a day or two late,
in Parliament. There is in fact much quotation from the British press, some
of it banal, as, for instance, when readers are informed that Queen Victoria
went walking on the slopes of Windsor Castle. However, an earthquake in
Martinique and fighting in India are fully covered. Social and theatrical
events are notified, as is the arrival in France of prominent visitors from
Britain and the USA. Shipping movements are regarded as important and
commodity and stock prices are listed. One learns too that Sergeant Seal of
the London police has returned to Paris in pursuit of a courier who is
believed to haven stolen property from Count Matuzevitch and robbed his
late employer, the Marquis of Clanricarde. From Bayonne comes the news
that Lord William Paget and a Mr Bell have fought a duel, but that there
were no injuries.

For an impression of ordinary life the advertisements are useful. An
English governess in Paris is available for work, as is another lady, a piano
teacher. French housemaids and cooks are looking for jobs in British
households. French tutors are there to teach the French language. Roberts'
London Dispensary in the Place Vendôme advertises 'genuine English
medicines', while a French dentist will supply teeth at 12 francs apiece.
British residents at Nice are advised that they can send property to Britain
more cheaply via the consul at Genoa than by using local agents. Families
coming to pass the winter in Paris are invited to try the Hôtel de l'Angleterre, 'where they will find English comfort combined with Parisian luxury'.
A more dashing attraction is Mr Bryon's pigeon shooting in the Tivoli
Gardens, while the nostalgic will be touched by an announcement that the

former gambling rooms of Frascati (closed down in 1837) are reopening, this time in another form as the Grand English Tavern. Through the newspaper's advertisements you learn where to hire horses or carriage or even houses in the country.

Most of the British who responded to a country house advertisement would probably have wanted to know if there was an Anglican church anywhere near to the house on offer. Political crises came and went; but religion remained as an important issue dividing the two peoples. The British were overwhelmingly Protestant and their French neighbours (in principle anyway) Catholic. There was sometimes difficulty about the burial of Protestants. As late as the 1850s in Brittany, despite the law, a local Catholic priest succeeded in preventing an Anglican burial in consecrated ground.[3] At Pau, when Lord Selkirk died, there was no Protestant cemetery and his body had to be taken to Orthez, 30 miles away, where during the nineteenth century there existed what is still known by older inhabitants of the town as the English Cemetery. (It now forms a corner of the town's ecumenical cemetery with almost all the old gravestones gone. One only survives – for a family called Pope.) British visitors generally, friendly to the French and admiring of France as they might be, reacted with what amounted to horror at what they saw as the gaudiness and vulgarity of the churches and ritual, and at the frivolity of the Continental Sunday. In its 1882 edition Murray's considered it necessary to rebuke the British tourist for behaving rudely in Catholic churches even during Mass. And the religious separateness was the more conspicuous given the importance to local British communities of possessing their own Anglican church. Simona Pakenham, who lived in Dieppe, could say that 'It was the possession of a church that really made a collection of British nationals abroad into a colony'.[4] (And for Scots and Welsh the same could be true of their own church or chapel.) Sometimes the government at home might help with funds for building or maintenance, but sometimes it balked, as in the case of Paris in the 1850s. A chapel in the rue d'Aguesseau, close to the British Embassy, was put up for sale by its owner, Mr Chamier, an ailing American minister. While in the end enough money was raised to buy it – and it is still the principal Anglican church in Paris – there were endless difficulties and embarrassments for the Ambassador personally. The House of Commons refused to vote the funds necessary, taking the view that the British in Paris were wealthy enough and could afford to pay themselves. But they aren't that rich, or only a few of them are, protested the Embassy. A public subscription in England was proposed. The reply to that was curt: 'very little sympathy is felt for Paris residents in such matters, and that if they could not maintain a place of worship for themselves they had better come home to their own parishes.' It was a good example of the impatience that expatriates could provoke in the homeland.[5]

While the British residents in Paris may or may not have been wealthy – and some certainly were – whatever happened, they could find a clergyman within easy reach. The situation in the provinces was much less clear-cut. The Reverend Francis Trench, planning with his wife a trip to the Pyrenees in search of better health, resolved to use the opportunity to investigate the state of Protestantism in rural France and to supply religious ministration himself wherever it was feasible. His wife and he landed at Dieppe, and moved on to Rouen, passing through Malaunay, which impressed them by its wealth, the number of its factories and the fine houses belonging to the factory owners. What was new – this being the early 1840s – were the numerous British workmen employed on the construction of the Paris/Rouen railway line, who, apparently being keen churchgoers, attended regular meetings conducted by a 'catechist', presumably paid by the contractors. It was a promising start. Trench held several services a week at Rouen or in its neighbourhood. At one of them, which took place in a room at his hotel, the congregation numbered between 40 and 50, all connected with the railway. Seven children were brought along to be baptized. There were children too at Orléans, a town, noted Trench, where Protestants abounded. He was introduced to three English children at the (French) Protestant pastor's orphanage, whose father, a workman, had died. They seemed, Trench wrote in his diary, much pleased at having a conversation in their own language. The encounter must have been the more poignant since he himself had been born at Orléans, where his parents had been interned.

And so the expedition continued. At Tours, where the Anglican church was firmly established, the resident clergyman told Trench that 70 or 80 British families lived in the neighbourhood. A service he conducted at Angers was well attended, and turned out to be the first held there in 12 years. Another, which he particularly remembered, took place at a country house on the Loire belonging to an English couple, for which the congregation arrived by steamboat. In the Vendée, a young Englishwoman working as governess for the local prefect's family attended his service. Trench was generally encouraged, coming to the conclusion that in places without a large British colony, it was worth posting a notice at the local hotel advertising such a visit as his: as well as ordinary families, the news might reach English students studying at the local college. A special effort, he thought, should be made where there was an iron- or gasworks since it might well employ British labour.

Francis Trench evidently got on well with French Protestant pastors, finding little in the way of doctrinal differences. At Nantes he attended a French Protestant service. (It was, incidentally, at Melleray nearby that English and Irish monks in 1824 had established one of the first schools of agriculture in France.) Indeed at Pau – Trench and his wife stayed with friends at a country house in the neighbourhood – a new church had been opened recently, run by a joint French and English committee and used by both congregations. Relations apparently were excellent. With the Catholic clergy, as was to be expected, they were less straightforward. Several, including a bishop who much impressed Trench, were distinctly friendly and helpful. But he was shocked on a visit to a convent to find that 40 of the 200 nuns were from Britain. He was unhappy at a Mass he attended at Rouen, though he admitted finding it 'most exciting to the outward senses'; at Paris, the officiating priest compared Protestants to murderers, slayers of Mother Church. There was one rather jarring note, which concerned politics, not religion, but which also illustrated the sometimes anomalous nature of Anglo-French relations. The British consul at Nantes told Trench that during one of the 'temporary excitements and ebullitions against England' a crowd of 1,200 men had collected to sing the Marseillaise under his windows and to shout slogans. But they followed their cry of 'Down with the English Consul' with – addressing him personally – '*Vive Monsieur N*'![6]

More even than clergymen, consuls were in touch on a day-to-day basis with the British in France, often as the de facto leaders of the local British community. And necessarily they were also in regular contact with officials and the general population. In the earlier years, consuls were sometimes a mixed lot, for the service served as a useful dumping ground for ruined playboys with good connections. One of Monsieur N's predecessors at Nantes was a Mr Richards, known in the fashionable world as Tom Pipes, so Captain Gronow recorded, who had run through an enormous fortune. In the end he had to be sacked. Thomas Raikes referred to Harry Scott, one-time consul at Bordeaux, a brother of the celebrated Lady Oxford. Above all there was Consul Brummell of Caen. It is hard to tell how he would have coped with circumstances such as confronted Monsieur N, for his consular career was short and his papers scanty. He reports on enquiries he has made over charges of encroachment of French waters by British fishing boats, and claims that he has succeeded in cutting expenses of what he calls the 'outposts' of his consulate by nearly half. But he does himself out of a job: writing to Lord Palmerston, the Foreign Secretary, he suggests that the consulate at Caen can be reduced to a vice-consulate and that he might himself be appointed to another post, Calais if possible. His resignation is accepted but no other job is offered.[7]

Disputes over fishing rights occurred regularly, and it was said that French naval vessels – the French navy being traditionally anti-British – were zealous in their intervention. In 1844 the consul at Bayonne reported a clash at sea between the crews of French and British boats that resulted in the British crew suffering a short spell in prison. In 1843 the Mayor of Le Havre complained that a boatload of paupers from Scotland had been dumped at Harfleur, shipped there by the Sunderland Board of Guardians. The local British consul was reluctant to believe the story; but it turned out to be true, and he had no alternative but to pay for their shipment back to Southampton. Sometimes it is hard to make out exactly what happened, let alone to apportion responsibility. In March 1855, Lord Zetland, Grand Master of the Grand Lodge of England, going over the consul's head, complained directly to the Ambassador of an incident at Dieppe involving a British mason set on at home by French cavalry officers, acting under orders from their colonel. 'They tore my wife from my neck with brutal violence, who had with heroic courage and coolness thrown herself between me and the brandished sabres', the victim reported.

Much of a consul's work was less exacting. He was required to supply regular statements of account, and provide information on coal imports into France, on the grain harvest, on French shipbuilding, on coastal fortifications and on marriages of British subjects. He might be required to wait on passing dignitaries: for instance, the consul at Boulogne assures the Foreign Office that 'due respect will be paid to the Bishop of London when he arrives tomorrow'; he will himself be on hand, accompanied by a clergyman, to greet the Bishop and his family. In the same week, this consul was also required to deal with Lord Mornington who, like many Boulogne visitors, was in financial difficulties. He was happy to say, he informed the Foreign Office, that he was 'now in a fair way of terminating his Lordship's liabilities'. A Mr Copland called on Consul Turnbull at Marseille furnished with a letter from the Ambassador in Paris. His daughter had been abandoned by her apparently bigamous husband, an Irish barrister, whom Copland was pursuing, intent on bringing him to justice. Most British subjects in need of help were, though, in a less favoured position than Lord Mornington or Mr Copland. Consul Turnbull in 1843 presented a list to the Foreign Office of those he had been obliged to assist over the previous year. Apart from seamen, it comprises clerks, domestic servants, mechanics, an interpreter, a courier, a groom, engineers, a mason (not Lord Zetland's kind), a blacksmith, two bookbinders and a 'language master'. The next year Turnbull records having had on his hands some Irish labourers back from Algiers where they had fruitlessly been looking for work. Some were suffering from dysentery and some were accompanied by wives and children;

for these last at any rate he was able to obtain a free passage up the Rhône by commercial steamers.[8]

Turnbull at Marseille would be spared the troubles which were to descend on many of the British workmen who had been assembled by the contractors Thomas Brassey and William Mackenzie to build the 82-mile railway line from Paris to Rouen. Francis Trench had been impressed by their bearing and by the 'handsome style of holiday dress so many wear on Sundays', but his ardent churchgoers were clearly untypical of the 5,000 British navvies who made up about half the multinational army that was working on the line, and was billeted in villages along the Seine valley. The British navvies stayed resolutely British, with a distinctive dress (not at all Sunday best) and manners. Unlike their French counterparts who made do with an apple or pear, they were gluttons for beef and bacon and beer. They were disinclined, as a doctor put it, to abstinence from drink, but they were inclined to riot. Still, they worked very hard and were very experienced, and as a result were paid more than the French railway navvies, receiving 4.50 francs for a ten-hour day in summer, and 4.25 in winter as opposed to 3.50 and 3. When the Paris–Rouen line was finished, many of them stayed on in France, splitting into smaller groups, going further afield, some to work on other railway lines, others moving to Paris to join the labour force engaged on the fortifications being constructed there. On the way, they might well pick up French girlfriends and French wives. On a much larger scale, the situation bore a distinct resemblance to that at the Manby and Wilson factory at Charenton in the 1820s. But worse. To start with, the risk of unemployment was high and those out of a job might well find themselves destitute, and, since consular funds were limited, dependent for their existence on local French communities. That is, they became a charge on the rates. This is an impossible situation, wrote a furious Mayor of Le Havre on one occasion to the local British consul: it threatens the public peace and will be dangerous if allowed to continue.[9]

The explosion occurred, not in isolation but as a consequence of the revolution which broke out in Paris at the end of February 1848 and was to spread through Europe. The King had fled, an unstable republic came into being, and the economy was in deep trouble, with the textile capital of Rouen especially vulnerable. General de Castellane, head of division at Rouen, recorded in his memoirs that he brought his troops into the centre of the city in response to a riot that had broken out. He found the mob, consisting of workers from local factories, had calmed down, and were rejoicing that they had forced the deportation aboard ship of forty British workmen.[10]

This was only the start. The new republican local authorities intervened to prohibit the employment of British workers, and ordered the owners of the Seine steamers to sack their British engineers. The problem for engineers and 'engine men' working on the French railways was the more serious since they often lost their tools of trade as well as their jobs. Lord Normanby, the Ambassador, agreed with the consul at Rouen that British workers should in any event be withdrawn to forestall worse violence on the part of the French unemployed. The stories of suffering were bad enough anyway, with reports of British men, women and children starving at the roadside on their way to the Channel ports. By April, a committee had been constituted in London to aid the 2,000 refugees reported to have arrived. Among them were children evacuated from the British Orphan School at Paris.[11]

While Lamartine, the President of the provisional government, assured Normanby that the quarrel was a purely local one between workmen, it was quickly evident that it had become part of a general breakdown in relations between the two countries, one that was still unresolved two years later when the French government withdrew its ambassador from London. It was not surprising that the British residents in Paris were alarmed, and that some panicked. Those living in hotels, *The Times* reported, got out quickly, but the majority, people in apartments that they had furnished themselves, were in a more difficult situation. 'Having the recollection of the fate of the *detenus* after the rupture of the Peace of Amiens', they were ready to sell their furniture at any price.[12]

There is no way of knowing how many of the British residents actually did go home. In any event, some at least would have returned a year or two later when relations between the countries improved and as the republic was replaced by Louis-Napoleon's Second Empire. But the point made by Elizabeth Carne when writing of Pau is worth bearing in mind: those who had become accustomed to living abroad found it hard to accommodate to life at home. She was thinking of adults, but children too were affected. Their situation was lucidly described by the great explorer Richard Burton who, though actually born in Torquay, spent virtually all the first nine years of his life, from 1821 to 1830, at Tours. It was not a question of shaking off French habits and attitudes. For one thing, Tours was 'an oasis of Anglo-Saxonism in a desert of continentalism', and for another, so Burton said, all Anglo-French boys were remarkable young ruffians who at ten years of age 'cocked their hats and loved the ladies'. Society at Tours, that is British society, resembled that of an English country town as it had been in 1800. It included a dentist, doctors and a surgeon, bankers and lawyers, as well as rentiers, and half-pay officers like Lt Colonel Burton, Richard's father. And of course a parson. (The English, according to Burton, knew as much about the Catholics on their doorstep as the average Englishman knew of the

Hindus.) Patriotism was intense: an Englishman who refused to fight a duel with a Frenchman was sent to Coventry and 'bullied-out' of the place. If you were a girl and you flirted with a Frenchman, you lost caste, it was like permitting the 'addresses of a nigger ... in black countries'. Yet it was not a community governed by Mrs Grundy. One of the reasons for residing abroad, explained Burton, was that though living a respectable life, one was free of 'the *weight* of English respectability'.

But in the long-term there was a penalty to be paid:

> We had no idea of the disadvantages which the new kind of life would inflict on our future careers. We were too young to know. A man who brings up his family abroad, and who lives there for years, must expect to lose all the friends who could be useful to him when he wishes to start them in life. The conditions of society in England are so complicated, and so artificial, that those who would make their way in the world, especially in public careers, must be broken to it from their earliest day. The future soldiers and statesmen must be prepared by Eton and Cambridge. The more English they are, even to the cut of their hair, the better. In consequence of having been brought up abroad, we never thoroughly understood English society, nor did society understand us.

In Burton's case, the disadvantages were magnified, for he and his brother and sister had been largely ignored by their parents and left to nannies, who were clearly unable to cope. While the school he attended at Tours included French as well as British boys, it was hardly ideal. His original teacher, an Irishman, disappeared, to be replaced by a 'Scotch pedagogue of the old brutal school' who was very free with his cane. He did, though, once take his pupils out for a treat: an excursion to watch the execution of a woman poisoner.

In 1830 the July Revolution in Paris and a cholera outbreak induced the Burtons to return to Britain. However, a year later they were back on the Continent, moving from one place to another all over France and Italy. As a result of these incessant travels, Richard Burton acquired an exceptional ear for languages and dialect, a fascination with gypsies, and a profound rootlessness. He spent almost all his adult life as a nomad, becoming one of the most illustrious of Victorian travellers, famous above all for his journey to Mecca. He was also an ethnographer, a writer of more than 20 travel books, and translator of the *Kama Sutra*.[13]

It was said by one who knew him that 'what a Bohemian is to ordinary persons, that Burton was to a Bohemian'. His friend, the famous and colourful journalist George Augustus Sala, must have run him close as a competitor for that distinction. Sala's father died soon after he was born, and his mother, the daughter of a ruined West Indian planter, was at once a second-rate actress, a teacher of singing and a 'grande dame'. Sala too passed an agitated childhood, and counted as a sort of involuntary refugee, for in the crisis of 1840 his mother thought it wise that she and he got out of Paris fast. In fact, Mrs. Sala was always on the move, and at another time, departing for London, she left behind the shy and nervous 11-year-old George Augustus as a boarder at the Pension Hénon. Years later, making no doubt some embellishments, he wrote of his time there in Dickens's *Household Words*, changing the name Pension Hénon to Pension Gogo. While some lessons were held at the Pension, others took place at the nearby Collège Bourbon, later the Lycée Bonaparte. It was nearby but not nearby enough, for Sala and his companions were obliged to run the gauntlet of those romantic urchins, the *gamins* of Paris, who flung 'offensive missiles' and splashed them with water from the gutters. (Burton and his fellows were less passive; they had a great time fighting the local boys.) There was nothing of the 'old brutal school' about Monsieur Gogo's regime, no cane, no strap, though solitary confinement was imposed in the case of serious misbehaviour. Hard work was encouraged, most effectively in winter by rewarding good marks with a place by the classroom stove. While the playground was large, there was less sport than there would have been at a British school. But the food was much better.

Monsieur Napoléon Gogo himself did not teach; he presided in a dig-nified way. His wife, who acted as matron, was large, vulgar and tender-hearted. The masters were an odd lot. The most junior – 'ushers' they would have been in England – were general dogsbodies who accompanied their charges on walks, though they appear to have been pretty ineffective at warding off the apparently ever-waiting street urchins. They were greatly despised. There was one master, very learned but inconceivably dirty and unkempt, who was much loved by the boys. He was one of four who actually lived in the Pension. Monsieur Lacrosse, in charge of mathematics, a 'scaly, hard-featured' man, was less likeable, while the master responsible for the smallest boys hated his job, and was reputed to have wept when his parents refused to allow him to be apprenticed as a hairdresser. The classics master, supposed by the boys to go out to dances every night, paid little attention to his pupils; he left suddenly, owing money to the washerwoman and to several of the senior boys. Teaching English was a Mr Jugurtha Willoughby whose memory of the language was distinctly rusty. Anyway, one French writer recalled that traditionally the hour nominally devoted to English lessons was actually spent playing leapfrog. At Monsieur Gogo's, French pupils seem never to have pro-gressed further than the knowledge of two words, 'God-dam' and 'Rosbif', which, said Sala, they 'delighted in applying to us, as a species of reproach for our Britannic origin'.[14]

These are words that went back a long way. 'God-dam' or 'Goddam' dates from the Hundred Years War when, according to Norman folklore, it was constantly on the lips of English soldiers. The expressions 'to swear like an Englishman' and 'to drink like an Englishman' also originated in the Middle Ages. In the eighteenth century at one time, British troops were known as 'lobsters' because of their red uniforms, and 'hermit crabs' because they were alleged to like nothing better than to take possession of other people's property. Then 'Rosbif'. As beef was expensive in France, its appeal to the English was particularly conspicuous. According to the *Illustrated London News*, as soon as the members of Thomas Cook's 'workingman's trip' reached Boulogne in 1861 they fell eagerly on 'biftecks'. The journal added that 'wherever an Englishman travels on the Continent he is sure to be persecuted [sic] with this national *morceau* as of course'. And of course the English equivalent, 'Frog' or 'Froggy', derives also from culinary preference. With attractive wit, Monsieur Paul Gerbod entitles his admirable 1991 book on British travellers in France, *Voyages au pays des mangeurs de grenouilles*.[15]

If catchwords can go back centuries and survive, as with 'rosbif', when they no longer have any particular relevance, so can perceptions of national character. Take Sir Robert Dallington's description, made after a tour of France in 1598. The French he counted as a very bellicose people – a mirror image of how the French thought of the English – who if they were not fighting some powerful outside enemy fought among themselves. France was a nation 'whose working spirits can never remaine long quiet'. The Frenchman 'sheweth his lightnesse and inconstancie, not only in matters of service and warre ... but also even in other his actions and carriages. But in nothing more, than in his familiaritie, with whom a stranger cannot so soone bee off his horse, but he will be acquainted'. A hundred years after Dallington, an English traveller described the French as very sociable, 'eternal babblers', inquisitive, witty rather than wise, credulous, 'in a word ... they are at all times what an Englishman is when he's half-drunk'.[16]

The British of the nineteenth century would not have disagreed with Dallington's opinion that the French were bellicose, nor, given the frequent revolutions and political disturbances, that they were quarrelsome among themselves. On one of Dickens's railway trips to France, a fellow passenger tells him that the French are 'no go' as a nation. Why? asks Dickens. 'That Reign of Terror of theirs was quite enough', says his companion. The French are revolutionary – 'and always at it'.[17] These successive revolutions, argued an article in *Bentleys Miscellany*, have destroyed all distinctions of rank and all respect for birth, and thus have done away with the moral example which an organized upper class can provide.[18]

Few British at mid-century would have agreed with Lord Normanby's opinion that the French were a 'grave' nation. Usually they saw them as volatile, even flighty, people. An elderly Englishman, years before, put this opinion in an original way. He was complaining about the Paris climate. But, protested the person he was talking to, now in November, London would be wrapped in its usual gloom and fog. 'I'm not one of those who find fault with that', replied the old gentleman. 'It's the right thing at this time of year; and if they had a little more of it in this country, it would be a good thing for them ... [A] reasonable degree of weight in the atmosphere steadies the brain.' He approved of the 'sedateness' of the English climate, he added.[19] For one anonymous English visitor during the 1830s, even the compromise, the 'half-drunk' suggestion, would not have done; the characteristics, one of another, conflicted too sharply. The Englishman is proud, the Frenchman vain, the one strong on judgement, the other full of verve, the Englishman in conversation leads steadily to his conclusion, the Frenchman is diverted by anything which catches his attention, the one generalizes, the other delights in the particular.

Americans might take a more objective view. Ralph Waldo Emerson in England wrote, 'everyone of these islanders is an island himself, safe, tranquil, incommunicable', and he says of the French that they are 'a most joyous race'. Hezekiah H. Wright, who is perhaps unusually anglophile, declared that the Frenchman lived in and for the present, and that,

> without possessing more kindliness of heart or as much sincerity as the Englishman, he contrives, by the greater courteousness of his manner, and his more winning volubility of tongue, to make himself the pleasanter companion, and imposes his tinsel upon you with an affectation of feeling and a seeming friendly earnestness of protestation, which throw into the shade the bullion of his more taciturn neighbour.[20]

The British Mrs Stothard, who at her hotel in Normandy had been so struck by the social freedom enjoyed by women in France, had a stab at a simile that expressed much the same idea, visualizing England as 'a plain steady gentleman, who wore a good, lasting cloth for his coat', and France as 'a light gay lady, with much powder, tinsel, and tawdry about her, who shakes some of it off as she moves along'.[21]

Whether or not the French had changed, certainly, by mid-century, the British had. The evangelical mood associated with Victorianism had created a very different atmosphere. A character in Wilkie Collins's thriller *The*

Woman in White says that 'I constantly see old people flushed and excited by the prospect of some anticipated pleasure which altogether fails to ruffle the tranquillity of their serene children'. Harriet Martineau described going to parties given by Mary Berry and her sister Agnes, in their eighties and unabashed survivors of another time, who were still wearing old-fashioned rouge and pearl powder and false hair, and crying out 'Oh Christ' and 'My God' in a distinctly unvictorian way.[22] What had not changed, however, insisted Léon Faucher in the 1850s, was the social structure. Manchester may have replaced Old Sarum, elected local authorities may have supplanted the family-controlled corporations, sinecures may have been abolished, but nevertheless the most extreme inequality of rank persisted.[23]

And the antithesis of Mrs Stothard's plain steady gentleman, the extravagant *milord*, is still around, splashing his money and bad manners about in the time-honoured way. Gloomily, it seems. Stendhal asserted that without an unhappy look one was not respected in England, and makes a character in his *Lucien Leuwen* declare that, whatever his temperament, an Englishman, first thing in the morning, looks as if he has just learned that he has gone bankrupt. Also in the book is a Lord Link (or, says the narrator, a name something like that), apparently ruined, but nevertheless with an income still of £4,000 a year (say £280,000 in our money). However, that is not enough to keep him in the West End of London, which is why he is in France. Even that pittance is not likely to last long, for he passes his time gambling, and – thinks the narrator – he longs to lose.

This is gentle enough satire. The genre is taken much further by Charles Marchal in his *Physiologie de l'Anglais à Pa*ris, published in 1844 as part of a series of 'physiologie' books with subjects such as ' "A Parisian in the provinces" by a Commercial Traveller', and ' "A Cuckold" by a bachelor' along with some dubious memoirs. Marchal's book is illustrated by drawings of recognizably English faces, mostly gloomy. None of these people has much of a 'plain steady gentleman look'. Nor have any of them much to do with business; Marchal states that few of the English who come to Paris are selling anything. The Englishman, he writes, is stubborn, irascible, greedy, fussy, capricious, hard to please, changeable, headstrong, ridiculous, debauched, excessively thirsty, and fatiguing, while his spoken French is bizarre, crude and laughable. He suffers from migraine, spleen and a tendency to suicide. (It is some compensation that he is allowed also to be enterprising, enquiring and cleanly.) He enjoys looking at pictures in the galleries and tips well, and visits the zoo mainly to watch the indecent antics of the monkeys. But Marchal is also using this figure of fun as a prop for his depiction of other victims, who include William the Conqueror certainly, but also Lamartine, Thiers, Victor Hugo and French 'lords' who, he claims, share the English taste for girls who have been 'a long time in circulation'. There are some elegant young English dandies, who spend the morning dressing, and, apart from clothes, are interested only in three things: women, wine and cigars. Oh cigar! apostrophizes Monsieur Marchal, broadening his thrust, you are to an Englishman what you are to a woman of letters.

At mid-century the French caricaturist sees the typical Englishman as having fair hair, a red beard, bright eyes, long arms, big feet. He is either obese or skeletally thin, and likely to be carrying an umbrella on his shoulder.[24] Léon Faucher stated that you would never mistake the Eng-lishman for anyone else: whether at Paris, Naples, Madrid or Berlin, he always stands out. Englishwomen do not figure much in Marchal's book. He describes them in fact in more or less flattering terms: fragile and pale, the sort of girl you dream about when you are 20 years old. (Stendahl, on the other hand, was struck in London with how much bigger they were than the Frenchwomen.) Hippolyte Taine saw the paleness and fragility, but in a different light. He recollected an evening at a spa in the Pyrenees. In the hotel was an elderly French officer grumbling away, used up by life in the country, by lack of conversation and by the fixity of his own habits. Beside him were a young English girl and her mother. For the girl there was no question of being used up; she had been frozen since birth. She sat quite motionless, wearing on her arms a whole shopful of jewellery: bracelets, chains of all kinds and metals which jingled like little bells. The mother was one of those crooked beanpoles (a favourite French epithet for middle-aged British women) hunched up in a balloon-like dress of the sort that can only flourish and go to seed under a London fog. These two were taking tea, and talked only to each other.[25]

In general terms, family ties in France, then as now, were closer than they were in Britain. There was also a different view of marriage. Frances Carey, on a tour of France with her husband, reported a sort of round-table discussion between French and British over what can only be called the function of wives. A Frenchman summed up: different customs suit dif-ferent people; Frenchmen take their wives for companions, the English choose them as playthings; the Frenchmen consider them as helpmates, the English as appendages. Apparently the Englishmen at the table did not demur. (The picture comes to mind of gentlemen in riding boots dallying over the port until they fall under the table, while the ladies, neglected, sit sewing in the drawing room.)[26]

Part of the explanation anyway lay in the difference of upbringing. John Stuart Mill, a determined advocate of women's rights, put it that:

The peculiar bringing up of women has on the whole from a multiplicity of causes having to do with the history of the nation & also with race peculiarities tended in England to make women both weaker & gentler than men; in France, to make them more energetic and passionate.[27]

Yet in one important respect Englishwomen (and men too for that matter) were subject to less constraint than their opposite numbers. The French, partly because of the law of equal, or near-equal, inheritance, were persuaded of the virtues of the arranged marriage, the *mariage de raison*. It would be easy to exaggerate the difference in custom between the two countries, for in England too you were expected to marry 'suitably' and to tie yourself up with a financial settlement. Nevertheless, there was latitude, as Jane Austen shows. Under the French system, Elizabeth Bennet would never have married Mr Darcy; in fact she might not have met him at all, for he would have been already married to the daughter of Lady Catherine de Bourgh, or at the least bound to her by contract. Elizabeth in her turn would have been landed with Mr Collins. To the British, the idea of a marriage that was explicitly materialist, without any emotional trimmings, was rather distasteful; certainly it was to the Scottish Miss Dempster who was staying with friends in Nice. She met a Picardy squire, a Monsieur de B, at a dance. The next day he called on her hostess to ask for her hand, drawing from his pocket 'a slip of paper on which were enrolled the names of five young ladies in society with their addresses, and a succinct account of their fortunes'. Miss Dempster's he regarded as *petite, mais sûre*! It was her second conquest, for just before, an Italian doctor, seeing her at a wedding, had also turned up with a proposal. His line was that 'I have a *leetle*, and she has a *leetle*, so it will do very well!' Really that one was going a bit far, she thought.[28]

The French and British had different ideas about children. For one thing, the French eschewed large families, partly again because of the difficulties relating to inheritance. For another, they did not dress them in a way the British considered appropriate. It had always been the problem, stated a pompous contributor to *Macmillan's Magazine* after a visit to Paris: they were got up like little men and women, and 'one quite sickens to see the tiny toddles [sic] that are made to flaunt in crinolines or to strut solemnly in jackets and trousers'. Very bad for them too, it makes them think only of their clothes and themselves. Some years later, Diana Craik, author of the best-selling *John Halifax, Gentleman*, also writing in *Macmillan's*, regretted that even at a carnival the French children were as grave as little old men and women. In Paris, she missed the 'constant gush of child-life which overfloods our London in park, street, alley and square'. Yet Thackeray, by no means an approver of all things French, praised the country fetes as much more fun and much less vulgar than the ones at home. Above all, he said, he enjoyed the great number of children there were to be seen, and the 'extraordinary tenderness' shown towards them by their parents.[29]

There was no doubt about warm feelings and children. At a school prize-giving ceremony in Tours, Frances Carey was struck by the sight of a boy, aged ten or eleven, sitting with his arm around the shoulders of a woman who was clearly his old nanny. In England, she wrote in her journal, a boy of that age would be ashamed to be seen doing such a thing publicly. The thought led her to write a powerful condemnation of the class system that had developed in her country.

> The fashion which has prevailed amongst us for some years, [she was writing in 1816] of entirely secluding the children of the family from the domestics, is big with evil: it assists to draw the line of separation between masters and servants, and to form them into distinct communities, with interests diametrically opposite each to other ... I cannot be persuaded that our young gentlemen and ladies, who have never spoken to a servant but to command, are better members of society than their grandfathers and grandmothers were; and assuredly the servants are much worse, less faithful in their calling, and more depraved in their general conduct.

That the French nobility were highly conscious of their social standing and far from indifferent to such matters as family quarterings is not for a moment in doubt. Nonetheless, in France, less deference was shown towards social superiors and, as we have seen, by servant to master. The difference in behaviour was obvious to the French. One visitor reported that when a carriage went by with a female servant sitting on the rumble seat and not beside her employer, the cry went up of 'There go the English'.[30]

How this dissimilarity in custom made itself plain in conversation comes out in an article published in *Fraser's Magazine* in 1851 and written (under a pseudonym) by the journalist Thomas Crofton Croker. It fastens on the use of 'Monsieur', and by implication 'Madame', in France, and the absence of an equivalent in England. Croker falls into conversation with a fellow passenger, a man he takes to be a lawyer, on the *diligence* between Marseille and Toulouse. 'I observe', said the Frenchman, 'that you never say Monsieur except when you prefix it to a name'. No, replied Croker, in England it is not the practice in good society to say 'Sir' or 'Madam' except in very special circumstances. A hundred years ago it was the fashion, but not now. 'And you don't say "Sir" to a shopkeeper?' 'Oh no! – he says "Sir" to his customer.' 'You are a singular people,' observed the lawyer, 'so free in your institutions – so aristocratic in your habits; you profess to uphold freedom and to put down slavery throughout the world, and yet you systematically meet the politeness of your inferiors with rudeness'. The Englishman, in the article anyway, avoids the point, arguing at great length that such forms do not matter, and, what is more, that the French also are in the process of throwing aside 'the tinsel and tricks of mere politeness' just as the British have done. But, of course, the convention survives in France to this day and adds greatly to the ease of social intercourse.[31]

Articles in *Macmillan's* or *Fraser's* or *Blackwood's* provide snapshots of French society. They have punch and a colour agreeably heightened by their authors' prejudices and foibles, and are usually based on a reasonable knowledge of their subject. Diana Craik, for instance, was to follow up the piece quoted earlier with a book about France. Nevertheless, by their nature they are superficial; for a closer analysis of the differences between the French and the British it is sensible to return to John Mill, qualified both by natural acuity and experience. He knew France and the French very well, and indeed he is buried at Avignon, to which he and his wife had intended to retire. Mill paid his first visit to France in May 1820, turning 14, a prodigy who had famously started learning Greek at the age of three. His father was the redoubtable James Mill, and a close family friend the even more redoubtable Jeremy Bentham. John – staying on the way in Paris with the great economist Jean-Baptiste Say – was to spend just short of a year with Bentham's brother, Brigadier General Sir Samuel Bentham, and his family, first on the Garonne, near Montauban, and then at Rétinclière, a château bought by the Benthams close to Montpellier, a city that conveniently possessed one of the best universities in France. At the university, John Mill attended courses in chemistry, zoology and logic and took private tuition in higher mathematics. He made an intense study of French, the language and literature, successfully enough to enable him later in life to carry on a long correspondence on philosophy with Auguste Comte.

The curriculum was varied by lessons in music and fencing, and in dancing which may have proved useful since the Benthams carried on a lively social life. They were on excellent terms with their French neighbours, partly no doubt because their daughter was married to the Marquis de Chesnel, a colonel in the French army. Close friends were a Dr Russell and his French wife, married during the Amiens peace, whose sons, still at home, were due to join the East India Company, as indeed was John Mill himself. In the late summer, there occurred a break in routine, with Mill accompanying the Benthams on an expedition to the Pyrenees that took in Bagnères-de-Bigorre (where they climbed the Pic du Midi) and Pau, where they arrived a few months after the death of Lord Selkirk. The trip was no rest cure: its purpose was serious botanical and entomological research in the mountains.

The influence of this visit to France on John Mill was considerable. It laid the foundation of a lifelong affection for the country and an interest in French life and affairs. He picked up all sorts of facts: as befitted a future economist he commented in his journal on the progress of French industry, noting that Lady Bentham had bought some stockings for 50 sous which a year or two before would have cost her four francs. Many of his impressions he would not analyse fully until later, but what he did feel at once, and passionately, was a sense of release, a joy at what he described as the 'free and genial atmosphere of Continental life'. For a boy whose life up to then had been nothing but very hard work with virtually no friends of his own age, perhaps any lengthy stay in a congenial setting would have had the same effect. Be that as it may, the experience was to make him reflect on how unusual his own life had been, and lead him to realize how unrepresentative of British society were his own family and their friends, people 'being mostly such as had public objects, of a large and personally disinterested kind'. In harsh terms he criticized what he saw as the utter selfishness of his fellow-countrymen in general, who acted as if 'everybody else (with few, or no exceptions) was either an enemy or a bore'. How refreshing then were the French with their frank sociableness and amiability.

On the Continent everybody, educated and uneducated, expressed what they felt, wrote Mill. An idea thrown into French soil takes root, blossoms and fructifies, which is why the works of Byron and Walter Scott struck home most deeply in France. With us it is common to repress both feelings and intellectual faculties so they remain undeveloped or at best develop in a narrow way. We suffer, as he expressed it to a French correspondent in 1829, from 'moral insensibility'. His exposition was the more pungent in that he himself as a young man had been appalled by what he feared to be the atrophy of his own emotional sensibility. Yet Mill was by no means an uncritical francophile. He saw vanity as a national failing and he deplored the love of display so common to what he termed their 'public men'. The French, he wrote in a review of Michelet's history, are like the Irish, with the same sociability and demonstrativeness and the same natural refinement of manners, but they share too the same weakness, an inordinate vanity, and – their more serious deficiency – the absence of a sensitive regard for truth. Indeed, 'they promise everything and do nothing'.

That the two countries should understand each other was of the utmost importance. 'There is something exceedingly strange & lamentable in the utter incapacity of our two nations to understand or believe the real character & springs of action of each other'. The ignorance of the British about France was reprehensible. *The Times*, for one, was quite ignorant, and the public 'are almost entirely ignorant that there exists a contemporary French literature; & their ideas of French writers are still those of the Voltaire period'. In a letter to Alexis de Tocqueville of 1835 he insisted that British politicians and publicists knew as much about France as they did about Timbuctoo. Writing in February 1841, in the immediate aftermath of a crisis that had brought the two nations close to war, Mill elaborated. When the French spend money on armaments and strengthen their Channel defences, it must, to the British, be a sure sign of aggressive intentions. It cannot be that they are just being prudent, for everyone in Britain knows the idea that we might attack them to be utterly absurd.

The trouble is that our minds work quite differently. The French distrust anything which does not emanate from general principles, while with the British it is the other way round. (Emerson gave a fine illustration of what Mill is saying when he averred that the English mind turns every abstraction it can receive into a 'portable utensil' or a 'working institution'.) The British look to order and compromise. Even as they love money, and engage in a universal and all-absorbing struggle to appear rich, they are driven to it not so much by passion as by simple habit, for habit governs the English mind more firmly than it does that of any other civilized people. Our tastes and inclinations become accommodated to our habitual practice, so that no principle is ever carried through, its application always stops halfway, we work always towards compromise. And Mill gives the institution of constitutional monarchy as an example. The difficulty is that 'few Frenchmen can understand this singular characteristic of the English mind: which, seen imperfectly and by glimpses, is the origin of those accusations of profound hypocrisy mistakenly brought by many foreigners'.[32]

7

The Riviera

There is something in the mere name of the South that carries enthusiasm along with it . . . Even those who have never been there before feel as if they have been; and everybody goes comparing, and seeking for the familiar, and finding it with such ecstasies of recognition, that one would think they were coming home after a weary absence.

Robert Louis Stevenson

The Pyrenees may have seemed like the end of the world, but nobody with a classical education would dream of describing the shores of the Mediterranean in such terms. To the contrary, they were the cradle of civilization, where everything had started. The novelist Anne Plumptre, arriving at Marseille at the very start of the nineteenth century, could say as she gazed about her that 'the mind is thrown into a sort of trance', and that 'We . . . might almost delude it into a belief that we are travelling back into past ages. We behold the waters that bore the ships of Tyre and of Sidon, of Egypt and of Carthage, of Greece and of Rome'.[1] In fact, this coast was still cosmopolitan. Even the Egyptians were around, in the shape of ladies who had acquired a taste for General Bonaparte's officers and followed them home when Egypt was evacuated. There were British too at Marseille, including an Irish lady married to the Swedish consul, and four daughters of the one-time British consul at Tunis, now married to local merchants. There were also British in residence at Nice and Aix-en-Provence. 'A parcel of English', was how Mary Berry termed the Nice ones, people who to her disgust kept English hours and ate English dinners. Anyway it did not matter, for also in town were her friends, the two Princes of Liechtenstein and Comte d'Attem.[2] These English, unassimilated as they might be, represented an old-established winter colony: 20 years before, it was estimated that there were perhaps 300 British in residence, of whom 69 were 'masters' and the rest domestic servants. It has been neatly put by a French scholar that the ties between the British and the county of Nice were those of 'a marriage of love with the region and a marriage of convenience with its inhabitants'.[3]

Still, one comparison with the Pyrenees is not out of place, for the glorious stretch of coast between Marseille on the west and the Italian border (or what is now the Italian border) on the east was to become a giant sanatorium. But in Anne Plumptre's time, the famous health resort on the Mediterranean coast was Montpellier, west of Marseille by more than 100 miles. It was the home not only of a great university, but also of an internationally famous medical faculty, at which John Locke had once studied. It professed its climate to be particularly healthy; to such effect apparently that several aspiring spas in England touted themselves as the English Montpellier. However, by Anne Plumptre's time, the city's appeal was waning, in part because medical expertise had become more widely diffused. And there were doubts about the climate as well: a few years later, Henry Matthews, a chronic invalid, delighted though he was with the view of the mountains, considered the air too sharp and the winds too biting. It must be, he thought, a very bad place for sufferers from pectoral complaints.[4] By that time, Marseille too was losing its allure, partly because of the dreaded wind, the *mistral*, to which it was especially exposed. British travellers continued to pass through for years to come since it was from Marseille that the mail ships to India set out. But its very importance as a port reduced its appeal to tourists and potential residents: in the 1860s a writer in *Macmillan's Magazine* stated that a stranger would as soon think of living there as he would in Liverpool or Manchester.[5]

The Côte d'Azur, the Riviera of the British and Americans, would take shape further down the coast, on past the naval base of Toulon and beyond little harbours like Le Lavandou, St-Tropez, Ste-Maxime and St-Raphaël. It was some miles on from the last that one arrived at Cannes, which was destined to become very much a British resort. The pioneer was Lord Brougham, ex-Lord Chancellor and a dominant and often unpopular figure in British politics during the earlier part of the nineteenth century. In 1834, after a holiday in France, he and his invalid daughter Eleanor were intending to move on to Italy. However, they were stopped at the frontier, unable to cross because of a cholera epidemic. After a brief stay at a filthy inn in the garrison town of Antibes – the inns at Antibes are quite frightful, said the Duchesse de Dino – they moved to the Auberge Pinchinat at Cannes. Brougham was pleased by the scenery and even more by the weather, writing to his wife in January 1835 that one wakes up in the morning to a temperature like that of England in July or August. He started painting watercolours, and – paying three times the going rate – bought some land on which to build a *château* that was to be named after his daughter. He would return to Cannes every winter until his death in 1868.[6]

Health was a decisive factor too in the choice made by Brougham's friend

General Sir Herbert Taylor, who has left the most complete record of the earliest days of Cannes as a resort.[7] He and his wife in 1837 drifted grandly through France – dining with the King, Louis-Philippe, on the way – before deciding on where to settle. Taylor had Pau in mind, but learning that it was packed with refugees in flight from yet another cholera outbreak in the south, selected first Tarbes, which he and his wife found clean but dull, and then, the cholera scare subsiding, Montpellier, 'although now out of fashion', which they did not care for either. So they moved on to Cannes which had been recommended to them by Lord Brougham, and, disliking the Auberge Pinchinat, looked round for a house to lease. The only tolerable one on offer had its drawbacks, not the least of them being that the coach house was occupied by 'a curious assortment of animals'. Still, Taylor took the place, beating down the asking price from 4,000 to 2,400 francs.

Taylor was a fastidious and also a prudent man: he had checked in advance that property bought by foreigners in France would be safe in the event of war, with rentals allowable for transmission abroad. So the climate and scenery being satisfactory and the real estate market encouraging, he decided to build his own house, employing Brougham's architect Monsieur de l'Arras to undertake its construction. He himself kept busy, admitting that it was not easy to know how to fill the time after so many years of hard work. Happily, Cannes was not as miserable and poverty-stricken a place as it has sometimes been represented. The hotel might be unsatisfactory but at least it was there. The population numbered between 3,000 and 4,000[8] and, Taylor noted, many of the inhabitants were rich enough to afford villas outside in the country. Some of the people around were distinctly congenial, the *curé* for one, and Monsieur de l'Arras and his wife, and Comte Rostand who turned out to be an excellent amateur violinist. Musical parties were arranged, with the local banker and the Director of Customs participating, and a Monsieur Front Michel who came over from Grasse.

However, since Lady Taylor was unwell, it was decided to spend time in Italy while the villa was being built. The Taylors left in April 1838, just missing Lord Brougham and his daughter. Sir Herbert never returned; he died in Italy. The house was completed, named the Château St George, and let, its tenants including the widow of Lord Nelson's brother, who had succeeded to his honours. By her time, however, the mid-1840s, Lady Taylor was about to sell. The buyer, Thomas Robinson Woolfield, discovered Cannes after years of travel in Spain, in Egypt, in Turkey as he searched in vain for somewhere to settle. Between them, Brougham and Woolfield launched Cannes as one of the world's paramount resorts, Brougham by word of mouth but also – he knew the King well – by persuading the French government to improve the road through Haute-Provence and make a grant for the development of the harbour, Woolfield by assiduous property investment and improvement.[9] Both men lived for a long time, Brougham (as noted above) dying in 1868 and Woolfield in 1888. Writing in the early 1850s, a traveller, Edmund Spencer, could announce that:

> English gold and English enterprise have wrought their usual wonders at Cannes, as elsewhere in the land of Gaul, where the wandering islanders have pitched their tent. Castles and villas have sprung, and are springing into existence, moulded according to the fancies of their owners, who it must be confessed, in the erection of some of their dwellings appear more solicitous to eclipse the neat, unpretending cottage of his Lordship [Brougham] ... than to display architectural taste and skill.*[10]

Spencer was writing at a time when the two founding fathers were joined by a third, the French Prosper Mérimée. After his death in Cannes, the former Mayor, in his funeral oration, declared that by opening doors long closed to the town, Mérimée had made Cannes rich and prepared the ground for its future. (Notably he had secured government funding for a freshwater canal nearly 40 miles long.) He was one of the most prominent men of his time. His novel *Colomba* was a classic to be studied in British schools, his *Carmen* supplied the basis for the famous opera, and his short stories above all gained him election to the Académie française. But much of his influence stemmed from his close friendship with the mother of the future Empress Eugénie. If he did not exactly dandle Eugénie on his knee – she was aged four when he first met her – he bought her cream cakes, and took her and her sister out to tea and entertained them with endless stories. During the Second Empire at Court, at Biarritz and at Compiègne, he carried on with stories for Eugénie, this time rendering them in the form of playlets for the house parties to act. He was appointed a senator and several times refused a post in the Cabinet.[11]

For his work as Inspector General of Historic Monuments Mérimée is credited with saving much of France's architectural heritage. Not surprisingly, he would have agreed wholeheartedly with Edmund Spencer's strictures on the architecture introduced by the British at Cannes. To Viollet-le-Duc he complained that the English have built 50 villas or *châteaux* here, each more extraordinary than the next and, writing to Madame de la Rochejaquelin, he spoke of a street a league long bordered by the most grotesque architectural fantasies that an Englishman could conceive: 'they have bought all the prettiest places and spoilt them with gothic châteaux and baroque cottages.' Referring to a hotel being constructed by Thomas

* In fact, Brougham's Château Eléonore was far from being a cottage.

Woolfield, he lamented that the English architects employed a style quite unsuited to the climate of the south of France.

Mérimée spoke English well and had a number of British friends. The daughter of one of them remembered that while his turn of mind, caustic and cynical, was very French, in appearance and demeanour – 'tall, rather gaunt, studiously quiet in voice and manner, stately and good-looking' – he was much more like an Englishman than a Frenchman. And his clothes, or at least the more formal ones, were supplied by the London tailor Henry Poole of 32 Savile Row. He knew Palmerston and Russell, and stayed with Gladstone at Hawarden. During the Empire he was frequently in London, sometimes on official business. He visited Scotland, staying with the Duke of Hamilton who had strong French connections, and with other grandees, and was astonished by the disparity in wealth between his hosts and their peasants, and intrigued by the quantity of rain, by the beauty of the Highlands, and the absence of trousers. (He wrote home gleefully that he was off to a place called Glenquoich where, he gathered, trousers were unknown.)

Mérimée certainly grumbled from time to time about the numbers of British at Cannes, as well as about their taste in architecture. There is a mass of English here this year, he wrote in November 1866 to Viollet-le-Duc; one hardly hears any other language spoken on the beach. Yet he was close to the British community. He was the enthusiastic President of the Cannes Archery Club, very much a British institution, though he drew the line at croquet, an 'irritating game', he thought. In particular, he played an important part in smoothing relations with local authorities. There was the old question of obtaining permission to build an Anglican church. The background was not propitious, for the Catholic clergy – to the fury of a populace eager to attract foreigners – had succeeded in securing the expulsion of a Swiss evangelical pastor and the closure of a Protestant chapel. Mérimée, said Woolfield, was most helpful both in drafting the petition and in piloting it through the right channels.

In letters written between 1856 and his death in 1870, Mérimée gave a lively picture of the crowd of British visitors who descended on Cannes each winter, many of them owners or tenants of the multitude of villas that went crowding down to the sea. Among the arrivals were the former Prime Ministers Earl Russell and the Earl of Derby, and Richard Cobden, the free-trader who did much to improve Anglo-French commercial relations, and by whom Mérimée was greatly impressed. A close friend was Francis Baring, the third Lord Ashburton. There was the painter Edward Lear to whom he was an occasional patron, and Lord Londesborough who was at first disconcerting. Londesborough was a large man with a beard, the sort of hat worn by millers, a coat the size of a handkerchief . . . and earrings. I hope, said Mérimée, with the earrings in mind, that he is not going to make me a proposition that runs contrary to my principles. And there was Lady Georgiana Fullerton from whom he anticipated a different sort of proposition: an ardent Catholic, she paid him repeated visits at a time when his health was failing – I am afraid, he wrote in a letter, that she has designs on my soul. Sometimes relations could be complicated by ill will between the British; once when Mérimée dined with Londesborough, Lord Brougham was much offended. The two men fought like cat and dog, Mérimée noted. A very different visitor was Queen Victoria's eldest daughter, the Crown Princess of Prussia, with whom he dined during her stay in Cannes in 1869. She was, he thought, very pretty, very gracious, but also very timid.

Mérimée was given to colourful descriptions: Lord Russell, he said, was dressed like Punch, and Lord Brougham, in extreme old age, with his great white hat and his 'incredible' cravat, resembled the ghost of Guy Fawkes. However, he makes little criticism of what the British men looked like. The women were a different matter. He was well enough acquainted with them; among his friends were the intellectual Mary Clarke, later Madame Mohl, and the widowed Mary Shelley, to whom he is thought to have proposed. He had written about British women. In *Colomba* the Anglo-Irish Miss Nevil, for whom 'the Mediterranean is too blue, and the waves lack grandeur', and who is longing to witness a vendetta, acts as counterpoise to the passionate Corsican, Colomba. Like Frenchmen in general, he admires the beauty of the younger ones. But he is not kind, to young or old, about their dress sense. He meets Baroness Burdett-Coutts, the hugely rich philanthropist, at the palace of Compiègne; very sensible and natural, he thinks, but her nose was as red as fire and she wore 'a dress representing the bars of a gate up to her neck, and everybody wondered why a gate when there was nothing there to be stolen'. A month or so later at Cannes he found a vast concourse of Englishwomen, 'unmarried and unmarriageable', with flaxen hair and long teeth, sporting the sort of hats worn by sailors.

There was no criticism, though, about what Edmond de Goncourt described as two old 'governess' [sic], two British sisters who in his last years accompanied him to the archery ground in Cannes, carrying the bows and arrows.[12] If they were not really governesses, they were by then more or less 'carers', whom he had known since boyhood. One of them, Fanny Lagden, to whom he left his property, had been his first mistress; or so it is thought, but Mérimée as a young man was so promiscuous that nobody can be quite sure who was first. (When he was elected to the *Académie*, a disabused fellow member observed ruefully that 'we needed a man of letters, and we've been given a stallion'.)

What Mérimée had made, some years earlier, of the strong-minded Scot Margaret Brewster is not known, although he would have been wary of her evangelical fervour. However, in her book *Letters from Cannes and Nice* she relates that Mérimée told her the true story of the Man in the Iron Mask, a topic doubtless suggested by an expedition he undertook with her father, a leading physicist, to the neighbouring Iles de Lérins where the Man had been imprisoned. Margaret Brewster delighted in Cannes: its climate she thought wonderfully strengthening, 'as if one were drinking champagne', and the blue, blue Mediterranean was like 'a huge sleeping lake'. She catches the Riviera in the winter of 1856/57, at a turning point, the moment of take-off. The first resident British doctor has just arrived at Cannes, the reservation of houses and apartments by the newly introduced telegraph has pushed up rents, she admires the 'pretty English church built by Mr Woolfield'. It is clear, though, that the existence of the church has not calmed the ardour of English Protestants: Miss Brewster reported that a Miss Marsh, staying with the Duchess of Gordon, who had provided funds for the church at Pau, was in trouble with the police for distributing tracts, and that another newcomer, Admiral Pakenham, had been ejected from Tuscany as a result of his 'efforts to spread the Bible'. The Catholic clergy might well have felt provoked.[13]

The Brewsters chose to reach the coast by way of a steamship down the Rhône. As usual it proved very uncomfortable and anyway got stuck in the mud. 'One lives and learns', commented Miss Brewster. Anyway it was always more agreeable to approach the Riviera from the west as Harriet Jephson and her husband did on their way to San Remo. They were in low spirits, what with bad weather at Pau, a near accident to the train from Toulouse, the fat man sitting on Harriet's hat, and general discomfort. But, with daylight, all was changed, it was summer again. 'We had closed our eyes on the Pyrenees & opened them on the Maritime Alpes & instead of bare leafless trees we found groves of stunted olives and avenues of cypress trees – the houses too with their red tiled roofs had an Italian Southern look'. As the train sped on from Marseille towards Nice, Harriet wrote in her journal that 'I defy even the most stolid of people to travel, without completely exhausting every adjective expressive of beauty in the English language'.[14] It is true that a train all the way made a great difference whatever the approach, but even then the hinterland of Provence, peered at from time to time through a train window, was depressing. Almost nobody wanted to stop and get out, for John Mill and his wife with their fondness for Avignon were exceptions. Dr Lee, writing a travel book for *Bradshaw's* in the 1850s, declared Provence to be without interest and to be unbearably hot in summer. Still, again, those with a classical education and some knowledge of history might have been expected to appreciate the cultural associations, Roman or medieval. After all, there were the great Roman theatre at Orange; the arena at Arles, one of the largest in the Ancient World; the Maison Carrée at Nîmes; and the great bridges, the Pont du Gard and the Pont d'Avignon and, also at Avignon, the gigantic papal palace. The British who did go were apt to admire rather cursorily and then hasten on. The French too shuddered at this bleak, arid land. To Mérimée, passing through in the 1830s, battling with mosquitoes, rats and fleas, Provence was like a foreign country. Margaret Brewster remarked on 'the apparent sterility', while T. Adolphus Trollope, elder brother of Anthony, let his habitual bad temper boil over. How misled we have been, he declared, by all the tales of seductive vineyards and olive groves, of limpid streams and verdant valleys – 'to my knowledge of Europe, there does not exist within its limits so arid, so monotonous, so ugly, and so every way unattractive a region as Provence'. When the vine-destroying disease of phylloxera took hold in the late 1860s and devastated the region's economy, Provence became even less prepossessing. Edward Barker, one of the few British tourists in the 1880s, found the gloom almost unbearable. At least in Roman times it must have been more inviting than it is now, he thought.[15] As for the Camargues, the territory directly south of Nîmes – that was described in *Blackwood's* in 1884 as desolate, 'really a piece of Africa, which has fallen by some mistake into Europe'. Perhaps the most perceptive comment was made by the romantically minded American Thomas A. Janvier, when he concluded that he had arrived a full half-century too soon.[16] Still, an Englishman, St John Harmsworth, brother of the press lords Northcliffe and Rothermere, unearthed an excellent business opportunity at Vergèze, now just off the motorway between Nîmes and Montpellier. In 1903 he bought a spring there, and bottled its sparkling water which he sold with great success as 'Perrier', the name of the French doctor from whom he made the purchase.[17]

Even though *coupé-lit* carriages permitted invalids to lie at full length, the train journey south by train could be exhausting, and was likely to leave them disinclined to enjoy the landscape through which they passed. What is more, on arrival, they might find themselves without much opportunity to enjoy anything more than the sliver of Riviera coastline which their doctor had pronounced to be suitable for their condition. Cannes, maintained Dr Lee, quoting a French doctor, was good for anaemia and scrofula, and for people 'weakened either from the abuse of pleasure, depressing influences or overwork'. But it was to be avoided by those suffering from an hysterical or nervous malady. The French doctor to whom Lee referred was explicit: patients from the south, 'in whom chronic affections are generally complicated with a state of nervous super-excitation', should go to Italy. Still, if you were not from the south but were nevertheless inclined to over-excitement, you could try Hyères, a town situated a few miles to the east of Toulon, which was much favoured by the British. A charming and elegant town still, its reputation was for an almost excessive quiet and, unlike Cannes, it possessed few houses large enough 'to accommodate families of distinction, who may require several servants'. It was also recommended for those suffering from pulmonary and lymphatic problems. And of course there was Nice. The American Dr Linn, with a practice in Nice, writing later in the century, was sceptical about the special characteristics of the various resorts. What was more, he urged, do not imagine that in mid-winter you will find a tropical climate on the Riviera; it is simply that the cold of the north is tempered and rendered less severe by the sun. He pointed out that the rainfall in Nice is greater than that of London; the difference being that in Nice, when it rains, it does so very heavily and gets it over with. For someone insisting on heat, Corsica might have been a reasonable choice. And while it is unlikely that London could provide any 'Corsica doctor', Edward Lear in the 1860s visited two Englishmen living in the little village of Olmeto, one of whom, a young man, was clearly dying. There was an Anglican colony of sorts at Ajaccio with its Anglican church, though Lear noted that the Hôtel de Londres was not one of the better hotels. However, any slight dinginess around was dispelled by a Miss Thomasina Campbell, the undoubted leader of the community, whom he described admiringly as 'a vast and man-like maiden who roars and raves about Corsica'.[18]

How lovely it all is, thought Harriet Jephson, firmly on the mainland; what a Paradise were it not for the *mistral*. For clearly that biting wind was not what invalids needed or doctors ordered, and the fact that it hit the western end of the coast with especial violence encouraged the development of the Riviera at the Italian end. Leaving Cannes out of account, the Riviera in its full glory was to centre on Nice, Menton and Monaco, places which were not in fact part of France at all until 1860; like Savoy they had reverted to the kingdom of Sardinia in 1814. Then, as a reward for French assistance in the Italian struggle with Austria, the first two were handed over to France in 1860, with Monaco becoming in effect a French protectorate. At this time, nobody in official Britain seemed to know much about Menton, or Mentone, to stick for the moment to its Italian name. The Foreign Office was evidently startled to receive a request that Mr Palmaro, a local Italian banker, be appointed British vice-consul at Menton. What do you know about the place? Do many British go there? Are there British residents? the Foreign Office demanded of the British consul at Nice. His reply, dated 20 July 1864, is admirably concise:

Mentone is a small Town of about five thousand Inhabitants, twenty three miles on the Riviera, East of Nice. The town had no Trade, Commerce, or Industry of any kind, and till quite recently being solely and entirely dependent on the produce of its Olive, Orange and especially Lemon trees, it was, like all the other small towns of the Riviera, poor and dirty, hardly possessing the means of affording even passing accommodation to Strangers and Travellers.

The mildness of its Climate, and its position, in a Kind of Amphitheatre, sheltered from Winds to which even Nice is partially exposed, having of late years attracted to it Invalids of all Nations, considerable private Capital has been expended to provide for their Reception and their comfort – Hotels, Villas and Lodging houses have been built – and this little Town is acquiring such repute as a winter residence, that very often the House accommodation it now possesses, does not suffice for the demand there is for it.[19]

The sudden interest in Menton was sparked off by a book *Winter and Spring on the Shores of the Mediterranean*, first published in 1861 and written by Dr J. Henry Bennet, himself a sufferer from tuberculosis. Two years before, on discovering his plight, Bennet had set off 'to die in a quiet corner, as I and many friends thought'. The corner he chose was Menton. He recovered, and returned to practise in the town every winter, becoming as important to its success as a health resort as Dr Taylor had been to Pau. In a later edition of his book, Bennet maintained that many patients had, like him, recovered, or at least found the disease arrested. He insisted, however, on two things: that a cure was unlikely if the illness had reached its last stages; and that the battle was half-won if the patient's general health could be improved to the extent that he or she could eat and sleep well. Bertall, the satirist who lampooned the British polo players and their spectators at Pau, turned his attentions to the doctors now crowding on to the Riviera. Well, he says, it is not going to be very rewarding if you have a patient for only six weeks; so stretch it out, make two visits a day, and 'too bad for the legatees'. At Menton, 'where you hear coughing in every language', there is Dr Bennet, and – he stops joking here – that man is the best of them all.[20]

Doctors necessarily were key figures in the British winter communities on the Riviera. At Menton in 1877, during the season, there were 20 of them altogether, of whom five were British. Other notables were the consul or vice-consul, the clergyman, the dentist and the estate agent who might well be a man of all trades. John Taylor at Cannes, for instance, starting out as Thomas Woolfield's gardener, accrued jobs rapidly. He was estate agent, wine merchant, banker, furniture dealer and eventually vice-consul as well, with his office serving as an information centre that published a regular bulletin listing arrivals at the town. Mr Willoughby, at Menton, initially a grocer, was also estate agent and wine merchant. Such people were on the spot all the year round and took care of the houses and apartments out of season. In the season they provided servants.

Servants were often a problem. In the 1840s, the *Boulogne Gazette* warned against allowing French servants to receive visitors, in particular women, who arrive in the morning before you are up, dressed in huge overcoats into which they may well load your coal and food. It was not easy to mix locals and those brought along from Britain. Sir Herbert Taylor had run into difficulties and so did Mr Thomas Stevenson, with his family from Edinburgh, who hired part of the Villa Bosano at Menton for six or seven weeks early in 1863. In their case a young local girl was provided, but since there was no cook, the evening meal was sent in by a confectioner. Obviously, though, there was still work to be done in the kitchen, and Alison Cunningham, known as 'Cummy', nanny to the 12-year-old Robert Louis, lent a hand. She knew a word or two of French – rather more, probably, than the local girl, who normally spoke Italian. The relationship between the two was uneasy and when it turned out that the girl, a good Catholic, would not eat meat on Fridays, Cummy lost her patience. 'Tuts', she remonstrated, 'take your dinner like other folk, and never mind'. She was shocked anyway by Catholic practices – all that show, and Sunday a carnival. Lewis (as he was called in the family) managed to get her away from one church where the priest, Cummy alleged, was 'scowling fearfully at me', only to be outraged himself at the English church – there being as yet no Scots one – when the clergyman preached against Presbyterianism.

Robert Louis Stevenson remembered that holiday at Menton with pleasure and returned ten years later when, already suffering from the tuberculosis that would eventually kill him, he was told by his London doctor to go south for the winter. He stayed six months, and with Dr Bennet's help achieved a respite. He lived a quiet life, sitting by the sea, reading, one after another, the novels of George Sand. He admired the orange and lemon trees and gazed over to the horizon at the smudge of Corsica, 'just a little darker than the pallid blue of the sky'. This time, Stevenson was living in a hotel, a cosmopolitan place. There was even a *milord* of the old type, 'Lord X', accompanied by some weedy-looking children under the direction of a Trollope-type clergyman-tutor 'who respires Piety and that kind of humble-your-lordship's-most-obedient sort of gentlemanliness noblemen's tutors have generally'. There were Americans, one of whom quarrelled with him over British support for the South during the Civil War, but then made it up, and Marie, a delightful small girl from Georgia. And two little Russian girls, the younger a polyglot three-year-old who criticized him for staring at her, doing so in Italian, German and what he assumed to be Russian, but said goodbye in 'very commendable English'.[21]

By then, the 1870s, there was a spread of nationalities, as the official figures for January 1870 at Menton show:

British	215
Germans	116 – accounted for largely by a translation of Dr Bennet's book
French	98
Russians and Poles	46
Americans	41
Other nationalities	66

A few years later, a British visitor described some of the visitors as they strolled past. The first of the British is a 'short Cockney, broiling in a long Noah's Ark Ulster', followed by three or four tall, lanky Dutchmen and some plump and rather good-looking German ladies accompanied by a male fellow-countryman with gold spectacles. There are Frenchmen, some in full Parisian costume with kid gloves, chimney-pot hats and smart canes or white parasols. And again the British, clergyman after clergyman it seems, Menton being much favoured by them. By mistake, one of the clergymen bumps into an old fisherman with a coil of rope in his hands, shoeless, unwashed and dressed in 'indescribable' trousers, 'in all likelihood the very personification of the fishermen of Caesar's time'. Then appear a young Englishman and a lady, mounted, out for a canter along the road to Cape Martin, and behind 'as in mockery, immediately follows an ass with panniers, in each of which will be found planted a fat, chubby, small child ... attended by donkey driver, pleased attentive nurse, proud mother, and a big little brother with toy whip in hand astride another donkey'.

These visitors may or may not have been in Menton for their health. As in the Pyrenees, ordinary holidaymakers were taking over. In the 1870 edition of his book, Dr Bennet stated that now much the greater proportion of the winter population were 'mere' sun-worshippers. William Chambers, an ex-Lord Provost of Edinburgh, was in Menton to convalesce, though not from tuberculosis, during the 1870/71 winter season. It was a very dull place, he considered, and pretty nearly destitute of means of intellectual recreation, although it was true that 'a little croquet' had been introduced. There were, though, some good walks and some tough walkers, notably lively English ladies ready for long hard walks in the hills and a dance at night. It was at night that the difference in types was most marked, with the more staid and sickly keeping to their hotels, while the others, presumably unsatisfied by the croquet, got reckless and joined the holidaymakers in the dancing, sometimes apparently with fatal results.[22]

The dancing must have encouraged those inhabitants of Menton who hoped that their town might come to rival Nice. Competition between resorts was tough. On one occasion Mérimée wrote to the Princess Matilde that the innkeepers of Nice and Menton were eagerly reporting and exaggerating news of a smallpox outbreak in Cannes. But the arrival of the railways – at Cannes in 1863, Nice in 1864, Monaco in 1868 – opened up glowing possibilities for everyone. Soon, express trains were to steam in direct from St Petersburg, Berlin, Rome, Hamburg and Amsterdam. For the British, there was the Calais–Nice–Rome express furnished with sleeping cars. By the 1880s you could reach Nice from Calais in little over a day.[23]

The Russians above all benefited from the railway to the South of France; they were to be seen everywhere, said one French writer. They shared with the British a love of travel and a propensity to spend freely. In 1831, well before railways materialized as a common form of transport, an Englishman observed that his countrymen's reputation as the greatest travellers in the world was in danger of being lost to the Russians. On the Riviera at mid-century, they were particularly in evidence at Villefranche, next door to Nice. In 1856 the King of Sardinia, Victor Emanuel II, and the dowager Tsarina met at Nice to discuss its use as a base for the Russian fleet. A few years later, with Nice and Villefranche now French, the Russians were back in force, this time including the Tsar himself. (They rather interfered, though, with the Nice season: Miss Dempster, having a marvellous time, took against the Russian officers as dancing partners – 'monsters', she said, all hideous and *mal élevés*.)[24]

But the French liked them. Emile Daullia, in his *La Vie à Evian-les-Bains*, gave sketches of the various nationalities.

> If, finding yourself seated beside a gentleman dressed as a foreigner, whose appearance seems to you respectable and whose bearing is outgoing, whose manners are affable and polite, and you chat with him and listen to his response, well-expressed, unhurried and without the least accent, you almost certainly have to do with a Russian. In fact it is only the Russians, apart from the French themselves, who enunciate and speak our language so correctly. As they do not have that haughtiness of the English, which makes the children of *perfide Albion* so totally disagreeable when they travel, one feels a great charm in their society.

Here is his picture of the British as seen on a luxurious cruise boat on Lake Léman in the Savoy:

> The inevitable English family, always numerous, encumbered with heaps of luggage, deliberately offhand, obstructing the passages. Mylord, stiff and bored,

despondently sweeping the horizon with a veritable telescope. Mylady, mature of age, in a waterproof, with angular features and blotchy complexion, deep in a Baedeker. There is a female companion, usually ageless and graceless, supervising four or five young girls.

One is again thankful for the girls: they come out as amusing, with laughing eyes and mischievous expressions.

But Daullia does not really like anybody much except the Russians and the French. Here are his Germans, a young couple – she, shy with languishing eyes and placid face, ruby and pink colouring, hair blonde as corn, he, arrogant, cold and stiff with a thick yellowish beard; they hold themselves aloof wrapped in their tartan plaids. The American women with their fresh little faces are a delight, a treat for the eyes, says Daullia, but the men are coloured either red-brick or *papier-mâché*, and are charmless with their odd bone structure and their little beards.

Daullia was writing near the end of the century. Well before then, the British, though well represented, were losing their primacy on the Riviera. The Duchesse de Clermont-Tonnerre, writing in 1928, recalled her childhood at Cannes where she had been sent, with her English governess Miss Johnson, to stay with an aunt, the Duchesse de Luynes. She remembered the exquisite twilight, the scent of flowers, the scattered villas set in immense gardens. She knew that Lord Brougham had, so to speak, founded this wonderful place. And there were still, she said, many English about, and one was very happy to see them in one's *own* house – her italics – but, she made plain, it was the French now who set the tone.[25] Cannes had become startlingly cosmopolitan and grand. Miss Dempster, who had suffered from the importunate suitors, spent most of each year there until her death in 1913, and recalled a party given by the (French) Duc and Duchesse de Vallombrosa for Queen Victoria's son, the Duke of Albany. It could be described as being *All London* had it not been also *All Paris*, observed the Duchess of St Albans. Miss Dempster added 'and *half New York*'. In the seventies and eighties, residents of the villas included not only the Vallombrosas and the long-lasting Thomas Woolfield (living at Sir Herbert Taylor's old Château St George, later the Villa Rochefoucauld), but the Comte de Paris, Orléanist claimant to the throne, a Rothschild, the Duc de Nemours, the Duchess of Montrose and Sir Julian Goldsmid, member of a very wealthy London Jewish family. Woolfield was not the only survivor of the earliest days. At the Villa Alexandra were the Tripet-Skrypitzines, he French, she Russian, others who had stumbled inadvertently on Cannes years back, in their case because of a carriage breakdown.[26]

In 1896 the President of the Republic, Félix Faure, and the Prime

Minister, Léon Bourgeois, paid an official visit to Cannes. The membership of the welcoming party is illuminating. It consisted of Lord Brougham (the nephew); the Grand Duke Michael, uncle of the Tsar, and his morganatic wife, the Comtesse de Torby; the Prince and Princess of Nassau; Prince and Princess Galitzine; the Grand Duke of Mecklenburg-Strelitz; and Mr Gladstone, who was a constant visitor to the Riviera in his last years.[27]

In the 1880s Stéphan Liégeard in his celebrated book *La Côte d'Azur* – he invented the name – described the 'promenade' at Cannes as the Bagnères-de-Luchon of the Alpes Maritimes. If there were parallels between the Pyrenees and the Riviera there was also competition. Early on, Dr Taylor had made the point that, while in Nice the annual death rate was one in 31, in Pau it was only one in 45. Were you a reasonably wealthy and healthy person, choosing where to go, perhaps the most telling argument in favour of the Pyrenees, and of Pau in particular, would be the sport available, the hunting, the polo, the racing, the mountain climbing. For the physical pursuits of the Riviera (in this sense anyway) were less demanding, especially before sea-bathing became widely popular. The Duchesse de Clermont-Tonnerre, for instance, remembered the atmosphere at Cannes as suggestive of utter indolence. One moved at night from party to party, from villa to villa, certainly, but as another writer said, one avoided the morning sun.

Liégeard wrote that the French and the British descended on Cannes in expectation of a mild climate and the pleasures of 'high life'. Cannes was outstandingly hedonistic. One jingle had it that Cannes was for living, Menton for dying and Monte Carlo for gambling. President Faure, in his speech at the Town Hall, exhorted his listeners to make Cannes pre-eminent among the Mediterranean ports (*le premier port de plaisance*). And the great yachts did come sailing in, to take part in the regattas that earned it the sobriquet of 'the Cowes of the Mediterranean'. That was one of the reasons the Prince of Wales liked it so much. Another reason is recalled by a further, sprightlier jingle that represents Nice as the World, Cannes as the Flesh, and Monte Carlo as the Devil. Whereas once Cannes had been definitely proper, 'la ville du *home*', as a French writer has put it, which left libertines and freethinkers to Nice and Monte Carlo, it had now become, under the weight of all that money, given over to gambling, parties and love-making, the town of the *dolce vita*. A whiff of another sort of Riviera decadence emerges from an article by the well-known writer Margaret Oliphant in *Blackwood's Magazine* published in 1889.[28] She refers with dislike to the many old men dragging out their lives 'after a sufficiently long life not well spent, one feels sure', who grumble that the sun is not warm enough and that the sea makes too much noise and interferes with their sleep. She goes on to describe those who will one day take their place, 'elderly young men' who, were they in Piccadilly, might be called men about town. This is a type, she says, to be found at its perfection on the Riviera, effete, careful of everything – their clothes, their manners, the avoidance of bores – 'who are acquainted with both the best people and the worst'.

It was not only the Prince of Wales and the Tsar of Russia among royals who enjoyed the South of France. The list was a very long one that included the Emperor and Empress of Austria, the King of the Belgians and Eugénie, the ex-Empress of France, with a villa at Cap Martin between Menton and Monte Carlo. And Queen Victoria who visited Menton in 1882, Cannes in 1887 – following the death there of her son, the Duke of Albany – and later Grasse, Hyères (which built a new road for her) and Nice, or more precisely Cimiez, just outside. She seems to have loved the Riviera and to have held a high opinion of its therapeutic powers, spending the mornings riding quietly in a donkey cart and the afternoons in carriage trips about the countryside. Her routine in the 1890s was to leave Windsor in the second week of March and return in the last week of April. Her visits much helped in attracting the rich and aristocratic from all over Europe.[29]

But royal or not, all these people were flooding in by rail. Understandably, the old-established residents in their villas had at best mixed feelings, threatened as they were by hordes of tourists whom they had no wish to see, and by railway lines which might affect their property and their view. Prosper Mérimée was unhappy and wrote to Princess Matilde that he was set to take refuge in the mountains. In fact, he played an energetic part in successful opposition to some of the railway company's original proposals at Cannes. However, Thomas Woolfield referred to the ground near the seashore as being ruthlessly cut through to make way for the line. The business communities, however, could not be expected to take the same view and, in the event, the railways were even more crucial to the success of the Riviera than they were for the resorts of the Pyrenees. Above all, they enabled the transformation of Monaco, which at the time it had passed under French protection was reputedly the poorest state in Europe. (Monaco, for at that time Monte Carlo was nothing but a bare hillside.) An attempt in the 1850s to establish a casino failed miserably, but the reigning Prince tried again, granting rights to the brothers Louis and François Blanc, proprietors of casinos at Wiesbaden and Bad Homburg. They were attracted by the climate of Monaco and the prospects to be opened up by the imminent arrival of the railways. The undeveloped hill was chosen as the site for the casino and named Monte Carlo – Mount Charles – after the Prince. The casino's success was extraordinary. In 1868 there were two hotels in the principality; 20 years later there were 48.

There was a great deal of very vocal opposition. It came from nearby towns fearful of losing business, and from foreigners, British, American, Russian, German, Italian. The Vatican also objected. And after all, public gambling had for years been restricted in France. A London Society for the Abolition of the Monte Carlo Casino was established, with a branch in Paris, and in April 1883 the Anglican Bishop of Gibraltar, within whose diocese Monte Carlo fell, wrote to *The Times* from St John's Parsonage, Menton, deploring the fact that doctors were recommending British families to take villas and apartments in Monaco. Many doctors, though, were worried on that score, with Dr Bennet believing that so unrestful an atmosphere must be harmful to the sick. Beyond this not unreasonable argument lay a general opposition to public gaming, a conviction that it was socially and morally retrograde, a step backwards in the nineteenth century's march to a better world. Queen Victoria noted after a visit to Monaco (which did not include the casino) that 'one saw very nasty disreputable people walking about ... though many respectable people go there for their health'. Sometime before, according to Miss Dempster, the Queen's son the Duke of Albany had requested from his host the loan of his yacht so that he might sail round to Monte Carlo. The host refused on the grounds that Queen Victoria would be sure to hear, and would be annoyed because of the bad impression such an outing would make on the British locally.[30]

In fact the British were in two minds. William Chambers, the ex-Lord Provost of Edinburgh, considered that it would be more seemly to remove the mote from one's own eye before criticizing others. After all, what else is betting on horses than disreputable gaming under cover of sport and fashionable usage? he asked. For the respectable there could be a delicious *frisson*. Harriet Jephson, for instance, went over to Monte Carlo from San Remo with her party. She and her sister, she noted in her journal, 'were horrified as became sober English matrons to see the "bedaubed bedizened women" ' who surrounded the tables. And it was not quite clear how far the casino really was a sink of iniquity. The Bishop of Gibraltar referred to 'the very scum of all Europe' who were to be found there, and a more sympathetic writer allowed that 'notorious' cocottes were more than welcome, gaining admittance with less fuss than beset plain decent Englishmen and Englishwomen.[31] But their outward behaviour was impeccable, he insisted, and the Casino was without doubt very well run and supervised. J. R. Green described the salon:

> The terrible 'Hell' which one has pictured with all sorts of Dantesque accompaniments, is a pleasant room, gaily painted ... and a huge mass of gorgeous flowers in the centre. Nothing can be more unlike one's preconceived ideas than

the gambling itself, or the aspect of the gamblers around the tables. Of the wild excitement, the frenzy of gain, the outbursts of despair which one has come prepared to witness, there is not a sign. The games strike the bystander as singularly dull and uninteresting.

As to the talk at the dinner table, Green goes on, it is quite unconcerned with the romantic or poetic side of gambling; you hear nothing about the wonderful runs of luck or those terrible stories of ruin and despair which are the stock in trade of novelists. It is all totally businesslike; you might be at a conference of commercial travellers.[32]

But you could not convince the respectable; they were not to be kept away, or so it appears from the article by Margaret Oliphant, quoted above. Along with the dilapidated old men and the odd younger ones, she mentions a batch of lively and straightforward women, some recently widowed, others 'recently released' by the death of a tyrannical father, all agog to see the sights, particularly the gardens and villas of the very rich. But then there are the tourists who eagerly seek out Monte Carlo to gaze at 'the painted ladies [and] equivocal men'. It is all part of the play they have come to see. There are respectable and wealthy families – nobody much around these parts is poor, she adds – usually a father and mother and grown-up daughters, unsure perhaps of what they are after, but anyway hoping to be caught up in the 'tourbillon' of joyous life, fascinated by the wickedness, while themselves staunch in their high principles.[33]

If Monte Carlo provided the excitement, Nice remained very much the largest town, a city in fact, which took in far more visitors than anywhere else. It was popular with the British throughout the nineteenth century. Alexandre Dumas recorded that while he was staying there in 1835 at the Hôtel d'York, a *diligence* drew up to disgorge some tourists. Dumas asked the manager who his guests were, to receive the reply that 'they are certainly English, but whether they are French or German I don't know'.[34] That was Sardinian Nice, agreeable but very dirty; the French cleaned it up and gave it more polish, and extended the attractions on offer. For it was no longer so much a health resort as simply a pleasant place to be with lots to do. By the 1890s, Monte Carlo too, while the gambling was what really mattered, offered a range of ancillary activities. There were lawn tennis, golf, pigeon shooting (which provided plenty of scope for betting) and a series of competitions – beautiful girls, lovely dogs, handsome parasols. It provided bicycle races and prizefights and, very early on, motor rallies. Both Nice and Monte Carlo paid attention to culture, Monte Carlo in particular becoming famous for the high quality of its concerts and later for the Diaghilev ballet company.

Nice prided itself on its elegance. Bertall described the procession of carriages in the afternoon on the Promenade des Anglais, the magnificent avenue along the sea-front built early in the century with British money. There were three or four lords mounted on magnificent horses, parasols in hand, then a Russian droshky driven by a bearded servant in national costume. Harriet Jephson, during a short stay, went there every day to be 'edified by a sight of the painted, powdered, squeezed-in, puffed out, high-heeled damsels who parade there'. Nice was very cosmopolitan – Russians, Spaniards, Germans, Dutch, Italians, Belgians, British, Americans – and given an extra vitality by the people passing through on their way to or from Italy. Its carnival was famous and the races in January among the most important in France.

There was another side too. The Australian Susan Duffy, at Nice in the 1890s, depicts a rather demure place with English churches, English doctors, English banks, English circulating libraries, English chemists and what she calls 'semi-English institutions' such as grocers, butchers and bakers. It reminded her in some ways of Melbourne, hardly then or for many years later the embodiment of sophistication. (Robert Louis Stevenson's Cummy had been put in mind of Edinburgh's Princes Street.) The British, said Susan Duffy, are less stiff than they are at home. Their hospitality is lavish and takes the form of tea parties (which went under the name of receptions) that are eminently suited to a semi-invalid population who perforce have to entertain themselves without too much fatigue or excitement. Few of these people are less than 65. Leaving Americans out of account – and they were well represented in the town – she adds that not many 'foreigners' are to be seen at these parties, hardly more than you would expect to see at their equivalent in Kensington or Bayswater. It sounds rather like Pau 30 or 40 years before.[35]

By the 1890s, the coast was dotted all along by a scarcely broken line of villas and hotels. The smaller resort-towns and villages flourished, providing an alternative to the main centres, cheaper probably and filling in gaps. St-Raphaël, for instance, catered for people who wanted something less exclusive than Cannes. Menton had not become another Nice, though one writer talks of a Monte Carlo contingent brought there by the railways. Hyères now had a substantial French clientele but still continued to attract the British, even if for them it was no longer fashionable. In fact the British residents of the period at Hyères are remembered, tangibly, to this day by a fountain donated posthumously by a Mrs Stewart who died in 1900. To the astonishment of the locals, it was intended not for ornament or for human beings but for animals needing to slake their thirst.[36]

Very large buildings were making an appearance: the modern hotel had arrived. Back in the 1860s Prosper Mérimée wrote in a letter that among the

effects of growing civilization was the construction in Cannes of an enormous hotel with 200 rooms which was to be both comfortable and cheap.
The British, he said, were fed up with the high rents charged for villas, and
this was the result. Anyway, traditional accommodation could no longer
cope with the huge increase in demand generated by the railways. The new
hotels were the children of the railways, and there were close financial links
between the two. In many towns, although less so on the Riviera, the hotels
clustered around the station. And, influenced by American design and
American demand, they were quite unlike the slovenly places to which
travellers in provincial France had been accustomed.

On the face of it, this does not look like Queen Victoria's *milieu*. In
practice, she proved a considerable factor: she travelled with a huge staff and
crates of luggage, she took up a great deal of room. At Menton in 1882 she
had taken a villa – one belonging, incidentally, to a railway builder – with
her entourage mainly lodged in a hotel. But when she wanted to stay in a
hotel at Nice, there was none to be found which was large enough. So she
settled in outside at the Grand Hôtel de Cimiez, formerly the more modest-
sounding 'Pension anglaise'. Later on, she switched to the newly built
Excelsior Regina, also at Cimiez. This hotel, which was opened in her
presence, was enormous, with five and, in part, six storeys, offering 400
rooms and suites facing the sea, and 233 bathrooms. It had in fact more
bedrooms than any hotel on the Riviera today. From then on, along the
coast, these monster buildings went up, the most famous being the
Négresco in Nice and the Carlton at Cannes, both opened in 1912. The
grandest hotels provided rooms for customers' more senior staff near those
of their employers, and a separate dining room for customers' servants. By
1909 there were a total of 332 hotels on the Riviera, 132 of them at Nice, 65
at Cannes, 55 in Monaco and 53 at Menton. They were needed, since
160,000 people were visiting the Alpes-Maritimes, with something like
20,000 staying for over a month.[37]

The big hotels of course catered for only a small proportion of the total.
They were for the rich, but then there were a lot of them in the years before
the First World War, and travel was in their blood. 'What was the life of a
rich man now?' Lady Dorothy Nevill, the doyenne of London society, asked
herself in 1906. A sort of firework, she thought! Paris, Monte Carlo, big-
game shooting in Africa, fishing in Norway, dashes to Egypt, trips to Japan.
What an astounding change within her own lifetime. When she had travelled to Munich as a child, the family party of six took with them two maids,
a footman, a French cook, a courier, two *fourgons* to hold the 'batterie de
cuisine', six beds – since there were no real hotels – the family coach and a
barouche, six horses and two attendant grooms.[38]

The flavour of the last winter season before the war can be captured in the columns of the *Menton & Monte Carlo News*, a less parochial paper than its name suggests since it included sections on Nice, Cannes and smaller resorts such as Beaulieu. Moreover, while intended mainly for a British and American readership, its coverage is a reminder that in this social world affinities of class prevailed over differences of nationality. In an issue of December 1913 the paper announces Princess Olga Gagarine to be staying at the Hotel Beau Rivage at Monte Carlo, while the Baron and Baroness Rosenkrantz are at the Hotel Helder. Nevertheless, it is the English-speaking grandees who get most space. Also at Monte Carlo is the Duke of Leeds, while Lord and Lady Charles Beresford have arrived at Cannes. The Earl and Countess of Lauderdale have chosen Menton, where the hotels bear reassuring names like Victoria, Anglais, St James, Balmoral. The villa owners are mentioned too. This season, for instance, it appears that the Duke of Sutherland has let his Villa Rosmarino to Mr J. C. Scott of Lancaster Gate. The paper is full of plans for Christmas and for children's parties; the Carlton at Cannes is planning 'Tango Teas' for January. The Menton Lawn Tennis and Croquet Club reports that a number of new members have joined; the town's Anglo-American Club advises that it still has room for more. There is a great deal about golf, now hugely popular. Then, in the issue for 17 January 1914, the paper reports the success of the Grand Prix de Nice where 'automobiles were present by the score', and that further entertainment was provided for spectators by a pair of aeroplanes.

Nothing more poignantly portrays the last fling of this world than the advertisements for spring and summer holidays, or rather, since for many of the readers of the *Menton & Monte Carlo News* life was one long holiday, where you might go to occupy your indefinite leisure. You could stay on, of course, for many of the hotels and boarding houses remained open, and certainly it would not cost you much out of season. However, as Robert de Souza put it in his *Nice, Capitale d'Hiver* of 1913, well before the first hot days Nice asked only to go to sleep. At Cannes the casino closed down on 15 May along with its programme of operas and musicals. The Monte Carlo croupiers headed northwards. Mr Ernest T. Bob, manager of Nice's Hotel Ruhl, was off to his summer post at the Salsomaggiore ('Salso as habitués prefer to call it') near Milan, and invited readers of the paper to follow him, particularly if they suffered from rheumatism or arthritis. In fact, the Italian lakes were a favoured location, as was Vichy. Or there was Aix-les-Bains where Lord Waleren, the most prominent member of the British community on the Riviera, had just accepted the presidency of a new bridge club. The Hotel Klinger at Marienbad was a possibility, as was the Le Zoute hotel at Knocke-sur-Mer in Belgium. An alternative was a *pension* in

Bruges. More dashing would be a yachting cruise or a trip to Egypt with P&O.

For the next season the news was full of promise. In January 1914, at Hyères, Lady Lampson laid the foundation stone of a Hotel Excelsior, pronouncing that it was as firmly fixed as the Entente Cordiale; and at Menton the new Hotel Lutetia was due to open in November, However, by November, every hotel room would be needed, not for holidaymakers and *hivernants* but for wounded soldiers and refugees, French and Belgian and Serb, some of whom, we are told, were staggered by the opulence of their surroundings. The Queen Victoria Memorial Hospital at Nice had at once been put at the disposal of the authorities. Many of the villas and private houses were called into use; some of the residents stayed on, helping with nursing or administration – many had nowhere else to go. For many too, money ran short. And supplies as well, with the Mayor of Nice reduced to deploring the amount consumed by those tourists who continued to turn up. Nice as a holiday resort never properly recovered, hit the harder in that something like 40 per cent of its pre-war visitors were Germans who, even after the war, were in no position to spend money on foreign holidays. The Riviera of course would survive and flourish once more, but fundamentally changed. The old winter life was over.[39]

8

Babylon

Paris, the City of Eternal Youth ... this city which possessed a special grace to give happiness to everyone who approached it.

Stefan Zweig

Most of the British residents in the South of France were there part time, occupying their villas, apartments or hotel rooms for only a few months in the year. The British expatriates in the Alpes-Maritimes, the department concerned, numbered 4,771 in 1891 and 6,067 in 1901, in the latter case amounting to just less than 40 per cent of those living in the Paris region. By then, the population of Britain had overtaken that of France and per capita income was more than 50 per cent higher. It meant that the British still had money to throw about. However, there are two points to be made. First, while in 1815 the cost of living in France was lower than in Britain, that was by no means the case later on. During the 1850s both countries suffered marked inflation – in Britain especially the effect of the Crimean War – but it was the more severe in France. Anecdotal evidence supports the statistics. It was reckoned in the 1870s that Paris rents had doubled in the previous 20 years, and in 1894 the American Dr Linn quoted figures showing the cost of living in France to be 15 per cent higher than in Britain. The other point is that the discrepancy in prices was not reflected in the exchange rate, which by later standards remained extraordinarily stable: apart from wobbles in moments of crisis, it stood between 25 and 26 francs to the pound all the way from 1802 to 1914.[1]

The only way then you could actually save money by moving to France or to most other countries on the Continent was by a reduction in your standard of living. In fact, that was not difficult. In Britain, according to an 1882 article in the *Cornhill Magazine*, the middle classes were driven to extravagance in an attempt to emulate what was an exceptionally wealthy upper class.[2] But in France there was less show, less necessity for parade, as Frances Trollope put it in 1836. Thirty years later Charles Lever (writing as Cornelius O'Dowd) suggested what to do. Paris was now much more expensive to live in than London, but there you could live in a more economical way: instead of occupying a whole house you made do with half of one; you employed fewer servants; your butler was a 'hairy rascal' who also cleaned the windows, polished the parquet and maybe did your wife's hair too.[3] You bothered less about carpets. Just before the outbreak of the First World War, Miss Betham-Edwards reviewed French spending habits with the aid of figures provided by 'experienced French householders'. Salaries in France were much lower than in England, and living proportionately dearer. The wages of a good servant had risen to a level that was beyond the means of many middle-class people, so they coped without anyone but an occasional charwoman. A French housewife, she went on, so long as her reputation and her toilette were irreproachable, troubled little about her standing in the world. What is more, an English family on £500 a year spent more on entertaining friends during a twelvemonth than did a French family of similar means and size in as many years.[4]

The *Cornhill* article of 1882 quoted above discussed the alternatives for those intending to settle on the Continent. Switzerland, at least in the larger towns, was very cheap out of season but very expensive between May and October. Belgium should be considered: Brussels and Bruges were crowded with British and there were smaller colonies in Antwerp, Ghent, Namur and Liège. Schools were good and cheap. When it came to Holland on the other hand, the article was distinctly sniffy. It was neither cheap nor pleasant; the Dutch were inhospitable, the houses small and the language useless for children to learn. Germany, however, was highly recommended: British and Germans got on well, there was much mixing – and intermarriage – between them and, while Berlin was expensive, Munich, Dresden, Leipzig and Stuttgart were all less costly than English cities. Italy was the cheapest country of all, but British there, if not careful, 'will be fleeced with a shamelessness hardly to be credited by those who have not witnessed it'. France is approached almost with resignation: many British go there and settle in the smallest towns as well as in the large cities, but nowhere do they 'amalgamate with the natives'. The differences in manners, customs and modes of thought run too deep.

Nevertheless, there were many more British expatriates in France than anywhere else – in 1881 they amounted to 36,447, in contrast to Germany, the next most popular, with 11,139. But while the number of ordinary tourists kept rising, that for expatriates in France remained remarkably static. In 1866 it came to just short of 30,000; after that, up to the census of 1911, it hovered between 36,000 and just over 40,000, always declining as a percentage of the total number of foreigners in the country and coming far behind the figure for Belgians, Germans, Spanish and Italians. Essentially it was a question of wages, for with wages (and salaries) much higher in Britain, manual workers would find little reason to emigrate, for the days when the French paid well over the odds for British workers were over. The British expatriates were often rentiers, particularly if they lived on the Riviera. Some were employed in commerce or the professions, and those who did work in industry were usually skilled workers. One important group was composed of domestic workers, who were sufficiently numerous, according to the 1911 census, as actually to outnumber their compatriots working in 'commerce'. Unfortunately, the governesses and nannies, such as the Duchesse de Clermont-Tonnerre's Miss Johnson or the governesses unearthed by Francis Trent, seldom left memoirs. Miss Bicknell wrote a book about her nine years at the Tuileries during the Empire, when she supervised the education of some well-born young ladies at Court, but she is not to be classed as a domestic servant.[5] Miss Shaw, also at the Tuileries at the time, served as nanny to the Prince Imperial but, so far as is known, she left no record of her experiences. Occasionally the British nannies and governesses crop up in memoirs, usually to be remembered favourably, although, were you unlucky, you might have got Miss Wyse, governess to Frederick Newte, an English boy born in Paris. Every day, never speaking a word, she took him and his sister to the cemetery at Montmartre to make them sit on a tombstone for two hours while she passed her time reading. (Happily, musical instruction was in better hands; the teacher was Dr Liszt.)[6] Elizabeth Smith refers to a governess at Pau who spent her time flirting in the drawing room. On the other hand, there was Anna Shackleton, of whom André Gide writes with great fondness in his autobiography. She started as governess to his mother, staying on into later life as her companion and friend. Her influence on the young Gide was considerable, but, he reflected, talented as she was, it was a life that must have imposed a suppression of thought and instinct.[7]

The British, observed the *Cornhill*, settled in small towns. But there is no mention of the countryside, where in our day they are to be found in great numbers, spread all over the place in *la France profonde*, deepest, rural France. In 1891 more than a third of the British lived in or near Paris, another 13 per cent (here including the Var as well as the Alpes-Maritimes) were in the South of France, and around 4 per cent in each of the Pyrenees and the region close to Calais. Even in the Gironde, which includes Bordeaux, they numbered less than a thousand. Should they have been so enterprising as to have penetrated inner France – like, for instance, Robert Louis Stevenson in his expedition with a donkey in the Cevennes – they would have felt very out of place. When they did go it was most likely to be for business reasons.[8]

An example is the Davies family living near Decazeville in a village, St-Martin, on the borders of the Aveyron and the Lot, where steep wooded hills loom over the River Lot. To a French visitor this was a *pays perdu*, a lost country, a land of ruins from the Hundred Years War and the Wars of Religion. It was sombre if to an extent picturesque, though the villages were dingy and the inns filthy. Tourists were unknown. There were pleasures: the Davieses enjoyed sitting out at night on their terrace, 'hatless and coatless', listening to the church bells ringing out the angelus, with the sound echoing round the hills. They got on well enough with the villagers, and the children were very friendly. But they were not there for pleasure. Henry Davies managed a mine on the edge of the river and, supported by two British assistants, employed a workforce a hundred strong. It was hardly relaxing, for he never went down the mine without his revolver. Labour relations in the area generally were wretched, not least because of the high mortality rate engendered by the work. This was in the late 1880s, near the end of a century of mining by foreigners, British and Belgian particularly, in the Decazeville region. The Davieses mined 'silver lead', their British predecessors at the start of the nineteenth century mined alum. Coal mines abounded, to continue in operation until a few years ago. In the 1830s a stream of Welsh and English families had arrived to work the mines and the ironworks, encouraged by the Duc Decazes, at one time the French Ambassador in London, bringing with them a clergyman (probably a minister) and schoolteacher. Boys followed fathers into the mines and workshops. Names like Lewis, Williams, Evans, Griffiths, Jenkins recur.[9]

The international character of the district persists to this day. The President of the local Historical Association and his colleague, who kindly briefed me on background, are by origin Spanish and Polish respectively. The one set of people you would have been unlikely to find in the time of the Davieses were Parisians. In 1911 no more than 0.02 per cent of houses in the department of the Lot belonged to Parisians, and 0.43 per cent in the Aveyron. Again and again, French visitors to Britain in those days contrast the difference in attitude towards the countryside held by Londoners and Parisians. Londoners, who could afford it, owned houses in the country as far afield as Scotland, or Northumberland or Cumberland, should that be where their roots lay, and to which they would hasten eagerly in July or August. And if they could not afford it, they sought every opportunity to get as near as possible by resort to suburbs such as Greenwich or Richmond. But apart from the Riviera, where in 1911 they owned 5.8 per cent of houses, Parisians hardly bothered with property in remote departments. Even in the Vendée on the Atlantic coast, their share was no more than 0.06 per cent. It was said that just before the First World War many areas of

France were almost as little known to Parisians as they had been in the 1820s.[10] Albert Vandam, a British journalist who lived for many years in France, went so far as to say that Parisians actually hated provincials, viewing them as needy and unscrupulous people whose yoke they could not shake off. The very provinciality of the provincials must to an extent explain why the British expatriates and visitors, usually educated people, found it difficult to mix socially.[11]

It is hard to exaggerate the importance and influence of Paris on France as a whole, though certainly Parisians did their best to do so. Sometimes they went further. Charles de Forster in his *Paris et les Parisiens* of 1848 asserts that:

> National prejudice aside, one is forced to agree that Paris as the personification of France, is the centre from which radiates upon the world the most generous, the most socially advanced, the most philosophic ideas, and one is obliged to acknowledge frankly that in the nature of things the French nation is placed at the head of social movement no matter where.

Pompously put, but with some degree of truth. But to many it was a short jump from social movement to all movement. Victor Hugo, going over the top, declared in a speech that 'Paris is the present capital of the civilized world. What Rome once was Paris is today: Paris has a dominating function among nations'.[12] The British journalist and playwright Blanchard Jerrold, writing in the 1850s, mocks the French attitude. 'We are barbarians, to be raised from our vulgar debasement by the surpassing excellencies of French artists and French authors. Poetry is to arrive in London, presently, from Paris direct.' In the years after Waterloo, the material superiority of London at least was undoubted. How far the French vision of the world had narrowed is illustrated by the reaction of the intelligent and (normally) informed Francis Wey, when he visited London in 1856. He observes how surprised a Frenchman must be by what he finds. He arrives, says Wey, full of a self-confident pride in his superiority, to find a nation as remarkable, as original and every bit as civilized as his own. This 'novel experience', Wey goes on, makes my compatriots uneasy, even intimidated.[13]

British influence and British associations in Paris survived, especially in high society. The Jockey Club, with its close social ties, flourished. British patricians were well received at Court both under Louis-Philippe and Napoleon III. They were still seen as rich, and as eccentric. In the chaotic and dangerous days that followed the collapse of the Orléans monarchy, Richard Monckton Milnes, politician and wit, gave a dinner party in Paris of which both Mérimée and Tocqueville left accounts. The company, three women and half a dozen men, was oddly assorted, thought Tocqueville: some people did not know each other at all, while others knew each other only too well – by that he meant Mérimée and George Sand who, years before, had been involved in a brief and turbulent affair that had ended if not in tears at least most uncomfortably. Tocqueville, who in a matter of weeks was to become Foreign Minister in the new Republican government, was almost as displeased as they were; he was placed next to Sand, against whom he was anyway prejudiced and who was on the opposite side politically. (In the event, though, he found what she said most interesting.) Only an Englishman, wrote Mérimée afterwards to a friend, could put a party like that together.[14]

Another eccentric British friend of both Tocqueville and Mérimée was Mary Clarke, married in later life to Julius Mohl, a distinguished scientist. She had been brought up in France and gone to school in Toulouse. To Stendhal, she was a 'a little humpbacked shrew', with a lively mind but hard and twisted. To the British writer and art critic P. G. Hamerton, she was the oddest-looking person, with original and unattractive notions about her toilette. Yet so celebrated did she become as a hostess and wit that she has been the subject of no less than four books (biographies and collected letters). Her purpose in life was running a salon, that institution so much at the centre of Parisian society. Her training was exemplary, undertaken by Madame Récamier and approved by Chateaubriand, while her success attained its zenith during the Second Empire when her salon served as a meeting place for intellectuals opposed to the regime. It was also a meeting place for British and French, with Robert and Elizabeth Browning among her guests, though it must be added that Madame Mohl had a low opinion of the conversational powers of British women. The English generally, she said, cannot hold their tongues in a drawing room and listen as the French do: they talk while the French converse. Nevertheless she kept close ties with her native country and in fact was in England when, in the summer of 1870, war broke out between France and Prussia. Parisian salons, and much else, were not to be quite the same again.[15]

On 30 June 1870 the French Prime Minister Ollivier declared that at no time had the peace of Europe been more assured than it was at present. But, a fortnight later, a dispute between France and Prussia over the nomination of a king for Spain, and a report doctored by Bismarck, provoked a rash and ailing Napoleon III to declare war. Within six weeks, the French armies were either crushed or trapped, and the Prussians were moving on Paris, to complete its encirclement on 20 September. The Emperor had been captured, the Empress, with the aid of an American dentist and a British yacht owner, had fled to England, a mob had stormed the Tuileries and a republican government was once more tenuously in power. The British community in Paris, like everyone else, was quite unprepared for the catastrophe. The Parisians could hardly believe what was happening. It couldn't be. The British Henry Labouchere, later a prominent radical politician, in Paris as correspondent for the *Daily News*, looked on cynically. To the Parisians, he wrote, 'their capital . . . is a holy city, and they imagine that the Christian world regards the Prussian attack upon it much as the Mahometan world would regard a bombardment of Mecca'. The Siege and the Commune, the revolutionary movement that took control of the city afterwards, were to have an enduring effect on French politics and French foreign policy.[16] A vivid impression of the British community at the time, and the initial shock, is given in the flood of letters that descended on the Ambassador Lord Lyons.[17]

Some of them must have been a particular trial. The Duchess of Newcastle asks him to arrange for a Queen's Messenger to carry her jewel box to England; the Honorary Secretary of the Acclimatisation Society of New South Wales is anxious for the Ambassador to send him some silkworm eggs. (That really will have to wait, is the ever-courteous reply.) An Englishman in Boulogne needs authority from the Ministry of Finance to dispatch his horses to Britain, the grounds for his application being that it was there they had been born and bred. More serious were the appeals for protection of buildings and shops. The British at Bordeaux want nothing less than the Royal Navy to keep intruders off. The Duchess of Hamilton wants protection for her house in Paris. A Mr Tucker, British-born with shops in central Paris, requests special protection, as does a Boot and Corset Merchant. Would hanging out the Union Jack help, or would it attract dangerous attention? This was the question of a Mrs Bishop, anxious about silver plate kept in her Paris apartment. Other letters ask the same thing. Many people want passports in order to escape. It has to be explained to Sister Mary of the Servite Sisters' convent at Raincy, who requested a 'certificate of safety' to protect her community, that the Embassy can do no more than to provide passports to British subjects. And it is necessary to point out – if not to Sister Mary – that British women who marry Frenchmen lose their old nationality.

Lord Lyons followed the French government on its withdrawal from Paris to Tours. But the letters kept pouring in. Some people needed protection not from German troops but specifically from the French. The Honourable Mrs Methuen and her husband, an invalid, were insulted by a man at Dinard who came up and, accusing them of being Prussians, pronounced that they should be killed. The British vice-consul at St-Valéry-sur-Somme was set on by a mob for allegedly having said 'Down with

France'; the local authority advised that for his own safety he should leave quickly.

There is one case of special interest. On 25 October, by which time Paris was under siege, Mr William Sisley, an exporter of silks and artificial flowers, wrote to the Ambassador from Le Havre asking that a letter (including, it seems, a cheque) be got through to his son Alfred, who missed the last train out of Paris, is without money and must be in serious difficulty. William Sisley pleaded for a pass across the Prussian lines for himself, writing 'that no risk or expense would deter me from the attempt' to cross over. Whether he got his pass is not known; what we do know is that his business collapsed as a result of the war and that Alfred Sisley, a British subject born in France of British parents, would eventually be acclaimed as the greatest British painter of the second half of the nineteenth century.[18]

The Sisleys represent an old tradition in the mixing of French and English. The business in silks and laces was inherited, but originally the family, agricultural labourers and small farmers in Romney Marsh, had conducted it as smugglers and, like others in the trade, intermarried. Alfred Sisley himself possessed some distinctly English characteristics: a certain reticence, a correctness of dress even, though in later life he was, with the business gone, often very poor. (A Frenchman remembered that his collars were 'irreproachably white'.) And his painting, however Impressionist, is restrained. On the other hand, he married a French wife, clearly felt more French than English (attempting unsuccessfully at the end of his life to acquire French nationality) and lived almost entirely in France. If his presence in Paris in October 1870 was involuntary, there were other British subjects who could not face the idea of leaving, and who ignored the Embassy's advice to get out. The Irish journalist John Augustus O'Shea met another, older British painter in Paris during the Siege who explained 'that my "household gods" are here. I'm an artist and an imperialist* . . . I must stay where my livelihood is; although a British subject, I would be a greater foreigner in London today than here.' And later on, during the Commune, the Reverend William Gibson, walking through the streets, was surprised at the number of Union Jacks he saw on the houses. It put him in mind that over his years in Paris he had become aware of numbers of English in the city, people who had given up English habits, dismissed English ideas, were English only in name and when there was something to be gained by manifesting their nationality. They hide themselves away from their countrymen, he said, and become French in their thoughts and modes of life.

---

* He would have meant he was a supporter of Napoleon III's Empire.

Labouchere was told the same thing, and that they 'emerge from holes and corners every day'.[19]

There were, though, British who deliberately arrived for the Siege, journalists like Labouchere and O'Shea, and Thomas Bowles, later an MP, who represented the *Morning Post* and proved a particularly bold war correspondent. The young Edwin Child, an apprentice to a jeweller who had fled, stayed on to see what happened and joined the *Garde Nationale*, the body formed to defend the city. Colonel Stanley of the Grenadier Guards arrived for 'Red Cross' work, serving with the much respected American Ambulance. (An Ambulance was a mobile field hospital with usually some 50 beds.) Dr Alan Herbert, a man of exceptional dedication and administrative ability, who had lived in Paris since 1859 and was to die there in 1907, played a large part in the British relief effort. However, the British – of whom there were some 4,000 in Paris during the Siege – were generally unpopular with the Parisians who believed, not very reasonably, that Britain should have entered the war to help them. An outstanding exception to this resentment was Richard Wallace, a man from whom on past experience of his family one might have expected nothing but selfishness and indifference. He was the natural son of the fourth Marquess of Hertford whose protracted illness and whose misanthropy and meanness were so grimly described by Edmond de Goncourt. Hertford died at the Bagatelle on 24 August 1870, just as the war turned into disaster. The title went to a cousin in England without any French affiliation, and the fortune, including the Bagatelle, to Wallace, who was to retrieve the reputation of his lamentable family. How different he was to his father is illustrated by another Goncourt anecdote. Sometime back in the past, Wallace had promised the courtesan Madame Sabatier that he would remember her should he ever become rich; a few weeks after the Marquess's death she received from him what amounted to a small fortune.[20] Wallace was a hero of the Siege, donating huge sums. He financed one of the balloons which kept the besieged city in touch with the outside world, he paid for a mobile field ambulance as well as two hospitals, one for war wounded and the other for civilian victims of the bombardment. Through the British Charitable Fund he supported an estimated 800 British in Paris, otherwise destitute and unable as foreigners to claim rations.

And everyone badly needed food. After Paris surrendered at the end of January 1871 the British exerted themselves to send supplies. The government provided Navy ships, and a Relief Fund set up by the Lord Mayor of London was inundated with donations.[21] But Parisians gained no more than a momentary respite from the horrors of war. The first siege was followed by another as government forces from outside struggled to suppress the Communard revolutionaries who took control of the city. Truly, we are again in the 'Reign of Terror', wrote William Gibson home to his wife. The rebellion, thought another Englishman, was more a furious instinctive response to humiliation than a calculated or conspiratorial political strategy. Be that as it may, many more people were killed during the Commune than during the siege by the Prussians, and many more buildings were destroyed – among them the Tuileries, the medieval Hôtel de Ville and much of the Palais Royal.

When at last it was all over, a massive clearance and rebuilding got under way. One British resident of Paris who had stayed throughout the Siege made a modest contribution. Charles Frederick Worth,[22] the most famous couturier in the world, 'a native of bucolic Lincolnshire', bought up some of the wreckage of the Tuileries to make sham ruins in his garden. There is a glimpse of him during the earlier stage of the Commune provided by the American socialite Lillie Moulton, who had just returned to Paris and was in need of clothes for whatever season the new Republic would be able to offer. As she neared Worth's premises in the Rue de la Paix (which had been used as a hospital during the Prussian siege) she found her way blocked by barricades. Leaving her carriage, she approached on foot and, aware of guns pointing in her direction, she hurried into Worth's building. Hardly had she arrived than growing commotion in the street brought her, along with Worth, his sons and members of his staff, out on to the balcony. A deputation of unarmed citizens was appealing to the men behind the barricades to take the guns away so that the life of the city could return to normal. Their leader called up to Worth to join them. 'But Mr. Worth wisely withdrew inside', wrote Mrs. Moulton, 'and, shaking his Anglo-Saxon head, said "Not I!" ' Then the firing started, and something like 300 people took refuge in Worth's showrooms.

Worth, the man who laid low 'the boasted superiority of the Parisienne in all matters relating to feminine fashion', came from a ruined middle-class family, starting off aged 11 as a printer's apprentice. A year on, he headed for London where he found a job in the drapery firm of Swan & Edgar at Piccadilly Circus. Aged about 20, he moved to Paris, without money and knowing no one in France. He picked up a job in a small drapers, working 12 hours a day, then progressed to a shop in the fashionable Rue de Richelieu and, with the help of his wife, a French girl who acted as his model, turned to making dresses. So good were they that customers, French and foreign, accumulated, among them, in 1860, Princess Metternich, as smart as anyone in Europe, who introduced him to the Empress. Worth became a star during the Empire and remained one under the Third Republic. Another glimpse of him, this time in August 1871, five months after the episode in the Rue de la Paix, reveals something of his force of personality. With the Commune now crushed, a British journalist, a woman, writing for *Blackwood's*, interviewed him at his country house.[23] The issue was the future of Paris, at least in the short term. Worth was ebullient, in an optimistic mood. He told her that he employed 1,200 people and had customers, Russians above all, who spent up to £4,000 on clothes every year, say £280,000 in our money. But, protested the interviewer, surely your business must suffer; what Paris sells is the frivolous and unnecessary, not the sort of thing for which there will be demand, at least for some time. 'Who were the silly people who said that?' demanded Worth, why, 'it is precisely the unnecessary and the frivolous that everybody comes to buy in Paris ... Do you ever hear of a woman – or a man either – who did come here for anything but the unnecessary?' The interviewer left, not wholly satisfied, her question not properly answered. But Worth was right; in a year or so, despite the ravages of the war and the Commune, despite Prussian occupation, despite the obligation to pay a huge indemnity to the victors, France and above all Paris achieved a quite remarkable and rapid recovery. What was to be called the *Belle Epoque* would follow very shortly, and with it, incidentally, would come numbers of other British couturiers.

Richard Wallace himself departed for London, taking with him his superb art collection – the Commune had been too much for him. He left behind some fountains for the city, a hospital for the British, and of course the Bagatelle, where he died in 1890 while on one of his regular visits. The most prominent British national in Paris during the later years of the nineteenth century was Sir Edward Blount, who had served briefly as chargé d'affaires during the Prussian siege. He was a banker of great eminence, closely involved with railway investment, a member of the Jockey Club and for many years President of the British Chamber of Commerce in Paris. Nevertheless, his career illustrates how business in France was made the more hazardous by political convulsion. A bank that Blount started with Charles Laffitte – Laffitte being a towering name in French banking – went under in the 1848 revolution, as, in 1870, did a bank he formed later which was backed by Thomas Brassey and other influential French and British investors. The British community in Paris changed; was more directed toward business and the professions – there were fewer duchesses around to bother the Ambassador about their jewel cases. In 1974, André Barblan, writing a book on the period, sought out old people in Paris, mainly from shopkeeping families, for their memories. The *Anglais*, he was told, were easily recognizable from the cut of their clothes and by their accent. They were recalled as business families, the father working for the branch of some large London commercial or financial business house, and there was a general impression that they were wealthy and often taken for a ride (*se faisaient rouler*) by their usually French maids. Frederic Marshall, writing in the *Fortnightly Review* in 1885, observes, however, that by far the largest proportion of the 10,000 British residents are servants, clerks and small traders, and doubts whether more than 300 live on a private income. Nevertheless, he goes on to discuss in some detail people who are clearly well off.[24]

The expatriates come to Paris, he says, to further their children's education and to save money. An agreeable life is possible for a family on £800 a year – half what it would cost in London – and that would include two months at the seaside in summer. A British family can enjoy a busy social life with small dinners and numerous tea parties, but they will know scarcely any French people, who, of all Europeans, are the least inclined to open their doors to foreigners. They were, however, likely to mix with the Americans, especially if they lived in the smart 16th and 18th arrondissements on the western side of the city. Marshall repeats that familiar warning. Should you succeed in fully adapting to Paris, or for that matter to anywhere else abroad, you pay the price: having done so you can never live agreeably in England again.

Of the British domestic servants and governesses, many were placed with most respectable and conscientious families. However, the 1870s saw an influx of young girls from Britain with little experience of life. Some came to enter domestic service, some to learn French or cooking or hairdressing, others intended to work in shops or offices or in the theatre. Some ended up as artist's models. It was the predicament of these girls, should they be unemployed or otherwise run out of money, that was the subject of a meeting at Manchester Town Hall in September 1874, with the Bishop of Manchester, in the chair, pointing out that Paris was not the safest place in the world. The moving spirit behind the meeting was a Miss Leigh who estimated that there were some 2,000 women who might be concerned. Miss Leigh had already undertaken to buy a large building in the Avenue Wagram to be used as hostel for up to 90 women in need. So effective was she, whether in raising funds or in administration, that, moving to Paris, she was to found a series of such hostels which over the years provided a refuge for thousands of women in difficulty. She also ran an orphanage in Neuilly.[25]

While Paris by mid-century had become a major industrial city, there were few British industrialists about. An exception was Isaac Holden from Bradford who in 1853 established a giant wool-combing mill at St-Denis just outside Paris, in partnership with Samuel Cunliffe Lister (later Lord Masham). Holden faced strong local competition but went on to open two

more factories, one of them at Reims, an important centre of the woollen
industry. By now, though, the textile industry, in which the British had
earlier excelled, was in general firmly in French hands.[26]

Holden, when he retired, went home, but his predecessors, the earlier
entrepreneurs and their families, had often stayed on. The most notable
were the Waddingtons, again in textiles, who were established at St-Rémy-
sur-Avre, near Dreux to the west of Paris. Two brothers, William, born in
1826, and his younger brother Richard were both remarkably successful and
an unusual amalgam of British and French. Richard, educated at Rugby and
at Woolwich, the army school, served several years in the Royal Artillery,
married an Englishwoman and, turned French, was deputy, senator and a
prominent industrialist; William went to Rugby and Trinity, Cambridge
(where he was a rowing blue) and also took French nationality. Early in life
he was an ardent traveller, acquiring a reputation as a numismatist. But then
he too switched to politics, serving as deputy, Minister of Education, Foreign Minister and in 1879 Prime Minister. Subsequently, he was for ten
years French Ambassador in London. He first married a Frenchwoman and,
after her death, an American, Mary King, whose grandfather Rufus King
had been the unsuccessful Federalist candidate for the presidency in 1816.
William Waddington, wrote his wife Mary, was in character very English.
Almost stage-English, it seems, represented in the press as a safe pair of
hands. One caricature pictured him as an English coachman, sitting straight
and correct on the box of a brougham, a man 'who has never upset or run
into anything'. In the chronically noisy Chamber of Deputies he was
imperturbable, remaining silent when interrupted until order was completely restored. Queen Victoria, intrigued by this ex-Englishman as Prime
Minister of France, told Lord Lyons (still Ambassador) after a long talk with
Waddington in Paris, that she had found 'everything about him ... so
absolutely English, figure, colouring, and speech'.[27]

Mary Waddington was thrown into political life during the first years of
the Third Republic. She was not impressed: she considered the officials and
politicians, and their wives, to be narrow in outlook, none, for example,
showing any interest in America or her life there, or for that matter in any
subject that ranged beyond France. Few could speak anything but French.
She tended to prefer life in the country, where the Waddingtons occupied
the wing of a *château*, La Ferté, north-east of Paris, which belonged to the
parents of William's first wife. It was set in a region of large farms and few
villages, on the edge of the extensive forest of Villers-Cotterêts, still, in the
1870s, profoundly rustic with very little traffic on the high road and utter
silence at night. At the same time, it was only an hour and a half by train to
Paris. Waddington's ex-parents-in-law were Protestants (as were the

Waddingtons themselves), people who had moved in the highest Protestant society. Most of the servants were Swiss Protestants, and, there being no local chapel, services were held in the library of the house on Sunday mornings. While again breezy chat about the USA would have been ill-received, the neighbours were curiously cosmopolitan. At the nearby Château de La Houssaye the mistress of the household was the former Miss Forbes, an American who obligingly served waffles for tea. Madame de Thury at Thury-en-Valois was also American. Some other friends, the Marquis and the Marquise de Lasteyrie had both inherited English blood. When Mary Waddington went over to stay with them she found two English couples staying in the house, who surprised her, given the usual shyness and self-consciousness of the English, by being better than anyone else at dumb-crambo (a form of charades). Closer home, at La Ferté itself, the lodge keeper's wife was a Scot who had once been a nanny in the family. The local doctor was married to an Englishwoman, and they often had English boys staying with them in summer to learn French.

La Ferté and the country houses visited by Mary Waddington were large, but they were hardly to be compared to Chenonceaux (sometimes Chenonceau), close to the Loire and described in *The Collins Guide to France* as 'arguably the most beautiful house in the world'. In 1864, this enormous *château* was bought by Monsieur and Madame Pelouze, the latter, 'English to her fingertips', being the daughter of Daniel Wilson, Aron Manby's partner at Charenton and in the introduction of gas lighting to Paris and other French cities. The Wilson and Manby children had remained in France. Dickens met one of the Manbys at Boulogne in 1863, where he was generously taking care of the ruined and disgraced ex-Railway King, George Hudson. But in terms of the noise they made in the world, the Wilsons, Madame Pelouze and her brother Daniel Wilson junior, were in a class of their own. The sister used her considerable fortune for the purchase and restoration of Chenonceaux; Daniel spent his on gambling, women and politics. His English blood – actually Scottish – was less obvious than his sister's, but he was nicknamed the 'Glaswegian', sported a long red beard and was held to possess British phlegm, even though, according to one observer, he looked more like a German or Austrian. His political career overlapped with that of William Waddington: both came in as deputies to the first republican chamber elected after the fall of the Empire; both had ties with President Grévy, who, on taking office, appointed Waddington as Prime Minister. When the Waddington government fell after nearly a year in office – a respectable term by Third Republic standards – Wilson joined the new Freycinet administration as an under-secretary. Here any connection ended. There was no similarity of character anyway: while Waddington was respectable and rather dull, Wilson was disreputable and prone to scandal. Still he had one very important thing going for him: his sister had for years been President Grévy's lover, and was able to arrange his marriage to the President's daughter, Alice. Wilson, installed in the Elysée Palace, started on the repair of his wasted fortune by selling honours, using the presidential letterhead and seal. The scandal broke, and forced the resignation of the government and the President.[28]

The sale of honours is not altogether unknown in Britain, but generally it is carried out with more discretion. To the British, the Wilson scandal, the Boulanger* crisis that followed, the Panama Company affair which revealed widespread bribery of deputies, were more or less what they expected of French politics. To an extent they even contributed to the allure of France, that land of excitement beyond the reach of ordinary restraints. Anthony Trollope expresses the feeling in *The Bertrams*:

> it was his purpose to go abroad again, to go to Paris, and live in dingy lodgings there *au cinquième*, to read French free-thinking books, to study the wild side of politics, to learn if he could, among French theatre and French morals, French freedom of action, and freedom of speech, and freedom of thought.

Paris was not Rome, as Hugo claimed, but it was Babylon – the great and vicious city – a title applied to it again and again. But perhaps it was Athens too, for Paris was the undisputed capital of art. 'It is in art', wrote the critic Albert Wolff in 1886, 'that Paris, after its disasters, had found the renewal of its high European standing'. The old English painter, the man who could never go home, encountered by the journalist J. A. O'Shea during the Siege, was one in a long line. In the 1900s Arnold Bennett records dining in Paris with a 'successful' painter, a British subject who had spent nearly all his life there, knew the city like a Frenchman, spoke the language like a Frenchman. I never heard him of him going to England, or wanting to go to England, said Bennett. They were joined by a Scottish painter, a man who never left Paris even in summer. Whatever their nationality, many other artists would have felt the same way.[29]

Babylon, Athens ... and 'Bohemia', celebrated at mid-century in Murger's *Scènes de la Vie de Bohème* and for the British in George Moore's *Confessions of a Young Man* and Du Maurier's *Trilby*. The close association of painting and the free life, dingy attics, a seamstress as mistress, crusts of bread but lots of wine – after all it was suicide to drink Paris water – and where everything was forgivable except lack of feeling. The real bohemian,

---

* General Boulenger's mother was British.

announced Murger, can only exist in Paris; Aubrey Beardsley, dying in Menton at the end of the century, would say much the same thing. George Moore, then intending to be a painter, who arrived in 1872 aged 21, with money in his pocket and accompanied by his valet, was not exactly typical.[30] But he enrolled at the Académie Julian which, next to the orthodox Beaux Arts, was to establish itself as the leading art school in Paris. Also working there he found eight or nine young English girls. A few years later, Clive Holland,[31] better known as a photographer, worked in a life-class at Colarossi's along with 'an Englishman or two, a few Americans, a couple of Japanese, a coloured gentleman' and some Poles, Austrians, French and Russians. A later student in Paris was the fine painter Gwen John who arrived in the early 1900s, stayed on, enjoyed an intense affair with Rodin and became, like Maria Cosway before her, a very devout Catholic.

The most entertaining account of life in Paris as an art student is provided by John Shirley Fox, whose father had taken a job in Paris. John arrived, a small boy, with his mother in 1878, travelling under 'the care of Cook's'. As they drove to their hotel he marvelled at the wide streets, at how strange everything was, at the number of soldiers and uniformed officials, to say nothing of the numerous priests and other 'ecclesiastical persons' in flowing black robes, 'which at this time were as plentiful as blackberries in the streets of Paris'. While attending day school he was allowed, aged 12, to enrol at the Académie Julian. His parents, obliged to return to England, decided not to interrupt his studies, and so left him behind at the Hôtel de Londres et New York in the care of some friends. John seems to have been quite unperturbed, and anyway was gifted with an exceptional knack for getting on with people. He was in demand as an interpreter and taken along to the Skating Palace in the Rue Blanche and to the Folies-Bergère. His popularity was unbounded and he was in effect adopted as a pimp by the 'gay ladies' who encouraged him to introduce to them his new grown-up friends. These ladies were a jokey lot and on one occasion, he remembered, they dressed him up as a girl to tease a Frenchman known to fancy 'nice little English girls'. His parents returned, and life reverted to a more orthodox pattern. He certainly did not see himself as having been debauched: by the time he reached his mid-teens, he was, he wrote in his memoirs, so blasé that in later life he found himself to be thoroughly bored on the rare occasions that he visited the Alhambras and Empires of London.[32]

If Paris was the capital of Art it was also the capital of Sex. Rudyard Kipling, a francophile, remembered that 'French as an accomplishment was not well seen at English schools in my time, and knowledge of it connoted leanings towards immorality'.[33] It is indicative that so many French words relating to sex (or made to relate to sex) have been incorporated into English – *roué*, *liaison*, *risqué*, *épris* are examples. In Britain, in less sophisticated circles at any rate, the mention by a man that he was off to Paris might well prompt a wink or a leer. Paris was the place for an illicit weekend; indeed so enduring has its reputation been that a year or two back lastminute.com was advertising it as 'The Hanky Panky City'. Some French were baffled. Prosper Mérimée wrote to his British barrister friend Sutton Sharpe that he could not understand why he needed to come to Paris for sex when the facilities were just as good in London. Charles de Forster protested that it was extraordinary that London should be taken for a puritan city and Paris as the capital of depravity, when in reality London was far more dissolute. Perhaps, but a calculation of the time came up with figures to show that while there were 24,000 prostitutes in London, in Paris, with half the population, there were 34,000.[34]

Still, the Second Empire would seem to have extinguished most of such doubts. There was so much noise about the sex and so much show. The bejewelled and bedecked courtesans were notorious, and sometimes important. It has been argued that without the money put behind her lover Louis Napoleon by Elizabeth Haryett from Great Yarmouth, later Elizabeth Howard, later Comtesse de Beauregard, there would never have been a Second Empire at all. An acquaintance of the fashionable Captain Bingham told him that he had met Mrs Howard on the train to Dover, transporting to Paris her jewels and all the money she could scrape together.* She was later to be dropped by the Emperor for reasons of state, though as some consolation was given a country palace and estate near Paris.[35]

Elizabeth Howard was very beautiful, very elegant, well educated and with irreproachable manners, and indeed she had been introduced to the future Emperor by the Comte d'Orsay, who was nothing if not discriminating. She was not typical. The other famous British courtesans of the time, Eliza Gilbert, better known as Lola Montez, and Eliza Crouch, otherwise Cora Pearl, were not noted for decorum or for high education. The latter, the daughter of a Plymouth music teacher who fled to America to escape his creditors, did, it is true, study at a Boulogne convent for a number of years, but she left early, so the story goes, in the company of a barber. Cora Pearl was raucous and wild, fond of playing tricks and adored gambling, but she did resemble Elizabeth Howard in that she 'rode like a jockey'. All agree that her figure was superb. At any rate, once established in Paris, she gathered to herself an unmatchable collection of lovers that included the Duc de Rivoli; the Duc de Morny, half-brother to the Emperor; the Prince of Orange; and

---

* She had been very generously provided for by a previous lover.

the Prince Napoleon, a cousin of the Emperor, who set her up in what amounted to a palace which got nicknamed the 'Petites Tuileries'. She was the height of fashion.[36]

For Cora Pearl, as for many others, the good times ended with the Empire. She was, though, still working in the 1880s when, approaching 50, she is described by the author of *The Pretty Women of Paris* as living at 6 Rue Christophe Colombe, 'undaunted', with her merry disposition still, but almost friendless and up to her neck in debt. *The Pretty Women of Paris* was published anonymously in 1883 and reprinted in 1996 as *The Pleasures of Paris: A Complete List of its Licensed Brothels or 'Maisons de Tolérance'*. As the editor of the reprint says, the book 'is as if a late nineteenth-century photographer's flash bar has brilliantly lit up the Parisian underworld', to reveal what many British visitors came to Paris to find: an exhilarating alternative to what – despite Mérimée – the author labels as the 'horny-handed whores' of his own country. Cora Pearl is far from alone in being British. There is Alice Gordon at 16 Rue Vézelay. And Alice Howard, 'the handsomest whore in Paris', whose majestic and disdainful bearing, the author thinks, may be the effect of the remorse and shame so often to be found among the British in her profession, and which leads them 'to drown their persistent regrets in the bottle'. The drinking anyway was true also of Nesta Needham – she rather resembled a man in woman's clothing – who drinks her English lover, himself a three-bottle man, under the table. Another English girl, Jenny Mills, a music hall performer, 'with her saucy screech' is quite free of the depression that afflicts Alice Howard. Her compatriot Elsie Murton, the author advises, is now in retirement but likely to be tempted back to work by a sufficiently substantial offer.

The USA is not always well represented. The Comtesse de Lansay (real name Mrs Jackson) is an old adventuress with dyed carroty hair. There is Camille Disney, 'a sober American woman of pleasure who like most of her countrywomen ... will never say "no" to anything'. The German Alice Scheresne has a problem given the anti-German feeling in Paris, so she sometimes pretends to be British. And pretending to be British can anyway be good for trade: one French girl with English looks calls herself simply 'Miss', while another, with nothing English about her at all, goes by the name of Fanny Jackson. A number of the courtesans award themselves the aristocratic *particule* 'de', and, like Mrs Jackson, adopt a title. Indeed, some may not need to: a Polish countess and a Neapolitan princess on the list are thought to be genuine. Several specialize in British customers: Marguerite Debreux, for example, understands the peculiar tastes of English rakes and, 'when dressed as a boy, she looks a picture'. One woman is the favoured whore of a British member of Parliament who spends most of his time in

Paris, while Gioja of the Avenue du Bois de Boulogne owes most of her colossal fortune to the 'liberalities' of a Scottish duke. The well-known brothel at 14 Rue de Monthyon contained a room called the 'Salon des Lords', presumably for the reception of wealthy British. The Prince of Wales is mentioned obliquely in the book, appearing as lecher and good fellow.

There are common denominators about the 'pretty women'. They are often lesbian, they drink hard, and while one of them was never anything more than a 'prowling whore at the skating rink', almost all are, or have been, actresses, whether in the orthodox theatre, the opera or the music hall. Many originate in the provinces, brought to Paris by a lover and then abandoned. In an extremely funny book on life in Paris, Marcel Boulenger advises that if you want to insinuate yourself into the good graces of a courtesan you should compliment her on her family's standing and say how proud her father, down in the country, must be of the success she has made of life.[37]

To the world, Frenchwomen became sex symbols. But were you really likely to find an impatient nymphomaniac in every bar? Alfred Hitchcock, who needed professionally to be right on the subject, put it that:

> I more or less base my idea of sexuality on northern European women. I think the northern Germans, the Scandinavians and the English are much sexier, although they don't look it, than those farther south – the Spaniards, the Italians. Even your typical Frenchwoman, the provocative one, is not the epitome of French sex. The girl who lives in the country, always wears black on Sunday, is guarded by her parents, wrapped in her family – that's your typical French girl, and it's nothing like what they give the tourists.[38]

'Nothing like what they give the tourists.' Many people quite unconnected with prostitution had a financial interest in boosting Paris as an erotic paradise. Obviously not all the male visitors were after Nesta Needham or Alice Howard or sex with anyone for that matter. Like the respectable family drawn to Monte Carlo described by Margaret Oliphant in her *Cornhill* article, people went to Paris not necessarily to join in the fun but to savour the titillation it provided. Maxime du Camp visualized the British back home again, sitting by their coal fires and holding boredom at bay by touching up their memories. They readily say of Paris that 'it's the most immoral city in the world and do not perceive that they are at least half the reason for the demoralisation with which they reproach us'. Looking back from 1919, Ernest Vizetelly, the son of Henry, a famous journalist and writer, made the same point in the preface to his book *Paris and her People*. The British, he said, wanted to see Paris as the city of frivolity, the world's favourite pleasure ground; they revel in its witticisms and 'spicy scandals'. In front of him, he writes, is a list of more than 70 books in English dealing with the frivolous side of Parisian life since the beginning of the Third Republic. Apart from ten or 12, they are all now absolutely dead, buried and forgotten.

John Stuart Mill believed that Frenchwomen were more active and more passionate than Englishwomen and that 'their energies are thus devoted in greater proportion than in England to rivalry with other women in dress, in love affairs, & in social success'. But many writers who knew France well doubted whether there was really more infidelity among the French than among the British. Some blamed the French novelists; the outside world took their lurid tales seriously, unaware that they let their imaginations loose, believing as they did that authentic representation would be dull. The irony was, as Hitchcock would assert, that French girls generally were brought up very strictly. One of the reasons that French and British did not mingle more was the reluctance of French mothers to encourage friendship between their respective daughters. To quote an article in the *Cornhill Magazine* attributed to E. C. Grenville Murray, the 'forwardness' and 'eccentricity' of English girls formed topics on which French mothers were never tired of expatiating. Indeed, French visitors to London remarked on the flirtatiousness of the girls. *'On est tutoyé par les regards des femmes'*, said one of them. (But it was agreed that once married, British girls – and American – became much more demure.)[39]

P. G. Hamerton, bilingual and married to a Frenchwoman, a man highly respected for his impartiality and judgement, devoted much of his life to analysing and explaining the differences between the two nations. It was particularly important, he wrote, to distinguish between behaviour in Paris and the country. He was careful to demolish some romantic ideas, denying for instance that the fine arts were beloved by all Frenchmen; they were, he said, more successfully cultivated in Manchester and Liverpool than in Rouen or Lyon. He insists that the two countries now – this in the late nineteenth century – view each other from quite different perspectives. France, he wrote, is very near to England, but England is as remote from France as some province in the heart of China. (One recalls Francis Wey's astonishment when he arrived in London.)[40] Another writer pointed out that while in England the stereotype of the typical frog-eating Frenchman had disappeared, in the café-concerts and music halls of France, the Briton was still portrayed in the old way, with long, flaming side whiskers and wearing a check costume.[41] A British writer during the Empire could say that 'no Frenchman knows anything about our history, our institutions, our manners, our economy or our position in the world. We loom upon them, as it were through a fog'.[42] That is not to say that anglophilia no longer existed; in fact, in high society, in the Faubourg St-Germain, it was commonplace: there was an enthusiasm that embraced 'five o'clock tea' with plenty of English words served up in the conversation. The Jockey Club, with its English associations, was as smart as ever. The Parisian anglophile, we are told, was likely to shake hands frequently – still regarded as a particularly English practice – and might even drop Bordeaux in favour of pale ale. But it seems superficial, and unreal, and certainly few French could speak English properly. In 1900 (that is during the Boer War when otherwise anti-Britishness was rife), Jean de la Poulaine in his book *L'Anglomanie* berated some of his fellow-countrymen for their anglomania which, he said, was worse than ever. But, he went on, few French anglophiles ever cross the Channel; they were not the sort of people anyway to suffer seasickness happily. If they do get to Britain they look only for the good. For the most part, asserts Poulaine, they are not people who welcome reality, and they are inclined to believe romantically in cottages along Piccadilly and in a Westminster surrounded by green fields and woodlands. And it does seem true, even when one recalls Mrs Waddington's life in the country, that few British by this time were to be found in Faubourg society. After all, none figures in Proust.

But anyway that was not very important. There is an old joke about anglophile Italians and italophile British; that they have nothing much to say to each other: the first want to talk about grouse shooting, the other about Piero della Francesca. If something of the same problem existed between French and British, it mattered little, for the fascination exerted by France, above all by Paris, on the British – and on many others as well – in the years following the Franco-Prussian war, owed little to individual friendships of the sort prevalent earlier in the century. If the appeal was particularly strong in the case of those interested in art and literature (and perhaps sex), it was broad enough to include a general public as well. Their numbers – and unfamiliarity with the French language – are reflected in the sales in Britain of conversation manuals. Five of these were published between 1850 and 1860, four between 1860 and 1880, but 24 between 1880 and 1890, and 17 between 1890 and 1900.[43] Then there was the architecture. Said Dickens of Paris, 'I don't know of any other place where there are all these high houses, all these haggard-looking wine shops, all these billiard tables ... all these dirty corners of streets'.[44] But now visitors, even if they were without any special acquaintance with architecture, could marvel at the magnificence of the new Paris created by Baron Haussmann with its wide, tree-lined boulevards, its great monuments such as the opera house, and that universal symbol of the city, the Eiffel Tower, completed in 1889.

This Paris was described by the Italian journalist Edmondo de Amicis as a 'vast gilded net, into which one is drawn again and again', which when you gaze on it at night 'seems like an immense display of fireworks'.[45]

An American, Richard H. Davis compared the difference in atmosphere to London:

> The crowd was strolling up and down the wide sidewalks. It was not one of those eager, breathless crowds that seem carried away in a vortex of business, such as one sees in London; it was composed of loungers who seemed to be walking about for their pleasure, who were cheering to the sight, and diffused, as it were, a feeling of happiness in the air.

This might almost be a description from the 1820s, when the little English girl quoted by Anna Jameson had pictured Parisians in the street as 'ladies and gentlemen going a visiting'. But with the wide sidewalks ('pavements' would not be the right word), the great sweep of Paris, the walker-about, the stroller, the *flâneur*, had taken on a new consequence, and seemed to many to epitomize the carefree quality of Parisian life. It went too with a sort of relaxed friendliness. In a street in London or New York, said Davis, you know virtually nothing of your neighbours, but in Paris people live in the street, or on their balconies or at their windows. We know what they are going to have for dinner, for we could see them carrying uncooked portions of it from the restaurant on the corner.[46]

Americans, wrote Davis in another context, go to London for social triumph or to float railroad shares, to Rome for the sake of art, and to Berlin to study music or to economize, but they go to Paris to enjoy themselves. And what of other cities? New York's time was yet to come. Vienna, like Paris, was cultivated and charming, but essentially defensive and 'somehow moving on the sidelines of European history'. Venice was unique and poetic, observed *Blackwood's Magazine*, but Paris possessed a more universal appeal – there is 'a certain breath of expectancy' about her. People came to learn how to live. George Moore may never have met an ordinary Parisian, or so it is said, but he believed that Paris would teach him not only how to paint but the meaning of life. Arnold Bennett, aged 30 non his first visit, came for the same reason, persuaded by his reading of Zola and Maupassant that here was to be found the 'authentic' atmosphere he required in order to develop into a realistic, genuinely modern writer. That is, he was to be persuaded by the very people, or some of the very people, who were accused of giving so false a view of French sexual morality. No wonder he found it difficult to sort out the truth when he did arrive.[47] People came to Paris to buy, to enjoy, what

Charles Frederick Worth had termed the 'unnecessary and the frivolous'. It provided the shops, it was the hub of women's fashion – but not men's, that was London's role – it was the home of *haute cuisine*, and of the arts, not just painting and sculpture, but also serious theatre and modern music. By 1900 France was a pioneer of cinema, a leader in the development of automobiles and, a few years on, in aircraft design. French men and women were making a formidable contribution to scientific advance.

There was extraordinary energy in the air and so much to enjoy. The British writer Arthur Symons insisted on the need for discrimination. Paris was indeed the most 'recreative' of all places for a holiday, but not the Paris familiar to the English tourist. Symons was not at all a 'conversation manual' sort of person. He allows the Champs-Elysées to be of some interest, and the Grands Boulevards as well, but they are cosmopolitan Paris, not the real thing. That is to be found in the Latin Quarter, on the Left Bank of the Seine, and in Montmartre, to the north of central Paris, at its most exuberant in the last 30 years of the century. In the 1870s, Montmartre remained in some ways the village on a hill that it had been before its annexation by the great city. But while cows still grazed among the windmills on its slopes, the character of the place was not at all bucolic. This was Paris at its most carefree, creative – and louche.[48] There are several notable British associations with Montmartre. In the 1830s, Hector Berlioz and his British actress wife Harriet Smithson had lived in the Rue du Mont-Cenis, and in the 1840s a rich coal owner from County Durham, John Bowes, withdrawing from a respectable political career in Britain, emigrated to France, joined the Jockey Club and bought a controlling interest in the fashionable and popular *Théâtre des Variétés* on the Boulevard Montmartre. The venture failed expensively, but Bowes married one of the actresses and with her formed a magnificent art collection which is now housed in the Bowes Museum at Barnard Castle.[49] The most significant association, however, was that of George Moore who, according to Philippe Jullian in his study of the district, provides the best account of Montmartre in its Impressionist days. (Manet in fact painted a watercolour of Moore at the café, the Nouvelle Athènes in the Place Pigalle.)

It was Moore's *Confessions of a Young Man*, published in 1888, that brought in the British visitors, not the people disdained by Arthur Symons so much as Anglo-Saxon Bohemia – artists, libertines and people who just enjoyed the music hall and cabaret shows. Visitors included the Prince of Wales, Oscar Wilde and Frank Harris. If you were looking for something close to home, you could listen to the Irish May Belfort running through her Franco-British repertoire, and, at the Moulin Rouge, Yvette Guilbert singing

'Miss Valerie', a song about an English maid preyed on by old men. Or 'La Valse des pantalons' which celebrated a pair of trousers – very English; not easy to wear; not attractive; but who cares; for on stage they are so fashionable. Hardly – that particular song – great art. But it had about it something of the originality which distinguished Montmartre, which inspired something more than ordinary music hall fare, and gave an immediacy to the music, a distinctive rendering of popular song that, over 50 or 60 years later, through performers such as Chevalier and Piaf, would touch the world's imagination. Montmartre itself would stay, indeed does still stay, in the mind as the very image of Paris in the *Belle Epoque*, idealized or traduced in films such as Minnelli's *An American in Paris* (1951), Huston's *Moulin Rouge* (1952), Becker's *Casque d'Or* (1955), Jean Renoir's *French Cancan* (1956) and more recently in Luhrmann's *Moulin Rouge!* Most hauntingly it survives in Toulouse-Lautrec's incomparable paintings and sketches of the Moulin Rouge. Sometimes he glamorizes. The circus clown Chocolat is transformed into an underworld dandy; the dancer Valentin Le Désossé, nothing very special in looks, appears on occasion as a sinister, almost macabre presence. As to the famous La Goulue – from photographs she looks just blowzy.[50]

But sometimes with Lautrec the magic vanishes, is replaced by the starkest realism in portraits of absinthe- and morphine-ridden, deviant Montmartre. A Paris in miniature. For many writers noted the brittleness, an underlying sadness, a sense of doom even. This astonishing city, wrote G. A. Sala, 'where no one thinks of to-morrow until to-morrow comes with a roar and a rush, such as those that whelmed the cities of the plain'. Roger Shuttock in his book *The Banquet Years* sees the Paris of the time as a stage, as a vast theatre for herself and for everyone else. And foreigners might be struck by Zelda Fitzgerald's perception of Paris, two or three decades later, when she wrote to her husband Scott that:

Paris comes to us second-hand. Our imagination has been there first, worked upon by the imagination of others. It is through the filter of their memories, desires, dreams, descriptions, lies, gossip that we experience the city.[51]

9

The Atlantic Coast

Runaway debtors, condemned bankrupts, false money makers, cashiered officers, discarded mistresses, poor widows of all ages and degrees of respectability, outlawed bachelors, rips of parsons, ... divorced wives, and conniving husbands.
Sir George Lefevre on the English at Dieppe in 1843

Perhaps the most enjoyable description by a Briton of living in provincial France during the nineteenth century was written by the Scottish Elizabeth Smith, born Grant, who in India had married Colonel Smith of the East India Company and proprietor of Baltiboys, a 1,200-acre estate 20 miles south of Dublin. Her journal, published – very posthumously – in 1996 as *A Highland Lady in France, 1843–1845*, has a distinctive flavour. For one thing, India is seldom far away. Colonel Smith has retired, but her father, a judge, is still there, as are her two brothers, both employed by the Company. (One of them was to become Lieutenant General of Bengal and Governor of Jamaica.) Elizabeth is intelligent and reflective, and during much of her life a contributor to *Chambers's Edinburgh Journal*. She follows the ups and downs of Irish politics closely, and takes a sceptical and often critical view of the English. The Smiths' reasons for their exile (as she regarded it) were commonplace: to economize by living for two years on Colonel Smith's pension while accumulating money from renting out the Irish estate; and to bring about an improvement in the Colonel's health. The money they saved was to be spent on alterations to the Irish property.[1]

So in the summer of 1843, the family – themselves, two daughters aged about 12 and 13, a son Jack aged 5 – set off for Pau where they were to join Elizabeth's youngest sister Mary Gardiner, also married to an old India hand who was very ill indeed. With them they took a governess, the housekeeper from Baltiboys (an old retainer of the Grant family), a man-servant and a cook. Accompanying them too was a bachelor, Colonel Litchfield, again from India. The association with India keeps recurring, be it in terms of the people they meet or the places they pass through. On the road from Bordeaux to Pau, for example, Elizabeth judged the dwellings of the poor (their 'cabins' as she put it) to be very Irish in the country but 'quite Indian' in the towns. Mont-de-Marsan, in effect the capital of the Landes, is described as a good town in the Indian style. At Pau, the days, though not at all the nights, are another reminder of India. The heat in the Garonne estuary she rates as worse than that of India.

At first, Elizabeth Smith has little good to say of Pau; still 'one can be happy anywhere so I will make the best of Pau'. A number of 'old Indians' turn up, and so does the Reverend Francis Trench, whose arrival takes Colonel Smith to church in the hope of hearing him preach. Mary Gardiner's health, though, is worse than ever, and she is kept going on drink and drugs. Moreover, she and her husband, driven by despair and boredom, are people who are always on the move, forever searching out some new spa. They decide on Avranches in Normandy where, after a short holiday in the Pyrenees, the Smiths, with Colonel Litchfield in tow, join them.

It was a poor choice. At much the same time John Hobbs, John Ruskin's valet (also in effect his secretary), left this account of the British at Avranches:

> It is amusing . . . to see the English, endeavouring to be taken for French and not of their own country, mustachios, beards, clothes cut to match as near as possible, but it's no use, anyone at all practised can see through them in a moment and when they are found out they talk of their chateaux and forests here, as big and as majestic as they possibly can, but in general they have a broken down, shabby genteel appearance about them, not at all the thing.[2]

The Smiths arrived only four years after the death of Beau Brummell at Caen. But there is in Elizabeth Smith not a trace of the raffish spirit of the Regency. She is already Victorian through and through. The world of my childhood, she says, and the period of my decline in life – she is in her forties – are a thousand years apart, in the immense material improvement, in the progress of science and, far more important, in the progress of virtue. She hears of someone she has known since childhood, a man of good background who threw his money away and ruined himself and his family – 'a common tale of the last age; I firmly believe that few such belong to this better era', is her comment. She comforts herself that now in Britain and in France there is no longer room for drones in the hive; they have had their day and will have to change their nature or go. The trouble was that a good many of the British drones appeared already to have gone – to Avranches. While an immediate and respectable neighbour, also an 'Indian', turns out to have been at school with Colonel Smith, Elizabeth was at once confronted by a number of highly doubtful persons.

Dr Pollard, her sister's doctor, for one. She likened him to Mr Quilp in Dickens's *The Old Curiosity Shop*. The 'doctor' seems to have been honorary, self-awarded. Though he had run a lunatic asylum in England, he had, so it was alleged, never practised medicine. 'A vile little man', Elizabeth called him, worse than tipsy, who fell down in the street. Phantoms emerge from the past. There was Mrs Turnbull, once the wife of a well-connected captain of a frigate who many years back had run off with the then dashing (but now quiet and grave and old) Lieutenant Turnbull. She is very ugly, but she has charm, conceded Elizabeth, and nobody here knows of her past. She would be terribly humiliated should the two of them happen to meet. While Elizabeth had a soft spot for Mrs Turnbull, she felt only loathing for another old acquaintance, Sandy Grant, 'the agent of my father's ruin, the mismanager of all his electioneering matters, who lined his pockets well, and lived and throve for a while on deceit and falsehoods'. Having run through his wife's money, he had represented himself as the elder brother of Elizabeth's father in order to raise funds. She recognized him instantly; how could she not, she said, when in her youth she had carried him tea in the study at Lincoln's Inn Fields where he and her father spent their evenings concocting electioneering schemes.*

Altogether Elizabeth Smith finds Avranches an odious place, though she likes what she sees of the local French, having in mind particularly the old legitimist nobility who live in the neighbourhood, people at odds with the Orleanist regime and rather impoverished. They are apparently well inclined towards the British. Still, since there is no time to cultivate their acquaintance, the Smiths are stuck with their fellow countrymen. No one has better expressed than Elizabeth Smith the monotony and pointlessness of this expatriate life. She records one dinner party, typical enough it seems, without music or conversation, though with plenty of wine. After dinner, the drawing room is filled with card tables, and those who are not playing – ladies as well as gentlemen – wander about jingling their purses and calling each other by nicknames. And then, Colonel Smith's asthma has worsened, although, so she claims, smoking his pipe does manage to hold it at bay. He gets no exercise at all beyond a walk from their house to the reading room, and then settles on a game or two of billiards and lots of drink. (According to one British expatriate, billiards and newspapers consume all the time of the English when they are not eating or drinking.)[3] Elizabeth's nerves are in a bad way.

I sometimes feel growing crazy, my head quite confused and temper souring. And that abominable husband of mine shaves away as unconcerned, two or

* Her father had only gone to India when all else failed.

three hours at the careful toilette, two or three more at his billiards, and then he
eats with the appetite of a school-boy . . .

A friend writes, suggesting they move to Florence. Colonel Litchfield is
restless and would like to leave. And Mary had died. Why then stay on;
would it not be sensible to modify their original plan and go back to Ireland
early? What held the Smiths in Normandy for a month or two longer was a
reluctance to interrupt the education of their two daughters and of the
Gardiner children. For one thing, it was important to learn the language.
Elizabeth was scathing about the narrowness of boys' education at home,
declaring that the neglect of modern languages in English education, 'certainly the most necessary of all the means of advancement in life', was
unpardonable. And she was irritated by the fact that neither her husband
(although he had served in the army of occupation after Waterloo) nor
Colonel Litchfield could speak French and made no effort to learn it. She
herself did speak French; for girls it was considered a necessary
accomplishment.

Schools for foreigners made a useful contribution to the economy of
north-west France, though they did not always deliver what was promised in
the prospectus or in an advertisement in *The Times*. On one occasion, the
British consul in Boulogne was reprimanded by the Foreign Secretary, Lord
Palmerston, for failing properly to investigate the facts behind a scandal
over a school run by a Monsieur de Brée where the boys were starved and
frozen, and kept in filthy conditions.[4] And Thackeray had depicted the
Reverend Mr Snodgrass's academy where the boys were shut away and saw
nobody but the French usher and the cook. Dickens, though, gave a very
different impression in an article he wrote for *Household Words* in May 1857
entitled 'Our Boys and Girls'. There are, he stated, schools catering for
foreign boys and girls scattered all over northern France, though they are
concentrated around the Channel ports. At the time he wrote, there were no
less than 120 boarding schools in Boulogne frequented by British pupils,
though some no doubt were very small. Pupils, Dickens said, live in roomy
mansions with names like Victoria House and Britannia House and are
escorted to and from London by masters and mistresses. Parents like Elizabeth Smith, keen for boys to learn French and with a low opinion of
British public schools – 'sinks of vice' in her words – might well be attracted.
Girls were instructed in deportment; fencing, riding lessons, gymnastics
might be on the syllabus. Pupils were often children of parents living in
India or some other distant part of the Empire; some were orphans who
remained at their French school all the year round. While Dickens did not
recommend the French schools for those seeking aristocratic contacts or

double-firsts at university, he considered them effective as crammers for an ordinary university place and for the military academies of Woolwich and Sandhurst. And these schools could claim one striking advantage over their counterparts at home, in that the French state imposed standards which were enforced through a strict system of inspection. Monsieur de Brée's academy was likely to be more of an exception than the real-life equivalent of Dickens's Dotheboys Hall. And, as George Augustus Sala bore witness, flogging was very rare.

There were some good reasons for visiting Normandy and the Pas-de-Calais region to the north. For one thing they were easily accessible, and for another the scenery of Normandy at any rate was appealing. John Sell Cotman went to Avranches, not for the social life, but to paint the Mont-St-Michel, seven or eight miles away across the shifting sands, a great rock surmounted by a castle, standing out to sea, an island at high tide. Cotman was fascinated – any painter of the Romantic period would have been – as he gazed at this 'gigantic vision' through the driving rain. The French greatly admired the British Romantic painters, who spent a good deal of time working in Normandy and Brittany, with Turner for instance painting in and around Rouen, Dieppe, St-Malo, Brest, Granville, Nantes, Avranches and the Mont-St-Michel. Bonington, who shared a Paris studio with Delacroix, painted in many of the same places. Everyone liked Bonington, wrote Delacroix to a friend many years later; none of the modern school before him possessed his particular lightness of touch, above all in water-colours. And Constable's paintings struck the French by their 'vivacity and freshness'. 'What an interesting collection could be put together of French landscapes as seen through English eyes: the rivers of France by Turner, Versailles by Bonington ... ', so wrote Proust in the preface to his trans-lation of Ruskin's *The Bible of Amiens*.[5]

Cotman provided a lively and appreciative description of Normandy in letters to his wife and to his friend and patron, the banker and antiquary Dawson Turner.[6] He made three journeys, in 1815, 1817 and 1820, equipped with a 'camera lucida, the latest aid to drawing in perspective'. There were problems. Once, when he climbed a church wall to get a better view, he was arrested as a Protestant missionary. He was arrested again, this time on the implausible suspicion that he was an Englishman mixed up in a recent conspiracy in Paris. At St-Lô, men, women and boys clustered round him while he was sketching the cathedral and cracked 'coarse jokes'. Nevertheless he was enchanted by the landscape. 'What a lovely country! Everything is picturesque' ... 'Nothing even as to colour can be seen in England like it.' He delighted in the forests and the meadows, and in the commons between Domfront and Mortain, covering more than 100 acres, which he depicted as being of a most beautiful green and, as in England, speckled with cattle of every description. And there were the close lanes, the hills and dales – 'in short everything a painter could wish for'. (The weather too he found a bit like England, with February fogs in July.) It was not just the landscape that was so appealing. At the Hôtel de Londres in Dieppe the catch singers outside in the street were altogether superior to those at home. And the plumber at work in the hotel sang with all the 'majesty of a Nobleman'.

There was then much to make British visitors feel at home. Moreover, they were conscious of historical, even racial, affinities. William the Conqueror was buried at Caen; the heart of Richard the Lionheart was interred at Rouen. The Normans themselves were considered to possess a congenial gravity; they were, thought one visitor, hardly French at all, they were less frivolous. Cotman compared Normandy's place in France to that of Yorkshire or Northumberland in England. It also tended to be cheaper than many parts of France; prices at Avranches were lower than at Pau, for example. It had its wild side. A British visitor in 1829 reported the neighbourhood of Alençon to be plagued by bands of arsonists who emerged at night to burn down farm buildings. (It was suspected that they were in the pay of insurance companies intent on persuading people to buy fire policies.) Grave robbers were rampant; so much so that it was customary to send home the bodies of British who died in Normandy.[7]

But Normandy was the modern world when compared to its neighbour Brittany, a province of France much less well known to the British and, indeed, to most French. It was famous for remarkable prehistoric sites, above all that of Carnac, for ancient legends and for 'ill-washed' bards. Even in the 1880s, by which time many of the old Celtic monuments had been destroyed by farmers, legends of strange happenings, the appearance of ghostly mules, the sound of tinkling fog-bells, all luring travellers to destruction, were still fresh in the memory. The coast was exceptionally beautiful but the weather resembled that of western Ireland, the hotels were awful and the railways inadequate – though it was a consolation to some that the Bretons were held to be untainted by revolution and civil discord. But in terms of civilization, *Murray's Guide* at mid-century declared Brittany to lag behind any other region of France. Another guide warned visitors not to expect to find any quiet villages fit for ladies and children.[8]

As was to be expected, Brittany was cheap; and stayed cheap, one reason being the discomfort of the sea journey from Southampton. C. T. Bidwell in his *The Cost of Living Abroad* of 1876 pronounced that one part of the province, the western department of Finistère that included Brest, Quimper and Roscoff, was probably the cheapest region, not just of France but of Europe. The journalist Henry Vizetelly came across two English spinsters at Dinan who had been compelled to abandon Tours by the rise in prices brought about by the influx of English residents. Since then they had wandered from place to place, finding each eventually too expensive. One of them said sadly to Vizetelly that the only place left to them was the mountains of the Auvergne. Then there was the British colony at St-Servan, a township now more or less incorporated into St-Malo. Its members, said Vizetelly who, with his wife, took a house there during 1868 and 1869, were 'distressingly poor'. Some were the familiar rejects from home, some Irish landlords driven abroad by fear of 'moonlighters'; and many, like the spinsters, migrants, in their case from Jersey. But St-Servan was no Avranches, the spirit was quite different; for these were proud people determined to maintain their dignity. The main reason for this, no doubt, was a contingent of colonels, the great feature of the colony, stated Vizetelly, men with gallant war records and troops of marriageable daughters, some rather good-looking, who studied tactics as fervently as their fathers had done, but in their case with the view not 'of taking any town or fortress, but of capturing one or other of the few eligible young Englishmen that the colony comprised'.[9]

On the other hand, Dinard, a few miles away, housed a prosperous British community. A number of well-regarded families were established there – Fosters, Forbes, Stevensons, Norths, Fabers – the most notable inhabitant being Lt Colonel Hamilton, an officer who had greatly distinguished himself in the Crimea. On first seeing the house that he had commissioned at Dinard, the Colonel was so startled by its convoluted layout and the mass of bits and pieces lying around that he called out 'My God, what a Bric-à-Brac!' And 'Bric-à-Brac' was what he called the house, and the name which the British community at Dinard then applied to their quarter of the town.[10]

Still, it was in the north that resorts multiplied most rapidly; by the 1870s, the coast from Trouville to Boulogne formed a chain of holiday places. Rosa Baughan in her *The Northern Watering Places of France* of 1880 listed dozens, many with names that meant nothing to most people then or now. Here is a sample: Ambleteuse, Berck-sur-Mer, Crotoy, Bourg d'Ault, Villers-sur-Mer, Veulettes, Cayeux, Lion-sur-Mer. The guide is very helpful, full of useful information about prices and the particular characteristics of each resort. Ambleteuse for instance is described as picturesque, appealing for those wishing to sketch, and with a wide and safe beach suitable for children, who may relish the tumbledown fort and the chance to play with the numerous French children they are likely to meet there. Hotels are listed and sometimes boarding houses; at Boulogne, for example, the author recommends Mr Howe in the Rue du Collège who boards families. She warns that at Cabourg and Villers-sur-Mer the society is thoroughly French. Virtually everywhere there is a casino, the centre of its social life and not necessarily concerned with gambling. The casino may be right on the beach and very simple, built of wood as at Houlgate, though it can usually be counted on for occasional theatrical entertainments, concerts and balls. The casino at the more fashionable Tréport contained an authentic ballroom, a reading room, a gymnasium, and 'gallery' in which to sit. This last was the more important since even at the smarter resorts the hotels often lacked salons. Deauville, Dieppe and Trouville notwithstanding, this was not the Riviera. Etretat, reasonably fashionable and charging prices on the same scale as Brighton and Scarborough, sounds less than lavish with its entertainments. Three times a week a blond young man in a white necktie played waltzes on the piano, but, 'the young ladies of France not being permitted to dance in public places' – though, in company of their mamas, they might sit and watch – 'the burden of gaiety is sustained by three or four rosy English maidens and as many of their American sisters'. Some places were trying to punch above their weight. Henry James in his *Portraits of Places* singles out Yport, which, he says, without much help from nature seems determined to be in fashion, even though she possesses only a meagre little wood at the back and an evil-smelling beach where bathing is possible only at the highest tide. Everything is on a Lilliputian scale, he adds.[11]

The resort above all associated with the British was Dieppe. It was the landing place for Thomas Cook's excursionists for one thing. Educationally it was important, specializing in schools for English young ladies – in the case of the academy run by the snobbish and hard-drinking Miss Cannick, rather grand young ladies. Walter Sickert (whose mother had been educated in Dieppe at Mrs Slee's academy for girls) studied at the Collège Jehan Ango, a school for mixed nationalities where the foreign boys slept in a separate wing, supervised by an English couple. Dieppe had long been famous for its sea-bathing. The future Napoleon III, aged four, had bathed there in 1812, and in the 1820s the Duchesse de Berry, the young widow of the assassinated heir to the throne, had been an ardent bather who had attracted to the town some of the most aristocratic families of France. It was attractive architecturally, with particular appeal to painters. In the early nineteenth century, Turner, Cotman and Bonington had worked there, and towards the end of the century, due mainly to Jacques-Emile Blanche, a Dieppe householder, visitors included Degas, Renoir, Monet, Pissarro and Whistler. Notwithstanding its popularity with the British, the atmosphere was emphatically French. In fact that was part of its attraction to the British, who formed a numerous and diverse resident community. Some were grandees – part-time residents – of whom the most eminent was the Marquess of Salisbury, the Prime Minister, who built himself a house, half-Swiss chalet, half-Gothic castle, on the cliffs two miles out of the town. The Prince of Wales, arriving by yacht, visited his god-daughter and her mother the Duchesse Caraciolo. Another well-connected resident was Lady Blanche Hozier, an obsessive gambler and mother-in-law of Winston Churchill. Along with the painters were writers and actors, some occasional visitors, some frequent. Walter Sickert for instance is said to have been seldom without a house or a room in Dieppe over a period of 30 years. Others were Max Beerbohm, Oscar Wilde and Aubrey Beardsley. George Moore came, and actors John Barrymore, Marie Tempest and Constance Collier, who was briefly engaged to Beerbohm. Henry James told Blanche that 'your Dieppe is a reduced Florence, every type of character for a novel seems to gather there'.[12]

Then there were the usual refugees, the people in difficulties or actual disgrace at home. Above all, there was Oscar Wilde who arrived in May 1897 immediately on release from Reading Gaol. It was not a success; British tourists ostentatiously left cafés when he came in, old friends like Sickert ignored or snubbed him. But admittedly Wilde played it up with a raucous dinner for a deputation of young French poets which led to a warning from the local sub-prefect advising more discretion. He moved on to the tiny village of Berneval-sur-Mer, ten miles away, which he liked, but by September was off again.[13] The 'respectable British' of Dieppe were careful people who, in Simona Pakenham's words, 'affected not to know about the numbers of their countrymen who had been lodged in the prison for unpaid debts, or who had their possessions auctioned on the pavement'. Tourists too could be an embarrassment: local French swimmers found it profitable to hang about the quays to rescue drunks who had fallen into the water. Most of the British were neither drunks nor in trouble, they were just unoccupied people who usually for financial reasons found it practicable to live at Dieppe. For some, though, the life could turn melancholy and demoralizing. In 1927 Blanche published a book about Dieppe dedicated to Walter Sickert, of whom he would later write that 'no other artist has so perfectly felt and expressed the character of the town'.

There were unoccupied French also in Dieppe. Blanche instances Parisians in exile to save money or for reasons of health, and elderly widows, at a loose end once the bathing season was over, dreaming of seasons past and those to come. He concentrates, though, on the frustrated British of before 1914. *Epaves*, he calls them, 'flotsam', killing time, waiting for something, anything, to happen. At midday they go to fetch their newspaper in the

Place du Puits-Salé, at three o'clock they wait at the end of the pier for the steamer from England, or run to the port to watch those lucky enough to be leaving. All of them, whether at Dieppe through their own fault or through other necessity, await deliverance, some substitute for flight, some tiny accident, some catastrophe even. They pass the winter without books, without parties, even without teas except at the pastry shop or with the parson's wife. Always the same faces, the same conversation, up and down the Grande Rue morning and afternoon, sunshine or rain, and in the evening on the unlit seafront. They go down to the shops to buy fish; they climb back again; they go down once more for the paper, or some needles, or to see whether the English biscuits have arrived at the grocer's. They promise themselves they will go away next winter, to Malaga, Cairo, Liverpool. Perhaps they do get eight days at home over Christmas, and return full of memories, the smell of London clinging to their clothes, with picture magazines for their compatriots back in France, and chat about the 'review' at the Alhambra and the latest musical comedy.

The Channel coast was early connected by rail to Paris, significantly sooner than the Riviera or the Pyrenees. In August 1848 the line to Dieppe was opened. A journey which by fast coach drawn by a team of horses had taken 12 hours now took half that time. A few years later and it was a matter of four hours. The railway promoted the idea of the weekend, if initially in a rather abbreviated form. Wives and children, holidaying on the coast, could be joined by husbands travelling on the *train jaune* which left Paris on Saturday night and returned on Monday morning. Steadily the trains, with restaurant cars and salons added, became more luxurious.[14] Money and fashion arrived. Henry Vizetelly in the late 1860s had witnessed the rather incongruous effect at Trouville, as he 'watched the stylish visitors who paraded the sands in piquant and costly costumes – the latest inspiration of crack Paris *couturiers*'. Parisian *élégantes* descended the steps of the church after Mass, 'while Norman crones in tasselled night caps and maidens in more picturesque headgear scanned them with open mouths and curious eyes'. Trouville was a good example of a town ascending the social scale, as was its immediate neighbour Deauville, constructed on the marshes by the Emperor's half-brother, the Duc de Morny, aided by his friend and doctor the Irish Sir Joseph Olliffe. Bertall in his *La Vie hors de chez Soi* declared that the railways had made the Norman coast 'veritable *faubourgs* of Paris'. Trouville itself was described as 'a well-aired quarter of Paris recommended by doctors in the months of July and August'.

Wealthier British were attracted to the smart resorts, to Deauville for example, with its horse racing, above all the Grand Prix for which Parisians arrived in special trains. There was pigeon shooting with pistol or carbine, duck shooting, polo, golf, tennis and yachting regattas. Interests and habits were converging. French enthusiasm for sport was an example, the idea of holidays another. A lecturer in Paris in 1880 pointed out that until recently no one in France left his native town in summer, people stayed in Paris all the year round. Now, 'if we don't take the waters, we go to the seaside or to Italy'. Socially speaking, a break from home was compulsory.[15] The coastal resorts provided fertile ground for the turn-of-the-century anglophilia. Marcel Boulenger along with helpful hints on how to behave, how to seduce a young girl or a woman of the world, and how to cope should you be caught cheating at cards, explained what to do if a friend discovered you in Paris in August. Speak very quickly, he advised, almost panting:

> Excuse me, I'm in a terrible rush with hardly an hour to spare in your Paris. I've just come from Dieppe where I went on leaving Deauville. I'm off now to Dinard and then to Biarritz and on to England. Goodbye, do forgive me, my train leaves in twenty-five minutes.

And when you actually do get to a beach, at Deauville, Biarritz or wherever, here is how you impress a snob. Start off with 'Good Morning, dear' – in English – and go on to complain about walking in the country what with the cowpats and the dust on the roads thrown up by cars. 'Ah', you say, 'it's not like that in England'.[16] The layout of the grounds to the Hôtels des Bains, we are told, was 'invariably' in the English style, and from around 1900 the hotels themselves were given names like The Modern Hotel or The Select Hotel.

By then, sea-bathing was more or less universally popular. Originally, despite the Duchesse de Berry at Dieppe, it had been more closely associated with health than with pleasure. The Channel resorts, with their excellent sandy beaches, advertised themselves (as in the case of Trouville) as spas of one sort or another. British doctors were much in evidence, hastening to leave their cards on new arrivals from home. There were specialists, French and British. English girls crossed to Boulogne for the services of Dr Charles Dunand, a specialist in the delivery of inopportune babies. Many women came to Boulogne or the other resorts because they actually wanted children, for bathing in the sea was recommended as a cure for sterility. Allegedly it was helpful too in alleviating constipation and as an antidote for the effects of bites by dogs or other animals. But caution was imperative. At one stage doctors advised against sea-bathing for those aged over 40. Preferably, bathing should take place between noon and 6 p.m. and not within three or four hours of a meal. And bathers should not stay in the water for more than a quarter of an hour at a time. All this advice could be confusing and contradictory: the British author of a book called *Tips for Travellers*, published as late as 1900, insisted that the safest time to bathe was after breakfast, and then only if your body was warm. Paddling by children was undesirable, since it made their feet cold and sent blood to the head. The beach itself was often intended less for bathing or sunbathing than as somewhere from which to admire the view, perhaps to watch the fishing boats and to inhale the wonderful sea air. (Though not too much of that: many expensive villas were built facing away from the sea to avoid the excessive humidity of the air.)[17]

But whatever the persisting reservations on the part of doctors, Henry James could report that the French love their beaches and take their bathing very seriously. They were, he added, excellent swimmers. Even he enjoyed the informalities of beach life, the opportunity to wear old clothes and canvas shoes. To Mr T. J. Hutchinson, the author of *Summer Holidays in Brittany*, sea-bathing was enjoyable because it was naturally so informal, so free of bothers about 'deportment' and 'proprieties', so unconcerned with the 'trammels of society'. Ladies got sunburnt and did not mind, said James. Indeed, matters went too far for some tastes. A British newspaper, published in Boulogne, complained about dress standards on the beach, declaring indecency to be the order of the day and that men's bathing dress amounted to nothing more than 'a few inches of rag'. The authorities, it claimed crossly, declined to intervene.[18]

But it would be a mistake to imagine that the Norman coast, let alone the Breton coast, of the late nineteenth century was an extended and anticipatory version of mid-twentieth-century St-Tropez. Hannah Lynch wrote in *Blackwood's* in 1899 that to the French a woman should be 'perpetually arrayed in the garments of seduction'. (A deep tan in those days was not considered fetching.) Certainly, there is nothing casual about beachwear in the paintings of Eugène Boudin, or in photographs, where the women seem dressed for Paris and the men wear top hats or bowlers and carry dark umbrellas.

According to *Dress Outfits for Abroad*, published 20 years after Henry James's tour, there was a vast distinction between *pension* life in 'quiet nooks' and the fashionable hotels. At the smart Norman resorts, clothes were changed two or three times a day. No one had a choice if they looked for acceptance into a society described by Bertall as one in which everybody was after someone: bankers and financiers were 'fishing' for foreign clients, and women on the hunt for sons-in-law, husbands or lovers. Grenville Murray in a skit on a small but fashionable resort he called 'Dip-sur-Mer', observed that holidaying there 'necessitated rather more dressing than in London, [and] infinitely more small talk than in Paris'. At Cannes, Nice and

Monte Carlo, standards were yet more exigent, with 'toilets' changed at all hours of the day. You are warned that the most elaborate petticoats are to be seen, and smart parasols, and that at the height of the season you will need fancy dress for the numerous balls.

An obvious difference between the Channel coast and the Riviera was the timing of the season: for the first it was in summer, for the other in winter. Biarritz, on the Atlantic coast close to the Spanish border, was a hybrid. The British – originally there to escape increasing rents in Pau – went to Biarritz in winter and spring, the French and Spanish during summer and early autumn. While this great resort lacked what Henry James called the 'superabundant detail' and softness of the Riviera, its climate was warmer than further north. Its beaches were sandy and its seas formidable and testing. Alexandre de la Cerda in his *La Tournée des Grand-Ducs* describes bathing at Biarritz for women and children. Taken in hand by a solidly built Basque professional, you were set down, your back towards the onrushing waves. The professional held your hand as a torrent of foaming, green water bucketed down, knocking your feet from under you. After a dozen of these somersaults, the professional, gleaming like a seal, led you, gasping for breath, shivering and crumpled, over the beach to 'an unforgettable old woman with grey hairs on her chin' who handed over a bathing robe and led you to a little cabin for rubbing down.

The Biarritz air was highly regarded and recommended for those who found Pau too relaxing. 'Old Indians', like Colonel Smith (though he personally was too early on the scene to go there) found the climate helpful for the sort of ailments from which they often suffered. Prosper Mérimée and his close friend Anthony Panizzi, the celebrated librarian of the British Museum, made ill by the waters at Bagnères-de-Bigorre, recovered at Biarritz. Victor Hugo, a visitor in 1843, adored what was still a straggling village with forests descending to the sea, and a coast lined with huge cliffs. He feared that it was too good to last, that fashion would take over. It did, ten years later, when the Empress Eugénie, partly because her native Spain was so close, fell in love with the village and built herself a spacious villa. In 1861, Mérimée, staying with the Empress, announced that the beach was crowded with people of all nations, and with women of every level of society and virtue, and that the place resembled a Carnival ball.[19]

The Empress was by nature charitable, and indeed at Eaux-Bonnes she established a refuge for soldiers and the poor who needed access to the waters. However, she had no intention of allowing Biarritz to be given over to invalids; it was to be 'a place for society' and she vetoed the establishment there of a clinic for the treatment of scrofulous children. The Empire fell, the Imperial villa survived, later on to be replaced after a fire, by the sumptuous Hôtel du Palais. The spirit was unchanged – it was still a place for high society. The people who go to Biarritz, commented Bertall, are those whose fortunes are already made. The Imperial family was replaced, at least partially, by sovereigns and princes from abroad: the ex-king of Hanover and his daughter; Queen Victoria in 1889; the King of Spain. The Russian Grand Dukes came to prefer this Atlantic resort even to Cannes, building there a magnificent church.[20]

It was in the years immediately before the First World War that Biarritz reached the peak of its success. By the 1880s, the British, less inclined towards Pau, turned in increasing numbers to Biarritz and nearby St-Jean-de-Luz. 'Nowhere else except in Pall Mall, the Champs-Elysées, or our own Fifth Avenue will you see so many beautiful motor cars in a single day as you will find here in April or September', observed the American Walter Hale at Biarritz in 1914.[21] One reason, perhaps the most important, was the presence at the Hôtel du Palais each March during his last years of King Edward VII, who brought with him a substantial entourage that included Mrs Keppel and Sir Ernest Cassel. Fashionable British who could afford it bought or rented a house at Biarritz as well as at Monte Carlo. It was a resort, so the King found, which allowed him more relaxation than was possible on the Riviera. Nevertheless he did not just rest, for he worked steadily at his desk for most of the morning. Afternoons were usually spent on expeditions by car into the countryside. The King loved cars and he loved speed. Once, after visiting Pau to watch a flight by Wilbur Wright, he insisted that his team of four cars drive back at such speed that every one of them shed fittings, lamps, bolts, nuts along the bumpy road. He loved noise too: his 'motor engineer' C. W. Stamper discovered in Biarritz a particularly noisy horn, comparable to one owned by the Kaiser. He could not, he said, blow it often enough to satisfy the King. (The police chief Xavier Paoli, responsible for the security of visiting foreign potentates – and a great admirer of Edward VII – said that 'a king abroad is something like a schoolboy on his holidays'.)[22]

The King was of course far from unique. Walter Hale in his *Ideal Motor Tour in France*, a book intended for British and American motorists, criticized the Americans for 'burning up' the roads between the historic towns of Europe, intent as they were on covering as much ground as possible each day. The ideal tour, Hale considered, would allow for stops of a day or two at Tours, Biarritz, Luchon, Marseille, Nice, Aix-les-Bains and Nancy. Tours, that old favourite of the British, on the main road southward and natural centre for excursions to the Loire *châteaux*, was a town revived by the car. The car, says Hale, has made it the rendezvous for fashionable tourists from all over the world. The Hôtel de l'Univers, recently just a good provincial inn, is now on a level with the better hotels of Paris and London.

The bicycle had given a glimpse of the possibilities of modern travel, but motoring was a revelation. The British Max Pemberton recalled a tour he made by car in the very early days, probably around 1900, driving south to Bordeaux:

> No sooner had we left Versailles behind us than we seemed to enter upon a great avenue, vastly wide, superb in its surface, everywhere bordered by acacias in full bloom; and this road, with scarce a break in its magnificence, was the one which carried us to the Garonne. If there were any criticism to be offered, it was that of the rural desolation, so marked, so weird, that, in the end, we seemed to be travelling almost through a depopulated land. I can well recollect one stretch beyond Tours of nearly twenty miles of absolutely straight road, upon which the only living thing to be discovered was an old priest sitting by the gate of a wood and diligently reading his breviary.[23]

The passage encapsulates much of what the British were to appreciate about travel in France during the coming century. The long straight roads, rare in Britain, so boring to travellers in coaches and *diligences*, were now a delight. What was more, they were empty and led to unspoilt countryside. Usually their surface was immaculate. On the Paris to Dieppe road, another driver said, the car 'bounded along as if it were on a billiard table'.

Travellers, for decades accustomed to view the countryside only as it rushed by their train windows, could renew acquaintance with *la France profonde*, deepest France. Other memories were given new life. As with your coach, you left a deposit for your car (unless of French make) with Customs on arrival, refundable if it remained in France for less than a year. Just as, in the past, travellers to the Continent, John Ruskin for one, paid a preliminary visit to Covent Garden's Long Acre to discuss fittings for their coach, so now the car-owner too went to Long Acre, to decide at Mulliners on the design of his car body.

France started well ahead of Britain in terms of motoring, for until the end of 1896, British law made driving cars on public roads all but impracticable. So whatever the fashion might be at the seaside or at the Faubourg tea table, with motoring it was French words that predominated. 'Garage' was one, 'chauffeur' another, though obstinately the British pronounced it 'shuvver'.[24] French mechanics and chauffeurs were likely to be more experienced and possibly better trained in mechanics, a very important matter given the high incidence of breakdown. According to Max Pemberton, they were also more energetic: he noticed that while the English drivers were still smoking their morning cigarette, the French, 'to a man', were busy cleaning car engines. Sometimes the French were too keen. Another British traveller, C. Neville, found that 'every locksmith, watchmaker and carpenter' in French country towns claimed to be a mechanic, the trouble being that they tended to recommend 'every remedy but the right one'. One supposedly qualified mechanic drove Neville's friend's car into a tram. The professionals in novels and memoirs often appear less than savoury. For instance, in perhaps the best known of the motoring novels written by the Williamsons, a successful husband and wife team, the (French) chauffeur runs off with money intended for the purchase of spare parts.[25]

Neville's book *Round France in a Motor* (1906) is amusing and packed with information and anecdote. He and his party wait for a new car in Paris, but, when delivered, it refuses to start; traffic is much faster than in Britain and his car will do 40 mph on a good road; they stick on hills, but get round the difficulty by driving in reverse gear; food in the French inns is good except in Provence. Sometimes one wonders, though, whether the authors of these reminiscences have not added some extra, fictional colour. Neville, for example, includes in his party a black servant Ali who proves especially popular with the French, while the American Michael Myers Shoemaker in *Winged Wheels in France* is accompanied by Yama, his Japanese servant. Still such companions are more plausible than the stock chauffeur character in novels, who turns out to be a handsome young nobleman in disguise.

Few pioneer motorists were more dedicated than Rudyard Kipling, who looked back nostalgically on the days when he and fellow-enthusiasts sat around the fireside discussing technical problems. Driving in France revived his latent francophilia. Along with a lot of other equipment, he remembered, it was wise to take a whip with a long lash to stop the 'temperamental dogs' of France from committing suicide under your wheels. Avoiding country people was almost as difficult, for they advanced down the wrong side of the road, seemingly absorbed in a dream, until the blast of the horn made them leap aside with the shout of *assassin!* He recalled the hostility of hotelkeepers in the very early days, in particular one at Avignon who refused to garage his car on the grounds that it would frighten the horses. Many of these hoteliers in fact took a long time to realize how profitable motoring would prove to them.[26] The *Michelin Guide* for 1900, its first edition, warned readers that hoteliers often charged for 'stabling' cars – the English word at the time – while accommodating horses and carriages free of charge. Object strongly, urged Michelin, and tell us what happened. The Guide, free to chauffeurs and anybody else buying Michelin's tyres, was even then astonishingly informative. Maps for the larger towns were included, hotels were 'starred' according to quality, with a note given of the number of cars they could accommodate. Mechanics were graded according to skill, the different types of petrol available were listed, and the reader could see at a glance whether or not some small town offered a doctor or a pharmacy.

The early days of motoring coincided with an enormous increase in cross-Channel traffic. Ferries to Calais took between an hour and ten minutes and an hour and 20 minutes to make the crossing, much the same as now. Tickets direct to Paris could be bought from Liverpool, Manchester, Birmingham and Dublin. The number of passengers to Calais, Boulogne and Dieppe rose from 224,626 in 1870 to just short of a million in 1910, most of them being British.[27] Even before motoring took hold, there was a marked increase in the number of 'excursionists', tourists who spent less than 48 hours abroad, people who made Bank Holiday forays to Boulogne. The local English-language newspaper *The Channel*, gave notice of an approaching bank holiday in Britain so that French shopkeepers, restaurateurs and barmen would have an opportunity to prepare for a burst of spending by holidaymakers coming over for the day. A British guidebook in the 1890s found a particular reason for welcoming the great increase in tourists to Boulogne: the 'annual invasion of worthy citizens' was swamping memories of those old-time debtors and bookies. Boulogne, unlike Dieppe, had a decidedly British atmosphere. *Murray's Guide* in 1848 put it that:

> The town is enriched by English money, warmed, lighted and smoked by English coal; English signs and advertisements decorate every other shop door, inn, tavern, and lodging-house; and almost every third person you meet is either a countryman or speaking our language.

And if the 'worthy citizens' were indeed introducing new standards, the bookies had undoubted staying power. In August 1891 the French bookmakers persuaded the authorities to order the expulsion of their British counterparts in Boulogne and Calais on the grounds of illegal competition. The local (non-bookmaking) French in Boulogne protested that the British bookmakers brought in good money to the town, doing so with enough force to have the injunction withdrawn.[28]

At the same time, the British traditionally came to this part of France, Picardy and Pas-de-Calais, to work as well as to play. At Boulogne, during the Second Empire, Hogwood of Belfast, partly attracted by nearby coal-mines, established a mill for linen manufacture. The Scottish Baxter brothers set up a factory close to Amiens at Ailly-sur-Somme. At Lille, an important manufacturing centre, there were in the mid-1860s more than a thousand British nationals; and also in the sixties, so a French writer declared, St-Pierre-les-Calais was like a suburb of Nottingham.[29]

Industry and tourism brought a lot of motor traffic. While in some country districts the automobiles, cars, buses, trucks and motorcycles would cause a stir for some time to come, it is noticeable how soon they were taken for granted in more populated areas. Mary Waddington, now a widow, taking a holiday during the mid-1900s in a 'funny little house' she had rented close to the beach at Boulogne, could say that cars kept going by all day. On another occasion she was in Normandy on the Domfront road that 80 years before had entranced John Sell Cotman – 'splendid automobile country', she thought. But the reason for her reappearance in this chapter is the vivid description she gives of an utterly different situation some ten years later, in 1916. She was back close to the Channel coast, this time for a prolonged visit to Hazebrouck, near the Belgian border. Sitting on the train from Paris she had found herself passing through what was a huge British military camp, with thousand upon thousand of huts and tents. This was country more or less taken over by the British Expeditionary Force.[30]

What brought Mary Waddington to Hazebrouck was the serious illness of one of her grandsons; what kept her there was the presence nearby of her son Francis who was serving as an interpreter with the Australians. She knew the British well, with friends that had included King Edward VII, who, to quote a French historian, was 'amused by her prattle'. She was, though, much more than a prattler, and was credited, during her husband's tenure as Ambassador in London, as having restored the rather damaged social reputation of the French Embassy.[31] From her photograph, she appears an indisputably imposing woman. One of her first impressions on arrival at Hazebrouck was of imperturbable British military police directing the traffic in the face of 'torrents of invective hurled at them by indignant natives'. Allowing for the circumstances, among them the hordes of refugees, German aircraft overhead, shrapnel from anti-aircraft shells, the curfew, it would be silly to press too far a resemblance to pre-war French towns with British communities. Nevertheless, Mary Waddington observed, shops in Hazebrouck are what one would find in any English provincial town. As usual, she went on, the English impose their habits wherever they are – church services, five o'clock tea for all classes, lawn tennis, football – with an absolute disregard of the customs of the country. Still there was one custom with a strong French correlation: there was always plenty of champagne, she said, where British officers were to be found. At the same time she was impressed by the efficiency, in particular, of the nursing staff, so well trained and marvellously organized. Moreover, despite the anglicization of the town, the 'Tommies' seemed to be on excellent terms with the townspeople.

But she thought how different they were to French *poilus*. They were not so gay, not so talkative, and their marches were less inspiriting, about them there was often a note of sadness. (The Australians reminded her of American cowboys, though perhaps not so rough in their language.)

'I suppose', remarked Mary Waddingon, with American objectivity, 'there are no two nations so unlike as the French and the British'. Pearl Adam, living in Paris during the war, emphasized the difference emotionally of the two peoples: how the French were hard-headed and expressive, and the British sentimental and inarticulate. The British often found it difficult to know how to approach the French, or how to respond to them. It was an old problem: during the Second Empire, Bayle St John commented on the absurdly 'boisterous enthusiasm' which Englishmen thought it proper to affect when in French company. In 1914, Rowland Strong watched British troops arriving in France, acknowledging the cheers of the crowd with 'certain curious twistings of the fingers and wrists', which they apparently thought to be what the French populace would understand and expect of them.[32]

But 'boisterousness', even exuberance, was out of place in wartime Paris, especially in the early years. A curfew dampened the nightlife and shut up the shops prematurely. There were no cars about, for they had been requisitioned and sent to the front; the foreigners were gone. For Gertrude Stein it was a return to the city of her childhood, even to the smell of the horse-drawn Paris of those days. To Madame de Pratz in September 1914 it was like a dead city, a perpetual Sunday afternoon in the Rue de la Paix and the Place Vendôme and suchlike fashionable streets. The 'exuberant Parisians of yore had suddenly become impressively solemn and sober-minded, disciplined and resolute', she said. It was only too understandable.[33] John Macdonald, writing in the *Fortnightly Review* a year later, recalled sitting in radiant sunshine on the terrace of a boulevard café as he watched the widows passing, one after another, young and old, dressed in deepest mourning, and how he could hear the dull muffled stump on the pavement made by mutilated soldiers on crutches. To Macdonald this not a 'new' Paris at all; the seriousness, the hard work had always been the real thing, not the 'stuff' about Montmartre and Maxims laid on for foreigners. Again the question arose, even if at that particular moment it mattered little – were the French, as foreigners persisted in seeing them, at heart lively and frivolous, or grave and serious?[34]

The British communities scattered about France, many of them much depleted, turned to nursing the wounded and making the lives of the convalescents and those on leave as agreeable as they could through organizations such as the 'Patriotic League of Britons Overseas' and the Paris

'Leave Club'. Elizabeth Le Blond, working as a temporary nurse in Dieppe, remembered that the patients in her British-run hospital were nearly all French, and that she and her colleagues raised in England sufficient transport to carry the wounded of five French divisions.[35] Some British communities found themselves under German occupation. J. P. Whitaker in his book *Under the Heel of the Hun* gave an account of life in the town of Roubaix, an industrial town with a population of 125,000, close to Lille and 36 miles over the lines from Mary Waddington's Hazebrouck. Roubaix, like other towns in the region, had enjoyed a long association with the British textile industry. Its football club, the second oldest in France, had been founded by British textile engineers. But although Whitaker likened it to 'one of the less attractive Yorkshire woollen towns', it was also, unexpectedly, a resort, a watering place to which British from other parts of France would come for holidays, staying with their compatriots who lived there. Whitaker, in woollen goods at Manchester, was called back to Roubaix, where he had previously worked, when the chief of his firm, a Frenchman, was called up. A few weeks after his arrival the Germans marched in, business collapsed and he found himself in imminent danger of deportation to Germany. With two friends he set out to walk to freedom, but they were stopped and sent back. For eight weeks he went to ground, staying most of the time indoors. On emerging, he worked on the principle that if he made himself as inconspicuous as possible, there was a reasonable chance that he might avoid detention. His fluent French helped. It was a very dull life, but he stuck it and eventually succeeded in escaping. Whitaker supplies one incongruous anecdote about the German occupation of Roubaix. There was still a British colony in the town, numbering 50 or 60 people. On Christmas Day in 1915 they trooped off to the English church for a service, only to find it occupied by German soldiers. The parson then conducted his service in the vestry, with the two nations singing their own carols and hymns, separated only by a thin wall.[36]

The hundreds of thousands of British tourists who visited France during the years leading up to the war would have included many whose knowledge of the country was rudimentary. But of the millions, the soldiers, who came over between 1914 and 1918 a large proportion would have known virtually nothing at all.[37] I myself remember mentioning to a friend, in his day a member of the British Expeditionary Force, that I was off to France. He looked at me doubtfully and said 'it's all trenches'. And what is noticeable in a random selection of soldiers' letters home deposited at the Imperial War Museum[38] in London is how little contact there appears to have been between the British troops and the French, in a sense with France itself. It has been put that 'for most front-line men the biggest town they ever knew was a semi-deserted village with a few cellars and perhaps a wrecked cottage producing eggs and chips'. The letters at the Imperial War Museum tend to be mainly from officers (often risen from the ranks) who might be expected to have had more contact than the average soldier. A Lieutenant Hill found the French peasants 'awfully weird' and while their houses are spotless, they have what he calls filthy habits. And they are hopelessly cruel to animals. Captain Lawrence of the Royal Welsh Fusiliers tells his mother of the small dirty village, dark and sombre, where he is billeted. Lieutenant Chappell, later a colonel, disagrees about the dirt. The poorer class of people, he writes, are much cleaner and tidier than at home, though the young ones start smoking very young and 'it is very funny to see little fellows about 3 foot high swanking about with huge pipes about 3 times as big as themselves'. Many of the correspondents, not surprisingly, refer to smells. Chappell claims that each village they pass through possesses its own distinctive odour. Lieutenant Macdonald, of the Middlesex Regiment, writing in his War Journal, relates that in the early morning a light breeze brought him the scent of English violets. He wonders, though, what 'strange medley of stinks went to compose it'.

The best opportunity to get to know French people most probably came from being billeted on them. Moreover the soldiers anyway, temporarily released from the trenches, were likely to be in a happy and outgoing mood. Sometimes the 'hosts' proved most friendly. Lieutenant Chappell wrote to his parents that he and his platoon were billeted on a farm owned by some very nice people. There was a little girl, presumably the daughter of the house, who reminded him of 'Marjorie', whom one assumes to be his sister at home. The only trouble was that 'Madame' had the 'occasionally rather embarrassing habit of coming upstairs to say goodnight to us every night'. (Again the British were taken aback by the ease with which the sexes mixed in France.) For a Captain Lyon (writing in his diary), however, Madame's visits could be 'quite delightful', for she and her husband sometimes dropped in after dinner with champagne for him and his brother officers. Captain Lyon's billet sounds like a *château*. That was not always an advantage. Another officer, allotted to a moated eighteenth-century *château* abandoned by its owners and recently used as a hospital, found it so uncomfortable that he preferred to sleep in his lorry.

In contrast to England, sizeable country houses, habitable ones at any rate, were thin on the ground in most of rural France. But here, in the area of the British armies, in Picardy, Artois and Flanders, there was one attached to nearly every village, maintained Colonel Nicholson in his book *Behind the Lines*. Their owners, the Counts and Countesses, usually descendants of the old nobility, might be without telephones or bathrooms, though sometimes possessed of an 'indifferent tennis court', but what they did have were the most charming manners in the world. Nicholson then qualifies himself to say that he is thinking mainly of the Countesses, for the Counts are usually 'scrubby little men', but their wives – what splendid women the French ladies are! It is a society with, on the one hand, the country gentry, the Counts and Countesses, and on the other, peasant farmers. And the middle class? They are recognizable by their ostentatious houses designed for show, but there are few of them around. In terms of billeting, thinks Nicholson, it cannot be much different from the days when English armies fought here during the Hundred Years War. Pleasing notion as that may be, it is hardly appropriate in terms of the British of the First World War. Rustic they were not. Another British officer described the juxtaposition, French and British, of 'the saving, careful, thrifty instinct of the peasant proprietor' set alongside 'the careless, spendthrift, looting ways of the ex-Cockney wage-earner, turned soldier and billeted in France'.[39]

By August 1917 the British Expeditionary Force, including Dominion and Indian troops, numbered over 2 million men and occupied a front line stretching 125 miles from north of Ypres to the River Somme. When out of the trenches, the troops inevitably affected rural life and its economy. A village for which Kenneth Bell was responsible as 'Town Major' contained precisely 130 inhabitants before the war; now, with the troops, the figure was something like 2,000.[40] There were advantages since the soldiers had money, much more than their French counterparts. Many of the locals responded in the natural and time-honoured way by opening or expanding shops and restaurants and cafés and bars. 'In the country', a French censor put it, 'the English are loved in proportion to the money they leave'.[41] There was a substantial shift in employment out of agriculture, already in difficulties with the younger men absorbed by the French army. And, as had happened so many times in the past, British money induced a local inflation, which this time piled itself on top of the general inflation produced by the war. There were other difficulties. The British Army requisitioned fodder and timber and cannibalized buildings to shore up trench walls and dugouts. What was taken officially was of course paid for, but nevertheless seizure of this sort caused many complaints. Then there was scrounging and sometimes looting on the part of those 'ex-Cockney' private soldiers. The officers did not always help; on occasion they took to hunting over precious agricultural land.

What little many of the soldiers knew about France before they arrived was that French women were sexy – news that would be speedily passed along to those who didn't. One young airman arriving in 1916 supposed Paris to be 'a sort of gigantic brothel where women wore nothing but georgette underwear and extra long silk stockings'.[42] And even outside Paris the women were supposedly sophisticated and erotic. The reality could be very different. For one thing, the daughters of those peasant proprietors were often distinctly prim. For another, the first encounter with a sexual scenario was probably in no way sophisticated; it was quite likely take the form of an urchin at the port of disembarkation pimping for one of his sisters. There were brothels, French and British, and there were many thousands of women – their husbands or boyfriends at the front or dead – who for money, for fun or for both were happy to go with British troops. Mary Waddington observed British soldiers in the park at Versailles, each with a girl on his arm. They foretold, she thought, an extraordinary increase in the population, but 'I would certainly prefer English babies to German if we are to have a great infusion of foreign blood'. For another slant on the subject, there was a jingle that ran:

Après la guerre fini,
Soldier anglais parti;
Mademoiselle française beaucoup pleurer
Avec petit bébé.[43]

Venereal disease was rampant, and extremely unpopular with the authorities for its effect on fighting capability.

It is calculated that altogether over 5 million British served in France between 1914 and 1919, 'making the most intense and numerous direct contacts that have ever occurred between the two nations'. There were marriages between troops and local girls. Some of the former stayed on afterwards. There were warm, sometimes tragic memories to be shared; after all, heroic French citizens had been executed by the Germans for sheltering stranded British soldiers, and many had taken serious risks. Different military priorities led to discord between the armies – the British were much preoccupied by the vulnerability of the Channel ports. One military expert has put it that the French considered the British temperamentally uncooperative and unreliable, a consequence of insularity and reserve, while to the British, the French were authoritarian, secretive, also unreliable, demanding and ungentlemanly. In the end the effect on personal relations was ambiguous. Rudyard Kipling, whose son, aged 18, had been killed at the battle of Loos, reflected that the two races had been utterly wearied of each other's enforced society through four years, and that there were a thousand points of friction and disagreement.[44] General Spears, then a relatively junior officer acting as liaison between British and French armies, wrote that by the end of the war, as far as the British were concerned, the French generally were in the position 'of a man tolerating for ulterior reasons the long-drawn-out visit of tiresome relatives'. Robert Graves in his widely read autobiography deplored what he saw as the meanness and avarice of French civilians and declared that anti-French feeling among most ex-soldiers amounted almost to an obsession. For all that, the traditional arrogance of the British was tempered by the experience; M. E. Clarke writing in the *Cornhill Magazine* in 1915 on 'British Women at Work in France' (mainly though not exclusively concerned with nursing) spoke of the burning memory 'that for the first time in our lives we see ourselves as others see us, and the picture is not always flattering. In a way England and the British people have walked among the nations of the earth a little mistily'.[45] And there is W. H. Auden's

> Where is the John Bull of the good old days,
> The swaggering bully with the clumsy jest?
> His meaty neck has long been laid to rest,
> His acres of self-confidence for sale;
> He passed away at Ypres and Passchendaele.[46]

10

Displacement

The Russians are gone, the British are beginning to be poor, the Germans are ruined.
Ernest Hemingway[1]

However arrogant and disagreeable he might be, John Bull, the stereotype, was at least more or less straightforward. But he could in French eyes assume a more equivocal form. An encounter in 1868 between two literary masters of the nineteenth century, Algernon Swinburne and Guy de Maupassant, provides an example. Swinburne, having drunk too much, collapsed in the British Museum Reading Room and was supposedly setting himself to rights swimming in the sea at Etretat. Maupassant, aged 18, was on the beach. Suddenly, Swinburne found himself in trouble, the alarm went up and Maupassant joined the rescue party. All was well, and Swinburne's friend and host George Powell, a Welsh landowner, invited Maupassant to lunch next day. He accepted, but not without a qualm, it seems, for Powell's reputation round about was questionable. He had renamed his rented house Dolmance Cottage, not 'Mon Repos', or after some wistful Pre-Raphaelite flower, Monsieur Dolmance being the hero in a work by the Marquis de Sade. Unlikely as it was that many of the holidaymakers or locals had read de Sade, rumours got about. Moreover, Powell's servants were unusual, being English, 14 or 15 years old, male and employed for only three months at a time. 'Extraordinarily neat and fresh', was how Maupassant described them to Edmond de Goncourt. Lunch was for four – Powell, Swinburne, 'a kind of fantastic apparition' who put the young Frenchman in mind of Edgar Allan Poe, Maupassant himself ... and a monkey, who qualified rather as a host than guest since it was soon plain that the *ménage* was *à trois*, and a very rough one at that. Maupassant, though struck by the extraordinary charm of Swinburne's conversation, resisted any participation, although he made one further visit. This time there was no monkey; it had been murdered by a jealous footman.[2]

Here was an example of what was known as the *vice anglais*, sado-masochism, a term also applied sometimes to designate homosexuality.

Later in life, Maupassant was to write an extended short story about another stereotype, the sexually repressed English spinster. The story, *Miss Harriet*, is set in Normandy, in a village not far from Etretat, where a young French painter stays at a farm as a paying guest. The only other lodger is Miss Harriet, tall, thin, withdrawn,

> One of those opinionated puritans that England produces in such numbers, one of those virtuous and insupportable old maids who haunt all the *tables d'hôte* of Europe … and make uninhabitable the charming towns of the Mediterranean, bringing with them everywhere their bizarre manias, the manners of a fossilized vestal virgin, their indescribable clothes.

But despite this fierce introduction, the story is written with remarkable tenderness. Gradually Miss Harriet thaws a little, accompanies the narrator on his painting expeditions, and falls in love with him. Unable to express herself or to cope with her feelings, she commits suicide, drowning herself in the village well.

If John Bull and Jane Bull (a term occasionally used) had really departed the scene after the war, how far had the fact been taken in by the French? Certainly the differences in temperament and behaviour had not melted away. Ivy Jacquier, her mother English, her father French (cut off by his family for marrying a Protestant), her childhood spent in both countries, one brother turning Frenchman, the other English, struggled to discover her identity. In a diary, mainly in English but partly in French, written between 1907, when she was 17, and 1926, she continually probes her feelings. Where should she live? When in France she feels safer if there are Anglo-Saxons about. She is proud of England – this in 1914 – but she loves France. An English teashop in Nice imbues her with nostalgia; but on a visit to the Lake District she longs to hear French spoken, to get letters written in French. She speaks of these 'two unblended nations, sapping our loyalty, our constancy'. There is a sense of liberty in England, she reflects, and at 25 you are not old as you are in France. But where the heart is concerned she is a Latin. There is so much disorder and dishonesty in France, but art in all things everywhere, and beauty. The faces are less kind, but they are more alive than in England.[3]

A lecture by Hilaire Belloc helps, but Ivy Jacquier draws scant comfort from the society of French anglophiles, from that of Jacques-Emile Blanche, for example – 'cold, *distingué*, well-balanced', she calls him. Sometimes they are rather a surprise: the 'exquisitely' Parisian Madame André Maurois, for example, announces that she reads only Jane Austen. The anglophiles, in the aftermath of the First World War, were warmly disposed towards an old-fashioned Englishness, as can be seen in the work of writers like André Maurois with his Colonel Bramble, René Bejamin with his Major Pipe, and in the books of Blanche and André Siegfried. Unfriendly French writers also look backwards, as for instance Pierre Frondaie whose twice-filmed, best-selling *L'Homme à L'Hispano* of 1925 exhibits Sir William Meredith Oswill, baronet, as so ludicrously eccentric as to be wholly implausible. Upper-class characters, as of old, are very much present in French minds. Louis Caza-mian, in his *Ce qu'il faut connaître de l'âme anglaise* (1927), observes that while most of the many British visitors who have come to France since the war are clearly *petit bourgeois*, 'we stick to the old idea that the Englishman is always more or less a lord'.

The distinguished journalist Claude Anet, writing in the popular *L'Il-lustration* under the heading 'Les Anglais chez nous', makes a distinction.[4] The *petit-bourgeois* British wintering at Hyères, for example, are not to be confused with their compatriots along the coast, on the Riviera proper. These are people who have little to do with the casino, and, while they play bridge, the stakes are very low. They are shopkeepers and small business-men; among them *le gentleman* is a rarity. Anet allows himself a note of regret; for, he believes, the gentleman is the best and the most representative type produced over the centuries by Anglo-Saxon civilization. There is an echo here of Taine's view that the English nobleman was a natural leader of the type that France had lost with the *ancien régime*.

Yet, 'gentlemen' or 'non-gentlemen', what sort of contribution did these British, wholly or partly resident, make to French life? Economically, a great deal. British money launched the Riviera and fostered many a spa and seaside resort. It paid, directly or indirectly, for improvements in hygiene and comfort, it enriched many French people. Culturally, however, the influence of the British was limited. They left buildings here and there, usually undistinguished, the odd street name, some fine Pre-Raphaelite stained-glass windows in what is now the Protestant chapel at Arcachon. But there is nothing English about even Pau now. The exception is Bor-deaux. The British concentrated in the smart Quartier des Chartrons, among the aristocracy of the city. It was an aristocracy of money where, to quote the historian Georges Dupeux, the great merchants, Catholic, Pro-testant and Jewish, belonged to *la Loge anglaise*. By the late nineteenth century it was not a particularly large community: by 1911 it numbered 370, by 1926 only 133, no more than 1 per cent of all foreigners. Many of the one-time British of course had turned French along the way, usually through intermarriage. But old names, Barton, Johnston, for instance, persisted. It was an enduring legacy. According to Monsieur Dupeux, the British colony, through its influence and its actions, has done much to promote the development of that urbanity of spirit which constitutes one of the most distinctive features of the city.[5]

Not all British investments in the region were successful. A General Palmer bought the Château de Gasq after the Napoleonic wars, renaming it Château Palmer. The *château* and its famous wine survived, but the General went bankrupt. More successful were the Gilbey family, 'the Victorian equivalent of Sainsburys and Marks and Spencer', who in 1875 bought the Château de Loudenne in the Médoc. The man they appointed manager was an Edouard Brown, a member of a prominent merchant family, its name one example of that Anglo-French fusion so characteristic of the region. (The Brown name survives still in the Château Cantenac Brown.) The Château de Loudenne, which remained in British ownership until very recently, was enthusiastically described by the Irish couple of Somerville and Ross, famous for their book *The Experiences of an Irish RM*, who stayed there in the early 1890s.

> English management and comforts were not made incongruous by the aromatic flavour of French surroundings and the vivid pageant of the vintage; each accented the other, and retired into the background with unfailing fitness.

The stables were occupied by great English carthorses 'such as had not been seen in France since the days of Agincourt', which were used instead of oxen for the roughest farm work.[6]

But the most important contribution to French life made by the British in France is of a different nature. In October 1959 the grave of William Webb Ellis was traced at a cemetery at Menton. The grave was renovated and a visit of respect was paid by the President of the French Rugby Union accompanied by a brass band. Ellis was an Anglican clergyman who had died at Menton in 1872. Fifty years before, at Rugby School, he was the person, so it is said, who grabbed a ball during a game and ran with it, thereby originating rugby football. But the gathering at the graveside can be held to have wider significance. According to Robert and Isabelle Tombs in their monumental book *That Sweet Enemy*, organized sport, along with parliamentary government, is France's most important import from Britain. The French of course had long been aware of the intense appeal of sport to the British: it seemed to answer an actual physical need, one that was as 'imperious as hunger or thirst', but to which they were immune. Physical training figured on the school syllabus, but not games. However, by the later part of the nineteenth century, interest quickened. The French were taking to golf and tennis and swimming, and now organized games began to look fun. What is more, intellectuals who might otherwise have been satisfied with physical training – at least for others – wondered whether this addiction to games might explain something of the economic dynamism of the Anglo-Saxon nations.[7]

The French nobility's relish of horse racing and foxhunting played no part in the conversion. (And certainly it did not appear to have injected them with any particular dynamism.) Had it entered the discussion at all, it might well, unconsciously perhaps, have been supportive of the anti-games lobby. For the Baron de Coubertin, the man above all instrumental in making organized sport acceptable in France, had no time for what he regarded as a decadent aristocracy. In fact, he visualized sport as a means to reconciliation between worker and employer. (In the 1920s, George Orwell noted that 'Football and Socialism have some mysterious connection on the Continent'.) Coubertin, influenced by Taine, visited Rugby and Eton, turned devotee of Dr Arnold and returned to France a convinced anglophile and a powerful campaigner for the introduction of sports and athletics into the secondary schools of France. He could also claim much of the responsibility for the first modern Olympic Games held in Athens in 1896.[8]

The growing enthusiasm for organized sport was fuelled by the example of local British clubs. The Havre Athletic Club was founded in 1872 by expatriate graduates of Oxford and Cambridge, while the English Taylors' Club came into being at Paris a few years later. As the Tombs point out, the regional pattern of French sport was shaped by social and economic contacts with Britain, and developed around the Channel ports and the Paris region, in the south-west, and in the industrial north, where the club at Roubaix serves as an example. In one case at least, schoolboys led the way: a contingent of British boys visiting Pau taught rugby to their French opposite numbers. Soccer took longer to catch on. Originally promoted by old boys of Scottish Catholic schools, it was not until the First World War – when it was encouraged by the example set by British troops – that its popularity surpassed that of rugby. By then, France was one of the leading nations in world sport: in 1931, when the French won the Davis Cup for the fifth year in succession, a French journalist could write that 'Sport is everywhere today, installed in our ways of life, imposing itself on our attention, reigning over our diversions'.[9]

Cricket, however, made few converts. Ivy Jacquier, her French side to the fore, considered that one must be at the end of everything to taste its joys. The French equivalent of cricket, it has been said, is cycling.

The British made another less flamboyant but not necessarily less exhausting contribution to French life with gardening, or more precisely with gardens. Nothing, wrote W. T. Williams, a detainee in Napoleonic times who showed a fine disdain for the tradition so famously exemplified by Le Nôtre at Versailles, nothing can surpass the false taste of the French in laying out gardens. They either torture their trees into straight-cut alleys or make what they call an English garden on a piece of ground about the size of a handkerchief.[10] Certainly the 'English gardens' cultivated by the British along the Mediterranean coast were on a very different scale. By common consent, the most distinguished was that created by the Hanburys at their Villa Mortola just over the border into Italy. But the celebrated Doctor Bennet, like many mid-Victorians a keen botanist, produced a worthy runner-up a few miles away near Menton. The local gardeners, the people who actually worked in the gardens, were sometimes unenthusiastic. Dr Bennet's head gardener, for instance, disliked gardenias and their smell, insisting that they poisoned the ground. Still, there was no labour shortage. At the Villa Victoria at Grasse, where was to be seen the most extravagant garden of all, Alice de Rothschild, of Waddesden in Buckinghamshire, employed 50 permanent gardeners in the years before the First World War, bringing in 30 to 40 more in preparation for the winter season. Grumbles would have gone down badly, for Alice de Rothschild was a perfectionist and a martinet, who would shout and scream if a weed were to be perceived in the lawn. She even went so far as to shout at Queen Victoria who inadvertently stepped on a flower bed. A simpler garden altogether was that of Lord Salisbury, who for reasons of health deserted Dieppe for the South of France, building himself a house in Beaulieu. He adored botany and gardens, and dressed the part, shambling about in the sloppiest of clothes. (He was shabby most of the time and, while Prime Minister, was turned away from the Monte Carlo casino on the grounds that he was improperly dressed.)[11]

Alice de Rothschild's Grasse, focal point of the scent industry as it now is, was propitious terrain for gardening, even though the climate was very dry. But over most of the Riviera the ground was poor and vegetation sparse. Establishing a garden was hard and expensive work. Turf might need to be brought from England. When Major Lawrence Johnston, well known for his superb garden at Hidcote in the Cotswolds, moved to the Riviera in the 1920s, he claimed that the garden he constructed at his property near Menton was stocked with plants either given by friends or picked up along the roadside. He did not mention, though, that he meant roadsides all over the world and that the friends were expert botanists.

Another fine garden, one covering 100 acres and tended by 14 gardeners, was attached to the splendid Château de la Garoupe built at Cap d'Antibes shortly before the First World War by Lady Aberconway. This property was also the last of its kind, designed specifically for winter holidays. So it was ironic that Cap d'Antibes and more particularly the beach at La Garoupe came to be regarded as the birthplace of the Riviera's summer season. Cole Porter and his wife rented the *château* in the summer of 1922 and were joined by their fellow-Americans Gerald and Sara Murphy. The next year, the Murphys, wealthy but not excessively so, returned to Cap d'Antibes to buy a house. Gerald was a painter, if hardly in the same league as the guests at his Villa America, Pablo Picasso and Fernand Léger. The Murphys' parties could scarcely have been more brilliant. Another guest was Stravinsky. Also around, from the Victorine Studios at Nice, were Rex Ingram, one of the most successful film directors of his time, with Rudolph Valentino, the star of Ingram's box office hit *The Four Horsemen of the Apocalypse.*

The atmosphere, the style of life (not least the drinking), on the beach at La Garoupe in the summer of 1925 has been captured in an unforgettable passage in Scott Fitzgerald's *Tender is the Night*, a book that is dedicated to the Murphys. The Fitzgeralds stayed, it seems, during August and September at Antibes' Hôtel du Cap which in the mid-1920s stood as the very symbol of the new Riviera, of the Jazz Age even. There, on 4 July 1926, took place a spectacular party attended by the Fitzgeralds, Ernest Hemingway, Noel Coward, the couturier Edward Molyneux, the film star Ruth Gordon and Alexander Woollcott. Few hotels can have ever enjoyed so exhilarating a resurrection. In 1921, if the Hôtel du Cap could be said to stand for anything, it was dreariness, its guests old and ugly and out of place in their 'city clothes', absurd when set against the bright sunlight. And such young guests as there were looked as 'stiff and starched as their collars'.[12]

The Murphys and their friends count as trendsetters, but they were not entirely out on their own. A shift of fashion was in the air. The Murphys' friend Ben Finney played a part in the transformation of the Hôtel du Cap. Edouard Baudoin was an entrepreneur who bought the casino at Juan-les-Pins and built a restaurant next door. Other people, including Elsa Maxwell and Frank J. Gould, have claimed credit.[13] The weather was an influence. People were put off by a series of wet and chilly summers up north. The international rich had taken to winter sports, with the first winter Olympics taking place at Chamonix in the Savoy in 1924. And the Americans, now around in great numbers, did not mind heat: they were used to it for, after all, Nice in summer was no hotter than Washington DC or Atlanta.[14] The war too played a part in the conversion to a summer season. In March 1918, 'Cousin Bette', the paper's gossip columnist, wrote in the *Menton and Monte Carlo News* that not many Riviera residents would want to go far afield this coming summer; travelling was no fun in these times. And, she added, the coast could be charming during the long summer days. Cousin Bette looked back as well, happy with what she called a very successful winter season. There had been royalty and dukes and duchesses simply falling over each other, and 'hordes of smart U.S. officers to compete with our khaki lads for the pretty girls' favours'. 'Hordes' was hardly an exaggeration; it was reckoned by May 1919 that 65,000 American soldiers had been lodged in Nice alone, usually convalescing from wounds or sickness. Never before had there been so many Americans in France, and many stayed on. Ben Finney for example came over in the army and had been badly wounded.[15]

Yet the change in emphasis from winter to summer was gradual. There were discouraging voices. The British Douglas Goldring warned honeymooners off the Riviera in summer: the heat has a disastrous effect on the Nordic male's virility, he claimed – 'the atmosphere of any ordinary country church during the vicar's sermon is more highly charged with sex-electricity than [a] sunbathed beach'. As late as 1939 another British writer could refer to January as being the high season.[16]

There was social change as well. There were fewer Russians among the leisured residents and holidaymakers. They were still around on the Riviera, but now for the most part they were refugees ruined by the Revolution, working as taxi drivers and garbage collectors, some as extras at Ingram's Victorine film studios. And there was a rebalancing in the relationship between the British and Americans. The two peoples had much in common, above all of course in their shared language, but also in attitude towards France and the French. To take an old example: At the start of the nineteenth century the American Colonel Pinkney noted that 'modesty is certainly no part of the virtues of a Frenchwoman'. He hopes that nothing 'will ever eradicate that modesty which is inseparable from a reflecting mind, and which acts as a barrier against inordinate passion'. It might be a contemporary Englishman speaking, John Scott for instance, the author of *A Visit to Paris*, who was quoted in Chapter 3. During the Second Empire, 'Cornelius O'Dowd' mentioned that Americans were constantly mistaken for English. Reasons for being in France were often much the same. For Americans too, Mrs Grundy was well installed back home; many were fleeing philistinism and puritanism, the more urgently in the 1920s when confronted with Prohibition. A cheaper form of living appealed to some of them too: for example, the parents of the august Edith Wharton (in the 1920s living opulently in a renovated convent at Hyères) had come to Europe after the Civil War as an escape from high inflation in the USA.[17] Sometimes the Americans too chose exile because of trouble at home. British and Americans read more or less the same newspapers and guidebooks. They might share clubs such as the Anglo-American at Menton and at Nice, and Americans would be welcomed at British clubs in such places as

Bayonne or Biarritz or Dinan. In 1913 the Secretary of the English Club at Pau was an Irish-American oilman. James Gordon Bennett, who died in 1918, was a leader of the foreign community on the Riviera and a one-time master of the Pau foxhounds. There were schools which catered for British and American pupils; and the Ada Leigh hostels, founded in Paris after the Franco-Prussian war, now called themselves the 'Ada Leigh Homes and Hostels for British Empire and American Girls'.

Nor were the Americans neglected when it came to circumstances particularly associated with the British. In 1934 an exhibition at the Musée Masséna at Nice celebrated the part played by the British in the city's history. The painters represented included Reynolds and Constable, Maria Cosway (a miniature) and Winterhalter. Queen Victoria was much to the fore. The advertisements in the commemorative edition of the *Riviera Magazine* are revealing. Admittedly, the Hotel Busby, founded by the current proprietor's mother in 1883, proudly proclaims itself to be the only English hotel in Nice. There is no mention there of Americans. However, the shops are at pains to stress their Anglo-American credentials. The Scotch Tea House offers its 'Scotch-English and American Specialities', and the Riviera Supply Stores stock 'English and American Products'. And the Old England Outfitters would without doubt have been eager for American customers.[18]

Now though, after the First World War, the relationship changed. The Americans had often possessed more money than the British, but there had been fewer of them to spend or flaunt it. Now they were numerous, decidedly richer, and more vigorous. The British had dwindled, had been supplanted in their old role. Philippe Collas in his book *Edith Wharton's French Riviera* put it that the British formed a small select world of their own alongside the brasher, more glitzy Americans.

Scott Fitzgerald was glitzy all right; *The Great Gatsby* just out, helping Ernest Hemingway along, the possessor of a glamorous wife. He was cutting about the British and, as he later admitted, rather unfair. 'England', he wrote, 'was like a rich man who makes up to the household ... when it is obvious that he is only trying to get back his self-respect in order to usurp his former power'. A cynical Frenchman could not have done better. One of the most unattractive characters in *Tender is the Night* is Baby Warren, the snobbish and anglophile sister of Nicole Diver, the wife of its flawed hero, a figure clearly based on Hoytie, Sara Murphy's sister. The Murphys, East Coast cosmopolitans, were not in principle anglophobe: Sara before her marriage had taken part in the London season. But they were very firmly not on the Riviera for a 'grand' social life or to mingle with the sort of people to whom it appealed. They were wary of the old British elite.

In one passage in Fitzgerald's book, Dick Diver – incidentally, so we are told, a Rhodes Scholar at Oxford in 1914 – contemplates other representatives of the old British Riviera:

> Fifty yards away the Mediterranean yielded up its pigments, moment by moment, to the brutal sunshine; below the hotel's balustrade a faded Buick cooked on the hotel drive ... Indeed, of all the region only the beach stirred with activity. Three British nannies sat knitting the slow pattern of Victorian England, the pattern of the 'forties, the 'sixties, and the 'eighties, into sweaters and socks, to the tune of gossip as formalized as incantation.

That there should still be plenty of nannies around post-war is easily understandable. They were probably employed by 35-year-old stockbrokers thrusting ahead in the bull market. The old elite needs little explanation either. Surprising though, given the financial effects of the war, is the survival in cheap hotels and lodgings of so many elderly and sick, people of the sort who had often found expatriate life difficult enough even before 1914.

The strength of the pound allowed it. During the 1920s, apart from a bout of vicious inflation during 1920, prices fell in Britain but rose in France. Such a trend in earlier times would have been uncomfortable for British residents and tourists. Now, it did not matter. The stable exchange rate – utterly stable except for a few brief flurries – that existed all the way to 1914 had gone. In 1914 the pound was exchangeable for just over 25 francs, in 1919 for nearly 32 francs, and four years later for over 75 francs. By 1926 the rate was 152 to the pound, and at one moment even more than that. In the past, the British in France saved money less as a result of lower prices than by being able to live, with dignity, in a more economical way than was possible for them at home. In the 1920s there was no need to bother about that any longer. They were simply much better off than at home.[19]

The effect on life in Paris was marked. Ralph Nevill, the author of numerous books on social history and high life, had known Paris well since the 1880s. He was back again in the mid-1920s, commenting on how short of money the French were and how rarely they were to be seen in the most fashionable restaurants; how too they resented the crowds of high-spending and ostentatious foreigners. Nevill refers to recent demonstrations in Montmartre and elsewhere directed against what are regarded as patronizing British and Americans. The hostility is understandable, he thinks. There were the tourists for instance who sat in their motor coaches – he is probably referring to an episode at Granville in Normandy – with five-franc notes pinned to their hats, and tossed money to children in the manner of alms to beggars. As a man who lived in the higher reaches of society wherever he found himself, who was anyway essentially an Edwardian if not a late Victorian, Nevill had little patience with uncouth behaviour. He could not welcome the appearance since the war of the sort of people who seldom used to go abroad but now crossed the Channel much as in former days they had made a trip to Brighton or Margate.

Paris has been far more affected than London by the Great War, Nevill says. Montmartre, which he remembers with affection from the days of La Goulue and Aristide Bruant, has changed its character; it is now a kind of 'pleasure fair' devoted to the exploitation of British and American visitors. All these visitors, whatever their class, hunger for relaxation and pleasure. They are, though, rather old, partly because night-life is expensive. (Partly too no doubt because so many younger men have been killed.) In the nightclubs and cabarets,

> grey-haired veterans and portly dames, in the intervals of bombarding each other with celluloid balls, may now be seen jazzing in a way which would seem to indicate that, in spirit at least, they have discovered the secret of perpetual youth.

Nevill adds that before the war many of these Anglo-Saxon women would have been in bed at their hotel with a hot water bottle by midnight at the latest. And then this American occupation of Paris is unfortunate. Still, there is one line of work where the British are in there with the best. Apparently no first-class Paris revue is complete without a troupe of English dancers, *les Girls*, as the theatre programmes call them. In fact, like rock stars later on in the twentieth century, French performers adopted English or American names, like the *Les 12 Nudyty's Girls* at Hyères or *Les Vamp Girls d'Hollywood*.* It seems that these English dancers led very well-ordered lives, for not only were they accompanied by a chaperone of mature years but they received the special attention of the Reverend F. Anstruther Cardew, Chaplain of St George's English church in Paris. A bemused French journalist observed:

> Formerly when a Lothario among the audience sent a dancer some flowers and a note the latter was not apt to resent his proposals. Today if anyone ventures to send a note to an English girl he ought to realise that it will have to be passed by a clergyman, who will not allow the damsel under his charge to reply to anything which is not a proposal of marriage.

Even in show business, though, the British were outgunned by the Americans. *Les Girls* could hardly hope to compete with the sensational Josephine

---

* Even that prodigy of Frenchness, Mistinguett, is supposed at one time to have called herself 'Miss Elliott'.

Baker at the Folies-Bergère. Some of the most famous names in American show business came to Paris. Nor was a London nightclub, should one be exported, likely to outshine Bricktop's, the favourite of the Fitzgeralds when they were in Paris. In London, said Nevill, anyone acting in a merely unconventional manner at a nightclub is at once treated as a dangerous criminal and handed over to the police.[20]

Yet whatever the tensions, the French were intrigued by the American invasion. Traditionally they had tended to lump together the British and Americans, the 'Anglo-Saxons'. But the Americans turned out to be the more friendly and more kind, although also less disciplined. Above all, that was true of the new arrivals in Paris, many of whom lived on the Left Bank, not usually rich, but well fortified by the strong dollar. Many were artists, above all writers or aspiring writers, and included such lustrous (or later lustrous) names as Hemingway and Fitzgerald, Pound, Dos Passos, Henry Miller and Sinclair Lewis – newcomers to reinforce the old colony of Gertrude Stein and Natalie Barney. There were British writers around too: Ford Madox Ford was writing his trilogy on the war and at one time editing the short-lived *Transatlantic Review*; D. H. Lawrence, mortally ill, was sometimes about; Nancy Cunard, mainly a publisher and a link with George Moore, her mother's lover and her own close friend, was anyway partly American. (There was also the Irish James Joyce.) And the composer Frederic Delius was still alive in the 1920s, living near Fontainebleau.[21]

That the numerous American chroniclers of the period should concentrate on their fellow countrymen is natural, but it is nevertheless significant that the British Vincent Cronin, under the heading 'The English-Speaking Enclave' in his *Paris, City of Light 1919–1939*, mentions only two British by name – one is Ford, the other a barman from Liverpool. The writer who slips through the net, though, is arguably the most influential of them all, British or American – George Orwell. No writer of the time would have noticed him unless perhaps, after a good lunch at the Crillon, he or she descended into the bowels of the hotel and stumbled over him as he washed a floor. Orwell was in his twenties, unpublished but attempting a novel, living in nineteenth-century style in a garret, and sometimes not far from starvation. There is nothing fancy about the comparisons or references he makes: London, he says, is the land of the tea urn and Labour Exchange, as Paris is of the *bistro* and the sweatshop. He gives a tip: in Paris always go to a pawnbroker in the afternoon, for the clerks, like most French people, are in a bad temper until they have eaten their lunch.

Orwell lived in Paris for over a year, arriving in the spring of 1928 to live in the middle of the Latin Quarter, in the Rue du Pot de Fer, called the Rue du Coq d'Or in his book *Down and Out in Paris and London*. His description of the neighbourhood and of his life in Paris is highly coloured but, he emphasized in the preface to the French edition, it is essentially accurate. The street he depicts is much like the one created by René Clair in his 1930 film *Sous les Toits de Paris*. It is, though, less jolly. 'It was very narrow – a ravine of tall leprous houses, lurching towards one another in queer attitudes, as though frozen in the act of collapse'. They were lodging houses packed to the roof with tenants, mostly Poles, Arabs and Italians, a representative Paris slum which yet included the usual respectable shop-keepers. It was extremely noisy, with 'a whole variegated chorus of yells, as windows were flung open on every side and half the street joined in the quarrel'. But mainly *Down and Out ...* is concerned with work in one of the city's great hotels and the author's relationship with an eternally opti-mistic White Russian refugee. The hotel (nameless in the text) is inde-scribably filthy, with year-old dirt in all the corners, and cockroaches infesting the bread-bin. The customers, though they did not realize it, were hardly better treated than the staff; they were cheated on every side by the proprietor.

The Duchesse de Clermont-Tonnerre, writing under her maiden name of Elisabeth de Gramont, describes some distinctive literary British residents of Paris, who, for better or worse, probably did lunch or dine at the Crillon – certainly, we are told, they ate oysters at Pruniers. They form a compact group, she says in an article published in the *Revue Hebdomadaire*, which, unlike the Americans, has no wish to mix with the natives. It is Paris they want and Paris they love; they are indeed its last true lovers, acquainted with the little restaurants as well as the big ones, savouring the wines, devotees who make expeditions to the countryside in search of a Gothic sculpture or a stained-glass window. 'It is with the English that I travel through my country and it is they who tell me of the latest French crazes'.[22]

'Paris', wrote the Swiss C.-F. Ramuz in 1939, 'has become a kind of theatre where everyone speaks and acts as if he were on stage'.[23] Certainly the city, and provincial France too on occasion, could inspire a theatrical response. Gush sometimes, as with the journalist Beverley Nichols who declaimed that 'all my life I had looked forward to the day when I should see the sun setting over the harbour at Villefranche'. But while the excitement, the allure and the artistic glory remained – the latter enhanced by the achievements of French cinema – the early 1930s brought about an unpleasant change for many British. The Depression was having its effect, and then Britain abandoned the gold standard. On 29 September 1931 a pound bought 124 francs, by 12 December only 84. According to the 1931 census, 50,000 British were living in France; by 1936, the figure was 30,000. Tourist numbers were also greatly affected: 870,000 in 1931 (more than half of all the tourists in France) but only 522,000 the following year.*[24] On the Riviera, the Americans fled, particularly affected by the Depression. The Jazz Age, what the French called *les années folles*, was truly over. The Fitzgeralds had already gone, the Murphys left in 1933, Ben Finney in 1937. In Somerset Maugham's novel *The Razor's Edge*, the narrator quotes an estate agent as telling him that 48,000 properties, large and small, were up for sale on the stretch of coast that ran from Toulon to the Italian border. It is significant that in the 1934 commemorative edition of the *Riviera Magazine* the Queen Victoria Memorial Hospital in Nice announces that its services are available to 'Necessitous British and American Nationals'.

With fewer Americans about, the British recovered something of their old standing, and it is noticeable that poorer tourists were often less affected by the financial upset of the thirties. In France, holidays with pay, made compulsory in 1936, did something to revive the fortunes of Nice, a city especially hit by the loss of foreign custom. In Britain, in the same year, the writer of a book on bicycling in northern France aimed it at people who had never travelled abroad before.[25] France, he said, is a 'decidedly dear country', but added that there must be a devaluation of the franc. He was right; it happened by the time his book appeared. The Channel coast resorts were popular, benefiting especially from the development of civil aviation. On 25 August 1919 a converted twin-engine Handley Page military aircraft, flying from Hounslow at 70 mph, inaugurated a regular passenger service between London and Paris. An experimental night service followed. The British 'Imperial Airways' and the French 'Air Union' established services operating between Croydon and Le Bourget, connecting with flights that brought passengers on to Le Touquet (or more precisely to Berck, a few miles away) and to Dinard. By 1925 some 7,000 tourists travelled by air; in 1930 the figure was over 20,000, in 1933 over 45,000.[26]

For the August races at Deauville, Imperial Airways laid on direct flights by 'landplane' and by seaplane. The sea played an important part in Deauville life, less perhaps for the bathing than for the yachts that lay superb in its harbour. 'The splendour of some of the yachts must be seen to be believed', commented *The Field* in 1938. Sailing had been at the heart of Deauville life from the start, from the 1860s when the town was developed as a resort by the Duc de Morny and Sir John Olliffe. In 1870, Sir John Burgoyne's yacht, moored in the harbour, was (with its owner) enlisted to ferry the fleeing Empress Eugénie across the Channel to safety. The great years were the 1920s. The 'Greek Syndicate' took over the casino in 1922, attracting the wealthy in droves, so many of them British clients – at a time

---

* Some tourists were merely passing through.

when public gambling was illegal at home – that it was thought sensible to employ an Englishman, formerly with Lloyds bank, Monte Carlo, to turn the cards.[27] It was not the place for a quiet holiday: it was very smart, very lively and with a strong raffish tradition. Even during the war, in 1916, a British resident of Paris could note in her diary that life at Deauville was 'an orgy of wealth and amusement'. (Appropriate enough for a creation of the Duc de Morny, who had died from an overdose of Sir John Olliffe's arsenic-based pills, provided to sustain his waning virility.)[28]

There was more to do at Deauville than anywhere else in the world, exclaimed *The Sketch*. Apart from any amount of sport, there were the motor shows and beauty contests. In 1923, a two-day beauty contest included Miss France, Miss England, Miss Germany and 17 others, who then went on to Rio de Janeiro to compete for the Miss Universe crown. There were dancing competitions, for the paso doble, the shimmy, the charleston, the foxtrot. While some of the villas bore rather coy names such as 'Darling Cottage', 'Emily Cottage' and 'Pretty Cottage', there was nothing demure about the magnificent hotels which emerged to serve the profusion of wealthy customers at Deauville and other smart resorts along the Channel coast. At Deauville were the 'Normandy', the 'Royal' and the 'Hôtel du Golfe'; at La Baule in Brittany, the 'Hermitage'; at Le Touquet, both of them completed in 1929, another 'Hermitage' and the 'Royal Picardy', so huge, it was said, that it could only be seen in its entirety from the air.[29]

Le Touquet, or Le Touquet-Paris-Plage, to give the resort its full name, rates as the last of the 'English towns', in the line of Pau and Cannes.* While in the 1890s the local French, considering things were going too far, vetoed a British-led real estate project, the architecture that emerged in the twentieth century possessed a quality of Gothic fantasy owing more to the British tradition than to the French; it was a *hommage aux Tudors*, in the words of Richard Klein, the towns's historian.[30] Claude Anet who spent some time at Le Touquet in the 1920s stressed the Britishness. He played golf with very pleasant old gentlemen, and ladies 'who did not put much powder on their faces'. When driven into the clubhouse by a shower you found the table covered by innumerable and very boring sporting magazines. There was tea. But then life looked up a bit. The English, said Anet, entered a 'rather mysterious room' carrying the three-letter inscription BAR. After a few moments, he goes on, their faces turn a sudden pink. He is reminded of the colour of mountain peaks in the Alps when touched by the setting sun.[31]

---

* Though there are villages now in France considered as given over to the British.

The Field, a weekly for the British landed gentry, certain of a place among the magazines on the clubhouse table, cast its eye over Le Touquet as well as over Deauville. It very much approved: 'Pleasure and comfort go hand in hand', there is 'a kind of politeness in the atmosphere', an absence of the vulgarities and trivialities common to so many seaside resorts on the Continent and at home. In a later issue the magazine alerted its readers to the historical links between Britain and nearby towns such as Amiens, Rouen and Beauvais. None of the 'exotic extravagance of Marseilles and Avignon'. It recalled the war, tapping other memories of France and the French. 'The quintessential Gaul is to be found not, perhaps, on the sunlit plages, but on the ridge and furrow of those small farms', was its refreshingly unconventional view. But perhaps Le Touquet sounds a bit dull, what with the old gentlemen and ladies with a powder deficiency, and the freedom from trivia. That, however, is only part of the story, for it was also very fashionable. Like Deauville, Le Touquet in the interwar years became less a purely bathing resort – though it prided itself on offering the 'most beautiful swimming pool in Europe' with 300 cabins – than a playground for the rich, with a flourishing casino and, by the 1930s, a direct air link to London, with a flying time of one and a half hours. A French visitor reported that everyone who counted in England was at Le Touquet. There were many lords attired in impeccable dinner jackets, rubbing shoulders with great French industrialists; a show-business Dolly Sister accompanied by 'Sir Selfridge' (Gordon Selfridge), and the Prince of Wales accompanied perhaps by the Duke of Westminster, who owned a property nearby.[32]

The Duke of Westminster was colossally rich, a grandee to rival the greatest *milords* of the past, who along with his place in Normandy and a suite at an expensive Paris hotel, owned (as well of course as a great chunk of London) a hunting lodge that he had built near Mimizan, standing deep in the great forest that enveloped the Landes. It served as a base for hunting wild boar. A string of hounds, hunters and hunt servants was brought there by special train, and the Duke himself dressed in the pink coat and velvet collar of an English master of foxhounds. According to Winston Churchill, a guest at Mimizan in 1927, the local people – well compensated for damage caused to trees or land – eagerly followed the hunt, by car or foot, or on horseback. The Duke 'who changed wives as if they were polo ponies' was a voracious sportsman, an enthusiast for powerboat racing, flying and yachting. One of his yachts, the *Cutty Sark*, was a converted destroyer which was staffed by a crew of 43. Motoring was another of the Duke's sporting enthusiasms. Like many people, he must have been excited when, in 1930, Woolf Barnato, son of the one-time bar-room bouncer and diamond king Barney Barnato, raced his Six-Speed Bentley from the Riviera against the

Train Bleu. Barnato was back in London before the train had reached Calais.[33]

The Duke of Westminster had no need to feel confined to Mimizan, Mayfair and so on. He also bought Les Zoraides, a villa on the Riviera for his mistress Coco Chanel. Still, he cannot be considered typical of the British nobility during the interwar period. Of some of them, Jean Bresson gives a striking picture, depicting those old and respectable 'ornaments' of Westminster, who for four months a year quit their massive Tudor country houses to shut themselves away with friends and grandchildren in a white villa above Cannes among orange trees and flowers. They are far removed from the jazz bands below, and from what Bresson describes as 'the playful world of young Americans with husbands unknown, flimsy goddesses with pink napes and virile hips, dressed in cashmere, shod with crocodile, their necks adorned with frills'. The Depression and the devaluation of the pound thinned down the wealthy and quietened the exuberance. Nevertheless, the villas at Cannes were not deserted. Some had passed to French industrialists such as Senator Meunier of the chocolate firm and Gabriel Voisin, the head of Voisin automobiles. But there were wealthy British about, like Lord Beaverbrook on Cap d'Ail, near Monte Carlo, in a house originally built for the couturier Edward Molyneux, and Somerset Maugham on Cap Ferrat. Lord Derby was at the Villa Sansovino, named after his Derby winner; the Château de la Garoupe was still in the family. H. G. Wells near Grasse was a celebrated resident, very much part of Riviera social life in the early thirties.[34]

Change was more noticeable in the towns: new money was less fastidious than old. Cannes is vulgarized, wrote Basil Collier in 1937, it has become the seaside dream of Surbiton and the Stock Exchange; this is the Riviera 'of the domestic servant's serial and *No, No, Nanette*'. The Cannes taxis are Hispano-Suizas, he grumbled superciliously, ignoring the extra comfort that they must have brought with them. To Aldous Huxley, living at Sanary, near Hyères, in the 1920s, the 40 miles of Riviera coast constituted 'a vast shuffling suburb – the suburb of all Europe and the two Americas – punctuated here and there with urban nuclei'.[35] It was a pity, there was no doubt of that; but suburban spread was conspicuous in most parts of developed Europe between the wars.

The differences between the British in France during the 1920s and 1930s and their predecessors can be exaggerated. There were now more shop-keepers and small businessmen; arguably some of the 'larger' businessmen – the people Basil Collier had in mind – were more flashy than in the past. There is much, though, that is familiar. Virginia Woolf visited the Monte Carlo Casino in 1935. She was unimpressed, writing in her diary of the 'dingy, sweaty rather sordid crew' at the tables. 'They had something peculiar. One couldnt place them. Some were dingy old governesses in spectacles, others professors with beards; there was one flashy adventuress; but most were small business men – only rather, not very vicious'.[36] The tone is much like that of J. R. Green in his description of 60 years or so before, quoted in Chapter 7. There were impoverished artists, driven, via Paris, to the Riviera when house prices rose in Chelsea, but impoverished artists had never been absent, they were always around. There were the disreputable, Somerset Maugham's shady people who live in sunny places, sketched so cleverly in his short story *The Happy Couple*. 'Synthetic Majors' was Douglas Goldring's term for some of the people he encountered in the South of France, and 'synthetic Princes' too, such as the Prince of Istria, the man who used to cut his hair in Bond Street. Giles Waterfield, in his study of his grandparents' life at Menton, identified another type, women who were 'elderly, dour and unattached ... propriety personified. They are spoken of as "worthy". Although not personally attractive they are eminent by reason of their intimate knowledge of the economics of life abroad'.[37]

Claude Anet's picture of the British he met on the Channel coast is particularly evocative. To the old reasons for being in France – health, money, whatever – is added the new, post-war 'impossibility' of finding domestic servants at home. These people, says Anet, adore England, setting it above everything else in the world, though they flee it like the plague if they can. But it comes along too. For the Englishman brings with him:

> His games, his sports, his drinks, his tobacco, his clothes, his phlegm and even that indefinable odour of fog, of leather, of coal-smoke and whisky that make up the special atmosphere of the Englishman and which one finds about him and around him in whatever part of the globe he lives.

There were travel books written about France in the 1930s, and novels by Elizabeth Bowen and Cyril Connolly and others set wholly or partly in France. Memoirists, though, are in short supply. Winifred Fortescue is the great exception, so much so in fact that her books, her enterprise and her intrepid character have earned her a place in the *Dictionary of National Biography*. The daughter of a Victorian rector, initially an actress playing minor parts, in 1914 she married John Fortescue, Librarian and Archivist at Windsor Castle and historian of the British army. When he retired (with a knighthood) they found themselves short of both money and good health, and in 1930 moved to the Riviera, to the slopes above Nice. Life was not easy: they were hit by the devaluation of the pound and then, after a few years, John Fortescue died. Winifred Fortescue, however, proved indefatigable. In 1935 she published *Perfume from Provence*, and two years later *Sunset House*, precursors of a number of other books. At the start, she was not much of a stylist: an article she wrote for *Blackwood's Magazine* is long-winded and whimsical as it chats on about her 'faithful little Morris Oxford "Sir William", and its replacement, a Fiat christened "Désirée" '.[38]

She is writing in stressful times. *The Sociological Review*, in 1937,[39] considering why so many British had returned from the Continent, referred to the fear of war and political unrest in Europe. Refugees had already arrived on the Riviera from Germany. In 1938, when war seemed close, Lady Fortescue and the other British in her neighbourhood put their houses and gardens and cars, as well as themselves, at the disposal of the French military authorities. (Désirée became an ambulance.) Nice after all was dangerously close to a bellicose Italy. For a change, in this corner of France, it was British households that were providing billets for French soldiers. Winfred Fortescue's natural feelings and her hard sense took definite shape, and her literary style became more taut. She watches a procession of:

> Thousands upon thousands of French soldiers, unshorn, sweat-begrimed, exhausted, marching, always marching in a kind of despairing sleepy stupor ... The peasants of our village lined the roads for hours to watch this endless sad procession. Their husbands, fathers, sons, and brothers had all been called up two days before ... Up and down and in between those dusty ranks of men ran lost and limping dogs, hunting and sniffing tirelessly along the lines in search of masters who had, perforce, left them at home.

From then on and through the icy winter of 1939/40 she lives what, with reason, she calls the strangest kind of life, 'with cars and motor-bicycles roaring ceaselessly along our mountain roads'.[40]

It kept her free from the complacency that afflicted many British in France during the 'Phoney War'. And tourists too for that matter. It was not until January 1940, four months after the outbreak of war, that a limit was imposed on money spent on foreign travel. The French, anxious about their economy, pressed that it should not be too rigorous, and the British Consul General in Nice argued about the importance of tourism for local morale. The Foreign Office, however, made plain that 'they would see considerable objection to facilitating lavish expenditure by British nationals abroad'.

When, so suddenly, the Germans shattered the Allied armies in May, the British living in France were unprepared. Winifred Fortescue left by car on 25 May, crossing to Britain via St-Malo. But many others remained. A Mr Woodhouse Lane (an MA, Cantab, as he made plain) wrote to the Foreign Office from St-Jean-de-Luz on 4 June – the day the Dunkirk evacuation ended – hoping that should the situation become urgent, a boat might be dispatched to rescue the small British colony there. He was told in reply that Bordeaux would be a more practicable point of departure. But across Mr Woodhouse Lane's letter someone at the Foreign Office scrawled that 'if Mr and Mrs WL choose to live in France, they must take the rough with the smooth & not expect to be able to run away'. A rare example of official opinion on expatriates. Anyway, policy clearly needed to be clarified, and after discussion – and argument – the Foreign Office issued an official ruling to the effect that everything should be done to evacuate British subjects wishing and able to leave territory under enemy domination or quasi-domination or threat of it. It was pointed out that they could not well be left in territories we proposed to bomb.

As it happened, the British authorities tried hard to rescue stranded nationals. A question was, should non-British judged to be at especial risk from the Germans be brought out too? Clement Attlee took a particular interest. The names of the ex-Spanish Republican Prime Ministers Largo de Caballero and Negrin were canvassed, as also were those of Léon Blum (who ended up in a concentration camp), the Joliot-Curies, some of the Roths-childs and General de Gaulle. It was impossible accurately to gauge how many British might be involved. The Foreign Office, working on admittedly incomplete consular records, estimated that a normal peacetime summer might have found something like 55,000 British living in France. But obviously many fewer would be there in 1940. Later in the year it was reckoned that some 8,000 troops were hiding with French families, an expense to those families as well as very dangerous for them.[41]

The most famous British captive was P. G. Wodehouse, who was possibly also the most easy-going and complacent; or, if not complacent, innocent, a trait evident later when he was persuaded to make a notorious broadcast on German radio. Rather ironically, Wodehouse was captured at his seaside villa, 'Lost Wood', at Le Touquet. This was ironic, since one reason he had chosen Le Touquet was because it was within easy reach of London. He did set out as the Germans closed in, but his car broke down in the heavy traffic. He borrowed another car from neighbours but that broke down too.[42]

Then there was the weird and wonderful Millicent, Duchess of Suther-land, charming, and enterprising – she wrote a number of books – first President of the Ladies' Automobile Club, and widow of the fourth duke. A fervent francophile, she harboured a particular dislike for hearing French spoken badly. On 8 August 1914, ahead of the British Expeditionary Force, she had arrived in France with her mobile ambulance to serve with the French Red Cross. They were soon captured by the Germans, though not long detained. It was helpful that the Duchess knew the Kaiser and the

Crown Prince personally. Allowed to return home by way of Holland, the Duchess was back in London in time to marry again on 18 October. She was soon once more in France, this time to organize the Millicent Sutherland Ambulance which she set up at Dunkirk. After the war, she made her permanent home in France, though exactly where she might be at any time must have been perplexing to her friends. To put it mildly, she was restless. First she took a house near Le Havre; then moved to Juigné, a village near Angers; next she chose the Vendée coast, and then turned inland again, to the neighbourhood of Tours. But anyone trying to track her down would have been advised to bear in mind that she possessed a suite at the Paris Ritz and at a hotel in La Baule. Wherever the Duchess found herself, she lived sumptuously. From 1936 she spent a couple of years not far from St-Jean-de-Luz, and finally, as it were, was back near Angers in a nineteenth-century *château*, La Froide Fontaine. It was there, having ignored warnings to leave, that she fell once again into the hands of the German army. No Kaiser this time, and she certainly had no acquaintance with Hitler. However, her fluent German helped, and so, as she remarked, did being a duchess. She remained under what amounted to house arrest, but stylish living was out of the question. For the first time ever, presumably, she was without money. After a time, authorization to leave was granted and, accompanied by her companion-maid Janet, she set out on a long, difficult and exhausting journey – she was in her seventies – to Madrid and then on to Lisbon, where to she hoped to find a ship to take her to the USA. Still financially stretched, she wrote 'letters' to the Foreign Secretary Lord Halifax asking permission to draw funds from Britain.* She got to America, and she and Janet were among the first foreign civilians to return to lib-erated Paris in 1944.[43]

The Germans arrested 1,452 British in Paris and its suburbs. They and the others captured elsewhere in Occupied France were interned, the women and children being sent to a camp in the mountains above Besançon, and later, from mid-1941, to the spa town of Vittel in the Vosges. The men, apart from some of the old, also sent to Besançon, were interned at Drancy, near Paris. They represented a good mix of professions: lawyers, teachers, businessmen, jockeys and blue-collar workmen. In the women's camp were to be found nuns, retired nannies, 'lots of dancers' (the next generation of Ralph Nevill's troupers) and prostitutes from the brothels of Calais and Boulogne. Some of the women considered themselves to be wholly French; it happened that at some point in their lives they had married British husbands.[44]

---

* There is no knowing Lord Halifax's response since the relevant archives have been culled.

Two who escaped from Paris were Rupert Downing and Peter Fontaine, both (separately) struggling by bicycle along roads clogged with refugees, bombed and machine-gunned, short of food and money, but intent on reaching Spain. They both succeeded eventually in getting back to England and speedily published books recounting their experiences. Neville Lytton, a painter, also wrote a book. He was better placed, living with his wife and daughter in Quercy, in Unoccupied France. He was able, before the family's eventual escape, to survive with the help of American friends who cashed his British cheques and with money earned from painting the portraits of Lyon notables.[45] The most exciting as well as the most entertaining account of a civilian's escape, however, is provided by Gael Elton Mayo in a book published long after the war. Like the Duchess of Sutherland she was unsettled and a francophile. She was to have two French husbands and, a Comtesse, would be chatelaine of a large and ancient castle in the remote Jura. She was a romantic and extremely resourceful, a painter, novelist and journalist. She was also very beautiful.[46]

But, she admitted, she was no good at choosing husbands. Anyway, in the summer of 1940, Gael Mayo, aged 18, was living in Paris, and married – on a rebound – to Vsevolod, a charming but feckless White Russian poet, a stateless person. It was this non-nationality that would be the cause of endless difficulties in getting away from France. The first difficulty was a classic case of bureaucratic obduracy. The law entitled a stateless person to an exit visa should he or she wish to leave France. That may be so, conceded the *Chef de Section* at the Prefecture, but it is a law that has never so far been put into practice. Moreover, it is usual for a letter of some sort to be presented along with applications. What sort of letter he would not specify – a bribe? they wondered. But 'he sat solid behind his desk, as if red tape were wrapped all round him, like a mad Magritte'.

Paris was in chaos, with the Germans close; it seemed best to head south. They caught the last train out of the Gare de Lyon and reached Bordeaux. But without an exit visa no ship was going to take Vsevolod to America, where Gael's parents were living, or to anywhere else. They were stranded, with a baby due. A private room in a hospital materialized, but Bordeaux was bombed and the hospital's director drove away in his car, with most of the staff disappearing soon afterwards. An old man, apparently the father of the regular gynaecologist, who was away with the army, turned up mysteriously and delivered the baby, a son, Stephen. Providentially, another mother in the near-abandoned hospital offered the three of them shelter in her home. But bureaucracy struck again: Gael, diagnosed as having developed puerperal fever – perhaps the old man was not as antiseptic as he might have been – was rushed by a doctor to another hospital. She was refused treatment. Her doctor-companion had no standing at this hospital and so was debarred from using the operating theatre. Even though all her doctors were somewhere else, the matron was adamant. Finally, after an agonizing delay, one of them was found and all was well.

The Germans, now at Bordeaux, summoned Vsevolod to Gestapo headquarters to explain why his wife, an enemy subject, had not been registered. She must remain where she was indefinitely. It was an impossible restriction; they had virtually no money and could not live on their hosts any longer. So, at considerable risk but with the connivance of the stationmaster, they caught a train back to Paris. There, Englishwomen, Jews and students were required to sign the police register daily. They had practically no money and very little food. 'We thought and talked about food the whole time.' Then – it was 19 December – the best Christmas present of Gael's life arrived, money sent by her father from the USA which unexpectedly got through. They could afford a *passeur*, someone to slip them over the border into what euphemistically was known as 'Free France', the Unoccupied Zone. But, before they could move, there came the dreaded hammering on the door at six o'clock in the morning. The police had arrived: all Englishwomen were being shipped off to Besançon. Vsevolod pleaded that Gael was very ill, and a friendly doctor, apparently in love with her, provided a medical certificate. That would not affect the internment order, but it did mean an ambulance, and maybe a day's delay. By the time the ambulance turned up, the three of them were on their way to an inn in Burgundy, from which, after several alarms, they were led nine miles on foot to the border and . . . a German patrol. But the bullets missed and they were across.

In the Unoccupied Zone, until November 1942 when the Germans marched in, the British were treated as rather undesirable aliens, enjoying a restricted liberty. You needed an exit visa to leave and, were you a man aged less than 48, you would not get one. Moreover, the best way out was through Spain which also imposed tight restrictions. There was no consular protection or advice: the Vichy government had broken off diplomatic relations with Britain after the Royal Navy's destruction of the French squadron at Mers-el-Kébir. British with houses on or near the Mediterranean coast were ordered to move away, although a number did manage to stay in place. Gael, her husband and Stephen got out of France in the end, travelling by train over the Pyrenees, on the first lap of an extremely uncomfortable sea journey to New York by way of Rio de Janeiro. First, though, they had to hang about for something like five months, waiting for visas. Most of the time they lived in Cannes. There too food was very short. Maurice Chevalier, bicycling along the Croisette, complained that his teeth would fall out because of the food. He got no sympathy, for he could afford the black market and was notoriously mean. Gael found a job as a photographer's model and her picture turned up on the front of the magazine *Marie-Claire*. Society was mixed, and sometimes unexpected. She met a woman, an Australian, with whom she had been at school; she was encouraged by the sight of a Welshman in a baggy suit at the bar of the Carlton Hotel. There was Jimmy, taken prisoner at Dunkirk, who had escaped, and was trying to get back to Britain. 'He did not seem to be trying very hard', though, sitting in the sun and living on a survival allowance presumably provided through the American consul. Jimmy disappeared; out during curfew hours, he was arrested, beaten and sent to prison. There was 'Barry the Beachcomber', a Canadian, ex-film actor and current drunk, but he too went missing, presumed arrested.[47]

Most of the British had gone. Some had made difficulties. The Duchess of Windsor had refused to fly. Those still there in June 1940 were notified that they should be on the quay at Cannes at eight o'clock one morning, equipped with handbag, blanket and three days' provisions, ready to board one of two colliers diverted from Marseille. There were 1,300 of them (possibly more), including Somerset Maugham who described the scene and the voyage which followed.

Some were invalids on stretchers (who had to be sent back to hospital); many were elderly, retired soldiers or civilians from India, with their wives. There were old governesses, teachers of English, chauffeurs and butlers, shopkeepers and businessmen, and young workmen employed on an engineering contract by the French government. Some were people who had probably lost all contact with Britain and would have no idea where to go when eventually they landed. Embarkation took four hours, Maugham said, and a woman died of heat while waiting. Even had these ships been intended for passengers, the space available would have been insufficient. So they were very uncomfortable indeed. Iron decks were icy for the many who slept on them at night. One of the boats, the *Ashcrest*, was attacked by an Italian submarine; luckily it managed to escape, lucky particularly since there were nothing like enough lifeboats or even lifebelts to go round. Some of the wealthier passengers found adjustment hard: one woman remarked with horror that it was the first time in her life that she had drunk tap water. Four people went out of their minds – in one case, Maugham thought, as a result of a 'sudden and enforced deprivation of alcohol'. One woman died. Still, they made it.[48]

11

The Rural Idyll

What the English look for in France is the England of past times. They find it in la France profonde.

Theodore Zeldin, quoted in *Le Monde*

France, in 1944 and 1945, was a shattered country. Old landmarks were hardly recognizable. Le Touquet, for instance, a German airbase, had been bombed by the RAF, with 300 of its 1,100 villas either demolished or seriously damaged. The magnificent Royal Picardy Hotel was wrecked. The prolonged fighting which followed the Allied landings left much of Normandy in ruins. Dieppe was a 'ghastly sight', said the wife of an American diplomat on her way to Paris. Nancy Cunard returned to find her house had been sacked, first by the Germans and then by local peasants. Robert Henrey and his wife were luckier, for Mrs Henrey's French mother, ill and penniless as she was, had kept their Norman farmhouse more or less intact. The Riviera was distinctly cheerless, with many of the houses and properties badly damaged, including Somerset Maugham's Villa Mauresque.[1]

There were shortages of just about everything. A pamphlet issued to British servicemen warned them not to expect any lavish entertainment from French people. Almost all French civilians were undernourished, it explained, because the Germans had eaten their food. In March 1945, Duff Cooper, the incoming British Ambassador, was told that there were about 8,000 undernourished British subjects in France.[2] Winifred Fortescue was in two minds about returning to her house above Nice. She was the sole survivor of the local British colony, and her close friend, the American (turned French) Elizabeth Starr had died of malnutrition. What persuaded her to go back, she said, was the conviction that Miss Starr would have wished her to continue the humanitarian work she had undertaken for needy Provençal children. What is more, the French authorities invited her to give them a report on conditions and to outline what could be done in the way of immediate relief. Being the woman she was, that proposal alone would have got her adrenalin flowing. So, in May 1945, the war in Europe just over, Lady Fortescue was back. She was appalled by the destitution, and embarked on a programme of relief, bringing money and clothes provided 'through the marvellous generosity of the readers of my books and the children and teachers of so many schools and convents in England'.[3]

The garden had run wild, but she found her house and its contents untouched, thanks to a conscientious domestic help. That a number of other, much larger, Riviera houses escaped serious harm was due to the energy and enterprise of John Taylor & Son, the estate agents at Cannes founded by the man who had started as gardener to Thomas Woolfield. While nothing could be done about the rows of Rolls-Royces, Daimlers, Cadillacs and Duesenbergs abandoned by their owners on the quayside, the senior partner Jack Taylor, in his capacity as British vice-consul, had personally paid for the costs of refuelling the two colliers which had come to the rescue – he had to wait ages for reimbursement – and organized the evacuation. He then split his firm in two, going himself to London. He persuaded the Treasury to authorize funds for the maintenance of his clients' properties, in particular the payment of taxes, so that the Vichy government would have no excuse for seizing them. When the Germans occupied the Riviera, Taylor continued to send money, now on behalf of his American clients as well, using Moroccan and Swiss intermediaries.[4]

'At least it's all still there', thought William Sansom, in Nice during the autumn of 1947, with that 'elegant parade of hotels', half-empty though they were. But prices had risen so much that it seemed incredible that anyone could live on the Coast. That was the opinion too of Colonel Harvey who arrived shortly afterwards: the cost of living he reckoned to be perhaps three times that of England.[5] There was a very flourishing black market. Gael Mayo, returned from the USA, wrote a story for the London *Picture Post* on Menton, which she dubbed the 'City of Unburied Dead'. The villas, and the gardens with 'their eerie, exotic lawns', were still there, just, for they were soon to be replaced by concrete blocks. Menton was a haunt of old people, who were almost in hiding, wrote Gael, shadows 'who wear lavender and grey, who are pear-shaped, whose skins are fine parchment'.[6] Some years later, in 1963, Malcolm Muggeridge noted elderly English ladies dressed in the fashions of half a century ago, 'frail, penurious ghosts who have somehow survived the wars, revolutions and disasters of our time, and still, with parasols and large flopping hats, emerge to take the air'. By then, the great Coast had indeed recovered. Rolls-Royces abound as perhaps nowhere else, says Muggeridge, but it is no longer the British who predominate, but rich Germans, Italians, Belgians and Scandinavians.[7] Geoffrey Bocca, in his *Bikini Beach*, also of 1963, dwelled on the perennial adaptability of the Riviera, surviving as the greatest resort in the world through 'apocalyptic' changes in society. 'Not once but several times,' he wrote, 'the very people for whom the Riviera existed were obliterated. Russian Grand Dukes and English royalty, the first families of the Almanach de Gotha, Indian maharajahs, flappers, black marketeers, Wehrmacht Generals, the United States Army, all came and departed'. What did change, though, was the dress code. At Monte Carlo, most of the people were hardly dressed at all, commented one journalist; never had he seen so much naked flesh of both sexes strolling down the street. Sam White, for 35 years correspondent in Paris of the London *Evening Standard*, described the emergence of St-Tropez, a resort without a casino or any large hotel, as the phenomenon of the time that had set its stamp on the 1950s as surely as the Charleston had done on the 1920s. Its overwhelming characteristic was youth. There was no drunkenness, no hooliganism and barely anything in the way of clothes. Nudism was publicly flaunted. Well could Sean Connery, a star at the 1965 Cannes Film Festival, look around him and say that 'I only knew the French Riviera through reading Hemingway and Scott Fitzgerald, it has changed a lot'.[8]

The sequence of hardship and recovery followed more or less the same pattern in Paris. Initially, food was very short and so was heating, with the icy winter of 1946/47 proving hard to bear. But then, stimulated by the flow of money opened up by Marshall Aid, recovery set in. For the British, there was a replay of sorts of the surges to Paris that had followed the Napoleonic wars, the Commune and the First World War, which was most evident perhaps in the exuberant embassy of Duff Cooper and his wife Lady Diana. It was the Paris of Nancy Mitford and of a Fleet Street seemingly intent on restoring the image of Gay Paree. But it was the city too of Sartre, Malraux and Camus and of the most famous painters in the world, from Picasso down. Once more it took the lead, spectacularly, in women's fashion. For the British it was a muted replay, for this time they were short of money, not so much the result of a general penury as of a meagre and strictly imposed allowance of foreign exchange for travel abroad.

Still, there were moments when it was like old times. In 1950, a sumptuous dinner for 40 guests (brought over on the Golden Arrow train) was held at Maxim's to celebrate the birthday of the young Lord Furness. To the head waiter it was 'just like old times – we dreamed of the day when the English *milords* would be back with us again; now here they are to show that Britain is not down and out'. But actually the party showed nothing of the sort: it was paid for in dollars by Furness's American mother and aunt. Sam White, anchored to his stool at the Crillon bar* – with which he claimed to have had an 'almost structural relationship' – reported the party as he did a

---

* The Crillon had been transformed since George Orwell's time.

myriad other bits of social news. And political and general news too. White paid a great deal of attention to those in trouble at home who found in Paris a convenient refuge. Such was Sydney Stanley, an archetypal conman claiming to work for MI5, who was at the centre of a political scandal in London that forced the resignation of a junior minister. (Stanley was inimitable: had he been Chancellor of the Exchequer, he declared, it would have been the Americans who owed us money.) Another who preferred the ease of life in Paris was the cockney George Dawson, with a fortune made from deals in scrap metal, who lived in the best hotels and owned an ocean-going yacht. White also closely tracked the career of the young Anglo-French James Goldsmith – a different matter altogether – who was to go on to build an astonishing fortune.

The difficulties with foreign exchange occupied a lot of space in White's columns. Max Intrator, born in Egypt – a bit sinister that sounded – accumulated a fortune in those early years, supplying francs to indigent British. However, there were dangers; one of them apparently was a Detective Inspector Tarr who 'haunted' the bars of Paris. And then there was the case of Sir Bernard Docker, by nature a rather self-effacing man, who had inherited a lot of money from his businessman father and was a generous donor to charity. The trouble for him was his wife Nora, 'a former dancing girl', who made a practice of marrying very rich husbands – she was the widow of two when she married Sir Bernard in 1947. Lady Docker was ostentation personified. The Dockers flaunted their money. Sir Bernard was Chairman of BSA (Birmingham Small Arms) which owned Daimler and the coachbuilders Hooper. His gold-plated Daimler stole the 1951 Motor Show but caused some disapproving comment. But it was on France and Monaco that the Dockers' troubles centred. Their lavish yacht *Shemara* seemed always to be moored at Monte Carlo, that is when Sir Bernard was not occupied with his campaign for economy in national spending. Anyway, in 1953 he was convicted at Bow Street magistrates' court of currency irregularities at Monte Carlo, and while his fine was negligible, he was obliged to resign from the board of the Midland Bank. From then on, the Dockers were always in the news – in 1955, when the directors of BSA sacked him for spending company money without consultation, not least on his wife's clothes. While he sought, in vain, to gather shareholders' support, she hired private detectives to investigate the personal and commercial activities of the directors. There was publicity about an insult to a Capri harbour official, and above all concerning outrageous behaviour at the casino, that caused them to be banned from Monaco. Their problem, as *The Times* put it in its obituary of Lady Docker, was that they were a 'symbol of fabulously expensive living in an age ruefully austere'.[9]

Yet the restriction on spending outside Britain and the sterling area did no more than curb the revival of tourism. The number of British tourists to France climbed. By 1949 it was higher than in 1938, although it was not until the mid-1960s that it overtook the record figure of close on 900,000 reached in 1928. Nevertheless, it was reckoned that the reduction in the annual travel allowance in 1952 from £100 to £25 meant a loss of 150,000 tourists for France. However, the importance of British tourism to the French economy was steadily declining. Whereas in 1938 the British constituted more than a third of all foreign tourists, by 1950 they made up no more than one in six, and by 1960 approximately one in nine. By 1980, with restrictions abolished, the proportion was roughly the same. They were far outnumbered by tourists from countries such as Germany, Switzerland and the USA. And the nature of tourism in France was changing. More visitors were using the country simply as a staging post to Spain or Portugal or Italy. They came from lower down the social scale – continuing the familiar trend – as holidays with pay became universal. 'The Grand Tourist of to-day is the Common Man', proclaimed *The Times* in 1956. That in its turn contributed to more backpacking and camping, and to the spread of youth hostels.[10]

What many tourists heartily desired was an escape from the glumness of post-war Britain. They went abroad now not so much for reasons of health, but to bask in the sun, to refresh themselves in a different and, as it seemed, exotic atmosphere. And, in France, they wanted to eat. French cooking, at least in Paris, had been long respected. From the eighteenth century, French chefs were employed in private houses as well as restaurants in Britain. 'I believe that jockeys are the exchange we make for cooks', said Dr Middleton in George Meredith's *The Egoist*, 'and our neighbours do not get the best of the bargain'. But now, the attraction of French cooking was stronger than ever. Food was rationed in Britain into the 1950s, and anyway what you did get was less inventive and less well cooked than in France. Indeed, according to Elizabeth David, it was not until the early 1960s that ingredients available in the shops became plentiful. In London in the early years, outside Soho, middle-range restaurants were few and far between, and some of them were less professional than plain eccentric. Outside London, restaurant food was often just bad. Another inconvenience in Britain was the licensing laws; frequently you had to bring your own (expensive) wine to a restaurant and even pay corkage for the right to drink it. None of that in France. You landed with your car at Calais or Boulogne or (by air) at Le Touquet and, in those pre-motorway days, sped south from Paris along the RN6 or the RN7, with a chain of fine restaurants waiting to claim you. The holiday started off with a good meal.[11]

Should, though, you venture on a detour off the main road, prospects were less appetizing. Deep France, *la France profonde*, might harbour excellent local delicacies, but tracking them down was not always easy. There was little in the way of a restaurant tradition, for until towards the end of the nineteenth century restaurants were very rare outside Paris and one or two other cities. The traveller depended on the *table d'hôte* at his inn or hotel which offered little individual choice. Ford Madox Ford, living in Provence during the 1930s, could refer to local restaurants, but Provence was far from typical of provincial France. The automobile had placed it within easy reach of what Ford termed 'the parasitic bathing towns of the Côte D'Azur'. Arid as it was, Provence had become fashionable, its antique and medieval monuments of great appeal to cultivated tourists. There remained, though, that great empty hinterland away from the tourist centres, unknown to all but a small proportion of visitors, and startling to occasional motorists.[12]

It is the occupation of that hinterland which above all characterizes the British presence in France during the last decades of the twentieth century. The contrast with the past is striking. Travellers' tales, in earlier days, even those by motorists, were sparse. The future, however, was anticipated by Aldous Huxley in the mid-1920s, as he mused on the suburbanization of England. Today, he thought, the Surrey he knew as a boy had disappeared. Hindhead was hardly distinguishable from the Elephant and Castle. 'There is no more country, at any rate within forty miles of London. Our love has killed it.' He turned to the emptiness of France, 'a delight to every lover of nature and solitude', and – author-to-be of *Brave New World* – he hazarded a prediction:

> In time, no doubt, the foreigners will begin to settle: the Italians in the south, the Germans in the east, perhaps even a few English in the west ... My children, I foresee, will have to take their holidays in central Asia.[13]

Huxley may have underestimated the British migration to France that was to come, but he shared that yearning for unspoilt land that was to be at its very heart.

In the event, to Huxley's Germans and Italians must be added the Belgians and Dutch, and the mass of urban French who, abandoning ancestral habits, have acquired second homes in the countryside. An authoritative estimate in 2007, which includes flats and chalets, comes out at three million homes altogether, of which close to 60,000 are thought to belong to British nationals and approaching 200,000 to other foreigners. The British and the Dutch particularly favour the departments that are remote from Paris and situated in the western part of the country. Though it is worth noting that thanks to Airbus there is now an important British community at Toulouse.[14]

In the past, the British had of course made tours in rural France, the prime example being the agriculturalist Arthur Young just before the Revolution. Particularly they had been attracted to the mountains and the territory along the Channel coast. When they settled they almost always did so within certain circumscribed areas, and Aldous Huxley's own French house at Sanary was firmly ensconced within the Mediterranean littoral. However, there were some very serious walkers: in the nineteenth century for instance, Charles Shaw, who started out from Tours in 1831 on a 200-mile hike, and followed it up with a walk from Avignon through to Chamonix and on to Switzerland and Italy. And, some years later, the young Edward Knight, bored with expatriate family life at Honfleur, who walked alone for thousands of miles in Brittany, the Jura and the valleys of the Loire, the Rhône and the Garonne.[15] In the twentieth century, more precisely in the 1920s, John Gibbons tramped from Mont-St-Michel to Lourdes, a distance of well over 600 miles. His account of the expedition tells much of conditions in provincial France between the wars. Gibbons was a devout Catholic pilgrim in his forties seeking the recovery of his wife, ill in a nursing home, and of their sick, newly born baby.[16] The terms he imposed on himself forbade any payment for transport or any request for a lift.* He had little money – his house in Hornsey, he said, was besieged by rate and rent collectors, and his food and very simple lodging were paid for mainly by an advance from a Catholic newspaper. Nor, except for a few words, did he have the language; anyway his French pronunciation was so poor that at best he was virtually incomprehensible. What John Gibbons did possess, however, was a lively sense of humour, and what H. V. Morton, a successful travel writer of the time, described as 'a certain disconcerting, child-like directness and clarity of mind'.

He was indeed direct. Why bother, he thought, to visit the famous Mont-St-Michel, when a couple of hundred thousand other suburban Englishmen have already seen it? Nor was he one for architecture. When a priest talked to him about the Norman architecture in the nave of his church, Gibbons tried his best, but feared that he was looking in the wrong direction. He met very few people who could speak English. A French General – he must be a General, concluded Gibbons, with that demeanour and so many medals – was most polite. It was just as well I could not speak French, he reflected, or it would have come out that I never rose beyond the rank of Lance Corporal. Sometimes he felt he should keep his end up, so he produced a

* He could accept one if proffered, but in fact walked almost all the way.

photograph of his stepson standing in what appeared to be a very grand private garden. In fact, it was the grounds of the Crystal Palace, but still they served their purpose. Sometimes there were embarrassments. Arriving at one village – the first Englishman there since the Middle Ages, he claimed – there was no choice but to pretend to understand a supposedly English-speaking girl pushed forward by her friends. She must have been boasting to them, he thought, on the basis of a correspondence course. At Limoges, where he was lodged at a school, presumably through the good offices of a local priest, the boys were trotted out to show off their English. 'They all told me in very correct phraseology how much they did admire our grand English Shakespeare. Personally, I have never read a line of him, except the *Venus and Adonis*; and that must have been thirty-five years [ago] or so, when another prurient-minded little beast told me there was something indecent in it.' Then there was the question of some lemonade for which he asked the landlady at an inn after a day's march in the sun. She was out-raged, for she thought he was asking for a loan: apparently an Englishman had once borrowed some money from her and never paid it back.

By this time Gibbons looked like a tramp and had got through almost all his money. (His description of life on the road without money is sometimes reminiscent of George Orwell.) People doubted he was an Englishman at all, for where on earth was his 'beautiful automobile'? Probably a Pole, they thought, a Polish tramp, which was a pity for it made it even more difficult to get lodgings for the night. He seems not to have encountered a single Briton on his journey. The nearest he got was an 'unpleasant American', the result of a confused introduction, and a French businessman on holiday in Gascony who happened to work in London.

Cecily Hamilton in her *Modern France as seen by an Englishwoman* of 1933 is more sombre. She describes the contrast between the new hotels on the Côte d'Azur, 'full to overflowing', and the empty farmsteads on the Garonne, and contrasts the decline of the countryside with the rapid growth of suburban Paris. In Burgundy, she came on a notice by the roadside advertising 'village for sale'. Between 1901 and 1962 the rural population fell from 60 per cent of the whole to under 40 per cent, the result of an exodus to the towns, but also of a perilously low birth rate, and of the terrible loss of life during the First World War, witnessed to this day by the long lists on the war memorials of what can never have been more than small villages.[17]

To illustrate the extent of the depopulation in the French countryside one can take an example, a very small example, from Lot-et-Garonne, a department of the south-west now full of British and with a northern boundary that adjoins the Dordogne. Within the canton of Monflanquin, essentially agricultural and fruit-growing, there are 12 communes. Between

1876 (the date of the first census under the Third Republic) and 1999, the population fell by nearly half; in no commune was it anywhere near its original level. Even the population of Monflanquin itself (1876 population, 3,299) dropped by a third. Moreover, in only two communes was the population in 1999 higher than it had been in 1954; overall, the fall since that date was more than 10 per cent. The trend was of long standing. In the commune of Paulhiac the high point was 1841 when the population reached 1,010. In 1999 it was 225.* A return of foreigners in the department made to the Prefect in 1924 came up with 24 British, including two children; though the real figure was probably 22 since two entries appear to be erroneous. Two men and six women lived in Agen, the principal town. Ali Shedded and Ahmed Mohammed, a shop and factory worker respectively, inhabited an Agen suburb, and possibly came from the Empire rather than the British Isles. A Mr and Mrs Barrett were living in another town, Villeneuve. The remainder are attributed to country communes. (A more colourful entry of this sort is provided by a 1935 police report from the Corrèze which names a Noel Lucas-Shadwell of the Château de Bity, an archaeologist, but 'considered by some' to be a member of the British Intelligence Service.)[18]

Back in the nineteenth century occasional British residents (such as John Mill's Benthams) come to light in faraway regions. In 1882, the *Cornhill Magazine*, in its article on 'Cheap Places to live in', observed that one of the 'most enticing features of life in France' was the vast number of *châteaux* dotted over the country. Partly as a result of the law concerning equal inheritance, these pleasant country houses were continually appearing on the market, and 'an Englishman with a little capital can make astonishing bargains if he picks the right time for buying or signing a lease'. That best time, added the *Cornhill*, was likely to be after one of the periods of political turmoil to which France was so susceptible.[19] In 1896, Mrs Courtney Bodley and her husband – who two years later was to publish his highly regarded *France* – were looking for a *château* to rent. They visited a dozen or more in various parts of rural France but none would do. Sometimes the owner really wanted to sell, not to rent; sometimes the buildings were hopelessly dilapidated; and most looked unfit for winter residence – their owners apparently almost always moved to Paris or another large town in winter. One property was too far from the railway, while another was practically on top of it. A resident steward refused them entry into one house; evidently he was not going to put his comfortable lodgings at risk. In the end, friends advised the Bodleys not to bother with the country, but to stick to the Paris region. Which is what they did, ending up very happily in a house with a

---

* There are signs now that the trend is at last broken.

view of the city and, what is more, with old oaks in the park that 'luckily hide the disgraceful Tour Eiffel'.[20]

Philip Gilbert Hamerton, a friend of the Bodleys, settled for a shooting lodge in Burgundy. He and his French wife had also considered *châteaux*, but, thought Hamerton, they were too gloomy. The dining room of one, he said, presented 'as cheerful an appearance as the vestibule of a solicitor's office in Lincoln's Inn Fields at about eleven o'clock at night'. Hamerton was original. Living in Lancashire, he decided it was time to be married. There were suitable rich girls around but they were not his type. He recollected that when in France to learn the language, he had been taken by the daughter of a former departmental prefect, Monsieur Gindriez. Having checked with a mutual friend that she was still unmarried, he sent her a letter, proposing. She accepted. (Definitely, this was a French way of going about things.) Initially, the Hamertons settled in the Scottish Highlands, deciding to move to France for several reasons, one of which, in contrast to the motives of their British successors a hundred years later, was to escape unspoilt nature in favour of something more sophisticated. And expense came into it: Hamerton explained that unless you were prepared to live on oatmeal and diseased meat, it was costly to live 'literally 12 miles from a lemon and 40 from the nearest hairdresser'. It was a question of a day's or half a day's drive.

Anyway they settled near Autun, beautiful country but no wilderness. Had the urge to revisit mountains seized them they could have made for the Alps in the east or the Massif Central to the south.[21] It was in the Massif Central, a year or so after the publication of Hamerton's book *Round my House* in 1876, that Robert Louis Stevenson made his famous trek with a donkey over the mountains of the Cévennes. And it was in the great desolate region of the Auvergne that were to be found the volcanic mountains close to Clermont-Ferrand and the upper reaches of the Dordogne river, which were to be popular with many British. For here were three spas, Royat, Le Mont-Dore and La Bourboule. They flourish still, like most of the spas of France thanks mainly to the resources of the French Health Service. But memories of more cosmopolitan days abound. At La Bourboule, for instance, strung out among a grandiose mixture of building styles, Gothic, Byzantine, Art Deco and Atlantic Seaside, are to be found an Avenue de l'Angleterre, an Avenue des Etats-Unis, a Rue du Canada [sic] and a Rue du Brésil. At Royat there is a Rue Victoria. John Mill described Le Mont Dore (which advertises itself as 'the Capital of Asthma'), where he was taking a cure, as 'a beautiful place, in the heart of a valley which is an old crater, surmounted by summits between 6 and 7,000 feet above the sea'. Louise Costello, who made the arduous ascent by *diligence* in the days before railways, was most enthusiastic. The Auvergne, she declared, is nearer to England than are the Alps and the Apennines. Every English seeker who is after the new and surprising should go to the Mont-Dores and pass a summer there among their 'wild solitudes'.[22]

But this could not be called friendly tourist country. The traveller Lady Verney[23] remarked on the grim poverty, the absence of children, and how in the uplands during the long cold winters the peasants seldom left their houses, but huddled in the barn with the cows. It is no wonder that emigration to the north was particularly marked among the Auvergnats. It was there, or nearby, that the Davies family were still, in Hamerton's day, running their mine near Figeac, and where, a few years later, James Elroy Flecker was to write his poem 'Rioupéroux', of a 'small untidy village' guarded by high and solemn mountains. The husband and wife travel-writing team of Jan and Cora Gordon tried out a summer in the 1920s in the Rouergue on the edge of the Auvergne. According to them, there was a Parisian saying that 'wherever you find an Auvergnat you'll probably find a bed-bug'. But what drove them out was the food. Five months of veal and goose grease, along with 'baccalla'o', a dish of salt and dried cod, were enough. Nor did they like the wine for that matter.[24]

Even the automobile did little to open out the wilder parts of France. Motorists like Francis Williams covered much of the country in an eight-week tour, but that gave little time for loitering. R. R. Gordon-Barrett, in his *Motoring in France* of 1925, discusses Brittany with enthusiasm but he observes that if ever a car can add to the enjoyment of a holiday it is on the Côte d'Azur. Most holidaymakers were likely to prefer the seaside and the nearer uplands. Gordon-Barrett passed through Bergerac in the Dordogne, in our day to possess an airport catering for 200,000 people a year, but considered it a dirty-looking place. Another motorist, 'Owen John', found it 'most picturesque' but unendurably smelly. The writer Peter de Polnay, after the Second World War, had a more serious choice to make. He had loved the Rivera, but arriving at Nice station in 1948 he at once felt that something had gone utterly wrong. There were bungalows everywhere, and the blue of the sky and the sea struck him as too theatrical, as insincere. He sought a region that had nothing in common with Provence except that it should be warm in summer. He hesitated between the Auvergne, warned though he was that it was very savage country, and the Périgord, the department of the Dordogne, which was recommended to him by Cyril Connolly, the editor of the much-respected journal *Horizon*.[25]

Yet supposing you were prepared to put up with some discomforts, bedbugs for example, did it matter much if the country was wild? The Gordons, experienced travellers, would have answered that at least you had to be careful: they were under no illusion but that their Rouergue villagers had the power to force them out should they want to do so. The dangers in romanticizing the remoter regions of France were proved dramatically and tragically by the murder of the Drummond family in the French Alps on 5 August 1952, an episode that captured worldwide attention. Sir Jack Drummond, a senior civil servant and fellow of the Royal Society, his wife and 10-year-old daughter were found dead near the village of Lurs, where they had set up camp for the night. Sir Jack and his wife had been shot and the daughter killed by a blow to the head. It was clear that the murders must have involved the local peasant family of Dominici. Jean Giono, the great expert and writer on peasant life, was in court for the trial of Gaston Dominici, the family patriarch – a figure out of the Middle Ages, a barbarian king, said Giono. The trial was complicated by confusions of language and meaning, by the accusations – and in one case a retraction – brought against the father by his sons, and by the evidence of a grandson, who, Giono noted, was a pathological liar, incapable of speaking the truth. Gaston Dominici was found guilty and sentenced to death. The sentence was never carried out and the case never properly solved.[26]

So outlandish a happening would have been unlikely in Cyril Connolly's Dordogne. During the war years, Connolly had longingly anticipated the first visit he would make to France once peace came. It would not be to Nice or Deauville, or even to Paris. He would land at Bordeaux or La Rochelle and go first to the valley of the Dordogne, 'that beautiful temperate Romanesque corner of France'. A land of friendly people, delicious food and – as was just becoming clear – astonishing prehistoric remains. Moreover, as Connolly[27] later explained in an article in the *Geographical Magazine*, 'If we go for a walk anywhere along the Dordogne we find everything is English – the flowers, the trees, the fields, the hedges – but multiplied to a vast size and enriched by the southern light with a kind of radiance'. Encouraged particularly, it seems, by Freda White's *The Three Rivers of France – Dordogne, Lot, Tarn*, first published in 1952, the British embraced the region, to the extent that by the mid-1950s the Dordogne had acquired for them an almost magical charm. A recent French survey states that for the Dordogne the British feel even now *une attractivité territoriale spécifique*.

There is, however, a distinction to be made between then and now. Freda White was thinking of tourists, not of full-time residents. On the high ground, she says, the winter is long and sometimes severe, but as 'few travellers will visit the country in winter this does not concern us'. Residents, whether full-time or part-time, for the most part came later, not until the 1960s in substantial numbers, even though the Treasury was helpful about allowing money to buy property. It was not until 1982 that the number of permanent British residents in France – 34,180 – attained normal pre-war levels.[28] Why do the British go and where do they choose? An article in the *Geographical Journal* in 1995 noted that:

> Those from south west England mainly move to France permanently due to cheaper costs of living; those from south east England use France as an accessible arena for acquiring a 'genuine' rural home. Buyers in Calvados [western Normandy] seek an 'escape' from Britain, those in Charente-Maritime are drawn to its cheap sun and sand environment: Dordogne and Lot buyers are attracted by traditional landscapes; Vaucluse receives wealthier buyers with stronger prior connections with France.

One could add to that admirably succinct answer. Magazines selling property in France, such as *France* and *French Property News*, make it clear that direct associations with English counties can be an attraction. For instance, some of the Vendée is described as having 'more than a touch of Lincolnshire about it', or alternatively some may be put in mind of Norfolk. However, even if buyers do not necessarily want the scorching summer heat of Provence and the Riviera, they do not look forward to East Anglian weather. Misapprehension about the weather can cause confusion. It always did, as with the invalids arriving at Pau in winter dressed in summer clothes. And the teenager Mary Browne on a tour with her family in 1821, who was shocked when confronted with rain at Calais. The writer Julian More, with a house in Provence, warned about the weather. His family had always envied his great-aunt Bessie, who had lived at Menton, partly on account of the reports she gave of the climate. But, says More, she was hardly in a position to judge, since she clocked into the casino for the day, each and every day, and 'never saw the howling, storm-tossed Mediterranean outside, and consequently reported all her days as halcyon'.[29]

Expatriate life can be very lonely. One writer, in his twenties, remembered being panic-stricken during the first three days in his new house. 'I had lost my habitual self completely, felt myself exposed, abandoned, around me colours I had never seen, forms I did not know, above me a sun such as I had never experienced.' His nearest neighbour was an old woman, obviously half-crazy with loneliness. Though half-crazy himself, he felt no inclination to talk. Dirk Bogarde, living on the Riviera, recalled that during the winter the telephone hardly ever rang, and never between Friday afternoon and Monday morning. Summer brought a complete change. The telephone shrilled, and people he hardly knew kept dropping in or inviting themselves to stay.[30] There is nothing so thick-skinned, declared Peter Mayle, as the seeker after sunshine and free-lodging; unless you are very firm, you will find yourself in summer running a small and highly unprofitable hotel. After the publication of Mayle's best-selling *A Year in Provence*, matters got worse still. Some of these uninvited visitors had not even read the book – they were waiting for the (cheaper) paperback version to come out. One of the funniest books about life in a French village was written by John P. Harris, who based it on a series of talks he gave on Radio Four during 1990 and 1991. Harris was not worried about loneliness but about the possible resentment felt by locals should he and his wife buy a house on their village square. So they consulted an aged inhabitant, Madame Julie. Oh no, she assured them, 'no one minds foreigners here. Why, the Mayor's a foreigner. He comes from somewhere near Millau'. (Millau was all of 50 miles away.) While the old hippy groups who used to camp in the region left when the weather turned cold, the village was momentarily unsettled by a couple of 'terrorists' who stayed on, pale people from up north, he with a beard and an earring and she who went shopping in bare feet. (They turned out to be very shy rather than malevolent.) Harris made it plain that the British in his part of the Languedoc did not want other fellow countrymen moving in on them, and so took pains to warn would-be house-buyers about the scorpions and wild boars.[31] Helena Frith Powell in her recent *More France please, we're British*, records that she and her husband, also in the Languedoc, encountered an English house agent who was reluctant to sell anything. On being reminded of what her job was about, she replied, 'I don't want the place overrun with foreigners. I liked it best a few years ago when it was quieter'.

There are shelves full of books about settling in France. Some are serious studies of life in the countryside. For instance, John Berger's *Pig Earth* was concerned with the disappearance of the peasantry in the French Alps and with such matters as the importance of formality and ritual in their lives. Books may follow a more or less set pattern: the arrival in the village; encounter with suspicious and taciturn locals; various misunderstandings and difficulties; acceptance, the locals eccentric still, but turned helpful and even chatty. There may well be some cheerful teasing about pea-soup fog, the Loch Ness Monster, mad cow disease and foot and mouth and, in the south-west, the Hundred Years War. Yet such descriptions of life and people, even if presented in fictional form, must prove tricky. The journalist Peter Forster in 1965 was asked by a Sunday paper to write an occasional column on life in his Provençal village. It was just not feasible, he considered. To represent the place as picturesquely comic, to turn it into a sort of Clochemerle, would be dishonest, while to carp and qualify would distress overmuch those anglophiles who had been welcoming.[32] But the comic angle is hard to avoid. For instance, in Peter Nichols's play *Chez Nous*, an old Frenchman is made to walk through the living room from time to time, oblivious of the fact that the house is no longer the barn that it once had been. Such a scene in a London play would no doubt slip through unnoticed by anyone likely to take offence. A film is a different matter: the recent film version of Peter Mayle's *A Year in Provence*, something of a travesty of the book, outraged the French critics by its caricature of French village life. Even jokey accounts in a novel or reminiscence written in English might be risky. And there is the case of the French novelist Pierre Jourde who was assaulted by a group of his neighbours in the Cantal for describing his and their village in a book as '*un pays de la merde*', and illuminating local indiscretions in too unguarded a way.[33]

The novelist Celia Brayfield, who spent a year in the Béarn in 2001 and 2002, managed a skilful balance between the comic goings-on and social comment by interspersing her narrative with bits of history and recipes for local food. At the same time, she is candid, pointing out how easy it is for expatriates with little to do to take to hard drinking or to live fantasy lives. Even if someone is not trying to pass him- or herself off as a former SAS hero or a brain surgeon or whatever, 'the neighbours may still prefer to think of them as a far more glamorous character than they really are. With this Walter Mitty spirit abroad, it is unusual for someone to produce concrete proof of their profession'. Here are modern equivalents of the 'synthetic majors' encountered by Douglas Goldring in the South of France during the 1920s. Marriages can be at risk, says Celia Brayfield, for in her experience it was rare for both partners to be equally happy in their unfamiliar surroundings.[34]

Celia Brayfield's acquaintance spanned a broad range in terms of age and profession. Of those who were actively employed, many were in the 'tourist industry', perhaps renting out accommodation to summer visitors. Her British friends included an interior designer, several painters, a writer on food, a couple of would-be arboriculturalists, and an art teacher. Many were retired and, indeed, in the Aquitaine region – of which Béarn forms a part – the British tend be older than the average member of the population. For instance, the 1999 census, the last comprehensive one, shows that 28.94 per cent of the British were aged more than 60 as opposed to an average of 24.9 per cent for the region as a whole. The discrepancy was particularly marked in the departments of the Dordogne and Lot-et-Garonne.

In November 2004, Marie-Martine Gervais-Aguer of the Université Montesquieu, Bordeaux published a detailed survey – the one mentioned above – of the British living as full-time residents in the Aquitaine, its basis the 1999 census.[35] She analysed replies made to a questionnaire, which were supplemented in some cases by interviews. Of the 77,250 British given as

living in France (there are at least 100,000 now), 7,133 were located in one
of the five departments that make up the region. The picture that emerges
may not be typical of the British in France as a whole, but it is at least
indicative. The more indicative since Aquitaine comprises two departments
with substantial urban characteristics, the Gironde (which includes Bordeaux) and the Pyrénées-Atlantiques, and three, the Dordogne, the Lot-et-
Garonne and the Landes, which are predominantly rural. In the first two
departments the British are younger, more likely to be employed and to live
in towns, and to be closer to the local French community. Many of them
form part of an Anglo-French household. Some are students and, though
counting for the census, only temporary residents of France. In the more
rural departments, almost all the British live in the countryside, with low
house prices a very important factor in their choice of where to live. Some
claim an affinity with French culture, for instance an attraction to the
medieval 'bastide' towns. Above all they are drawn by the prospect of an
improved 'lifestyle', a term that tends largely to comprehend a good
(though unreliable) climate and environment. In contrast to the past, health
plays virtually no part, or no direct part, as a reason for immigration,
although the French Health Service is admired. Surprisingly, given their
propensity to mix with fellow countrymen once they have arrived, the
presence of other British appears to be of slight importance when selecting a
place to live.

Marie-Martine Gervais-Aguer's respondents are on the whole highly
satisfied with what they have done. In this they are not quite typical.
(Perhaps it is the happier people who bother to fill in questionnaires.) For it
is clear from statistics and other sources that many would-be expatriates
give up and return to Britain within a few years of arrival. It may be that
they cannot find a job – and that is often not easy in France, even for the
French – or fail to make their own business work. Or it may be that they
have underestimated the cost of setting up a house or simply failed to adapt
to unfamiliar language and customs. A few years back, the choice of where
to live in France was likely to be influenced by the level of importance
attached to easy access to Britain. The recent introduction of cheap flights
and the development of local airports have done much to alter the balance.
It is increasingly common for a family to move to the Pyrenees or nearby,
with the man – usually – working in London during the week. Carola Mills
reports that in her village in the Midi-Pyrénées there is a London Underground train driver in his twenties who does precisely that. She goes on to
say that, after five happy years, she and her husband have decided to sell up
'in order to move on to another project in France'.[36]

It is unlikely that Claude Anet's club-house British in 1920s Le Touquet could have raised a single 'project' among them. However their successors – such of them as exist – view the matter now, they will certainly find plenty of commuters, day commuters often, close to hand. Housing in the area of Le Touquet, Calais and Boulogne is much cheaper than in Kent, and travel by the Tunnel (which of course has greatly simplified connections to France) or ferry or air to a job in Britain is often no great problem.

There are two sets of British visitors to the Channel coast who evoke mixed reactions. One consists of day-trippers over for some vigorous shopping in the supermarkets and other shops of Calais and Boulogne. The other is the product of cheap flights. In October 2006 the *Sunday Times* carried a headline announcing 'Normandy to fight budget Brit invasion', accompanying the article with two photographs, one of the beautiful and chic film star Emmanuelle Béart, the other of a decidedly unchic and less than beautiful British male on the beach with his can of beer. The question was whether Madame Béart and Gérard Depardieu and Kevin Spacey, let alone a host of other elegants, would continue to patronize Deauville should they find themselves in the company of such an unkempt individual.

Also at risk presumably could be the well-heeled French reported to be arriving in Normandy from the Riviera, driven out by the heat, the crowds and the crime. One local estate agent is on record as saying 'We've even sold property here to Brits who've moved up from the south because it was too hot'. The 'even' shows, though, that such sales are rare, for the South exerts a very strong pull on the British. During the later twentieth century, the Riviera continued to provide a home for British literary figures: Graham Greene, Anthony Burgess and Bruce Chatwin all lived there. But now, to inhabit the most desirable places, you would have to sell very well indeed. For they are where the very big money goes. Property at St-Jean-Cap-Ferrat (permanent population 1,895) is the most highly priced of any holiday resort in the world, with British, Irish and American money particularly evident. And the Russians are back in strength. Here the houses are protected by high walls and set at the end of long driveways. Depressingly, many of them are seen, particularly by the Russians, as pure investments to be inhabited by caretakers but seldom by their owners. The British of yesteryear, apparently, are regretted, for at least they occupied their houses for several weeks in summer and the occasional weekend at other times. St-Jean-Cap-Ferrat is in fact just one of four Riviera resorts that rank among the top ten in the world in terms of high property values. And France can claim another two in this select list: Courchevel and Val d'Isère in the Alps. Here a direct correlation has been made with high bonuses paid out in the City of London. Estate agents locally are quoted as saying that a large proportion of their clients are British and are 'nearly all men, single or "dual income no kids", high net worth, 25–35 years old and professional'.

Paris is a different matter, not because it is cheap, but because over the decades the seemingly perennial charm has faded. According to Sam White, to speak ill of Paris in the days after the war was to brand oneself a barbarian. But 30 years later, in the 1970s, he was lamenting that the city had now come to be widely thought of as a clip joint, a cultural desert, an architectural eyesore and a gastronomic poor relation. The American journalist Mary Blume, on 'the Paris beat' between 1965 and 1998, found the younger generation self-absorbed, with little sense of curiosity.[37] Still, no one ever expected Parisians to be cosy.

The South African Suzanne Gordon, selling real estate there, loved the city but warned that while you may not quite require nerves of steel, it is undoubtedly a hard place. 'The front-on British way of doing things doesn't go down well', she says: you must accept people the way they are, and navigate your way around obstacles.[38] Never raise your voice, advises the American David Applefield, thinking mainly in terms of business life, never curse in English, never moralize and never disagree – always agree, but repeat what you want. Among older foreigners the memory has lingered of May 1968 when everything broke down, when there were no buses, no underground, no schools, no newspapers, no banks to cash cheques. What an extraordinary dream it seems now, reflected one writer. For Sarah Turnbull from Sydney, that was all part of the appeal: 'France conjured up thrilling images of radical philosophers and cobblestone-throwing students into marijuana and all sorts of sex'. While her clearly delightful French boyfriend made things easier for her, she found Parisians very un-Australian; cool and restrained towards a stranger who rushed up to them at parties to introduce herself.[39] The best mixer must be the Englishman Michael Sadler. 'I have never met an Englishman who is so thoroughly French', wrote Peter Mayle in his preface to Sadler's *An Englishman in Paris*. 'As noon approaches', observes Mayle, 'I feel sure I can hear a low, persistent sound ... it is the discreet rumbling of a stomach that is ready for lunch'. The book is very funny, but there is room here for only two of Sadler's tips on how to get on in Paris. If renting a flat, remember you may be in competition with 50 other people. What you must do is convince the landlord that you are a rich Catholic, a right-wing non-smoker with no pets and 'not the slightest predilection for chaining girls to radiators after eight o'clock at night'. And, be careful not to give a Parisian the impression that his house in the country is far from Paris.[40]

In fact, Michael Sadler himself has a place in the country, in the Touraine, within fairly easy reach of Paris. His neighbours' idiosyncrasies seem as marked as you might expect from inhabitants of other, more remote departments. Their speciality appears to be hard drinking, so hard in fact that Sadler finds it tough going merely to keep up. (Reassuring this, since the British in France have a lamentable reputation as drinkers.) They sound a good deal jollier than Peter Mayle's Provençal peasants, obsessed by the need to haggle on every occasion. Should the other party to a transaction agree at once to the asking price, they are tormented by the thought that they have not asked enough. As in old times, the British may be regarded as fair game. Foreigners in general may collect whatever blame is going. Bill and Laurel Cooper, living on their houseboat in the Camargue, found during one harsh winter that everyone seemed to come down with flu. The only question was which foreigners were to be blamed; was it Spanish flu perhaps, or was it Chinese or Russian?[41] That the presence of so many foreigners in the countryside is sometimes resented cannot be surprising. Occasionally it boils over, as in Brittany in 2005 when Breton nationalists, brandishing anti-British placards, demonstrated at Bourbriac on the theme that 'Brittany is not for sale'.[42] It must be irritating sometimes to hear almost nothing but English spoken in bars and at country markets. It was that apparently which prompted an old inhabitant of Eymet in the Dordogne, with the Hundred Years War in his mind, to remark of the English now that 'what they could not get by arms, they have by money'.[43] But the money which they and other foreigners and Parisians (to many people in the country there is not much difference) brought with them has been welcomed gladly in a countryside often so badly in need of it. Jobs have been created, buildings and land resurrected, the *patrimoine* sustained. If there are social problems – the effect of increased property prices on the young being one – they have been far outweighed by the advantages.

And of course when a Briton is challenged on the lines of 'how would you like to have French neighbours living next to you at home?', there is a simple answer. We do have, and we do not seem to mind at all.[44] For after all, there are more French residents in Britain than British in France – 300,000 it is estimated, of whom something like two-thirds are in London, a situation which was thrown into high relief by (the now) President Sarkozy's highly publicized visit to London in January 2007 in his quest for votes in the forthcoming election. That is an answer (a somewhat disingenuous one) which would have appealed to Major Marmaduke Thompson.

Major Thompson, an upper-class Englishman living in Paris, was the hugely successful creation of the author Pierre Daninos shortly after the Second World War. He was an attractive and original character close to standard caricature: he parades prominent front teeth, and was in his day a big-game hunter, but is now devoted to golf and gardening. The British, he announces, claim two possessions of outstanding value: their tweeds and their silences. Sometimes there is a good aphorism, for instance, 'The English call themselves sportsmen when they practise some sport: the French call themselves sportsmen when they look on'. Major Thompson is married happily to a French wife. His English first wife, who had died, was less satisfactory, following, as she did, her mother's advice that the best thing to do when making love was to 'close your eyes and think of England'. The French devote to love, said Major Thompson, the care we bring to making tea. (This book, one might note, came out at a time when Frenchmen were coming to London because the women there were more accommodating than at home.) The Major was the end of a line, though even later, in 1958, Edith Piaf named one of her most successful songs 'Milord', its theme a girl in a dance hall who consoles a 'gentleman' whose girlfriend has gone far across the sea.

But Major Thompson was soon a pointless joke, drowned out by the Beatles and the Rolling Stones and by the roar of Carnaby Street and Swinging London. 'England', in the words of Bernard Lemonnier, 'became a model of permissiveness and fantasy', a society in 'full mutation', appropriated by the young.[45] London emerged as the 'the coolest city in the world'. To quote the writer and broadcaster Agnès Catherine Poirier, who lives there, 'the London of 2000 is 1920s Paris: cosmopolitan, full of energy, daring, heroic, untidy, a microcosm of the world'. Echoes of the past of course remain. The Dordogne Organisation of Gentlemen, predominantly British, with dinner jackets obligatory on appropriate occasions, qualifies. Though currently its Chairman is French, and it is worth noting that the English-language newspaper *French News* is far from parochial. But eccentric behaviour is not yet smothered. The French papers recently were full of the late Earl of Shaftesbury – resident in the South of France, genial and generous, murdered for his money by his wife and her brother – whose drinking started before breakfast and carried on the whole day and most of the night. But there are no *misses* of the old school, many fewer nannies and governesses and no ubiquitous Anglican clergymen.

On the cover of Agnès Catherine Poirier's *Les Nouveaux Anglais*, a 'revisitation' of French clichés about the English, there appears a man in a state of frenzy (apparently Damian Hirst). While phlegm itself may be spattering all over the place, old-fashioned phlegmaticism is wholly absent. A stiff upper lip? The one shown here is spongy. What has happened to that staple of staples, good old English hypocrisy? Thinned away into elaborate unmeaning conversational gesture on the lines of 'I'm *dreadfully* sorry' ... for being two minutes late! Very much to the point – this from her companion-book in English – is Poirier's perception of violence in the

English character, expressing itself in part through a habitual forcefulness of language. If that recalls the old idea of 'Goddams', her impression of the essence of British maleness as 'restrained violence' evokes the more virile dandies of the early nineteenth century, above all the threatening figure of Lord Henry Seymour.[46] Then there is the violence of binge drinking and binge sex: for that the British abroad are notorious. The online travel service Expedia's survey of tourist boards worldwide ranked the British as the most 'obnoxious' tourists of all.

José-Alain Fralon, in his witty *Au Secours, les Anglais nous envahissent!* (Help, the English are invading us!) quotes another inhabitant of Eymet (apparently a very articulate place) who identified two sorts of British: the summer ones and the winter ones. The first, the tourists, are noisy, stingy and disorderly – bingers in fact – while the others, the residents, are *sympa*, generous and discreet. 'Like us', he added.

In terms of those British more closely engaged with France, homeowners and those who spend much time there, there are two profound differences with the past. Their nineteenth-century predecessors came, not to be reminded of home, but, their health permitting, to experience and enjoy what was unfamiliar. Now one of the greatest pleasures is the unspoilt countryside of France, with the reminder it brings of what was once so dear in England to their grandparents or their great-grandparents. Of what, in Huxley's words, 'our love has killed'. Secondly – and this must apply mainly to expatriates – while they may spend much of their time with fellow countrymen, they do not relish the idea of a life apart, in fact they long for acceptance as part of the local community.[47]

Notes

Abbreviations: FO: Foreign Office records, deposited at The National Archives, Kew
DNB: Dictionary of National Biography, Oxford edition

Notes to Chapter 1: The False Start

1 Chevrillon on 'Nos Anglais' in *La Revue de France* April 12, 1925
2 Martineau
3 Berry v. 2
4 'a demoniac' – Weston
5 This quotation and most of those which follow are taken from Wilmot, edited by Mavor. Also however see T. U. Sadleir. I have preferred Mavor's 'Katherine' to Sadleir's 'Catherine'.
6 Plumptre v. 1
7 F. E. King
8 Blagdon
9 For Lille see Trotter.
10 See Paul.
11 Sir G. Jackson v. 1
12 For 'dreadful associations' see J. King; and, for private mansions, Carr.
13 Warren
14 Burney (1904/5)
15 Greatheed; and Opie
16 Berry v. 2 and Blagdon
17 For Yorke see Sykes, and for the British in Paris during the Revolution and during the Amiens peace see Alger (1889) and Lewis. Also see Alger's article in the *English Historical Review* v. 13, 1898.
18 Burney (1975)
19 Edgeworth
20 For Cornwallis see DNB, Wickwire and Cornwallis 'Correspondence..'and for the high spending Warren. For relations with Bonaparte see Poniatowski (1986).
21 For C. J. Fox see L. G. Mitchell; and the *Gentleman's Magazine* May 1802.
22 Trotter and, for Napoleon's later view, Crouzet. Also see Opie.
23 Roget

24 For British in Paris and at Verdun see Boutet de Monvel (1911), Lewis and Alger (1904). F. E. King

25 For Italy, see Wilmot and, for Lord Bristol, Fothergill.

26 Wilmot

27 Elgin

28 For Talleyrand and the Americans see Poniatowski (1982). For 'De Bathe' see Alger.

29 Greene's escapade is related in Burney (1975); see also Greene.

30 For 'Cosway' see Berry, Greatheed and Barnett.

31 Pinkney

32 Life at Verdun is described by Bussell, Sturt, Lawrence, Wright, Forbes and Langton. For the English nanny see Davies.

33 The papers of the Lloyd's Patriotic Fund are held at the Guildhall Library, ms 35166, v. 3.

34 For Sir Joseph Banks and Edward Jenner see Williams.

35 The fire-lighter reference is from Lawrence v. 1 and the quotation on the 'Grande Rue' from Langton.

36 Boutet de Monvel (1911) comments on the 'debauchery' at Verdun. For the French mistresses see Alger (1904) and for the Anglo-French offspring below an article by B. Govett in the *Genealogists' Magazine* v. 21, Mar. 1983.

Notes to Chapter 2: Travelling before the Railways

1 Irving is quoted in J. Taylor. See Best.

2 Statistics from Gerbod

3 Ellis

4 Bordeaux families from Butel

5 For 'Potter' see Greene. Derainne & Veglia, *Les Etrangers en France* v. 2 (1999), a guide to archival sources, refers to the unemployed British workmen.

6 Wansey

7 For British industrialists in France at this period see Dunham, Heywood and Ballot.

8 Raffles

9 Stothard

10 E. J. Eyre

11 Berry v. 2; Eyre; the 'cormorant' quotation is from Plumptre.

12 Paul

13 Roots

14 Paul

15 Plumptre; Carr describes the released prisoners.

16 F. E. King

17 For French postillions see D. Carey.

18 Berry v. 2

19 F. J. Carey; Bunbury. V. Hugo is quoted by Fourcassié. Ellis

20 For tourist transport before the railways see Withey and F. E. King.

21 For wheels dashing through the water see 'Anon': *A Spinster's Tour'*, For the continued 'shake, shake' of steamboat engines see 'Anon': *The Bull Family*. See Hazlit.

22   The *Blackwood's* reference is v. 42, 1837.

23   For 'Ruskin' see Links.

24   The differences between Paris and the provinces are discussed in Playfair. See Stendhal and Fournier-Verneuil.

25   Kitchiner

26   For Yorke see Sykes.

27   For Quillacq's see Thackeray, and Eagles for Sydney Smith's eulogy.

28   Pinkney

29   Holcroft, Mayne and Wilmot

30   Shepherd

31   The 'Goddam' in the diligence is described by Reboul.

32   Campbell; Bunbury

33   Hazlitt

34   Strachey

35   The arrival at the Hotel Meurice is described by MacDonogh.

36   J. A. Scott

37   For Yorke see Sykes.

38   For Dormer and the Tuftons see Calton.

39   Campbell

40   For Brummell see Raikes; Woolf; Boutet de Monvel (1908); M. Boulenger

Notes to Chapter 3: A Tumultuous Entente

Mansel and Elkington provide comprehensive studies of the British in Paris during the years following the restoration of the Bourbons in 1814.

1   Hazlitt

2   Roots

3   Jameson

4   Berry v. 3

5   Sir W. Scott

6   Weston; Clayden

7   Jameson

8   For the country gentleman's library see Hall.

9   Stanley

10   Vandam

11   For Quintin Craufurd see in particular Elkington, M. Sadleir and Lapie.

12   For Egerton see Boutet de Monvel (1911).

13   Gronow

14   Reboul

15   Broglie

16   Granville

17   Haydon

18   Gerbod

19 For backgound on Manby and Wilson see Dunham and the *Transactions of the New-comen Society* v. 29, 1953.

20 *The Times* reported the events at Charenton on April 22, May 4 and May 17, 1824.

21 Police surveillance of foreigners is recorded in Guyot.

22 For alleged conspiracies see Forgues. Lord Kinnaird's involvement in plots to kill the Duke of Wellington is given by Elkington.

23 For the alarmist report of the effect of the withdrawal of the occupying forces see *The Times* Aug. 28, 1818.

24 For Stendhal's articles see Dollot.

25 Lady Morgan (1817)

26 Granville

27 The Scottish soldiers are discussed in Boutet de Monvel (1911).

28 For Lord J. Russell see Prest.

29 For Wright see Mansel.

30 Castellane v. 2, 1895. For clubs see Yriarte.

31 For the ball see Mansel.

32 For names lifted from Scott see Wagener.

33 Lady Morgan (1830)

34 *Blackwood's* March 1846. The attitude of the French nobility is discussed by Reboul. For Bryon see J. Boulenger.

35 See also J. Boulenger for the extraordinary family of Seymour-Conway, marquesses of Hertford. They figure in many of the memoirs, including those of Gronow, Raikes and Greville, and as collectors in Mallet and Hughes. They figure as debauchees also in Connolly.

36 Goncourt referred thus to Hertford on July 7, 1869.

37 For Henry Seymour see in particular Roy, Guyot and Yriarte.

38 For dandies see Boutet de Monvel (1911) and Reboul.

39 Dino v. 3

40 H. H. Wright

41 For the 'superbly dressed' British at Court see Martin-Fugier.

42 See Elgin and DNB.

43 For Admiral Sir Sidney Smith see Pocock.

44 *The Times* report on debtors in France is dated August 30, 1816.

45 Boutet de Monvel (1911) comments on Potter, and Gronow on Livry and his parties; Haydon

46 Maclean and Elkington. The ruined gamblers figure in Gronow and Raikes; for Scrope Davies also see Burnett.

47 His interview with Gronow is described by H. de Villemessant in his *Mémoire d'un Journaliste* v. 1 (1867).

Notes to Chapter 4: Pau and the Spas

1 Thornton, and also 'Col.T. Thornton' in DNB

2 Haydon

3 Pinkney

4　Boddington

5　Dormandy; Castellane v. 1, 1895

6　Tucoo-Chala

7　The welcome to Wellington's army is recorded in Vigny as below.

8　Lefevre

9　Hardy

10　For the clergyman see Trench.

11　The cows feature in *Blackwood's* v. 130, July/Dec. 1881; the peasants on stilts and the dandy in Grattan; the Spanish Customs Officers in *Fraser's Magazine* v. 44, July 1851.

12　See Packe.

13　The guide's revenge is from Fourcassié.

14　Wittitterly; Ellis

15　Duloum describes the early days of the British in Pau; see also Fourcassié.

16　See Vigny: paper presented by Y. Legrand.

17　The less than exclusive balls are recorded in Wittitterly.

18　Harriet Jephson's (unpublished) journals are in the author's possession.

19　Duloum

20　Bertall

21　Murray

22　Costello (1844)

23　Taine

24　*Galignani's Messenger* Mar. 9, 1840

25　Murray is the witness to the arrivals at Bagnères-de-Bigorre while Bunbury deplores the mix of visitors in the Pyrenees.

26　See Paris for Eaux-Bonnes.

27　Fourcassié for the medical facilities at Eaux-Bonnes; see Senior.

28　M. Eyre

29　Bunbury

30　Jarrassé. For the statistics relating to the resorts see Gerbod and Fourcassié.

31　The *Blackwood's* volume number is 59.

32　Newton and Wallon

33　*Plombières et ses Thermes* was published anonymously at Nancy in 1880. For Brainne see Wallon.

34　The close links within European high society are described by Rauch.

35　Granville. Ring (2000) for the British in the Alps

36　See Wallon for Contrexéville, and Achard and Wechsberg for Aix-les-Bains.

Notes to Chapter 5: The Transport Revolution

1　For Jephson see note 18 in Chapter 4 above.

2　Mill: *Collected Works* v. 14

3　J. B. Drayton, writing in *Chamber's Journal* v. 8, 1904/1905

4　For 'sheep pen' see Miller; see Siebecker.

5　Desportes, Schivelbusch and O'Moore

6　Talfourd

7   Desportes quotes Napoleon III
8   Dickens's description is from *Our Mutual Friend*.
9   Faith (1990). *The Calais Night Mail'* is published in 'Dickens in France'.
10 See Thackeray
11 'Dickens in France' as above and Delattre
12 For 'Luchon' see Cazes; Siebecker
13 For 'Arcachon' see Marandon and Moncrieff
14 Dino v. 2, May 1840
15 *A Flight* is published in 'Dickens in France'. This is Stevenson's *Ordered South* published in *Macmillan's Magazine* v. 30, May 1874.
16 Ruskin is quoted in Schivelbusch; also see Links.
17 Articles on the Pyrenees were published in *Blackwood's* v. 62, Dec. 1847 and v. 130, July/Dec. 1881.
18 See A. Trollope.
19 *Blackwood's* v. 97, Feb 1865 – an article entitled *Knight Errantry in the Nineteenth Century*
20 Viator Verax; Siebecker
21 O'Moore
22 Advice about tainted water is given by Miller. Gerbod enumerates hotels with British associations.
23 For Ruskin see Links; Ahn
24 Mallock
25 For Thomas Cook see Brendon, Swinglehurst, Withey.
26 The *Illustrated London News,* 'The Whitsuntide Trip to Paris', June 8, 1861
27 Bertram's 'Fish Culture in France' was published in Galton: *Vacation Tourists* for 1864.
28 Garvey
29 For Layard see DNB and reports in *The Times* for July 3 and Aug. 26, 1867.
30 Gerbod
31 Buzard

Notes to Chapter 6: Rosbif and Frog

1   The 'authority' was writing in the *National Review* v. 25, Mar.–Aug., 1895.
2   For Bordeaux see the *Revue Historique de Bordeaux* t. 23, 1974. See Crouzet. The 'Jekyll and Hyde' comparison is made by Dabernat.
3   For Brittany see FO 146/672.
4   Pakenham
5   The difficulties about the church are set out in FO 97/202 and 203.
6   Trench; and for the monks see Barou & Prado.
7   For Consul Brummell see FO 27/435 and 453.
8   Consular correspondence more generally is included in the Foreign Office files. FO 27/673, 27/731, 27/760, 27/673. For the Bishop of London and Lord Mornington see 27/731; for Copland see 27/760. Consul Turnbull's list is given in 27/675.
9   For the railway navvies see Henderson, Coleman and Faith (1990); the Mayor of Le Havre's protest is recorded in FO 27/673.

10   Castellane v. 4, 1896
11   For the expulsion of British workers see Tombs.
12   *The Times* reports are in issues for Apr. 4 and 21, 1848 and May 22, 1850.
13   See Burton and Kennedy.
14   Sala 1894 v. 2 and 1895; also Straus. *Monsieur Gogo* was published in 'Household
     Words' v. 4, Jan. 24, 1852; 'leapfrog' is quoted by Hamerton (1889).
15   For folklore see Johnson in the *Contemporary Review* v. 134, July–Dec. 1928.
16   Dallington. The 'half-drunk'description is by Dr Veryard, quoted in Watrin.
17   *A Flight* is from 'Dickens in France'.
18   *Bentley's Miscellany* v. 51, Jan. 1862
19   The Englishman who prefers a sedate climate appears in Sir G. Jackson v. 1.
20   For Emerson see Rahv; H. H. Wright.
21   Stothard
22   For Berry see Jaeger.
23   Faucher
24   Marchal; Lapie
25   Taine
26   F. J.Carey
27   For Mill on women see *Collected Works* v. 17, Oct. 5, 1869.
28   Dempster
29   *Macmillan's Magazine* v. 5, 1861–62. For Craik's 'A City at Play' see *Macmillan's
     Magazine* v. 18, 1868. For Thackeray and tenderness to children see Moraud.
30   'There go the English' comes from Lamont.
31   For Croker's article see *Fraser's Magazine* v. 43, Feb. 1851.
32   For 'Mill' see *Boyhood Visit to France*. The other direct references are taken from Mill:
     the *Collected Works*; v. 1 (Autobiography), pp. 58–61; v. 20, pp. 184, 235, 331, 332, 343;
     v. 2, letter of July 28, 1837; and letter to Tocqueville, p. 271; v. 13, a letter of Feb. 23,
     1841; v. 23, a book review, p. 717.

Notes to Chapter 7: The Riviera

Excellent studies of the Riviera in the nineteenth century are provided by Howarth and
Blume (1992).

1   Plumptre v. 2
2   Berry v. 2
3   See Féliciangeli for the British in Nice in the eighteenth century.
4   The 'English Montpellier' reference comes from Conway. H. Matthews.
5   *Macmillan's Magazine* v. 15, Nov. 1866
6   For Brougham see T. H. Ford. Dino, v. 3, Dec. 20, 1841.
7   Sir H. Taylor
8   The population figure for early Cannes is provided by Bianchi.
9   For Woolfield see Mossop.
10   Spencer

11   For the freshwater canal see Antier. See Mérimée and Raitt; Mérimée's letters are dated Dec. 17, 1856, July 26, 1856, and Nov. 24, 1861.

12   Goncourt writes on Mar. 3, 1869.

13   Brewster

14   For Jephson see note 18 in Chapter 4 above.

15   For Mérimée's reaction to Provence in the 1830s see Pope-Hennessy. See also on Provence T. A. Trollope and Barker.

16   Janvier; the *Blackwood's* reference is v. 35, May 1884.

17   The information on Harmsworth has been provided by Mme Costes of Nestlé Waters UK. There was a *Times* obituary on May 5 1933.

18   Linn describes Hyères; Lear

19   For the Foreign Office and Menton see FO 27/1545.

20   Bertall

21   Chambers. R. L. Stevenson's boyhood visit to Menton is described in the diary of his nurse Alison Cunningham, published as *Cummy's Diary* in 1926. For Stevenson's second visit to Menton see 'Ordered South' in the *Works of Robert Louis Stevenson* v. 23, 1912. (The epigraph to this chapter is also taken from 'Ordered South.)

22   Chambers; Miller

23   For railways and the Riviera see Withey and Page.

24   The Russians as travellers are mentioned by Conway; see Cane for Villefranche; Dempster.

25   Daullia; Clermont-Tonnerre

26   Bresson

27   Antier describes the welcome given to the President of the Republic.

28   Liégeard; Dr Taylor; *Blackwood's* May 1889.

29   Queen Victoria's high opinion of the Riviera's therapeutic powers is reported by Paoli.

30   Blume (1992) and Howarth. See 'Monte Carlo and Public Opinion'. The Bishop's letter to *The Times* was published Apr. 3 1883. For Dr Bennet see Pemble. Dempster

31   The reference to 'cocottes' is provided by Goldberg; see also C. Graves (1951)

32   J. R. Green

33   Oliphant's article was published in *Blackwood's* v. 145, May 1889.

34   T. Jones

35   Duffy

36   Information on Mrs Stewart of Hyères was provided by Mme Grimaud of the Hyères Public Library.

37   Mérimée, Dec. 4 1864. See Nelson, Pemble, Gerbod, Souza and Gonnet for the development of the Riviera.

38   See Lady D. Nevill for her account of the revolution in travel.

39   R. Schor wrote of 'Nice pendant la Guerre de 1914–1918', a thesis issued by *Annales de la Faculté des Lettres, Aix-en-Provence* (Travaux et Mémoires 32, 1964).

Notes to Chapter 8: Babylon

1   For the cost of living, and the economic influence of foreigners see Mauco, Singer-Kérel and Gerbod and, for the exchange rate, B. R. Mitchell (1975).

2   The *Cornhill* article, v. 45, 1882 was entitled 'Cheap Places to Live in' – see also Moncrieff and Bidwell.

3   O'Dowd

4   Miss Betham-Edward's article on household budgets abroad was published in *Cornhill* July–Dec. 1904.

5   For numbers see Mauco and Gerbod; Bicknell

6   Newte

7   For E. Smith see Grant; Gide

8   Barblan

9   For the Davies family see Davies & Broughall.

10 Daumard

11 Vandam (1895)

12 For Hugo see Mansel

13 Jerrold; Pirie

14 See Mérimée; and Tocqueville, pp. 859–60.

15 For Miss Clarke see Stendhal (1975), Hamerton (1897) and Marandon.

16 Horne (1965) and Labouchere

17 The Ambassador's problems are revealed in FO 146/1507 and 146/1504.

18 For Sisley see also Shone.

19 O'Shea and Gibson

20 Goncourt on Mme Sabatier: letter of Nov. 9, 1871. For Richard Wallace see references under Hertford in notes to Chapter 3; and Lapie.

21 For British food gifts after the siege of Paris see *Blackwood's* v. 124 for August 1878 and v. 157 for 1895.

22 For Worth see Horne (1965) and Saunders.

23 The interview is reported in *Blackwood's* v. 157, May 1895, under heading of 'Mr Worth'.

24 Blount, Barblan. Marshall's article 'Paris as an English Residence' was published in the *Fortnightly Review* v. 43, 1885. For living in Paris see also P. E. Ogden, *Foreigners in Paris. Residential Segregation in the Nineteenth and Twentieth Centuries*, Occasional Paper 11, Department of Geography, Queen Mary College, University of London (October 1977).

25 Miss Leigh's work in Paris is recorded in *The Times*, Sept. 17 and 21, 1874; Dec. 21, 1876; Feb. 26, 1880; Aug. 28, 1883; Oct. 26, 1888.

26 For Holden see Henderson and Honeyman & Goodman.

27 Waddington 1908 and 1914; Lequin

28 For the Wilson scandal and its background see Chapman, Dansette and Lequin.

29 For Wolff see Milner; Bennett (1913)

30 See Beardsley and Moore

31 For Holland see *The Studio* v. 27, 1902.

32 S. Fox

33 Jones for Kipling, and Campos

34 Mérimée wrote to Sharpe on June 3, 1829. See Forster (1848). Prostitute numbers are supplied by Zeldin.

35 For E. Howard see Maurois and Bingham.

36 For Cora Pearl see Richardson.

37 M. Boulenger

38 McGilligan

39 Du Camp is quoted in Rearick (1985). Rudorff; *Cornhill*, 'Englishmen and "Foreigners"' Dec. 1884, The 'forwardness' of English girls is alleged in *Cornhill* v. 45, 1882.

40 Hamerton (1889)

41 Rhodes and Alb

42 B. St. John

43 Marandon

44 Parisian architecture is described by Dickens in *Dickens in France*.

45 Evenson for the illumination of Paris

46 Davis 1892 and 1895

47 Moore; and for Arnold Bennett see Drabble.

48 Symons and Jullian (1977)

49 For the Bowes see I. V. Wilkinson's 'John and Josephine Benoite Bowes and France of 1870–1871' in the *Durham University Journal* v. 51, March 1959.

50 Also for Montmartre see Lapie and Rudorff.

51 Zelda Fitzgerald is quoted in Littlewood.

Notes to Chapter 9: The Atlantic Coast

1 See Grant

2 John Hobbs is quoted in Links.

3 The British expatriate is J. A. St. John.

4 Watrin

5 For painters see Leribault and Faber

6 For Cotman see H. I. Kay (ed) 'John Sell Cotman's Letters from Normandy', published by the *Walpole Society*, vs. 14 & 15, 1926 and 1927.

7 Marandon for the British in Normandy. The British visitor was J. A. St. John.

8 For Brittany see Baughan and *Cornhill* v. 45, June 1882.

9 H. Vizetelly v. 2

10 The Dinard families are noted by C. Anet in an article in *L'Illustration* July 26, 1924. 'Bric-à-Brac' comes from *Le Pays Malouin* (local St Malo paper) Aug 3, 2006

11 James

12 For Dieppe see Pakenham; for Sickert see also the *Listener* Dec. 23, 1954 and Blanche (1937). Henry James's reaction to Dieppe is reported in Blanche (1937). The *épaves* are described in Blanche (1927).

13 For Wilde at Dieppe see Jullian (1969) and Goodman.

14 For the railways see Rauch.

15 Weber

16 M. Boulenger

17 Watrin. The dangers of sea-bathing are described in Désert, Morand, Weber and O'Moore.

18 The newspaper is *The Channel*.

19 *Blackwood's* v. 166, Sept. 1899. For Mérimée recovering at Biarritz, see letter Sept. 22, 1862. For 'Dress Outfits for Abroad' see A. Holt.

20 For keeping Biarritz smart see Barthez.

21 For fashionables see Thompson. Hale

22 Stamper

23 Pemberton

24 J. Bolster in his *The Upper Crust* wrote on motoring language.

25 Neville

26 Kipling

27 Gerbod for cross-Channel traffic

28 Moncrieff welcomed the arrival of 'worthy citizens'. For bookmakers see *The Times* Aug. 24 and 29, 1891.

29 For British industrialists see Daumard, Fohlen and Lequin (1988). Henderson refers to the 'suburb of Nottingham'.

30 Waddington 1908 and 1918

31 Jullian (1967) writes on Mme Waddington in London.

32 See B. St. John, Adam, Strong.

33 For Pratz see the *Contemporary Review* v. 108, July 1915.

34 *Fortnightly Review* v. 98, July–Dec. 1915. Marandon for change in temperament.

35 Le Blond

36 Whitaker

37 For background on relations between British soldiers and the French civilians, see Tombs, Holmes and Liddle.

38 The references in the Imperial War Museum, the Department of Documents, are to the Papers of Lt L. J. S. Hill; Lt Col H. J. C. Chappell; Lt D. Macdonald; Capt. P. H. B. Lyon MC and Lt W. M. Peto.

39 For the contrast of peasant and soldier see K. Bell's 'Joys and Sorrows of a Town Major in France' in the *Nineteenth Century and After* v. 81, Jan. 1917.

40 *Ibid.*

41 For this reference and general background see K. C. Gibson's articles in the *History Workshop Journal* v. 55, Spring 2003; and in *Past & Present* v. 178, Feb. 2003.

42 C. Lewis

43 The jingle is from Guyard, quoting L. Lemonnier.

44 Kipling

45 R.Graves, and for Clarke, *Cornhill* v. 39, July–Nov. 1915.

46 Auden's view of John Bull appears in his *Letter to Lord Byron*.

Notes to Chapter 10: Displacement

1 From *The Garden of Eden*

2 For Maupassant see Troyat, and for Swinburne, D. Thomas.

3 Jacquier

4 For Anet, *L'Illustration* July 5, 1924. For Taine see *French History* v. 14, June 2, 2000.

5 See Desgraves and *Revue Historique de Bordeaux* t. 23, 1974.

6   Dupeux's article is entitled *L'Immigration britannique à Bordeaux au xix siècle et au début du xx*. Faith 1978 and 1983

7   For Ellis see DNB and for sport in general see Barblan.

8   Coubertin – see *Journal of Contemporary History* v. 5, April 1970. Orwell.

9   Tombs and R. Holt. The French journalist is quoted in Rearick (1997).

10 Williams

11 For gardens on the Riviera see Quest-Ritson, Collas and Johnston.

12 On the change in the 1920s see Bocca, Howarth, Silver; and for tourism more generally, Turner & Ash. C. Matthews writes of the effect on hotels.

13 Blume (1992)

14 The Americans' taste for summer heat is referred to in Ring (2004).

15 For the American soldiers see Schor, reference as in the notes to Chapter 7.

16 Goldring

17 See Pinkney, Wharton and Tombs.

18 The exhibition at Nice was celebrated by 'Les Anglais sur la Riviera' in the *Riviera Magazine*, Nice, Feb.–April 1934.

19 For exchange fluctuation see B. R. Mitchell (1988).

20 For French resentment see Schor (1985), R. Nevill and Collier. The journalist (unidentified) is from Nevill as above. For Mistinguett see White.

21 Collier; Cody

22 Orwell; D. J. Taylor. Revue *Hebdomadaire* July 18, 1931

23 Ramuz

24 Gerbod; B. R. Mitchell (1988)

25 Newman. Robb is interesting on earlier British cyclists in France.

26 For links by air see Rauch, Cronin (1994) and Macmillan.

27 Margetson describes the British on the Channel Coast. See too C. Graves (1963).

28 Adam on Deauville. For the poisoning of Morny see Reyt.

29 For Beauty Queens at Deauville see Désert.

30 For Le Touquet see Klein.

31 Anet is writing in *L'Illustration*, June 14, July 5 and 26, 1924.

32 *The Field*: articles appeared on Aug. 8, 1936; July 19, 1937; Aug. 6 and 20, 1938. Again Klein

33 For the Duke of Westminster see Field, C. Graves (1963) and Cannadine. The Barnato race was described in the *Financial Times* Nov. 1/13, 2005.

34 Bresson. For Lord Derby see Bocca.

35 Collier; Huxley is quoted in Turner & Ash.

36 Morris for V. Woolf

37 Waterfield

38 For Winifred Fortescue see also *Blackwood's* 'Driving a Car in Provence', July 1934.

39 *Sociological Review* April 29, 1937

40 Fortescue (1941)

41 The Foreign Office references in the National Archives are 371/24310, 310/25194,371/24326 and 369/2744.

42 Donaldson for Wodehouse

43 Sutherland and Stuart (unpublished). For the letters to Lord Halifax see K.9949/9949/ 236 (Portugal) in the original register.
44 For internment see Blume (1999), Gerbod.
45 Downing, Fontaine, Lytton
46 Mayo
47 For difficulties with Vichy see Howarth and R. T. Thomas.
48 For the evacuation from Cannes see Maugham and Bocca.

Notes to Chapter 11: The Rural Idyll

1 War damage at Le Touquet is described by Klein; see Alsop, Henrey; and for Cunard see Cody.
2 Cooper
3 Fortescue (1948) and DNB
4 For John Taylor see Wilkinson.
5 Sansom in the *Geographical Magazine* Oct. 1947. Harvey in the *Contemporary Review* v. 172, Dec. 1947.
6 Mayo
7 Muggeridge, *New Statesman and Nation* Mar. 1, 1963
8 Bocca. For nudity see P. Carr in *The Spectator*, May 28, 1948. White. For Connery see *Cannes Memories*, 'The Official album of 50th anniversary of international Film Festival' (2000).
9 White for the Furness party; for the Dockers see *The Times* Feb. 25, 26 and 28, 1953 and (for the obituary) Dec. 22, 1983. Also see Bocca.
10 For tourist numbers, see Gerbod; the 'Common Man' article was published in *The Times* Aug. 4, 1956.
11 David; for restaurants on roads see Pitte.
12 For earlier provincial restaurants Spang and Ford
13 Huxley
14 An estimate of the number of secondary homes was given in *Le Monde* May 13 and 14, 2007.
15 For Shaw and Knight, see Jebb.
16 Gibbons
17 For statistics on emigration from the countryside see Kedward.
18 Population statistics for Lot-et-Garonne are taken from *Sous les Arcades*, numéro spécial, Canton de Monflanquin, juillet/aôut 2004, and from the departmental archives at Agen, série M, no. 4, 825. For Lucas-Shadwell, see Derainne & Veglia, *Les Etrangers en France* v. 1 1999.
19 For *châteaux*, see *Cornhill* v. 45, 1882.
20 Mrs Bodley's article appeared in *Blackwood's* v. 159, Jan. 1896.
21 Hamerton 1908 and 1897
22 For Le Mont-Dore etc. see Mill: *Collected Works* v. 20 and Costello (1842).
23 Lady Verney described the Auvergne in the *Contemporary Review* v. 42, Dec. 1882.
24 See Gordon
25 'Owen John' and Polnay

26   The Drummond case is reported in *The Times* Aug. 6, 1952 and in Giono.

27   See Connolly and, for his description of the Dordogne, the *Geographical Magazine* Mar. 1952.

28   Gerbod has calculated the number of residents.

29   Browne; Barou & Prado; see Forster in *New Statesman and Nation* Dec. 3, 1965.

30   White; Bogarde

31   Harris

32   Powell; Forster's 'An Expatriate for me' was published in the *New Statesman* Dec. 3, 1965.

33   Pierre Jourde's problem was reported in *Le Monde* June 22, 2007.

34   See Brayfield.

35   The survey was published in November 2004 for the Groupement de Recherches Economiques et Sociales for the Université Montesquieu-Bordeaux 4, under the title *Les fondements de l'attractivité territoriale résidentielle. Les enseignements d'une recherche portant sur les résidents britanniques en Aquitaine (France).*

36   Carola Mills writes in *French Property News* June 2006. For 'internal migration', see *Financial Times* Sept. 9/10, 2006.

37   For property on Riviera now, see *Le Monde* May 11, 2007 and September 7, 2006, *Sunday Times* Feb. 11, 2007, see Blume (1999).

38   Suzanne Gordon is reported in *Financial Times* Sept. 30/Oct. 1, 2006.

39   See Applefield; the 'extraordinary dream' comes from Gallant. See Turnbull.

40   Sadler 2002 and 2004

41   B. & L. Cooper

42   Fralon

43   The old inhabitant is quoted in Guiffan.

44   The French neighbour's challenge is reported in the *Guardian* Jan. 4, 2007.

45   For Lemonnier's 'La Culture Pop' see Bonnaud. Dabernat

46   Poirier

47   Fralon, and for the survey of tourist boards, *Le Monde* June 2, 2007 quoting the *New York Times*. Generally also see Tombs and, for changing British character, Faber.

Bibliography

Achard, A. (1850) *Une Saison à Aix-les-Bains*. Paris: Ernest Bourdin

Adam, H. P. (1919) *Paris sees it Through*. London: Hodder & Stoughton

Ahn, F. (1862) *Manual of French Conversation*. London: G. Bell & Sons

Alb, [H.Whiteing] (1886) *Living Paris and France*. London: Ward & Downey

Alger, J. G. (1889) *Englishmen in the French Revolution*. London: Sampson Low

Alger, J. G. (1904) *Napoleon's British Visitors and Captives*. London: Constable

Alsop, S.M.(1976) *To Marietta from Paris*. New York: Doubleday

Anon. (1829) *The Bull Family at Boulogne*. Paris: J. Smith

Anon. (1828) *A Spinster's Tour in France ... 1827*. London: Longmans

Antier, J-J. (1872) *La Côte d'Azur*. Paris: Editions France-Empire

Applefield, D. (2003) *Paris: Inside Out*. Guildford, CT: Globe Pequot

Ardagh, J. (1989) *Writers' France*. London: Hamilton

Auden, W. H. *Collected Longer Poems*. London: Faber & Faber

Autin, J. (1984) *Les frères Pereire*. Paris: Librairie académique Perrin

Avenel, P. & P. Vaydat (2000) *La France Fascinante et Détestée*. Arras: Artois Presses Université

Ballot, C. (1923) *L'Introduction du Machinisme dans l'Industrie française*. Lille/Paris: Marquant/Rieder

Barbey d'Aurevilly, J-A. (1845) *Du Dandysme et de G. Brummell*. Caen et Paris: B. Mancel.

Barblan, A. (1974) *L'Image de l'Anglais en France pendant les querelles coloniales*. Francfort: Herbert Lane/M. Peter Lane

Barker, E. H. (1890) *Wayfaring in France*. London: Bentley

Barnett, G. (1991) *Richard and Maria Cosway*. Tiverton: Westcountry Books

Barou, J. & P. Prado (1995) *Les Anglais dans nos Campagnes*. Paris: L. Harmattan

Barthez, Dr E. (1912) *The Empress Eugenie and her Circle*. (trans. Miall) London: T. Fisher Unwin

Baughan, R. (1880) *The Northern Watering Places of France*. London: 'The Bazaar'

Beardsley, A. (1971) *The Letters of Aubrey Beardsley* (ed. Maas & Ors,) London: Cassell

Bedford, S. (1973) *Aldous Huxley*. London: Chatto & Windus/Collins

Beevor, A. & A. Cooper (1994) *Paris after the Liberation 1944–1949*. London: Hamish Hamilton

Bennet, Dr J. H. (1870) *Winter and Spring on the Shores of the Mediterranean*. London: J. Churchill

Bennett, A. (1913) *Paris Nights*. London: Hodder & Stoughton

Bennett, A. (1932) *The Journals of Arnold Bennett, 1896–1910* (ed. Foster) London: Cassell

Berger, J. (1979) *Pig Earth*. London: Writers & Readers Publishing Co-operative

Berry, M. (1831) *Social life in England and France* .... London: Longman, Rees, Orme, Brown & Green

Berry, M. (1865–6) *Extracts of the Journals and Correspondence of Miss Berry* (ed. Lewis) London: Longmans

Berry, M. & A. (1914) *The Berry Papers* (ed. Melville) London: Bodley Head

Bertall [C-A. d'Arnoux] (1876) *La Vie Hors de Chez Soi*. Paris: Plon

Bertier de Sauvigny, G. de. (1974) *La Restauration*. Paris: Flammarion

Best, H. (1826) *Four Years in France*. London: Henry Colburn

Bianchi, B. (1964) *La Saison d'hiver à Cannes de 1870 à 1914*. Cannes: L'Equipe des Historiens Cannois

Bicknell, A. L. (1895) *Life in the Tuileries under the Second Empire*. London: Unwin

Bidwell, C. T. (1876) *The Cost of Living Abroad*. London: Sampson Low

Bingham, Capt. Hon. D. (1896) *Recollections of Paris*. Vol. 1. London: Chapman & Hall

Blagdon, F. W. (1803) *Paris as it was and as it is*. London: C. & R. Baldwin

Blanche, J-E.(1927) *Dieppe*. Paris: Eds Emile-Paul Frères

Blanche, J-E (1937) *Portraits of a Lifetime*. London: Dent

Blount, E. (1902) *Memoirs of Sir Edward Blount*. (ed. Reid) London: Longmans

Blume, M. (1992) *Côte d'Azur*. London: Thames & Hudson

Blume, M. (1999) *A French Affair*. New York: Free Press

Bocca, G. (1963) *Bikini Beach*. London: W. H. Allen

Boddington, Mrs (1837) *Sketches in the Pyrenees*. London: Longman, Rees, Orme, Brown, Green & Longman

Bogarde, D. (1993) *A Short Walk from Harrods*. London: Viking

Bolster, J. (1976) *The Upper Crust*. London: Weidenfeld & Nicolson

Bonnaud, L. (ed.) (2004) *France-Angleterre*. Paris: Harmattan

Boulenger, J. (1907) *Sous Louis-Philippe les Dandys*. Paris: Librarie P. Ollendorff

Boulenger, M. (1913 ed.) *Cours de vie parisienne*. Paris: Librarie P. Ollendorff

Boutet de Monvel, R. (1908) *Beau Brummell and his Times* London: Eveleigh Nash

Boutet de Monvel, R. (1911) *Les Anglais à Paris, 1800–1850*. Paris: Librairie Plon

Bowman, W. & E. Leadham (eds.) (1923–24) *The Peerless Riviera*. London: McCorquodale

Brayfield, C. (2004) *Deep France*. London: Pan Books

Brendon, P. (1991) *Thomas Cook*. London: Secker & Warburg

Bresson, J. (1981) *La Fabuleuse Histoire de Cannes*. Monaco: Eds du Rocher

Brewster, M. M. (1857) *Letters from Cannes and Nice*. Edinburgh: Constable

Brightwell, C. L. (1854) *Memorials of the Life of Amelia Opie*. Norwich: Fletcher & Alexander

Broglie, duchess de. (1896) *Lettres de la duchesse de Broglie, 1814–1838* (ed. Broglie) Paris: duc de Broglie

Brooke D. (1983) *The Railway Navvy*. Newton Abbot: David and Charles

Browne, M. (1905) *The Diary of a Girl in France in 1821* (ed. Shore) London: John Murray

Bruccoli, H. J. (1981) *Some sort of Epic Grandeur*. London: Hodder & Stoughton

Bunbury, S. (1884) *Rides in the Pyrenees*. London: T. C. Newby

Burnett, T.A.J (1981) *The Rise and Fall of a Regency Dandy*. London: Murray

Burney, F. (1904/5) *Diary & Letters of Madame d'Arblay*. (ed. Barrett) London: Macmillan

Burney, F. (1975) *Journal and Letters of Fanny Burney*, vols 5–6 (eds Hemlow & Ors) Oxford: Oxford University Press

Burton, I. (1893) *The Life of Captain Sir Richd F. Burton*. London: Chapman & Hall

Bussell, P. (1931)*The Diary of Peter Bussell* (ed. Turner) London: Peter Davies

Butel, P. (1991) *Les Dynasties Bordelaises*. Paris: Perrin

Buzard, J. (1993) *The Beaten Track*. Oxford: Oxford University Press

Calton, R. B. (1852) *Annals and Legends of Calais*. London: John Russell Smith

Cameron, R. (1975) *The Golden Riviera*. London: Weidenfeld & Nicolson

Campbell, T. (1849) *Life and Letters of Thomas Campbell*, vol. 3 (ed. Beatty) London: Edward Moxon

Campos, C. (1965) *The View of France*. Oxford: Oxford University Press

Cane, A. (1978) *Histoire de Villefranche-sur-Mer*. Nice: Claude Boumendil

Cannadine, D. (1990) *The Decline and Fall of the British Aristocracy*. New Haven, CT: Yale University Press

Carey, D. (1822) *Life in Paris ... Dick Wildfire*. London: John Fairburn

Carey, F. J. (1823) *Journal of a Tour in France*. London: Taylor & Hessey

Carne, Elizabeth. See Wittitterly.

Carr, Sir J.(1807 ed.) *The Stranger in France*. London: J. Johnson

Castellane, B. de (1895–6) *Journal du Maréchal de Castellane 1804–1862*. Paris: Librarie Plon

Cazamian, L. (1927) *Ce qu'il faut connaître de l'Ame Anglaise*. Paris: Boivin

Cazes, G. (ed.) (1964) *Le Tourisme à Luchon*. Toulouse Association Marc Bloch

Cerda, A. de la (1999) *La Tournée des Grands Ducs*. Biarritz: Atlantica

Chambers, W. (1870) *Wintering at Mentone*. London & Edinburgh: W. &. R. Chambers

Chapman. G. (1962) *The Third Republic of France, The First Phase*. London: Macmillan/St. Martin's

Christiansen, R. (1994) *Tales of the New Babylon*. London: Sinclair-Stevenson

Clark, R. (1953) *Victorian Mountaineers*. London: Batsford

Clayden, P. W. (1889) *Rogers and his Contemporaries*, vol. 1. London: Smith, Elder

Clermont-Tonnerre, duchesse de (1928) *Mémoires – Au Temps des Equipages* (ed. Halévy) Paris: Bernard Grasset

Cody, M. (1984) *The Women of Montparnasse*. New York: Cornwall Books

Coleman, T. (1965) *The Railway Navvies*. London: Hutchinson

Collas, P. & E. Villedary (2002) *Edith Wharton's French Riviera* (trans. Pickford). Paris: Flammarion

Collier, B. (1977) *To Meet the Spring*. London: J. M. Dent

Connolly, C. (1945) *The Condemned Playground*. London: Routledge

Conway, D. [H. D. Inglis] (1831) *Switzerland, the South of France, and the Pyrenees in 1830*. London: Edward Moxon

Cooper, A. (1999) *Writing at the Kitchen Table*. London: Michael Joseph

Cooper, B. & L. (1992) *A Spell in Wild France*. London: Methuen

Cooper, D. (2005) *The Duff Cooper Diaries* (ed. Norwich) London: Weidenfeld & Nicolson

Cornwallis, C. (1945) *Correspondence of Charles, First Marquis Cornwallis*, vol. 3 (ed. Ross) London: John Murray

Costello, L. (1842) *A Pilgrimage to Auvergne*, vol. 2. London: Richard Bentley

Costello, L. (1844) *Béarn and the Pyrenees*. London: Richard Bentley

Cronin, V. (1989) *Paris on the Eve, 1900–1914*. London: Collins

Cronin, V. (1994) *Paris. City of Light 1919–1939* London: HarperCollins

Crouzet, F. (1990) *Britain Ascendant* (trans. Thom) Cambridge: Cambridge University Press

Dabernat, R. (1976) *Messieurs les Anglais*. Paris: Eds Robert Laffont

Dallington, Sir R. (1605) *The View of Fraunce in 1598*. London: T. Creede

Daninos, P. (1955) *Major Montagu Thompson lives in France* (trans. Farn) London: Jonathan Cape

Dansette, A. (1936) *L'Affaire Wilson et la Chute du Président Grévy*. Paris: Librairie Académique Perrin

Daullia, E. (1890) *La Vie à Evian-les-Bains*. Paris/Nancy: Berger-Levrault

Daumard, A. (ed.) (1973) *Les Fortunes françaises au xix siècle*. Paris/LaHaye: Mouton

David, E. (1984) *An Omelette and a Glass of Wine*. London: Hale

Davies, C. (1841) *Eleven Years' Residence in the family of Marat, King of Naples*. London: How & Parsons

Davies, G. C. & Mrs Broughall (1890) *Our Home in the Aveyron*. Edinburgh/London: W. Blackwood & Sons

Davis, R. H. (1892) *The Great Streets of the World*. London: Osgood, McIlvaine

Davis, R. H. (1895) *About Paris*. New York: Harper

Delattre, F. (1927) *Dickens et la France*. Paris: Librarie Universitaire

Dempster, C.H.L. (1920) *The Manners of My Time* (ed. Knox) London: Grant Richards

Derraine, P-S. & Veglia, I. (1999) *Les Etrangers en France*. Paris: Génériques

Désert, G. (1983) *La Vie quotidienne sur les Plages Normandes*. Paris: Hachette

Desgraves, G. & Dupeux, G. (eds) (1969) *Bordeaux au xix Siècle*. Bordeaux: Fédération historique du Sud-Ouest

Desportes, M.(2005) *Paysages en mouvement*. Paris: Gallimard

Dickens, C. (1865) *Our Mutual Friend*. London: Chapman & Hall

Dickens, C. (1996) *Dickens in France*. Brighton: Print Publishing

Dino, duchesse de (1901) *Chronique de 1831–1862*. (ed. Radziwill) Paris: Plon

Dollot, R. (1944) *Une Chronique de la Restauration*. Grenoble: Univ. de Grenoble

Donaldson, F. (1982) *P. G. Wodehouse*. London: Weidenfeld & Nicolson

Dormandy, T. (1999) *The White Death*. London: Hambledon

Downing, R. (1947) *If I Laugh*. London: Harrap

Drabble, M. (1974) *Arnold Bennett*. London: Weidenfeld & Nicolson

Duff, D. (1970) *Victoria Travels*. London: Muller

Duffy, S. (1894) *The English Abroad*. London: T. Fisher Unwin

Duloum, J. (1970) *Les Anglais dans les Pyrenées* ... Lourdes: Les Amis du Musée pyrénéen

Dunham, A. L. (1955) *The Industrial Revolution in France*. New York: Exposition Press

Eagles, R. (2000) *Francophilia in English Society*. Basingstoke: Macmillan

Edgeworth, M. (1894) *Life and Letters of Maria Edgeworth* (ed. Hare) London: Edward Arnold

Edmondson, J. (1997) *Travellers' Literary Companion to France*. London: 'In Print'

Elgin, M. (1926) *Letters of Mary Nisbet, Countess of Elgin* (ed. Grant) London: John Murray

Elkington, M. E. (1929) *Les Relations de Société entre l'Angleterre et la France sous la Restauration*. Paris: Librairie ancienne Honoré Champion

Ellis, Mrs [Sarah Stickney] (1841) *Summer and Winter in the Pyrenees*. London: Fisher

Evenson, N. (1979) *Paris: A Century of Change, 1878–1978*. New Haven/London: Yale University Press

Eyre, E. J. (1803) *Observations made at Paris during the Peace*. Bath/London: Robinson/Longman & Rees

Eyre, M. (1865) *A Lady's Walks in the South of France in 1863*. London: Richard Bentley

Eyre, M.(1865) *Over the Pyrenees into Spain*. London: Richard Bentley

Faber, R. (1975) *French and English*. London: Faber

Faith, N. (1978) *The Winemasters*. London: Hamish Hamilton

Faith, N. (1983) *Victorian Vineyard*. London: Constable, in association with Christie's Wine Publications

Faith, N. (1990) *The World the Railways Made*. London: Bodley Head

Faucher, L. (1856) *Etudes sur l'Angleterre*, vol. 1. Paris: Corbeil

Féliciangeli, D. (1967) *Le Développement de Nice*. Monaco: série Annales de la

Faculté des Lettres et Sciences Humaines de Nice, 19 vols. Paris: Minard lettres modernes

Field, L. (1983) *Bendor, the golden Duke of Westminster*. London: Weidenfeld & Nicolson

Fitzgerald, F. Scott (1955) *Tender is the Night*. London: Penguin Books

Fohlen, C. (1956) *L'Industrie textile au temps du Second Empire*. Paris: Librairie Plon

Fontaine, P. (1941) *Last to leave Paris*. London: Chaterson

Forbes, J. (1806) *Letters from France*, vol. 2. London: J. White

Ford, F. Madox (1935) *Provence*. Philadelphia/London: J. P. Lippincott

Ford, T. H. (2001) *Chancellor Brougham and his World*. Chichester: Barry Rose Law

Forgues, E-M. (1908) *Le Dossier Secret de Fouché*. Paris: Emile-Paul

Forster, C. de (1844) *Paris et les Parisiens: physiologie de l'Etranger*. Paris: Firmin. Didot Frères

Forster, C. de (1848) *Paris et les Parisiens: quinze ans à Paris*. Paris: Firmin. Didot Frères

Fortescue, W. (1941) *Trampled Lilies*. Edinburgh: W. Blackwood

Fortescue, W. (1948) *Beauty for Ashes*. Edinburgh: W. Blackwood

Fothergill, B. (1974) *The Mitred Earl*. London: Faber

Fourcassié, J. (1940) *Le Romantisme et les Pyrénées*. Paris: Gallimard

Fournier-Verneuil, M. (1826) *Paris*. Paris: Guiraudet

Fox, S. (1909) *An Art Student's Reminiscences of Paris in the Eighties*. London: Mills & Boon

Fralon, J-A. (2006) *Au secours, les Anglais nous envahissent!* Paris: Michalon

Gallant, M. (1988) *Paris Notebooks*. London: Bloomsbury

Galton, F. (ed.) (1862) *Vacation Tourists*. London: Macmillan

Garvey, M. A. (1852) *The Silent Revolution*. London: Cash

Gerbod, P. (1991 *Voyages au pays des mangeurs de Grenouilles*. Paris: Albin Michel

Gibbons, J. (1929) *Tramping to Lourdes*. London: Methuen

Gibson, Revd W. (1872) *Paris during the Commune*. London/Nottingham: Whittaker

Gide, A. (1945) *Si le grain ne meurt*. Paris: Gallimard

Giono, J. (1955) *Notes sur l'affaire Dominici*. Paris: Gallimard

Goldberg, W. & Piesse, G. (1891) *Monte Carlo and how to do it*. Bristol: Arrowsmith

Goldring, D. (1945) *The Nineteen Twenties*. London: Nicolson & Watson

Goncourt, E. de (1896) *Journal des Goncourt 1886–1892*. Paris: La Renaissance

Gonnet, P. (1993) *Les Alpes Maritimes d'autrefois*. Lyon: Eds. Horvath

Goodman, J. (ed.) (1988) *The Oscar Wilde File*. London: Allison & Busby

Gordon, J. & C. (1925) *Two Vagabonds in Languedoc*. London: John Lane

Gordon-Barrett, R. (1925) *Motoring in France*. London: Methuen

Gramont, E. See Clermont-Tonnerre.

Grant, E. (1996) A *Highland Lady in France* (eds Pelly/Todd) East Linton: Tuckwell Press

Granville, H. (1894) *Letters of Harriet Countess Granville* (ed. Leveson-Gower) London: Longmans Green

Graves, C. (1951) *The Big Gamble. The Story of Monte Carlo.* London: Hutchinson

Graves, C. (1963) *None but the Rich.* London: Cassell

Graves, R. (1929) *Goodbye to all that.* London: Jonathan Cape

Greatheed, B. (1953) *An Englishman in Paris: 1803.* (eds Bury/Barry) London: Geoffrey Bles

Green, F. C. (1965) *A Comparative View of French and British Civilisation.* London: J. M. Dent

Green, J. R. (1876) *Stray Studies from England and Italy.* London: Macmillan

Greene, J. (1986) *History of Parliament, The Commons 1790–1820* (ed. Thorne) London: Secker & Warburg for the History of Parliament Trust

Gronow, Captain (1862) *The Reminiscences and Recollections.* London: Smith, Elder

Guiffan, J. (2004) *Histoire de l'Anglophobie en France.* Rennes: Terre de Brumes

Guyard, M.-F. (1954) *La Grande Bretagne dans le Roman français 1914–1940.* Paris: Librairie Marcel Didier

Guyot, R. (1926) *La Première Entente Cordiale.* Paris: F. Rieder

Hale, W. (1914) *Ideal Motor Tour in France.* London: G.Bell

Hall, Lt F. (1819) *Travels in France in 1818.* London: Longman, Hurst, Rees, Orme & Brown

Hamerton, P. G. (1889) *French & English.* Leipzig: B.Tauchnitz

Hamerton, P. G. (1897) *An Autobiography.* London: Seeley & Co

Hamerton, P. G. (1908 ed.) *Round my House.* London: Seeley & Co

Hamilton, C. (1933) *Modern France as seen by an Englishwoman.* London: J. M. Dent

Hardy, J. (1825) *A Picturesque and Descriptive Tour ... in the High Pyrenees* London: R. Ackermann

Harris, J.P. (1991) *An Englishman in the Midi.* London: BBC Books

Haydon, B. J. (1990) *Diaries of B. J. Haydon* (ed. Joliffe) London: Hutchinson

Hazlitt, W. (1826) *Notes of a Journey through France and Italy.* London: Hunt & Clarke

Hemmingway, E. (1986) *The Garden of Eden.* New York: Sribner's

Henderson, W. O. (1954) *Britain and Industrial Europe, 1750–1870.* Liverpool: Liverpool University Press

Henrey, M. (1952) *A Farm in Normandy and the Return to the Farm.* London: Dent

Heywood, C. (1977) *The Cotton Industry in France, 1750–1850.* Loughborough: University of Loughborough

Hibbert, C. (ed.) (1991) *Captain Gronow.* London: Kyle Cathie

Holcroft, T. (1864–5) *Travels from Hamburgh through Westphalia 1804*, 2 vols. Glasgow.

Holmes, R. (1985) *Footsteps.* London: Hodder & Stoughton

Holmes, R. (2005) *Tommy ...* London: Harper Perennial

Holt, A. (1904) *Dress Outfits for Abroad.* London: Edward Arnold

Holt, R. (1981) *Sport and Society in Modern France*. London: Macmillan, in association with St Antony's College, Oxford

Honeyman, K. & J. Goodman (1986) *Technology and Enterprise. Isaac Holden and the Mechanisation of Woolcombing in France*. Aldershot: Scolar

Horne, A. (1965) *The Fall of Paris*. London: Macmillan

Horne, A. (2004) *Friend or Foe*. London: Phoenix

Howarth, P (1977) *When the Riviera was Ours*. London: Routledge & Keegan Paul

Hughes, P. (1981) *Founders of the Wallace Collection*. London: Trustees of the Wallace Collection

Hugo, V. (1891) *En Voyage: Alpes et Pyrénées*. Paris: Bibliothèque Charpentier

Hutchinson, T. J. (1876) *Summer Holidays in Brittany*. London: Sampson Low, Marston, Searle & Rivington

Huxley, A. (1925) *Along the Road*. London: Chatto & Windus

Jackson, Sir G. (1872) *The Diaries and Letters of Sir George Jackson* (ed. Jackson) London: Richard Bentley

Jackson, J. (2001) *France. The Dark Years*. Oxford: Oxford University Press

Jackson, W. J. (1893) *James Jackson et ses fils*. Paris

Jacquier, I. (1960). *The Diary of Ivy Jacquier 1907–1926*. London: V. Gollancz

Jaeger, M. (1956) *Before Victoria*. London: Chatto & Windus

James, H. (1883) *Portraits of Places*. London: Macmillan

Jameson, A. (1826) *Diary of an Ennuyée*. London: Henry Colburn

Janvier, T. A. (1893) *An Embassy to Provence*. London: Unwin

Jarrassé, D. (1992) *Les Thermes Romantiques*. Clermont-Ferrand: Institut d'études du Massif Central

Jebb, M. (1986) *Walkers*. London: Constable

Jerdan, W. (1817) *Six Weeks in Paris* ... London: J. Johnston

Jerrold, W. B. (1867) *Paris for the English*. London: Bradbury, Evans

Johnston, S. (1998) *The Villas of the Riviera*. London: Thames & Hudson

Jones, T. (2004) *The French Riviera*. London: I. B. Tauris

Jullian, P. (1967) *Edward and the Edwardians*. London: Sidgwick & Jackson

Jullian, P. (1969) *Oscar Wilde* (tr. Wyndham) New York: Viking Press

Jullian, P. (1977) *Montmartre* (tr. Carter) London: Phaidon

Kedward, R. (2005) *La Vie en Bleu*. London: Allen Lane

Kennedy, D. (2005) *The Highly Civilized Man*. Cambridge, MA: Harvard University Press

King, F. E. (1808) *A Tour in France*. London: J. Booth

King, J. (1803) *Letters from France*. London: W. Flint for M. Jones

Kipling, R. (1933) *Souvenirs of France*. London: Macmillan

Kitchiner, Dr W. (1827) *The Traveller's Oracle*. London: Henry Colburn

Klein, R. (1994) *Le Touquet Paris-Plage*. Paris: Institut français d'architecture/ 'norma'

Labouchere, H. (1871) *Diary of the Besieged Resident of Paris*. London: Hurst & Blackett

Lamont, M. W. (1844) *Impressions, Thoughts and Sketches*. London: Edward Moxon

Langton, R. (1836) *Narrative of a Captivity in France*. London/Liverpool: Smith Elder

Lapie, P-O. (1976) *Les Anglais à Paris*. Paris: Fayard

Lawrence, J. H. (1810) *A Picture of Verdun*, 2 vols. London: Hookham

Lear, E. (1870) *Journal of a Landscape Painter in Corsica*. London: R. J. Bush

Le Blond, Mrs A. (1928) *Day in, Day out*. London: Bodley Head

Lee, Dr E. (1865) *The Health Resorts of the South of France*. London: W. J. Adams

Lefevre, Sir G. (1843) *The Life of a Travelling Physician*. London: Longmans

Lequin, Y. (ed.) (1984) *Histoire des Français xix-xx siècles*, vol. 1. Paris: Armand Colin

Lequin, Y. (ed.) (1988) *La Mosaïque France*. Paris: Larousse

Leribault, C. (1994) *Les Anglais à Paris au 19 siècle:* Paris: Paris-Musées

Lewis, C. (1936) *Sagittarius Rising*. London: Peter Davis

Lewis, M. (1962) *Napoleon and his British Captives*. London: George Allen & Unwin

Liégeard, S. (1887) *La Côte d'Azur*. Paris: Maison Quantin

Liddle, P. H. (1985) *Home Fires and Foreign Fields*. London: Brassey's Defence

Links, J. G. (1968) *The Ruskins in Normandy*. London: John Murray

Linn, Dr T. (1894 ed.) *The Health Resorts of Europe*. London: H. Kimpton

Littlewood, I. (1982) *Paris. A Literary Companion*. London: Murray

Lytton, R. (1942) *Life in Unoccupied France*. London: Macmillan

MacDonogh, F. (1824) *L'Hermite Rôdeur*, vol. 1. Paris: Malepeyre Librarie

McGilligan, P.M. C. (2003) *Alfred Hitchcock. A Life in Darkness and Light* Chichester: Wiley

Maclean, Dr C. (1804) *An Excursion in France ...* London: Longman & Rees

Macmillan, Capt N. (1929) *Air Travellers' Guide to Europe*. London: Duckworth

Mallet, D. (1979) *The Greatest Collector*. London: Macmillan

Mallock, W. H. (1892) *In an Enchanted Island*. London: R. Bentley

Mansel, P. (2001) *Paris between Empires*. London: John Murray

Marandon, S. (1967) *L'Image de la France dans la Conscience Anglaise, 1848–1900*. Paris: A. Colin

Marchal, C. (1844) *Physiologie de L'Anglais à Paris*. Paris: Fiquet Editeur/Galerie de l'Odéon

Marès, A. & P. Milza (1994) *Le Paris des Etrangers depuis 1945*. Paris: Publications de la Sorbonne

Margetson, S. (1974) *The Long Party*. Farnborough: Saxon House

Martineau, H. (1869) *Biographical Sketches*. London: Macmillan

Martin-Fugier, A. (1990) *La Vie Elégante*. Paris: Fayard

Massingham, H. & P. (1961) *The Englishman Abroad*. London: Phoenix House

Matthews, C. (1971) *A Different World*. New York/London: Paddington Press

Matthews, H. (1820) *Diary of an Invalid*. London: John Murray

Mauco, G. (1932) *Les Etrangers en France*. Paris: Armand Colin

Maugham, S. (1941) *Strictly Personal*. Garden City, NY: Doubleday, Doran

Maurois, S. (1957) *Miss Howard and the Emperor* (tr. Hare) London: Collins

Mayle, P. (1989) *A Year in Provence*. London: Hamish Hamilton

Mayle, P. (1991) *Toujours Provence*. London: Hamish Hamilton

Mayne, J. (1909) *The Journal of John Mayne during a tour . . .* (ed. Mayne). London: John Lane

Mayo, G. Elton (1983) *The Mad Mosaic*. London: Quartet

Mérimée, P. (1953–61) *Correspondence générale*, 2 ser, 17 vols. (ed. Parturier) Toulouse: E. Privat

Mill, J. S. (1960) *John Mill's Boyhood Visit to France* (ed. A. J. Mill) Toronto: University of Toronto

Mill, J. S. (1984) *Collected Works of John Stuart Mill* (ed. Robson/Stilling), Toronto: University of Toronto

Miller, W. (1879) *Wintering in the Riviera*. London: Longmans, Green

Milner, I. (1988) The *Studios of Paris*. New Haven/London: Yale University

Mitchell, B. R. (1975) *European Historical Statistics 1750–1975*. London: Macmillan

Mitchell, B. R. (1988) *British Historical Statistics*. Cambridge: Cambridge University Press

Mitchell, L. G. (1992) *Charles James Fox*. Oxford: Oxford University Press

Moers, E. (1960) *The Dandy*. London: Secker & Warburg

Moncrieff, A.R.H. (1893) *Where to go Abroad*. London: A & C. Black

Monte Carlo and Public Opinion (1884), edited by a Visitor to the Riviera. London: Rivington

Moore, G. (1928) *Confessions of Young Man*. London: Heineman

Morand, P. (1960) *Bains de Mer*. Lausanne: Eds. Clairfontaine

Moraud, M. (1933) *Le Romantisme français en Angleterre*. Paris: Librairie ancienne Honoré Champion

More, J. (1985) *Views from a French Farmhouse*. London: Pavilion

Morgan, Lady S. [Owenson] (1817) *France*. London: Henry Colburn

Morgan, Lady S. [Owenson] (1830) *France in 1829–30*. London: Saunders & Otley

Morris, J. (1993) *Travels with Virginia Woolf*. London: Hogarth

Mossop, J. (1890) *Thomas Robinson Woolfield's Life at Cannes*. London: Kegan Paul, Trench

Murray, E. C. G. (1885) *Under the Lens*, vol. 2. London: Vizetelly

Murray, Hon. J. E. (1837) *A Summer in the Pyrnes*. London: John Macrone

Nelson, M. (2001) *Queen Victoria and the Discovery of the Riviera*. London I. B. Tauris

Nevill, Lady D. (1906) *The Reminiscences of Lady Dorothy Nevill* (ed Nevill) London: Edward Arnold

Nevill, R. (1927) *Days and Nights in Montmartre and the Latin Quarter*. London: H. Jenkins

Neville, C. (1906) *Round France in a Motor*. Dublin/Birmingham: Combridge

Newman, B. (1936) *Cycling in France (Northern)*. London: Herbert Jenkins

Newte, F. (1869) *Twenty Years Wanderings* ... London: Simpkins, Marshall

Newton, S. (1852) *Essais Divers. Lettres et Pensées de Madame de Tracy* vol.1. Paris: Typographie Plon frères

Nicholson, Col W. N. (1939) *Behind the Lines*. London: Cape

Normanby, Lord. (1828) *The English in France*. London: Saunders & Otley

Normanby, Lord. (1857) *A Year of Revolution*. London: Longmans

O'Brien, P. & C. Keyder(1978) *Economic Growth in Britain and France*. London: Allen & Unwin

O'Dowd, C. (1864)] *Upon Men and Women*. Edinburgh: Blackwood

O'Moore, M. (1990) *Tips for Travellers*. London: Elliot Stock

Orwell, G. (1933) *Down and Out in Paris and London*. London: Victor Gollancz

O'Shea, J. A. (1886) *An Iron-Bound City*, vol. 1. London: Ward & Downey

'Owen John' (1919) *Towards the Sunshine*. London: Cassell

Packe, C. (1862) *A Guide to the Pyrenees*. London: Longman, Green

Page, M. (1975) *The Lost Pleasures of the Great Trains*. London: Weidenfeld & Nicolson

Pakenham, S. (1967) *Sixty Miles from England*. London: Macmillan

Paoli, X. (1911) *My Royal Clients*. London: Hodder & Stoughton

Paris, T. C. (1843) *Letters from the Pyrenees*. London: Murray

Paul, Sir J. D. (1802) *Journal of a Party of Pleasure to Paris*. London: T. Cadell jnr. & W. Davies

Pemberton, M. (1907) *The Amateur Motorist*. London: Hutchinson

Pemble, J. (1987) *The Mediterranean Passion*. Oxford: Clarendon

Pinkney, Lt Col (1814 ed.) *Travels through the South of France*. London: Gale, Curtis & Fennel

Pirie, V. A. (1935) *A Frenchman sees the English in the Fifties*. London: Sidgwick & Jackson

Pitte, J-K. (2002) *French Gastronomy*. New York: Columbia University Press

Playfair, W. (1819) *France as it is, not Lady Morgan's France*. London: R. C. Chapple

Plumptre, A. (1810) *A Narrative of a Three Year's Residence in France, 1802–1805*. London: Constable

Pocock, T. A. (1996) *A Thirst for Glory*. London: Aurum

Poirier, A-C. (2005) *Les Nouveaux Anglais. Clichés revisités*. France: Alvik

Poirier, A-C. (2006) *Touché, A French Woman's Take on the English*. London Weidenfeld & Nicolson

Polnay, P. de (1952) *Unfinished Journey to South Western France and the Auvergne*. London: Allan Wingate

Poniatowski, M. (1982) *Talleyrand et le Directoire*. Paris: Librairie Académique Perrin

Poniatowski, M. (1986) *Talleyrand et le Consulat*. Paris: Perrin

Pope-Hennessy, J. (1952) *Aspects of Provence*. London: Longmans, Green

Poulaine, J.de la (1900) *L'Anglomanie*. Paris: Librairie Plon

Powell, H. F. (2005) *More France please, we're British*. London: Gibson Square Books

Prémaray, J. de (1851) *Promenades Sentimentales dans Londres*. Paris: D. Giraud & J. Dagneau

Prest, J. (1972) *Lord John Russell*. London: Macmillan

Quest-Ritson, C. (1992) *The English Garden Abroad*. London: Viking

Raffles, T. (1818) *Letters during a Tour*. Liverpool: Thomas Taylor

Rahv, P. ed. (1960) *Discovery of Europe*. Garden City, NY: Doubleday

Raikes, T. (1856) *Portion of a Journal kept by Thomas Raikes Esq from 1831 to 1847*. London

Raitt, A. W. (1970) *Prosper Mérimée*. London: Eyre & Spottiswoode

Ramuz, C-F. (1939) *Paris*. Paris: Gallimard

Rapport, M. (2000) *Nationality and Citizenship in Revolutionary France*. Oxford: Clarendon Press

Rauch, A. (1996) *Vacances en France*. Paris: Hachette

Rearick, C. (1985) *The Pleasures of the Belle Epoque*. New Haven: Yale University Press

Rearick, C. (1997) *The French in Love and War*. New Haven: Yale University Press

Reboul, P. (1962) *Le Mythe Anglais dans la Littérature Française sous la Restauration*. Lille: Univ. de Lille

Reyt, D. (1982) *Deauville et la Côte Fleurie*. Condé-sur-Noireaud: Corlot

Rhodes, A. (1885) *Monsieur at Home*. London: Field & Tuer

Rice, H. C. (1976) *Thomas Jefferson's Paris*. Guildford: Princeton University Press

Richard, M. [Audin, J.M.V.] (1824) *Guide du Voyageur en France*. Paris: Audin, Librarie

Richardson, J. (1967) *The Courtesans*. London: Weidenfeld & Nicolson

Ring, J. (2000) *How the English made the Alps*. London: John Murray

Ring, J. (2004) *Riviera*. London: John Murray

Robb, G. (2007) *The Discovery of France*. New York/London: Norton

Roberts, A. (1999) *Salisbury*. London: Weidenfeld & Nicolson

Roget, S. R. (1921) *Travel in the Two Last Centuries of Three Generations*. London: T. Fisher Unwin

Roots, Dr W. (1909) *Paris in 1814*. (ed. Ogle) Newcastle-upon-Tyne: Andrew Reid

Roy, J-A. (1958) *Histoire du Jockey Club de Paris*. Paris: Librarie M. Rinère

Rudorff, R. (1972) *Belle Epoque*. London: Hamilton

Russell, V. (1993) *Gardens of the Riviera*. Boston, MA/London: Little, Brown

Sadleir, M. (1947) *Blessington-D'Orsay*. London: Constable

Sadleir, T. U. (ed.) (1924) *An Irish Peer on the Continent 1801–1803* London: Williams & Norgate

Sadler, M. (2002) *An Englishman in Paris*. London: Simon & Schuster UK

Sadler, M. (2004) *An Englishman à la Campagne*. London: Simon & Schuster UK

Sala, G. A. (1894) *Things I have Seen*, vol. 2. London: Cassell

Sala, G. A. (1895) *The Life and Adventures of George Augustus Sala*. London: Cassell

Saunders, E. (1954) *The Age of Worth*. London: Longmans, Green

Schivelbusch, W. (trans. 1880) *The Railway Journey*. Oxford: Blackwell

Schor, R. (1980) *Nice et les Alpes maritimes de 1914 à 1945*. Nice: C.R.O.P.

Schor, R. (1985) *L'Opinion Française et les Etrangers, 1919–1939*. Paris: La Sorbonne

Scott, J. A (1816 ed.) *A Visit to Paris in 1814*. London: Longman, Hurst, Rees, Orme & Brown

Scott, Sir W. (1972) *The Journal of Sir Walter Scott* (ed.Anderson) Oxford: Clarendon Press

Senior, N. W. (1871) *Journals kept in France and Italy 1848–1852*. London: Henry S. King

Shattuck, R. (1969) *The Banquet Years*. London: Cape

Shepherd, Revd W. (1814) *Paris in 1802 and 1814*. London: Longman, Hurst, Rees, Orme & Brown

Shoemaker, M. M. (1906) *Winged Wheels in France*. New York/London: Putnam

Shone, R. (1979) *Sisley*. Oxford: Phaidon

Siebecker, E. (1867) *Physiologie des Chemins de Fer*. Paris: J. Hetzel

Silver, K. E. (2001) *Making Paradise*. Cambridge, MA: Institute of Technology

Singer-Kérel, J. (1961) *Le Coût de la vie à Paris de 1840 à 1954*. Paris: Colin

Somerville, E. & M. Ross (1893) *In the Vine Country*. London: W. H. Allen

Souza, R. de (1913) *Nice, capitale d'hiver*. Paris/Nancy: Berger-Levrault

Spang, R. L. (2000) *The Invention of the Restaurant*. Cambridge, MA: Harvard University Press

Spencer, E. (1853) *Tour of Enquiry*. London: Hurst & Blackett

St John, B. (1854) *Purple Tints of Paris*. London: Chapman & Hall

St John, J. A. (1831) *Journal of a Residence in Normandy*. Edinburgh: Constable

Stamper, C. W. (1913) *What I Know*. London: Mills & Boon

Stanley, Revd E. (1907) *Before and after Waterloo*. London: T. Fisher Unwin

Stamper, C. W. (1913) *What I know*. London: Mills & Boon

Stendhal (1981 ed.) *Mémoires d'un Touriste*, vol. 1. Paris: François Maspero

Stendhal (1975) *Memoirs of an Egotist* (trans. Ellis) London: Chatto & Windus

Stevenson, R. L. See under notes for Chapter 7, and Holmes (1985).

Stothard, Mrs C. [Elizabeth] (1820) *Letters written during a Tour of Normandy*: London: Longman, Hurst, Rees, Orme & Brown

Strachey, Lytton (1989) *The Shorter Strachey* (ed. Holroyd) London: Hogarth

Straus, R. (1942) *Sala: The Portrait of an Eminent Victorian*. London: Constable

Strong, R. (1915) *The Diary of an English Resident in France during Twenty-Two Weeks of War Time*. London: Eveleigh Nash

Stuart, D. (1982) *Dear Duchess*. London: Gollancz

Sturt, C. (1810) *The Real State of France in the Years 1809–10*. London: J. Ridgway

Sutherland, M. Duchess of (1914) *Six Weeks at the War*. London: *The Times*

Sutton, D. (1976) *Walter Sickert*. London: Joseph
Swinglehurst, E. (1974) *The Romantic Journey*. London: Pica Editions
Sykes, J. A. C. (ed.) (1906) *France in Eighteen Hundred and Two by H. R. Yorke*.
    London: Heinemann
Symons, A. (1918) *Colour Studies in Paris*. London: Chapman & Hall

Taine, H. (1858) *Voyage aux Pyrénées*. Paris: Librairie Hachette
Talfourd, T. N. (1845) *Vacation Rambles and Thoughts*. London: Edward Moxon
Taylor, D. J. (2003) *Orwell*. London: Chatto & Windus
Taylor, Sir H. (1913) *The Taylor Papers* (ed. Taylor) London: Longmans
Taylor, Dr A. (1842) *On the Curative Influence of Pau, and the Mineral Waters of the
    Pyrenees*. London: J. W. Parker
Taylor – John Taylor & Son. See Wilkinson
Taylor, J. (1993) *The Travellers' Quotation Book*. London: Hale
Thackeray, W.M [Mr Titmarsh] (1840) *The Paris Sketch Book*. London: John Macrone
Thomas, D. (1999) *Swinburne*. London: Univ. of London
Thomas, R. T. (1979) *Britain and Vichy 1940–42*. London: Macmillan
Thompson, P. (1975) *The Edwardians*. London: Weidenfeld & Nicolson
Thornton, Col T. (1806) *A Sporting Tour through France*. London: Longman
Tocqueville, A. de (2003) *Lettres Choisies. Souvenirs 1814–1859*. Paris: Gallimard
Tombs, R. & I. (2006) *That Sweet Enemy*. London: W.Heinemann
Trench, Revd F. (1845) *Diaries of Travels in France and Spain*. London
Trollope, A. (1866) *Travelling Sketches*. London: Chapman & Hall
Trollope, T. A. (1850) *Impressions of a Wanderer* ... London: Henry Colburn
Trotter, J. B. (ed.) (1811) *Memoirs of the Latter Years of ... Charles James Fox*.
    London: R. Phillips
Troyat, H. (1989) *Maupassant*. Paris: Flammarion
Tucoo-Chala, P. (1979) *Pau, Ville anglaise*. Pau: Société Nouvelle d'Editions Régio-
    nales et de Diffusion
Tucoo-Chala, S. (1992) *Quatre Siècles de Protestantisme à Pau*. Pau: C.E.P.B.
Turnbull, S. (2002) *Almost French*. Sydney/London: Bantam Books
Turner, L. & I. Ash (1975) *The Golden Hordes*. London: Constable

Urbain, J. D. (1993) *L'Idiot du Voyage. Histoires de touristes*. Paris: Payot
Urbain, J. D. (2003) *Sur la Plage*. Minneapolis: University of Minnesota Press

Vandam, A. D. (1894) *My Paris Notebook*. London: W. Heinemann
Vandam, A. D. (1895) *French Men and French Manners*. London: Chapman & Hall
Viator Verax [Revd G. Musgrave] (1863) *Cautions for the First Tour*. London: W.
    Ridgway
Vigny. Colloque Alfred de Vigny (1978) *Les Pyrénées & l'Angleterre*. Pau: Académie
    de Béarn.
Vizetelly, E. A. (1919) *Paris and her People*. London: Chatto & Windus
Vizetelly, H. (1893) *Glances back through Fifty Years*. vol. 2. London: Keegan Paul

Vovelle, M. (ed.) (1989) *Paris et la Révolution*. Paris: Publications de la Sorbonne

Waddington, M. K. (1908) *Chateau and Country Life in France*. London: Smith, Elder
Waddington, M. K. (1914) *My First Years as a Frenchwoman*. London: Smith, Elder
Waddington, M. K. (1918) *My War Diary*. London: John Murray
Wagener, F. (1997) *La Comtesse de Boigne*. Paris: Flammarion
Wallon, A. (1981) *La Vie Quotidienne dans les Villes d'Eaux*. Paris: Hachette
Wansey, H. (1814) *A Visit to Paris in June 1814*. London: J. Robinson
Warren. D. (1913) *The Journal of a British Chaplain in Paris* (ed. Broadley) London: Chapman & Hall
Waterfield, G. (2000) *The Long Afternoon* London: Review
Watrin, J. (1986) *Boulogne sur Mer. Vingt ans d'occupation anglaise, 1840–1860* Aire-sur-la Lys: Watrin
Weber, E. (1986) *France, Fin de siècle*. Cambridge, MA: Belknap Press
Wechsberg, J. (1979) *The Lost World of the Great Spas*. London: Weidenfeld & Nicolson
Weston, Revd S. ['WS'] (1803) *The Praise of Paris*. London: C. & R. Baldwin
Wharton, E. A . (1934) *A Backward Glance*. New York: D. Appleton-Century
Whitaker, J. P. (1917) *Under the Heel of the Hun*. London: Hodder & Stoughton
White, K. (1966) *Letters from Gourgounel*. London: Cape
White, S. (1983) *Sam White's Paris*. Sevenoaks: New English Library
Wickwire, F. & M. (1980) *Cornwallis. The Imperial Years*. Chapel Hill: N. Carolina University Press
Wilkinson, G. K. (1964) *John Taylor & Son. Un Siècle d'Histoire*. Cannes: privately printed
Williams, W. T. (1807) *State of France* .... London: Phillips
Wilmot, K. (1992) *The Grand Tours of Katherine Wilmot* (ed. Mavor) London: Weidenfeld & Nicolson
Withey, L. (1998) *Grand Tours and Cooks Tours*. London: Arum Press
Wittitterly, J. A. [Elizabeth Carne] (1860) *Three Months' Rest at Pau*. London: Bell & Daldy
Woolf, V. (1930) *Beau Brummell*. New York: Rimmington & Hooper
Wright, H. H. (1838) *Desultory Reminiscences of a Tour ... by an American* Boston: W. D. Ticknor
Wright, W. (1803) *A Narrative of the Situation and Treatment of the English*. London: J. Badcock & Ors

Yeo, Dr J. B. (1890) *Climate and Health Resorts*. London: Cassell
Yriarte, C. (1864) *Les Cercles de Paris 1828–1864*. Paris: Librarie Parisienne

Zeldin, T. (1979) *France, 1848–1945. Ambition and Love*. Oxford: Oxford University Press
Zweig, S. (1943) *The World of Yesterday*. London: Cassell

Index